'Talking Proper'

'Talking Proper'

The Rise of Accent as Social Symbol

LYNDA MUGGLESTONE

CLARENDON PRESS · OXFORD

Oxford University Press, Great Clarendon Street, Oxford OX2 6DP

Oxford   New York

Athens   Auckland   Bangkok   Bogota   Bombay
Buenos Aires   Calcutta   Cape Town   Dar es Salaam
Delhi   Florence   Hong Kong   Istanbul   Karachi
Kuala Lumpur   Madras   Madrid   Melbourne
Mexico City   Nairobi   Paris   Singapore
Taipei   Tokyo   Toronto
and associated companies in
Berlin   Ibadan

Oxford is a trade mark of Oxford University Press

Published in the United States
by Oxford University Press Inc., New York

British Library Cataloguing in Publication Data
Data available

Library of Congress Cataloging in Publication Data
Data available
ISBN 0–19–823706–5

1 3 5 7 9 10 8 6 4 2

Printed in Great Britain on acid-free paper by
Biddles Ltd., Guildford and King's Lynn

ACKNOWLEDGEMENTS

My thanks are due to Cambridge University Press for allowing me to use data from Peter Trudgill, *The Social Stratification of English in Norwich* (CUP, 1974), and to the Bodleian Library Oxford, for permission to reproduce the advertisements for Thomas Sheridan's lectures on elocution of May 1759 (fo. 66 items 67(a) and 67(b) entitled 'Oxford, May 25, 1759. Mr Sheridan'. Shelfmark = *Don. b. 12*). I am grateful also to the readers of Oxford University Press for their many helpful comments, and to Professor Eric Stanley in particular for his time and energy in discussing the various drafts of this book.

CONTENTS

LIST OF FIGURES

INTRODUCTION

Accent as Social Symbol

'ACCENT and Pronunciation must be diligently studied by the conversationalist. A person who uses vulgarisms will make but little way in good circles . . . A proper accent gives importance to what you say, engages the respectful attention of your hearer, and is your passport to new circles of acquaintance.' So wrote the anonymous author of *Talking and Debating* (1856),[1] a manual of linguistic etiquette which, like many others published during the late eighteenth and nineteenth centuries, sought to teach the social proprieties of linguistic usage to those who felt themselves disadvantaged in this respect. Pronouncing dictionaries, works on elocution, tracts on speech and articulation, and handbooks of social advice were regularly to unite over this time in stressing the social import to be conveyed within the nuances of speech. As *Talking and Debating* indicates, accent was itself to be regarded as a marker of social acceptability, facilitating or impeding social advance; it alone could secure deference or disrespect, acting as an image of 'worth' in a culture increasingly attuned to the significance of phonetic propriety. 'No saying was ever truer than that good breeding and good education are sooner discovered from the style of speaking . . . than from any other means', the Reverend David Williams affirmed,[2] similarly endorsing the stated importance of assimilation to the 'correct' forms of speech. Nor, it seemed, was that blend of both social and linguistic prescription which commonly resulted to pass entirely unheeded: George Gissing read Thomas Kington-Oliphant's *The Sources of Standard English*, as well as George Craik's *Manual of English Language and Literature*, eagerly absorbing their dictates on the shibboleths and social markers to be found in the spoken English of the late

---

[1] *Talking and Debating* (London, 1856), 15.
[2] Revd D. Williams, *Composition, Literary and Rhetorical, Simplified* (London, 1850), 5.

nineteenth century. George Bernard Shaw, 'a social downstart', devoted himself to works on elocution in the British Museum, as well as to *The Manners and Tone of Good Society*[3] with its subtitle *Solecisms to be Avoided*, and its advice that 'the mispronunciation of certain surnames falls unpleasantly upon the educated ear, and argues unfavourably as to the social position of the offender'. Thomas Hardy purchased a copy of Nuttall's *Standard Pronouncing Dictionary*,[4] as well as *Mixing in Society: A Complete Manual of Manners* with its assertion that 'the best accent is undoubtedly that taught at Eton and Oxford. One may be as awkward with the mouth as with the arms or legs.'[5] Hardy's application in this context was, however, apparently to leave something to be desired, at least in terms of George Gissing's high standards in matters of accent. As Gissing commented in his diary on 13 July 1895: 'With Hardy I talked a little, and he asked me to write to him . . . I caught a few notes of the thick western utterance.'[6]

Gissing's own hypersensitivities to the social symbolism contained within contemporary notions of 'talking proper' exemplify in many ways the preoccupations, and prejudices, about speech which came to form a hallmark of the late eighteenth and nineteenth centuries. The interrelationships of language and identity form recurrent images in his novels, iterated again and again in terms of articulation and the spoken word: 'His utterance fell short of perfect refinement, but seemed that of an educated man', we are, for example, told of Mr Widdowson in *The Odd Women*.[7] 'Her intonation was not flagrantly vulgar, but the accent of the London poor, which brands as with hereditary baseness, still clung to her words, rendering futile such propriety of phrase as she owed to years of association with educated people', runs the description of Mrs Yule in *New Grub Street*.[8] Accent assumes a role

---

[3] *The Manners and Tone of Good Society By a Member of the Aristocracy* (London, 1879), 172.

[4] Peter Austin Nuttall was the author of a number of frequently reprinted pronouncing dictionaries published in the latter half of the nineteenth century, including *The Standard Pronouncing Dictionary of the English Language* (London, 1863), *Routledge's Pronouncing Dictionary of the English Language* (London, 1867), and a revised edn. of *Walker's Pronouncing Dictionary of the English Language* (first published London, 1855; later edns. published 1868, 1872, and 1873).

[5] *Mixing in Society. A Complete Manual of Manners* (London, 1870), 91.

[6] P. Coustillas, *London and the Life of Literature in Late Victorian England: The Diary of George Gissing* (London, 1978), 329.

[7] G. Gissing, *The Odd Women* (London, 1893), i. 87.

[8] Id., *New Grub Street* (London, 1891), i. 154.

as prime social signifier for Gissing's characters, their ears ever alert for the dropped [h], a shibboleth which was itself encoded over the course of the eighteenth and nineteenth centuries,[9] or for the imperfectly articulated vowel sounds which might label them as members of the working class: ' "How I like your way of speaking . . . your voice—accent" ', says Mrs Wade to Lilian in *Denzil Quarrier*. ' "As a child I had a strong northern accent; you don't notice anything of it now?" ', Lilian immediately replies, seeking reassurance that her voice conforms to the models of true propriety located in 'good' southern speech.[10] As Gissing recognized all too well, and as Phyfe cautioned his audience in *How Should I Pronounce?* (1885), by the late nineteenth century popular attitudes towards acceptability were all too willingly to endorse assumptions that it was accent, together with appearance, which formed the dominant images within any impression that one made: 'The first impression made upon a person's mind by the presence of a stranger is gathered from his personal appearance; the second, from his speech. In spoken language the most conspicuous element is pronunciation, and we naturally estimate one's condition, both mental and social, by his practice in this regard.'[11]

Subject to a veritable barrage of information on this head, it was, it appeared, difficult to remain completely unaware of the repercussions which speaking with the 'right', or indeed the 'wrong' accent might have. Popular penny journals such as the *Family Herald* or the *London Journal*, with combined circulations of *c.*750,000 by the 1850s, urged their readers, largely located among the upper working and lower middle classes, to improve their modes of speech and, in turn, improve their station in life (or, at least, perceptions of it). Readers responded by writing in, asking for precise instructions on articulation, the 'proper' ways to speak. As Mitchell notes of this process:

The readers of the *London Journal* and the *Family Herald* actively sought information about the values, standards, and mechanical details of living in a milieu that was new to them. Their letters to the correspondence column reveal their conscious mobility. They want to eradicate the traces of their origin that linger in their grammar and pronunciation. They ask the kinds of questions about etiquette and general knowledge that would

---

[9] See Ch. 3.   [10] G. Gissing, *Denzil Quarrier* (London, 1892), 168.
[11] W. Phyfe, *How Should I Pronounce? Or the Art of Correct Pronunciation* (London, 1885), 6.

be impossible for anyone with a polite background and more than a rudimentary education. The advertisers urge them to buy textbooks, life assurance, and fashion magazines, to learn elocution, French, Italian, and music.[12]

Sixpenny manuals, such as *P's and Q's. Grammatical Hints for the Million* (the opening pages of which admonish that 'A knowledge and practice of the rules of the English language are absolutely essential to respectability and a comfortable passage through decent life'),[13] or *Poor Letter H. Its Use and Abuse* also by the anthropomorphized 'Hon. Henry H.', were correspondingly sold in their thousands. As the latter opined in the preface to the fortieth edition, in this context the public displayed a seemingly voracious appetite for instruction in the proprieties of speech ('the circulation of forty thousand have been but as drops poured into the mighty tide of human life, whereon float hundreds and thousands who don't know an H from an A'),[14] though that this should be the case was not, in fact, entirely surprising given a cultural climate in which accent had increasingly assumed a role imbued with social meaning, especially in terms of /h/. 'Social suicide' was committed by its omission in words such as *house* or *heart*, as the philologist Alexander Ellis, one of the more objective observers of the language, recorded in 1869.[15]

The new popularity of elocution, as a private as well as public pursuit, likewise stressed the importance of 'talking proper': five times as many works on elocution appeared between 1760 and 1800 than had done so in the years before 1760,[16] and this tendency did not abate with the coming of the nineteenth century. Works on the arts of speech were published and republished in a way which clearly attests contemporary interest in the issues of articulation, especially given the growing conviction that accent could provide a way of articulating social identity as much as words in themselves. Whether in terms of Thomas Sheridan's early *Lectures on the Art of Elocution* (1762), or George Vandenhoff's *Art of Elocution* of 1855,

---

[12] S. Mitchell, 'The Forgotten Women of the Period: Penny Weekly Family Magazines of the 1840s and 1850s', in M. Vicinus (ed.), *A Widening Sphere: Changing Roles of Victorian Women* (Bloomington, Ind., 1977), 34.

[13] Hon. Henry H., *P's and Q's. Grammatical Hints for the Million* (London, 1855), 8.

[14] Id., *Poor Letter H. Its Use and Abuse*, 40th edn. (London, 1866), pp. iii–iv.

[15] A. J. Ellis, *On Early English Pronunciation* (London, 1869–89), i. 221.

[16] See W. Benzie, *The Dublin Orator* (Leeds, 1972), p. vi.

the central tenets were clear: 'pronunciation . . . is a sort of proof that a person has kept good company, and on that account is sought after by all, who wish to be considered as fashionable people, or members of the beau monde', as the former averred.[17] 'Pronunciation distinguishes the educated gentleman from the vulgar and unpolished man', wrote Vandenhoff in his own later endeavours to inculcate a due sense of phonemic propriety in his readers.[18]

It is this shift in sensibilities surrounding accent and the role it was to play in assumptions about social definition and notions of social standing which is to occupy this book. Language rarely exists in a vacuum, and its interactions with prescriptive ideology and the attempt to codify one 'standard' accent for all, its links with developments in educational provision, and its reflection in contemporary literature, which also served to encode common preconceptions about the social alliances of speech and speaker, will all be considered in the following chapters. Though when Sheridan wrote it was seen as no disadvantage for either upper or under class to speak in a way influenced by their regional location —as Dorothy Marshall notes of the late eighteenth century, 'even the gentry thought it no disgrace to speak with a provincial accent'[19] —by the end of the nineteenth century such attitudes had changed. Notions of a non-localized accent (and assimilation to it) had come to act as a dominant social symbol, the salient element in what the phonetician Henry Sweet defined as 'a class-dialect more than a local dialect . . . the language of the educated all over Great Britain'. As he added, 'the best speakers of Standard English are those whose pronunciation, and language generally, least betray their locality'.[20] It is this creation of a set of non-localized and supra-regional norms, or of what can be seen as a set of 'standard pronunciation features' which provides a major focus of the late eighteenth and nineteenth centuries, as writers on the language endeavoured to supplant the heterogeneities of actual usage in terms of accent with the homogeneity of the 'correct' way to speak, regularly asserting the assumed values of the monolithic and the unilinear as they did so.

[17] T. Sheridan, *A Course of Lectures on Elocution* (London, 1762), 30.
[18] G. Vandenhoff, *The Art of Elocution* (London, 1855), 43.
[19] D. Marshall, *Industrial England 1776–1851* 2nd edn. (London, 1982), 8.
[20] H. Sweet, *The Sounds of English* (Oxford, 1908), 7.

Culminating in notions of 'received pronunciation', the period from the late eighteenth century onwards was to see the creation, and consolidation, of a number of national stereotypes to this end in terms of speech: the 'educated accent', the 'public school' accent, the 'Oxford' accent, 'talking without an accent', 'talking proper', and eventually 'BBC English' too. It was witness to the rise of a range of socially sensitive variables for the spoken word, in which notions of the 'dropped letter', such as the 'h' in *house*, or the 'g' in words such as *walking*, can still, of course, remain prominent. Revealing the integration of accent within the concerns of prescriptivism, and its attendant ideologies, the late eighteenth century (and afterwards) emerges as a period in which issues of correctness and purism relating specifically to matters of accent attained a hitherto unprecedented significance. Articulated in treatises on education and on elocution, in manuals of etiquette and handbooks of social advice, in the grammars and pronouncing dictionaries intended for private as well as for educational use, and in the many works explicitly devoted to creating the 'right' accent which were published over this time, notions of 'talking proper' were subject to a large-scale shift in terms of both perception and attitude. Though language was, and is, innately variable, with speakers locating themselves on continua of formality (and 'proper' language) depending on their immediate audience and varying the way they choose to speak accordingly, this fact was commonly ignored. Writers, whether in works of fiction or of fact, affirmed the hegemony of one way of speaking while they attempted to exert its persuasions upon their readers, pointing out aspects of 'deviation' in ways unparalleled in earlier writings on the language. Like class itself, accent was, in effect, to become a major national obsession over this time. 'Classes are getting mixed, confused . . . we are so conscious of the process that we talk of class distinctions more than anything else,—talk and think of them incessantly', as Gissing stressed in *Born in Exile*.[21] Since it was accent which popularly came to be conceived as a prime marker of such class distinction, this habit was, in many ways, thus almost guaranteed to ensure its prominence in the public mind.

---

[21] G. Gissing, *Born in Exile* (London, 1892), iii. 35.

I

The Rise of a Standard: Process and Ideology

IN a number of ways, how one speaks has of course almost always been bound up with conceptions of social identity. In the fourteenth century, for instance, those seeking to stress their superiority sought to speak French, the language of the court, rather than an English which was, as Caxton later declared, fundamentally 'rude and barbarous'. Then, as now, language varieties seemed emblematic of the social order. 'Gentilmens children ben lerned & taught from their yongth to speke frenssh', Ranulph Higden noted in his *Polycronicon*,[1] revealing the shared forces of social and linguistic emulation in his comment that 'vplondissh men wyll counterfete & likene hem selfe to gentilmen / & arn besy to speke frenssh for to be more sette by'. The ambition to 'be more sette by', and the linguistic ways in which this might be achieved, are clearly of long standing in England, their fourteenth-century resonances encapsulated by Higden in the proverb he provides: 'Jack wold be a gentilman if he coude speke frenssh.'

Seeking to establish status by the habits of speech one adopted was nevertheless signally different at this time. It relied, for example, upon choice between two different languages, rather than between different varieties of the same language, or, as in the nineteenth century, between different ways of pronouncing the same word, articulating the same thing. The notion that 'a provincial dialect should always receive a check, since however good a speaker's argument may be, it becomes ridiculous by the manner in which it is conveyed', a precept encoded by the grammarian Thomas Smetham in 1774,[2] would have been meaningless at a time when

---

[1] Ranulph Higden wrote *Polycronicon* in Latin in the mid-14th c. It was translated (with additions) into English by John of Trevisa c.1387, and afterwards printed as *Description of Britayne, & also Irlonde taken out of Policronicon* by William Caxton in 1480. All citations are from the latter, ch. XV.

[2] T. Smetham, *The Practical Grammar* (London, 1774), 36.

all native varieties of the language were fundamentally perceived
as 'dialects'. In the absence of a 'standard', in the sense later to
emerge, all dialects in Middle English assumed an equality they
were never after to attain; though Chaucer in his *Reeve's Tale* does
indeed pick out dialect difference in the Northern markers allotted to the two Cambridge men, Aleyn and John, it is worth re-
membering that in this tale it is they who are the 'educated' and
'superior' characters, and the miller who, in spite of his London
forms, takes on the implications of lower status, and of loser too.

It is the presence or absence of standardization, both as a process, and, perhaps more significantly, as an ideology, which provides
the major difference between these fourteenth- and eighteenth-
century conceptions of language, linguistic choice, and language
variety; an examination of this, with reference to both written and
spoken language, should make these implications clear. Though
the emergence of 'incipient standards' can, for example, be detected in the Wycliffite writings of the late fourteenth century,
and, in the fifteenth century, in the development of 'Chancery
Standard' (the widely disseminated and highly regular form of
written English used by the scribes of the Chancery in official
documents), even these differ somewhat from the notions of a
'standard' which were later to develop. As David Burnley points
out:

In modern times ['Standard English'] denotes a form of language—that
is, of its phonology, morphology, syntax, and lexis—which is superordinate
to geographically variant forms, and which is realised in both spoken and
written modes, and in the latter by a consistent orthography. Middle
English standards differ sharply from this modern conception, firstly in
that they exist . . . *only* in the written mode, for standardization in spoken
English belongs to a much later period . . . Secondly, they are distinct in
that the consistency of their orthography does not approach that of Modern
Standard English.[3]

Moreover, in the fourteenth century, the absence of a dominant,
non-localized, or superordinate standard variety meant that all
regional varieties of language had not only spoken, but also written forms: the author of *Sir Gawain and the Green Knight* wrote

---

[3] J. D. Burnley, 'Sources of Standardization in Later Middle English', in J. B.
Trahern, Jr. (ed.), *Standardizing English. Essays in the History of Language Change
in Honor of John Hurt Fisher* (Knoxville, Tenn., 1989), 23–4.

in the dialect of the north-west Midlands, while Chaucer selected that of London English, not by virtue of any intrinsic merit he happened to perceive in it, but simply because it was the form of language current in the area where he lived. Once a standard variety does emerge, however, discernible in the written language with the rise of fifteenth-century Chancery English as a non-localized written norm (and a transition especially marked after the emergence of printing in the 1470s), perceptions of dialect, status, and appropriate usage tend to change accordingly.

'After a speach is fully fashioned to the common vnderstanding, & accepted by consent of a whole countrey & nation, it is called a language', stated George Puttenham in 1589.[4] This is, in effect, what happens over the course of the fifteenth and sixteenth centuries as one variety of London English, originally perceived as a 'dialect', shifts status to function as a non-localized, and superordinate, written 'language'. The sense that other dialects are subordinate to this emergent standard is in turn reflected in their displacement from the written, and statusful, channels of communication to which they too previously had access; it was, for instance, into this one variety that literature, itself a statusful domain of usage, was henceforth also to be largely confined, and into which the Bible was translated. As Manfred Görlach notes, as early as 1450 'written evidence had generally become impossible to date or localize so great had the adoption of London English become'.[5] Though private documents could, and did, continue to betray the influence of regional variation, public documents make this development particularly clear; one variety of written English, and one alone, was disseminated all over England in the form of print.

These processes of standardization are not, of course, limited simply to the means by which one variety of language is endowed with a national and written mode of communication. An ideal standard language can, for instance, additionally be defined in terms of a formula which combines 'maximum variation of function' with a 'minimal variation of form'. With reference to the former therefore, a standard must be omnifunctional, able to fulfil a range of prestigious and official roles within the nation, rather

---

[4] G. Puttenham, *The Arte of English Poesie* (London, 1589), 120.
[5] M. Görlach, *Studies on the History of the English Language* (Heidelberg, 1990), 23.

than merely being the coin of common exchange. In the use of English (rather than French) in the domains of government and law after the mid-fourteenth century, one can see moves towards precisely that elaboration of function deemed significant in such definitions, a movement further aided by the later biblical translations into the vernacular. This development alone was notably to assist the claims of English to be considered a language just as worthy as Latin for the writing of important texts and, over the course of the seventeenth century, English continued to consolidate its hold over the transmission of intellectual discourse. Though More wrote *Utopia* in Latin, the language of international scholarship and cultured erudition, as did Isaac Newton his *Principia* in 1689, nationalism, and the role of language within it, nevertheless came to ensure that the emergent standard variety was ultimately to encompass these functions as well. As Richard Mulcaster, headmaster of Merchant Taylors' School and author of *The First Part of the Elementarie* (1582) had asked, 'why not all in English?'. By the end of the seventeenth century, his question would have been largely rhetorical. The texts written in Latin after this date, such as Newton's *Opticks* of 1704, appeared significantly out of tune with the prevailing climate of linguistic (and cultural) thought in which the standard variety of English was regularly praised for its copious vocabulary, its qualities of elegance, its capacities for rhetoric, and its potential for stylistic and intellectual polish.

By the late seventeenth century, a sense of a 'standard' of English was thus clearly in existence, at least in terms of the written language, though in popular opinion even this was seen as particularly deficient in the rules by which a standard should 'properly' be used (and with which Latin was of course abundantly supplied). It is this perception, articulated by writers such as Jonathan Swift in his 1712 proposal for an official academy which might regulate such matters, or in Addison's plea in 1711 for 'superintendents' to curtail aspects of change deemed 'incorrect', which heralds the era of codification, an important stage in notions of standardization. In simple terms, this can be seen as the endeavour to control language by the attempted imposition of 'ordered' and 'reasoned' patterns of 'correct' usage. Relevant and newly perceived norms of 'correctness' were encoded in the spate of prescriptive grammars and dictionaries produced over the eighteenth and nineteenth centuries; it was by such means (at least within the tenets of prescriptivism) that the 'minimal variation of form' deemed essential to a 'standard', and standardized, language, might itself be achieved. 'The foundation of the rules is reason', stressed John Dryden in this context, and criteria based on logic, on the application of analogy, and on affinities with mathematical thinking were indeed often to dominate approaches to language over the course of the eighteenth century, as writers attempted to formulate rules by which 'proper' English was to be regulated, and the 'best' speakers in turn recognized. Dryden himself set forth early on the 'incorrectness' of using prepositions in final position, as in 'Where are you going to?', for, although such constructions were long legitimized by usage in English, they were absent from Latin, the language deemed paradigmatic of grammatical perfection. Moreover, 'logically', a preposition implied that the word in question should come before the verb, and Dryden accordingly changed all relevant constructions in the 1668 edition of his *Essay on Dramatic Poesy*. Dryden was not alone in such preoccupations, and self-appointed regulators of the English language flourished. Robert Lowth, archdeacon of Winchester, and later Bishop of London, assumed seemingly divine rights on linguistic legislation too in his *Short Introduction to English Grammar* (1762). Asserting that 'in many instances [English] offends against every part of grammar', he castigated a range of constructions in normal use, such as *you was* ('an enormous Solecism'), the 'improper' use of *who* and *whom* (so that Dryden's own 'Tell who loves who' comes in for condemnatory comment), as well as the use of the flat adverb, as in *extreme unwilling* ('Adjectives are sometimes employed as adverbs; improperly, and not agreeably to the Genius of the English Language'), and the use of the double negative. In other words, grammarians such as Lowth formulated and endorsed many of the rules by which 'correct' language is now popularly thought to be ascertained, regularly disregarding the realities of linguistic usage in favour of these somewhat more theoretical (and tenuous) notions of correctness. As Dick Leith adds in his own social history of the English language, 'to a large extent, our whole perception of grammar has been distorted by their work'.[6]

'The principal design of a grammar is to teach us to express ourselves with propriety; and to enable us to judge of every phrase

---

[6] D. Leith, *A Social History of English* (London, 1983), 89.

and form of construction whether it be right or not', wrote Lowth, expressing his own belief in the binary oppositions of 'right' and 'wrong' which prescriptivism was often to endorse above the heterogeneities of actual usage. It is in these terms that codification, and its accompanying traditions of proscription, operate as an ideology, a set of assumptions about language behaviour and usage which can, in real terms, sometimes exert more influence on speakers' attitudes than does direct observation of the actualities of the language itself. Standardization too is best seen in similar terms, consisting not only of these processes by which one variety of the language assumes superordinate and non-localized roles within the nation, but being formed equally of a complex of beliefs and attitudes which evolve around the 'standard' which results. Like the processes of standardization themselves, such notions undergo a slow and gradual development, underpinning a history of the language which is, in reality, far from unilinear (though paradoxically, such images of unilinearity are often fostered as a salient part of their operation). Renaissance debates about the status of English as a language for intellectual expression exemplify, for instance, the increasing consolidation of one variety alone in the functional roles by which a standard may be determined, but they also, and more pertinently, reveal advances in accompanying ideologies, whereby this one variety of the language comes to be conceived as the language itself, and as exemplifying its 'best' qualities. Joseph Priestley, scientist, theologian, and grammarian, likewise reveals the operation of exactly these ideas in his eighteenth-century conviction that the standard variety emerges not as a result of external circumstance (the prominence of London as capital, the role of the Chancery, Caxton's decision to set up his printing press outside Westminster), but rather as the consequence of some superior merit and inherent value intrinsic to this one variety: 'the best forms of speech, the most commodious for use, and the most agreeable to the analogy of the language, will at length establish themselves and become universal, by their superior excellence.'[7]

Attempted codification of this variety thus tends to take all these conceptions a step further as the grammars, dictionaries,

---

[7] J. Priestley, *A Course of Lectures on the Theory of Language and Universal Grammar* (Warrington, 1762), 178–9.

and manuals of linguistic usage of the eighteenth and nineteenth centuries strive to set down intentionally invariant norms of usage by which 'correct' English is to be recognized, and 'incorrect' English to be proscribed. Often choosing to set forth for the erudition of users of the language patterns in which what 'ought' to be predominate over what is, manuals of this order have important implications for pronunciation too, and for those issues of 'propriety' and 'impropriety', 'correctness' and 'mistake', which also came to infuse attitudes towards it at this time. In that search for a standard of spoken language which preoccupies many writers of the late eighteenth century and afterwards, it was in many ways this ideology of standardization which was to be most significant.

In terms of pronunciation therefore, the same set and stages of development can, on the whole, be observed. In the sixteenth and seventeenth centuries, for example, phoneticians such as John Hart, William Bullokar, and Christopher Cooper had written extensive and detailed works on the articulatory mechanisms of English, classifying sounds, and demarcating the distances between grapheme and phoneme in a language which, as William Bullokar urged in 1580, merited a new orthography on these grounds alone ('fower and twentie letters, are not sufficient to picture Inglish spéech: For in Inglish spéech, are mo distinctions and divisions in voice, than these fower and twentie letters can seuerally signifie, and giue right sound vnto').[8] Writers such as George Puttenham with his clear depiction of an emergent standard of speech (based in 'the vsuall speach of the Court and that of London and the shires lying about London within lx. myles')[9] moreover evince the marked awareness that the speech of London was, in a number of ways, already to be seen as 'better' than that of the provinces. Similarly, Hart's principles of reformed spelling are set down in his *Orthographie* of 1589 with the intent that, by their use, 'the rude countrie Englishman' will be able to pronounce English 'as the best sort use to speak it'.

London, as political, legal, administrative, commercial, and cultural centre of the country naturally assumes prominence in such comments, as does the language of the learned above that

---

[8] W. Bullokar, *Booke at Large for the* Amendement *of* Orthographie *for English* (London, 1580), repr. in Bullokar, *Works*, ed. J. R. Turner (Leeds, 1970), vol. iii, C2ᵛ.

[9] Puttenham, *Arte of English Poesie*, 121. See also pp. 16–19.

of the majority of the populace; Alexander Gil, High Master of St Pauls and author of the *Logonomia Anglicanu* (1619), hence expresses his notion of standard speech in the precept that all spelling is to be accommodated to the sounds used, not by ploughmen, maidservants, and porters, but by learned or elegantly refined men in speaking and reading. As the poet and essayist, James Beattie, was later to write, it was natural to 'approve as elegant what is customary among our superiors',[10] and the superiority vested in knowledge of the written word, and in familiarity with the metropolitan above the provincial, readily served as major determining factors in these early perceptions of linguistic elegance with regard to speech. Over the course of the sixteenth and seventeenth centuries, a clear sense of an emergent standard of spoken as well as written English does therefore become perceptible. The schoolmaster and writer on language Owen Price notes in *The Vocal Organ* that his work 'has not been guided by our vulgar pronunciation, but that of *London* and our *Universities*, where the language is purely spoken'.[11] Elisha Coles in *The Compleat English Schoolmaster* (1674) specifies that the basis of his work is 'the present proper pronunciation of the Language in OXFORD and LONDON'.[12]

Nevertheless, it should not be assumed that such statements indicate the existence of a 'standard' of speech, either in terms of process or ideology, which is akin to that described, and, more importantly, prescribed in the late eighteenth and nineteenth centuries. Coles, for example, writing in the late seventeenth century, evidently feels constrained to defend his choice of the one variety of 'proper' pronunciation which he documents in his book, a situation inconceivable a century later:

because men usually espouse that pronunciation as properest which they have been accustomed to, therefore they will be quarrelling at some particulars.

Let them know, that in these things I have been jealous of, and have oftentimes divorc'd my self, and have followed that pronunciation which I have for many years observ'd to be most in use among the generality of Schollars.[13]

'I have had opportunity of making observations', he admonishes in further justification of these preferences for London speech.

---

[10] J. Beattie, *The Theory of Language* (London, 1788), 92–3.
[11] O. Price, *The Vocal Organ* (Oxford, 1665), A3ᵛ.
[12] E. Coles, *The Compleat English Schoolmaster* (London, 1674), title-page.
[13] Ibid. 103.

Likewise, John Hart's specification of the 'flower' of speech which is located in London does not, at that date, exclude all other modes of speech from consideration. His tolerance and, moreover, acceptance of the validity of pronunciations used in other parts of the country provides a striking contrast to later comments in which such varieties are, in the words of Thomas Sheridan, lexicographer, elocutionist, and one of the foremost writers on pronunciation in the late eighteenth century, necessarily to be conceived as a sign of 'disgrace'. As Sheridan asserted in 1762, 'all other dialects are sure marks, either of a provincial, rustic, pedantic, or mechanic education, and therefore have some degree of disgrace attached to them'.[14] Hart, two centuries earlier, instead proffered his conviction that speakers of dialects outside the standard variety have a right to spell as they pronounce, and that their way of doing so should give no more offence than should the fact of their speaking differently:

if any one were minded at Newcastell uppon Tine, or Bodman in Cornewale, to write or print his minde there, who could iustly blame him for his Orthographie, to serue hys neyghbours according to their mother speach, yea, though he wrate so to London, to whomsoever it were, he could be no more offended to see his writing so, than if he were present to heare him speake.[15]

Christopher Cooper, phonetician and headmaster of the Grammar School in Bishop's Stortford, expresses a similar belief in his *English Teacher* of 1687. Though choosing to describe 'the best dialect' of London speech himself,[16] which is, in his opinion, the 'most pure and correct', his attitude to variation, and variant articulations of words, is nevertheless strikingly liberal. 'Everyone pronounceth them as himself pleases', he notes on page 105. As Eric Dobson comments on this position, Cooper 'admits that there are variants, and that some men use dialectal pronunciations; he is quite content that they should, but he himself will describe a defined pronunciation, that of the South'.[17]

Though sixteenth- and seventeenth-century observations about language thus do make plain notions of an emerging standard of

---

[14] Sheridan, *Course of Lectures*, 30.
[15] J. Hart, *An Orthographie* (London, 1569), fi^r–fii^v.
[16] C. Cooper, *The English Teacher or the Discovery of the Art of Teaching and Learning the* English Tongue (London, 1687), 77.
[17] E. J. Dobson, *English Pronunciation 1500–1700*, 2nd edn. (Oxford, 1968), i. 309.

speech, they do not do so with that highly normative, prescriptive, and codifying zeal which characterizes their later counterparts. Cooper, for example, aims simply to describe his 'best dialect'; Thomas Sheridan, a century later, aims instead to disseminate its eighteenth-century equivalent and hence to displace all other 'inferior' forms of speech. The pronouncing dictionaries which flourished at the end of the eighteenth century and throughout the nineteenth are, in Sheridan's terms, to act as a means by which 'the pronunciation of each word' can be reduced 'to a certainty by fixed and visible marks; the only way in which uniformity of sound could be propagated to any distance'.[18] The change lies both in the process and the ideology of standardization; whereas Cooper wrote in an era more concerned with the status of English as a language in itself, Sheridan wrote in one inspired by its codification, its reduction to rule. Whereas Hart and Puttenham described, and were moreover content to describe a still largely localized form of spoken English, Sheridan and other writers of the late eighteenth century (and afterwards) sought instead to codify a non-localized, supra-regional 'standard', and thus to displace the linguistic diversities of accent which currently pertained. As Sheridan notes with disfavour of regional markers of speech, 'the pronunciation of all natives of these Countries, is entirely formed, from the Custom which prevails in the places of their respective birth and education'.[19]

The precise nature of this transition within attitudes to pronunciation, and its framing ideologies, is perhaps made most clear through a more detailed comparison of notions of a standard, and its social role, in the work of George Puttenham in the sixteenth century, and that of Thomas Sheridan in the eighteenth. Puttenham's *Arte of English Poesie* (1589) is often, and rightly, cited for the valuable information which it provides about the rise of perceptions of a standard in English usage. As we have seen, he locates this in the usage of London and the court, in 'southerne' speech ('the vsuall speach of the Court, and that of London and the shires lying about London within lx. myles and not much aboue'). He goes on, moreover, to develop its social affiliations,

---

[18] T. Sheridan, *A Rhetorical Grammar of the English Language* (Dublin, 1781), p. xviii.
[19] Id., *A Dissertation on the Causes of Difficulties, Which Occur, in Learning the English Tongue* (London, 1761), 17.

placing his linguistic model in 'the better brought vp sort . . . men ciuill and graciously behauoured and bred', rather than in 'the speach of a craftes man or carter, or other of the inferiour sort, though he be inhabitant or bred in the best towne and Citie in this Realme'.[20] As he adds in explanation, 'such persons doe abuse good speaches by strange accents or ill-shapen sounds and false ortographie'. Puttenham's standard is self-evidently a sociolect—at least in part—and one which is to be sought in the 'courtly' and 'currant' use of the southern counties around London, and specifically in those of breeding and education who inhabit these regions. It is the conjunction of these two factors which gives the 'standard'. For those born beyond the Trent, as he says, 'whether they be noble men or gentlemen or of their best clarkes all is a matter'.[21]

This concept of a standard has a number of marked affinities with that later discussed by Thomas Sheridan in his own work. As Sheridan states in 1761, 'the standard of pronunciation is affixed to the custom which prevails amongst people of education at the Court, so that none but such as are born and bred amongst them, or have constant opportunities of conversing with them . . . can be said to be masters of it'.[22] Both Sheridan and Puttenham thus apparently describe what is a largely localized standard of speech, based primarily in the capital, and used by those with access to this 'best' London society. Just as Puttenham notes that those living beyond the Trent, irrespective of their rank, are not to be adopted as linguistic models, so too does Sheridan comment on the linguistic infelicities which can mark the social élite outside London: 'there are few gentlemen of England who have received their education at country schools, that are not infected with a false pronunciation of certain words, peculiar to each county.'[23] As he remarks in further corroboration of a shift in attitudes, however: 'Surely every gentleman will think it worth while, to take some pains, to get rid of such evident marks of rusticity.' Though both describe speech in terms of social markers, both therefore make it plain that elevated status is in fact to be no guarantee of linguistic propriety. Similarly, though both indicate that there may indeed be in existence a non-localized and supra-regional standard

---

[20] Puttenham, *Arte of English Poesie*, 120.   [21] Ibid.
[22] Sheridan, *Dissertation*, 17.   [23] Sheridan, *Course of Lectures*, 33.

for the written language, they also make clear that there is, on the whole, still no corresponding one for speech. As a result, when Puttenham asserts that 'I say not this but that in euery shyre of England there be gentlemen and others that speake but specially write, as good Southerne as we of Middlesex and Surrey do, but not the common people of euery shire',[24] he merely confirms the fact of a written standard which has assumed a supra-localized role for those of good standing and education, against a spoken one which, influenced by social factors, still remains localized to a larger degree. The fact that the whole sentence is in the subjunctive (following the negative) makes this still more plain. Puttenham doesn't deny that, outside the confines of the capital and the southern counties which surround it, there *may* be those of superior status who approximate to the emergent standard of speech based in London. He simultaneously reveals, however, that it is much more likely that such assimilation has been achieved in terms of the written rather than the spoken forms which they employ.

The real difference between Sheridan and Puttenham lies in the attitudes they express towards the language varieties they describe, and in the framing ideologies of a standard to which they adhere. For Puttenham, the fact that spoken language varies throughout the country, even among the 'better brought vp sort' is, for example, of far less import than is the ability to handle the 'currant' termes of the 'courtly' and 'southerne' language variety. His text is, after all, addressed to the 'maker or Poet' and, as he states in this context, 'common desiphers of good vtterance . . . resteth altogether in figuratiue speaches'.[25] Sheridan instead devotes his work to the spoken language and, as already indicated, more specifically to the need to create a uniform, and non-localized, variety of pronunciation which was to be used throughout the entire country. As he proclaims upon the title-page, his *General Dictionary* of 1780 is expressly written with the intent to define 'a plain and permanent STANDARD of PRONUNCIATION'. Standardization itself is his major motive, for, as he adds, 'in order to spread abroad the English language as a living tongue, and to facilitate the attainment of its speech, it is necessary in the first place that a standard of pronunciation should be established, and a method of acquiring a just

---

[24] Puttenham, *Arte of English Poesie*, 121.   [25] Ibid. 117.

one should be laid open'.[26] As a result, whereas for Puttenham it had been possible, and indeed acceptable, for a gentleman to speak in ways manifestly influenced by the area where he lived (even if in his written discourse he ought to approach and adopt court standards), for Sheridan the retention of such markers was to be connotative of 'disgrace', capable of contravening the status of 'gentleman' in itself. The right accent is, for him, a social testimony, 'a sort of proof that a person has kept good company', and it is presented in terms far more rigid, and socially aware, than those preferred by Puttenham. Sheridan, for example, formalizes the socio-symbolic affiliations of accent in ways expressly designed to appeal to a society in which, as contemporary commentators observed, emulation and social ambition seemed to operate as a dominant social force.[27]

Sheridan's prescriptive crusade is, as a result, explicitly constructed in terms of furthering the framing ideologies of a standard for pronunciation, and heightening awareness of its import. As he lectured his audience in Oxford in 1759, his aim was, in effect, to raise the linguistic consciousness not only as it applied to language in general, but specifically in terms of accent. 'No man can amend a fault of which he is not conscious; and consciousness cannot exert itself, when barred up by habit or vanity', he expounds,[28] setting forth familiar prescriptive paradigms in which 'habit', as for the split infinitive or the preposition in final position, was to be no safeguard against newly perceived 'incorrectness'. He thus urges an education into a proper consciousness of pronunciation so that its 'faults' may be recognized and its analogies restored; as for the written language, with its stronger sense of error and mistake, pronunciation too was, at least intentionally, to be endowed with the sense of a norm. Prevailing imbalances in attitudes towards acceptability are, in consequence, duly pointed out: 'it is reckoned a great disgrace for a gentleman to spell ill, though not to speak or read ill'.[29] The long-established leniency in terms of divergent pronunciation and difference of accent is berated: 'many provincials have grown old in the capital, without making any

---

[26] T. Sheridan, *A General Dictionary of the English Language* (London, 1780), Br.
[27] See ibid. 94.   [28] Sheridan, *Course of Lectures*, 37.
[29] Id., *A Discourse Delivered in the Theatre at Oxford, in the Senate-House at Cambridge, and at Spring-Garden in London* (London, 1759), 24.

OXFORD, May 25, 1759.

Mʀ· SHERIDAN

TAKES this Method of acquainting such Gentlemen as are desirous of improving themselves in the manner of reading the Liturgy, that he will be ready to give his Assistance in that Way, by entering into a Practical Course for the Purpose, as soon a sufficient Number shall offer themselves.------All who want farther Information on this Head, may know in what Way, and upon what Terms the Design is to be executed, by applying to Mr. Sʜᴇʀɪᴅᴀɴ at Mr. *Kemp*'s in the *High-Street*, any Time before *Thursday* the 31ſt Instant.

Such as ſhould chuſe private and ſeperate Inſtruction, may alſo know upon what Terms it is to be obtained.

And as Mr. Sʜᴇʀɪᴅᴀɴ has heard that many young Gentlemen are inclined to form themselves into ſmall Claſſes, in order to practiſe together the Art of reading aloud and reciting under his Inſpection, He likewiſe gives Notice, that upon Application to him, he will inform ſuch Gentlemen how far, and in what Way he can be of Service to them during his preſent Stay at *Oxford*.

Fɪɢ. 1.1. Advertisements for Thomas Sheridan's Lectures in Oxford, 1759

change in their original dialect'.[30] As Sheridan states with similar disapprobation in 1781: 'In general . . . speakers content themselves with the thought, that they are not worse than their neighbours.'[31]

---

[30] Id., *Course of Lectures*, 37.   [31] Id., *Rhetorical Grammar*, p. iii.

OXFORD, *May* 16, 1759.

MR. SHERIDAN's General Courſe of Lectures on
ELOCUTION, and the ENGLISH LANGUAGE
(ſo far only as relates to Elocution), will commence
on *Wedneſday* next the 23d Inſtant ; will be continued on
the ſucceeding *Friday* and *Wedneſday*, and conclude on
Friday the firſt Day of *June* : To begin each Morning
preciſely at the Hour of Ten. Price to each Subſcriber
one Guinea. Such Gentlemen as purpoſe to attend this
Courſe, are requeſted to ſend their Names to Mr. *Fletcher*,
Bookſeller in the *Turl*.

N. B. As Mr. SHERIDAN's Illneſs when he was laſt at
Oxford, prevented his going through the Courſe in the
Time propoſed, by which Means many of the Subſcribers
were abſent during Part of the Courſe, and Others heard
it in ſuch an interrupted Manner as could not be ſatis-
factory, Notice is hereby given, That all Subſcribers to
the former, ſhall be entitled to their Admiſſion, during
this Courſe, by Virtue of their firſt Subſcription.

The Lectures will be delivered at the Muſic Room *as before.*

The hitherto habitual exclusion of pronunciation from the normative paradigms of prescriptivism was evidently to be regarded as
untenable; Sheridan's self-appointed task is to provide, and moreover to disseminate, the 'information' which might decisively raise
or awaken 'consciousness' in this context for, as he affirms, it is
impossible for 'consciousness' to 'be awoken without information'.

It is, for example, clear that though the 'consciousness' Sheridan
advocates had proceeded apace in terms of attitudes to grammar,

and to spelling too, attitudes to accent had, in a number of ways, indeed seemed to lag behind, even during the eighteenth century with its habitual prescriptive zeal. Provided with the 'information' to inspire the requisite sensitization, Lord Chesterfield in 1750 could advise his son on the importance of good spelling: 'orthography, in the true sense of the word, is so absolutely necessary for a man of letters, or a gentleman, that one false spelling may fix a ridicule upon him for the rest of his life'.[32] Joseph Priestley in 1762 similarly stresses that the ability to use grammar with accuracy and precision functions as a major signifier of the educated and urbane whereas, in marked contrast, pronunciation and accent were to be adjudged 'a matter of ornament only'.[33] It was the use of the double negative or the double comparative rather than the dropped [h] which, in then dominant conceptions of linguistic propriety, served to reveal the provincial rather than the polite, and which, in turn, was seen as allied with the stratified patterns of an ordered society. In Fielding's *Tom Jones* (1749), for instance, the 'illogical' double superlative consistently characterizes the speech of servants, but its use is absent from the discourse of those higher in the social sphere: ' "That he is, the most handsomest Man I ever saw in my Life . . . his Skin be so white, and to be sure it is the most whitest that ever was seen" ' Mrs Honour, the maid, declares.[34]

Writers on the language in the earlier part of the eighteenth century make these disparities in terms of language attitude even clearer. The grammarian and schoolmaster James Greenwood, for example, simultaneously reveals the ways in which the legacies of prescriptivism are beginning to be felt in the context of pronunciation, as well as his impotence to do anything about them. As he states in this context in his own highly popular grammar of 1711: 'I cannot dissemble my unwillingness to say anything at all on this head [orthoepy]; first, because of the irregular and wrong Pronounciation of the *Letters* and *Words*, which if one should go about to mend, would be a business of great Labour and Trouble, as well as Fruitless and Unsuccessful.'[35] Ten years

[32] Cited in D. Scragg, *A History of English Spelling* (London, 1974), 90.
[33] Priestley, *Course of Lectures*, 250.
[34] H. Fielding, *The History of Tom Jones* (London, 1749), ed. F. Bowers (Oxford, 1974), 205.
[35] J. Greenwood, *An Essay Towards an English Grammar* (London, 1711), 231.

later, the hymn-writer and educator Isaac Watts, in a text explicitly intended to delineate 'the Chief Principles and Rules of *Pronouncing our Mother-Tongue*', in effect abdicates entirely that authority which Sheridan (and others) arc later so willing to wield. Making with reference to accent only a token gesture towards the prescriptive sensibilities then dominating comment on grammar, he appears content simply to describe the fluctuations which currently held sway. With marked tolerance, Watts thus states after a list of words illustrating variant pronunciations 'according to the Custome of the Speaker': 'I do not suppose both these Ways of Pronunciation to be equally proper; but both are used, and that among Persons of Education and Learning in different Parts of the Nation; . . . Custom is the great Rule of Pronouncing as well as of Spelling, so that everyone should usually speak according to Custom.'[36]

A similar pattern can be discerned in Owen's *The Youth's Instructor* of 1732; again aiming to assist in the acquisition of a 'right pronunciation', he is nevertheless forced to admit that "tis difficult (and therefore I do not pretend absolutely) to determine in so nice a Point, wherein the learned themselves are not agreed'.[37] Likewise, though Dr Johnson had originally aimed to include the 'ascertainment' of pronunciation in his *Dictionary* (his 'idea of an English dictionary' in 1747 is specified as a work 'by which the pronunciation of our language may be fixed, and its attainment facilitated'),[38] a later linguistic realism, induced by the subsequent years of lexicographical toil, retracted such ambitions. As he states in the Preface of 1755, 'sounds are too volatile and subtile for legal restraints; to enchain syllables, and to lash the wind, are equally the undertakings of pride, unwilling to measure its desires by its strength'.[39]

It is perceptions such as these which change so radically over the next few decades. In the hands of Thomas Sheridan, John Walker, Benjamin Smart, and many others, belief in notions of a spoken standard, and notably in a minimal variation of form which might extend to sounds as well as spelling, did in fact lead to a general attempt to 'enchain syllables', regardless of Johnson's own

---

[36] I. Watts, *The Art of Reading and Writing English* (London, 1721), 101–2 n.

[37] J. Owen, *The Youth's Instructor* (London, 1732), p. ii.

[38] S. Johnson, *The Plan of a Dictionary of the English Language* (London, 1747), 32.

[39] Id., *A Dictionary of the English Language* (London, 1755), C2^r.

belief in the futility of such endeavour. 'No evil so great can befal any language, as a perpetual fluctuation both in point of spelling and pronouncing'[40] Sheridan asserts, and in line with this maxim the inherent variabilities of usage were, at least ideally, to be reformed by the authoritative imposition of norms; in the words of John Walker (another of the foremost writers on pronunciation, whose *Critical Pronouncing Dictionary* was acclaimed as 'the statute-book of English orthoepy' in his obituary notice in the *Athenaeum*),[41] 'custom' (ordinary usage) was to be corrected wherever it was 'silent or dubious', a formula which seemed to permit a particularly wide latitude of operation. Concisely betraying the normative parameters in which 'custom' was now to be confined, Walker, for example, added: 'as the venerable garb of custom is often borrowed to cover the wantonness or ignorance of innovators, it will be highly necessary to view this legislator in language as closely as possible, that we may not mistake him for novelty or caprice.'[42] Walker's *General Idea of a Pronouncing Dictionary*, formulated in 1774, was in a number of ways inspired by the possibilities which prescriptivism might offer for constraint in this context. Though forced to acknowledge the realities of usage ('custom is not only the law of language, but strictly speaking it is language itself'), Walker nevertheless adheres to the prescriptive impulse behind his forthcoming dictionary of pronunciation, emphasizing the need for rational guidance in all matters where 'custom' might err; 'the most disgraceful irregularities are daily screened under the specious authority of custom', he adds.[43]

Variation was therefore intentionally to be resisted wherever possible, for, though Walker admits that it is in fact intrinsic to language ('indeed, a degree of versatility seems involved in the very nature of language'),[44] this was, as expected, to encourage rather than inhibit the operation of future prescriptive sanction: 'indeed . . . [variation] is one of those very evils left by Providence for man to correct: a love of order, and the utility of regularity, will always incline him to confine this versatility within as narrow

[40] T. Sheridan, *Elements of English* (London, 1786), p. v.

[41] *Athenaeum Magazine*, 3 (1808), 81.

[42] J. Walker, *A General Idea of a Pronouncing Dictionary of the English Language on a Plan Entirely New* (London, 1774), 7.

[43] Ibid. 7.

[44] J. Walker, *A Critical Pronouncing Dictionary and Expositor of the English Language*, 1st edn. (London, 1791), p. vi n.

bounds as possible.'[45] The tolerance which had earlier marked attitudes to accent variability was also to shift. Johnson, for example, epitomizes earlier attitudes to acceptability in his conviction that provincial markers were not necessarily at odds with the polite and that 'little aberrations' in this context were to be seen as 'of no disadvantage'.[46] His reactions to variation in accent were positive: 'a small intermixture of provincial peculiarities may, perhaps, have an agreeable effect, as the notes of different birds concur in the harmony of the grove, and please more than if they were all exactly alike' he affirmed, similarly pointing out that people who listened to him carefully would readily discern his own geographical origins: 'When people watch me narrowly . . . they will find me out to be of a particular county', just as 'Dunning may be found out to be a Devonshire man'.[47] By the time John Walker produces the first edition of his own *Critical Pronouncing Dictionary* in 1791, such variability in pronunciation is, at least within the prescriptive paradigms adopted, instead presented as 'ridiculous and embarrassing', to be avoided by all 'elegant speakers' and the truly genteel.[48]

The relevant paradigm was, it seemed, that of 'neglect', a term also selected by Walker in this context. Its effects were rendered even more conspicuous by the apparently contrastive achievements of grapheme and phoneme in this respect in a post-Johnson age: 'wherever English is taught', as Sheridan averred, 'all may attain a uniformity in spelling; but, with respect to pronunciation it is left entirely to chance.'[49] Or as Walker more pertinently expressed it: 'written language, without any considerable variation, extends to the remotest distances, . . . but speaking not only differs widely in different places at different times, but in the same place, and at the same time.'[50] In these terms, the codifying impulses already applied to grammar and especially to spelling did indeed, by contrast, seem to intensify perceptions of these continuing inadequacies and instabilities of pronunciation. Published texts, for example, tended to reproduce on a national scale the grammatical

[45] Ibid.
[46] Boswell, *The Life of Samuel Johnson LL.D*, ii: *1766–1776*, ed. L. F. Powell (Oxford, 1934), 159.
[47] Ibid.   [48] Walker, *Critical Pronouncing Dictionary*, 1st edn. (1791) p. vi.
[49] Sheridan, *Elements of English*, p. v.
[50] Walker, *General Idea of a Pronouncing Dictionary*, 1–2.

and orthographical proprieties endorsed by the prescriptive tradition, thus also of course achieving a nationwide exposure for their use within the authoritative registers of print. Double negatives and double comparatives were, in turn, gradually eliminated from these particular public discourses over the whole country, though their use could and did continue in the localized norms of speech. In a similar way, printing as well as the popularity of the dictionary as reference book encoded national norms of spelling which increasingly tended towards that invariability deemed both necessary and correct. In comparison, pronunciation continued to vary widely, not only in the realizations of individual words in London that Walker had pointed out ('the same words are often differently pronounced by different speakers, and those perhaps, of equal numbers and reputation'),[51] but also in the way that, all over England, localized norms rather than national standards seemed to prevail, a situation from which, as we have seen, not even the gentry were exempt. As Walker stressed in the introduction to his own pronouncing dictionary:

the grand difference between the metropolis and the provinces is, that people of education in London are free from all the vices of the vulgar; but the best educated people in the provinces, if constantly resident there, are sure to be strongly tinctured with the dialect of the country in which they live.[52]

In terms of the standardizing impulse which becomes increasingly perceptible in the writings of Walker and others on the subject of pronunciation, the desired standard of speech was to be identical in enunciation all over the country, regular rather than irregular, and endowed with rules of usage whereby 'good' and 'bad', as in grammar, might perhaps be ascertained. The 'best' accent was, in other words, not only to be 'correct', but it was also to be nonlocalized. In the language of the time, 'nature' was to be reformed by reason and by art, or, as expressed by Alexander Bicknell in 1796, 'as nature leaves us in a rude and uncultivated form, it is our business to polish and refine ourselves. Nature gives us the organs, it is ours to acquire the skilful performance upon them.'[53] Polishing and refining the language, in its broader ideological

---

[51] Id., *Critical Pronouncing Dictionary*, 1st edn. (1791), p. vi.
[52] Ibid., p. xiv.
[53] A. Bicknell, *The Grammatical Wreath* (London, 1796), ii. 101.

implications, was, however, to become a matter of public as well as private responsibility, and, significantly, of national as well as social honour.

The engagement of national sensibilities in issues of linguistic 'refinement' of this order was, of course, of long standing, being closely linked, for instance, to the rise of foreign language academies such as the Accademia della Crusca in 1584 and the Académie Française in 1635. In the continuing absence of a corresponding academy for England, the periodic decrees of these institutions had indeed often been seen as evincing a superior concern with the precision and purity which language, and specifically a 'standard' language, ought to manifest. Already in 1640, for example, Simon Daines had opened his introductory address to his readers:

> grieving at the strange neglect of our English Nation, that suffer our selves to be outstripped by almost all Forreigne Countries, in their daily endevours for the perfection of their Tongue . . . when we, as it were, lulled asleep with a kind of stupid remissenesse, forget the necessity of Precept.'[54]

It was, as this and similar appeals imply, the responsibility of a good nation to refine its language; achievements in this sphere were in turn felt to redound upon conceptions of the nation's own prestige.

Though the pleas for an equivalent foundation to reform English were ultimately to fail, notions that attention to language could be a matter of national honour did nevertheless remain prominent, naturally being integrated into that set of beliefs surrounding those notions of a 'correct' and perfected 'standard'. The publication of Johnson's dictionary was lauded as a national as well as a linguistic triumph—or as Garrick declaimed in his celebratory poem 'On Johnson's Dictionary':

> Talk of war with a Briton, he'll boldly advance
> That one English soldier will beat ten of France;
> Would we alter the boast from the sword to the pen,
> Our odds are still greater, still greater our men:
>
> .   .   .   .
>
> Johnson, well arm'd like a hero of yore,
> Has beat forty French, and will beat forty more![55]

[54] S. Daines, *Orthoepia Anglicana* (London, 1640), A3^r.
[55] Boswell, *Life of Johnson*, i: *1709–1765*, 300–1.

Moreover, since the state of the language was regularly interpreted as a mirror of the state of the nation, precepts of this order gave additional force to the rhetoric of nationalism which many writers also chose to employ in the context of language and correctness. As the anonymous author of *The Many Advantages of a Good Language to any Nation* (1724) asserted: 'an uncouth, ambiguous, imperfect Language, is a sure Sign of a slothful or low Genius in the People'.[56] The converse of this is made equally plain: 'a Language that is copious and clear . . . shews a good Understanding and Capacity'. Even though the proclamations of academies abroad tended to reveal, at least to an objective observer, the dichotomies which must exist between principle and practice (or ideology and process) in matters of linguistic control (as Johnson had noted in 1755, 'academies have been instituted, to guard the avenues of their languages, to retain fugitives, and repulse intruders; . . . their vigilance and activity have hitherto been in vain',[57]) this did not diminish the impact of their reforming zeal. They exemplified above all the ideology of standardization, and its power, and it was this that they disseminated so effectively through their respective nations, and, indirectly, through England too.

Writers on pronunciation were likewise subject to the legacy of these ideas, and it was in terms of national honour, and national shame, that Sheridan, for one, also sought to bring out the deficiencies of the English with regard to their spoken language. 'The Italians, French, and Spaniards, in proportion to their progress in civilisation and politeness, have for more than a century been employed, with the utmost industry, in cultivating and regulating their speech', he stressed in 1780,[58] effectively pointing up the contrast between 'civilisation' and its antonyms in his subsequent description of England, and English: 'we still remain in the state of all barbarous countries in this respect, having left ours wholly to chance'. It was neglect of this order which, from a European perspective, formed the true hallmark of the nation: 'the English are still classed by the people of these countries, amongst the more rude and scarcely civilized countries of the North. They affix the term of barbarism to this country, in the same manner as the Greeks did to the rest of the world; and on the same principle, on account of the neglect in polishing our speech.'[59]

---

[56] *The Many Advantages of a Good Language to Any Nation* (London, 1724), 4.
[57] Johnson, *Dictionary* (1755), C2r.
[58] Sheridan *General Dictionary* (1780), A1r.   [59] Id., *Dissertation*, 1.

Albeit 'the last refuge of a scoundrel' according to Dr Johnson, patriotism was thus readily to be employed in order to instil this necessary consciousness of 'correctness'; in these terms, the absence of national standards of use was to lend additional force to the often-stated impulses to standardize an accent for all speakers of English. Since differences of accent manifestly divided the country, revealing place of origin for virtually every speaker, the intention, at least within the self-expressed tenets of prescriptive ideology, was therefore to dispel these distinctions by formalizing one pronunciation, wherever possible, for each word, just as each word had, on the whole, received one spelling. With a certain naïvety (and no little irony in view of the consequences it was ultimately to have), early conceptions of a non-localized accent hence stressed the role it would play in creating a new equality in speech, and indeed in uniting a nation hitherto characterized by difference and diversity in terms of the spoken word. In Sheridan's words, since the introduction of a 'proper' standard would mean that all people would speak in the same way, the 'odious distinctions' which had previously prevailed in England would, of course, necessarily be eliminated: 'Would it not greatly contribute to put an end to the odious distinctions kept up between subjects of the same king, if a way were opened by which the attainment of the English Tongue in its purity, both in point of phraseology and pronunciation, might to rendered easy to all inhabitants of his Majesty's dominions?'[60]

Both altruism and egalitarianism are thus overtly made to predominate in the texts of Sheridan and other writers on this subject, the former's aims to disseminate a set of supra-regional norms of accent over the whole country being phrased not only in the familiar terms of national honour, but equally in terms of the need to increase access to a 'standard' seen as bound up with social and linguistic advantage. Since, as Sheridan justifiably contends, 'the standard of pronunciation is affixed to the custom which prevails among people of education at the Court', it was, in consequence, confined to the habits of a social élite to which relatively few have access. Social (as well as geographical) barriers impeded the spread of the 'proper' norms of speech which all should rightly use, for, as he adds, 'none but such as are born and bred amongst them, or have constant opportunities of conversing with them . . . can be

---

[60] Id., *Rhetorical Grammar*, p. xv.

said to be masters of it'.[61] Since this inequality of opportunity could moreover extend even to those of polite and educated rank located outside the capital, the role of accent as social symbol as it existed in the late eighteenth century was, in conceptions such as these, to be regarded as fundamentally divisive, promoting an unnecessary exclusion, and exclusivity, at the expense of creating a proper, uniform, and above all, non-localized standard for the nation. In contrast to the deft manipulations of social nuance which predominate in later accounts of accent, such as that expressed in *How to Shine in Society* ('Purity of accent is the grand distinctive feature of an educated gentleman. It belongs to no city or district, and is acknowledged and accepted as current coin with all grades of society'),[62] the prime motivation in these earlier texts on language is often not the fostering of emulative paradigms for their own sake. Instead, adopting ostensibly different ideological strategies, it is commonly presented in images of a greater good which advocate the social utility of standardization as well as seeing it as a linguistic process.

'Talking proper', in such socially motivated rhetoric, is thus made into a social right, utilizing conceptions of a standard which acts, as William Downes confirms, as 'part of the abstract, unifying identity of a large and internally differentiated society'.[63] Those with direct access to fashionable modes of speech in London are, Sheridan stresses, 'but few compared to the millions who speak the same tongue, and cannot have such opportunity'[64] and it is this 'opportunity' which he, and many other writers, were to attempt to change and to extend. A spoken standard was, at least in theory, to manifest a new equality within the nation, removing, by means of its convergent specifications, the 'disgrace' of dialect and the 'inequalities' of regional markers from rustic aristocracy, northern gentry, and commoner alike. As Sheridan affirms:

an uniformity of pronunciation throughout Scotland, Wales, and Ireland, as well as through the several counties of England, would be a point much to be wished; as it might in great measure contribute to destroy those odious distinctions between subjects of the same king, and members of the same community, which are ever attended with ill consequences,

---

[61] Id., *Dissertation*, 17.   [62] *How to Shine in Society* (Glasgow, 1860), 20.
[63] W. Downes, *Language in Society* (London, 1984), 34.
[64] Sheridan, *Dissertation*, 17–18.

and which are chiefly kept alive by differences of pronunciation and dialect.[65]

Social harmony rather than social hegemony will, such comments suggest, emerge as a consequence of prescriptive endeavour in this context, the 'ill consequences' of accent difference being removed with the adoption of a new and, in particular, a neutral standard for all. Language and nation are again linked, and not only, of course, by Sheridan. William Johnston offers his pronouncing dictionary as a means 'by which, Both his Majesty's Subjects, and Foreigners, may correct an *Improper*, or acquire a *Right* Pronunciation of the English Language'.[66] John Murdoch, in his 1809 edition of Walker's *Critical Pronouncing Dictionary*, commends as 'a real service to society' those who aid in 'an acquirement so desirable and important'.[67] Walker himself depicts his own prescriptive zeal as inspired by his recognition of 'duty to the nation', stressing the fact that though 'Accent and Quantity, the great efficients of pronunciation, are seldom mistaken by people of education in the Capital . . . the great bulk of the Nation, and those who form the most important part of it, are without these advantages, and therefore want such a guide to direct them as is here offered'.[68] Samuel Oliver in the early nineteenth century is, in a similar vein, driven to express his own 'due reverence for the enlightened, and patriotical spirit which has produced in Ingland so large a number of grammatik works'.[69] The central tenet of such positions is, however, perhaps best summed up by Henry Alford, Dean of Canterbury and writer on language, in 1864: 'the national mind is reflected in the national speech', as he proclaimed in yet another call to individual and national responsibility in matters of linguistic correctness.[70]

Prescriptive texts, as this indicates, can operate very effectively as ideological discourses, and in such formulations duty to the nation was regularly to reside not only in the specification of

---

[65] Id., *Course of Lectures*, 206.

[66] W. Johnston, *A Pronouncing and Spelling Dictionary of the English Language* (London, 1764), title-page.

[67] J. Walker, *Critical Pronouncing Dictionary*, ed. J. Murdoch (1809), p. i.

[68] Id., *Critical Pronouncing Dictionary*, 3rd edn. (1802), 13.

[69] S. Oliver, *A General Critical Grammar of the Inglish Language on a System Novel and Extensive* (London, 1825), p. xiii.

[70] H. Alford, *A Plea for the Queen's English* 2nd edn. (London, 1864), 5.

convergent patterns of usage, but also, of course, in the censure, and proposed elimination, of divergent ones. Since it was above all regional accents which were deemed to be a primary cause of these 'odious distinctions' among the population, their 'refinement' in the direction of London norms could only be a social good. Clearly regarded as 'other' within the rhetoric so often employed, such enunciations were necessarily 'deviant', and in need of due correction, a notion which in itself rapidly exposes the ideological flaws within the egalitarian ideals overtly endorsed. In the stated terms, 'ill consequences', whether social or linguistic, could be mitigated by such prescriptive means, while differential value, long embedded in the modes of metropolitan against provincial speech, might thus be brought to disappear. In such ways, the intolerance of optional variability which is a staple of the standardizing impulse was made to fuse both social and linguistic ideology, a circumstance which had seemingly obvious appeal in a society in which notions of mobility, self-help, and as Bulwer Lytton termed it, 'the aristo-cratic contagion',[71] were all deemed to operate as significant social stimuli.

The framing ideologies of a standard might indeed be brought to shift ground on the subject of pronunciation, fostering a new sensitization to its norms as well as a sense of its social values in ways which, at least ostensibly, were more philanthropic than those which were later to pertain. Nevertheless, as Sheridan stressed, there still remained no 'method', and no easy way, in which knowledge of this non-localized and neutral accent was to be acquired. This had indeed initially been the factor inhibiting any earlier application of prescriptive sensibilities to the realms of speech. As Swift, one of the major writers on the initial ambitions to reform English, had indicated in the early eighteenth century, though grammar and lexis were properly to be subject to linguistic legislation, it seemed impossible to apply this to the domains of spoken English, and to accent in particular; he therefore describes with complete acceptance 'a country squire having only the provincial accent upon his tongue, which is neither a fault, nor in his power to remedy'. By the end of the eighteenth century, how-ever, such 'remedy' seemed perhaps within reach. Pronunciation

---

[71] E. Bulwer Lytton, *England and the English* (London, 1833), ed. S. Meacham (Chicago, 1970) 27; see pp. 66–7.

too, as we have seen, was to become part of the taught language, its principles described, prescribed, and, perhaps most importantly, transcribed in the flood of works devoted to it, and its attendant ideologies, which appeared from the mid-eighteenth century onwards.

As Sheridan had already realized in 1761, 'if a method of acquiring a just pronunciation by books, as well as conversation, were established [its] acquisition would not be circumscribed within such narrow bounds, but would be open to all British subjects wherever born'.[72] It was this 'method' on which he and others were to concentrate their energies, not least in terms of the dictionary and the systematic details of pronunciation which it could perhaps be made to provide for all users of the language. Almost twenty years before his *General Dictionary of the English Language* of 1780, Sheridan had noted his general aims:

The object ... is, to fix such a standard of pronunciation, by means of visible marks, that it may be in the power of every one, to acquire an accurate manner of uttering every word in the English tongue, by applying to that standard. In order to do this, the author of this scheme proposes to publish a Dictionary, in which the true pronunciation, of all the words in our tongue, shall be pointed out by visible and accurate marks.[73]

The power of the press was to act as a prime agency in the dissemination of this intended phonemic 'remedy'. 'This would be making a noble use of the invention of printing',[74] stated Sheridan in 1761; to reduce 'the pronunciation of each word to a certainty by fixed and visible marks' was in fact 'the only way in which uniformity of sound could be propagated to any distance'.[75] This was of course the aim, phonetic notation serving, in the ideal world, as a means by which a non-localized accent might be defined, and in turn disseminated. Many others were naturally to think along the same lines and, guaranteed a national distribution, it was print, in the form of books, manuals, pamphlets, and dictionaries, which was envisaged as being able to provide the non-localized access to non-localized norms which, as we have seen, was widely propagated as essential. Though condemned later in the nineteenth century by the philologist (and founding father of the *OED*), Richard Chevenix Trench, as 'the greatest of all

---

[72] Sheridan, *Dissertation*, 38.   [73] Ibid. 29–30.   [74] Ibid. 18.
[75] Sheridan, *Rhetorical Grammar*, p. xviii.

absurdities',[76] it was, in this context, the development of the pronouncing dictionary which was nevertheless perhaps to be of notable importance.

In line with the previous absence of sensitization towards the proprieties of accent (and its needful correction), pronunciation had in fact not been indicated in the early dictionaries. Nathan Bailey in the fifth edition of his *Universal Etymological Dictionary* (1731), for example, merely marks the position of main stress (ABA'NDON, A'NTICHAMBER), though even this represents an advance in lexicographical practice from the neglect with which pronunciation had previously been treated. Samuel Johnson too adheres to this method, in keeping with his rejection of the possibility of enchaining syllables by prescriptive means. As he notes: 'In settling the orthography, I have not wholly neglected the pronunciation, which I have directed, by printing an accent upon the acute or elevated syllable.'[77] Later dictionaries, however, began in addition to include the marking of vowel length, so that two years after the first edition of Johnson's own dictionary James Buchanan, in *A New English Dictionary*, is already deploying a macron (–) for a long vowel, and a contrastive breve (˘) for a short one.[78] Reflecting the gradual shifts in thinking about accent, even this was later considered inadequate, especially given the growing convictions about the utility of the written language for the intended reform of the spoken. William Kenrick in his *New English Dictionary* of 1773, is, as a result, the first to utilize the possibilities of a series of small numerals appended above individual letters in order to signify still finer details of enunciation. Sheridan himself is the first writer to combine this, in his *General Dictionary of the English Language* (1780), with the systematic respelling of the entry word, thus introducing the method which, with individual modifications of notation, was to be adopted by Walker, Smart, and many others over the later eighteenth and nineteenth centuries, as in the following entries in Walker's dictionary illustrated in Figure 2.1.

The pronouncing dictionary was, in a number of ways, to be of fundamental importance in furthering these notions of 'proper' speech. Trading on the popularity of the dictionary in a post-Johnson age, and on a public increasingly habituated to consult,

---

[76] R. C. Trench, *English Past and Present* (London, 1855), 171.

[77] Johnson, *Dictionary*, A2ᵛ.

[78] J. Buchanan, *A New English Dictionary* (London, 1757).

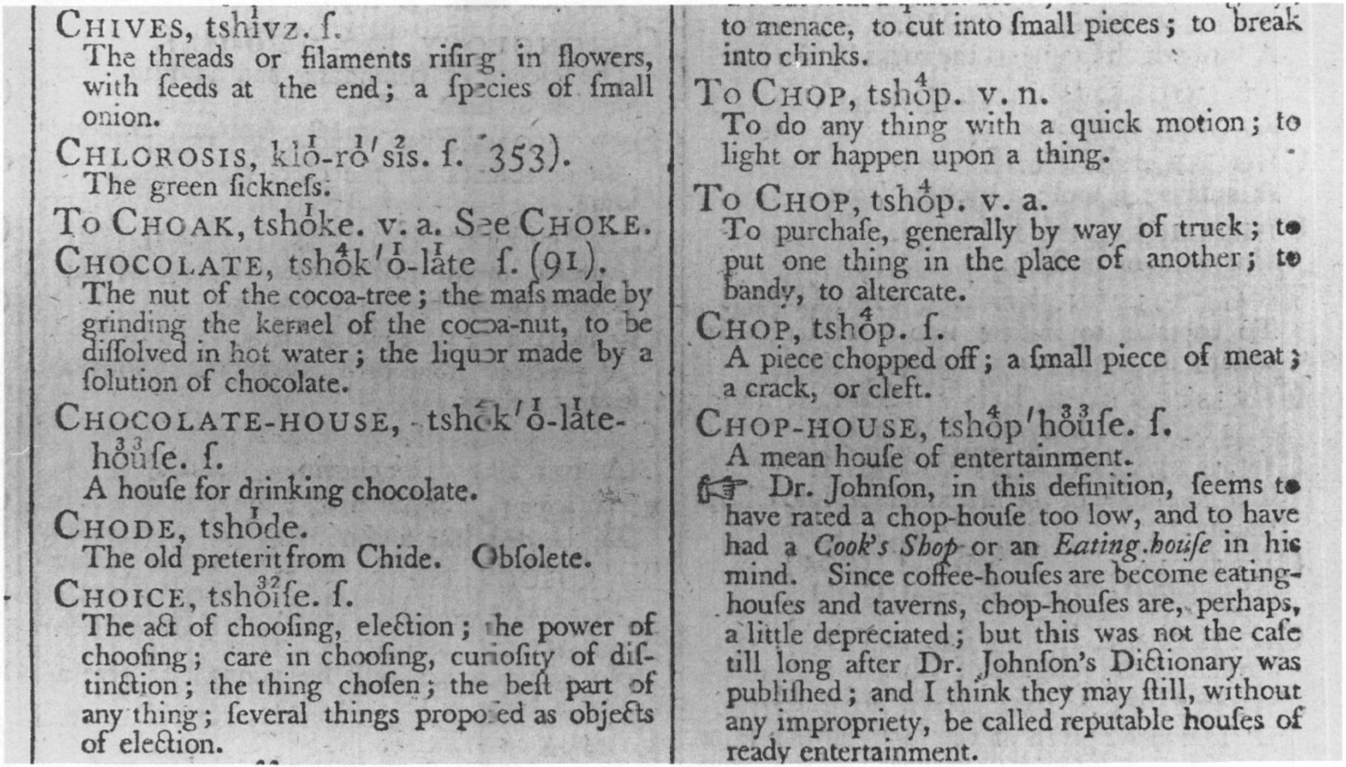

CHIVES, tshívz. f.
The threads or filaments rising in flowers, with seeds at the end; a species of small onion.

CHLOROSIS, klŏ-rṓ'sis. f. (353).
The green sickness.

To CHOAK, tshṓke. v. a. See CHOKE.
CHOCOLATE, tshŏk'ŏ-láte f. (91).
The nut of the cocoa-tree; the mass made by grinding the kernel of the cocoa-nut, to be dissolved in hot water; the liquor made by a solution of chocolate.

CHOCOLATE-HOUSE, -tshŏk'ŏ-láte-hŏúse. f.
A house for drinking chocolate.

CHODE, tshṓde.
The old preterit from Chide. Obsolete.

CHOICE, tshŏíse. f.
The act of choosing, election; the power of choosing; care in choosing, curiosity of distinction; the thing chosen; the best part of any thing; several things proposed as objects of election.

to menace, to cut into small pieces; to break into chinks.

To CHOP, tshŏp. v. n.
To do any thing with a quick motion; to light or happen upon a thing.

To CHOP, tshŏp. v. a.
To purchase, generally by way of truck; to put one thing in the place of another; to bandy, to altercate.

CHOP, tshŏp. f.
A piece chopped off; a small piece of meat; a crack, or cleft.

CHOP-HOUSE, tshŏp'hŏúse. f.
A mean house of entertainment.
☞ Dr. Johnson, in this definition, seems to have rated a chop-house too low, and to have had a *Cook's Shop* or an *Eating-house* in his mind. Since coffee-houses are become eating-houses and taverns, chop-houses are, perhaps, a little depreciated; but this was not the case till long after Dr. Johnson's Dictionary was published; and I think they may still, without any impropriety, be called reputable houses of ready entertainment.

Fig. 2.1. Extract from John Walker's *Critical Pronouncing Dictionary*

and defer to, its authority on all matters of doubt, writers such as Kenrick, Johnston, Walker, Browne, Longmuir, and Nuttall, amid many others, all yoked Johnson's definitions to increasingly complex systems of transcription. Their work often met an audience which seemed to subscribe all too readily to the ideologies of a standard manipulated within the prescriptive tradition. William Cobbett, for example, became word perfect on the nuances of correctness offered by Lowth's *Grammar* ('I wrote the whole grammar out two or three times; I got it by heart; I repeated it every morning and every evening, and . . . I imposed on myself the task of saying it all over once every time I was posted sentinel').[79] Similarly, as Adam Smith's review of Johnson's own dictionary reveals, it was common for still more stringent, and still more rigorous guidance to be demanded on this subject of linguistic correctness: 'we cannot help wishing, that the author had trusted less to the judgement of those who may consult him, and had oftener passed his own censure upon those words which are not of approved use, tho' sometimes to be met with in authors of no mean name.'[80] Certainly, once the pronouncing dictionary was instituted, demand for the instruction it claimed to offer was high and, together with attendant texts on the same subject, it too was seemingly assimilated within the consequences of that 'consumer revolution' documented by Neil McKendrick.[81] Walker's *Critical Pronouncing Dictionary* went through well over a hundred editions, appearing in a wide variety of formats over the late eighteenth and nineteenth centuries; as he noted already in 1802, it acquired a popularity which was difficult to satisfy: 'The rapid sale of the Second Edition of this Dictionary called upon me for a Third, at a time of life, and in a state of health, little compatible with the drudgery and attention necessary for the execution of it.'[82] In this, as in any other area, supply and demand were to be closely linked, and a public whose attitudes to language were often constructed in terms of prevailing

[79] W. Cobbett, *The Life and Adventures of Peter Porcupine* (Philadelphia, Pa., 1797), 22.

[80] Unsigned review A. Smith of '*A Dictionary of the English Language* by Samuel Johnson', in *The Edinburgh Review. Containing an account of all the Books and Pamphlets Published in Scotland from June 1755 (to January 1756)* (Edinburgh, 1755), 62.

[81] N. McKendrick, J. Brewer, and J. Plumb, *The Birth of a Consumer Society: The Commercialization of Eighteenth-Century England* (London, 1982); see also p. 82.

[82] Walker, *Critical Pronouncing Dictionary*, 3rd edn. (1802), 13.

prescriptive (and fashionable) thinking, was likewise, according to contemporary accounts, increasingly attuned to the validity and virtues of linguistic correction too. As William Johnston affirmed as early as 1764, again encoding these stated affiliations of altruism and prescriptive censure: 'many who labour under the disadvantages of a wrong pronunciation, are so sensible of these things, as to have earnest desires to acquire a right one: and for that end, may have kindly endeavoured to furnish them with some suitable assistance.'[83]

Even individuals whose incomes precluded their purchase of these dictionaries in their entirety (Walker's, for example, cost over a pound at a time when, as Richard Altick confirms, the average salary of an usher in a school was only between four and eight shillings a week)[84] were to be made so aware of their own inadequacies in this respect that they issued public demands for more economical formats, or for separate and thereby cheaper publication of the extensive descriptions of 'good' speech prefacing these works. Russel in 1801, for instance, earnestly importuned Walker in these terms, desiring a format for the *Critical Pronouncing Dictionary* which would 'be portable with convenience' and priced so that it did not prohibit access to those 'who cannot, without inconvenience, spare a guinea'.[85] William Kenrick, among others, was to accede to similar requests, publishing the original introduction to his *New Dictionary of the English Language* as a work in its own right in 1784 on the grounds that 'the expence of that work [the original dictionary] must have for ever precluded its merits from being generally known to those who stood most in need of it'.[86]

Of course, not all responses to the pronouncing dictionary as a social and linguistic institution were unreservedly favourable. Johnson for one had serious misgivings early on about its potential utility as a means of standardization, at least in practical terms. As

---

[83] Johnston, *Pronouncing and Spelling Dictionary*, p. v.

[84] R. D. Altick, *The English Common Reader: A Social History of the Mass Reading Public 1800–1900* (Chicago, Ill., 1957), 51.

[85] W. P. Russel, *Multum in Parvo* (London, 1801), 13 n.

[86] Advertisement for W. Kenrick, *A Rhetorical Grammar of the English Language* (London, 1784). The price of the dictionary is given as one guinea. Sheridan also published the *Rhetorical Grammar* which formed part of his *General Dictionary of the English Language* as a separate work. First appearing in 1781, this proved highly popular, and went through a number of further editions.

he pointed out with reference to Sheridan's dictionary: '[the pronouncing dictionary] may do very well; but you cannot always carry it about with you: and, when you want the word, you have not the Dictionary.' Potential problems are further illuminated by a typically Johnsonian simile: 'it is', he adds, 'like a man who has a sword that will not draw. It is an admirable sword, to be sure: but while your enemy is cutting your throat, you are unable to use it.'[87] Though Russel, as we have seen, did campaign for a smaller version of Walker's dictionary 'so as to be portable with ease', thereby envisaging one solution to those more practical difficulties foreseen by Johnson, other writers made it clear that the proper use of works on pronunciation of this kind was not by any means to require their constant presence about the person. As they stress in their own claims for the processes of standardization which might thereby be enacted on the spoken word, it was to be conscientious application rather than occasional reference which would ensure command of the 'proper' and non-localized accents which such dictionaries so eloquently offered their readers.

This is perhaps expressed with greatest clarity by the lexicographer and clergyman William Johnston in 1764, for, although not dismissing the use of his *Pronouncing and Spelling Dictionary* as a reference book to be consulted in moments of phonetic indecision, he makes it plain that a somewhat more regular engagement with the text is advisable if the full benefits it offered were to be derived. Like Sheridan, he places due emphasis upon the agency of the dictionary, and the 'fixed and visible marks' of its transcriptions, in facilitating the acquisition of a 'standard' accent:

I herein offer a help to the right Pronunciation of the english Language, whereby those who generally speak well, may with great facility, rectify their peculiar Improprieties, and by which, I sincerely think, the youth of Cornwall and Cumberland, of Scotland and Ireland . . . may learn by themselves to pronounce english tolerably well; and by which, were they, after this, to reside for some time in London, their pronunciation might soon, become hardly distinguishable from that of the inhabitants.[88]

This rectification of regional 'error' is clearly not to be arrived at by mere consultation of the dictionary in moments of uncertainty. Instead, both text and dictionary proper were (at least ideally) to

---

[87] Boswell, *Life of Johnson*, ii. 161.
[88] Johnston, *Pronouncing and Spelling Dictionary*, p. viii.

be worked through systematically, each and every word being articulated in accordance with the notation supplied until true propriety is not only achieved, but is, in addition, assimilated. The recommended method is intensive, but will, the reader is assured, bring its own rewards:

> Three quarters of an hour, employed in pronouncing words in this distinct manner, in the order in which they occur, would be a sufficient exercise at a time; for both the attention, and capacity for pronouncing well, will by that time generally flag: But in the interval of an hour or two, they will be revived again. And this exercise repeated two or three times in a day, as affairs will permit, for a month together, will carry you several times through the book, and give you a general knowledge and practice of a right pronunciation.[89]

Johnston is not alone in such specifications. *Live and Learn: A Guide for All Who Wish to Speak and Write Correctly*, a later text which went through twenty-eight editions in seventeen years, proffers similar counsel, recommending both patience and industry in its 'general advice to those who find themselves deficient in the art of pronunciation':

> Take, every morning, some passage from a good writer, poetry or prose; mark every letter and syllable with respect to which mistake is likely to occur, using a good dictionary in every case of the slightest uncertainty; pronounce each word several times by itself, and then go through the whole passage until you can read it correctly, in a graceful and natural manner, and with ease to yourself. N.B.—A great deal of care, as well as humility, is required for the discovery of one's own faults.[90]

Sheridan too envisaged application of similar thoroughness on the part of his readers. As he notes with reference to [h]-dropping, a shibboleth which he is the first writer to record in terms which reveal negative sensitization to its use: 'The best method of curing this will be to read over frequently all the words beginning with the letter *H* and those beginning with *Wh* in the dictionary, and push them out with the full force of the breath, 'till an habit is obtained of aspirating strongly'.[91] It was modes of usage on these lines, stressing methodical, dedicated, and practical use rather

---

[89] Ibid. 41.
[90] *Live and Learn: A Guide for All Who Wish to Speak and Write Correctly* 28th edn. (London, 1872), 160–1.
[91] Sheridan, *Course of Lectures*, 35. See also pp. 113–15.

than incidental checking, which had of course initially led to
Sheridan's belief in the value of the pronouncing dictionary as an
agent of standardization for the spoken word. By individual industry, users of the dictionary would be able to eliminate those features, and their connotative values, which 'in a manner proclaim
the place of a man's birth, which otherwise could not be known
by other means in mixed societies'.[92]

'A Pronouncing Dictionary is almost a necessary appendage to
every library',[93] declared David Booth in 1837, and edition after
edition of such works was in fact brought out, the introductory
principles of pronunciation which they contained being reduced,
expanded, printed in miniature, printed in paper or hard covers,
or condensed to their utmost essentials so that they might come
within the means of every pocket. Moreover, it is important to
recognize that private individuals were by no means to provide the
only readership for these pronouncing dictionaries. On the contrary, they often became essential tools in educational institutions,
as pupils were drilled in the requisite proprieties of speech while
they learnt to read. The parsing of sounds in line with the principles
used by Walker became, for example, a commonplace mode of
instruction,[94] while familiarity with Walker's *Critical Pronouncing
Dictionary* was often recommended by government inspectors for
teacher and pupil alike ('The master should have at hand a good
English dictionary (Walker's may be purchased for 4s. 6d.) and not
be afraid to make use of it in the presence of his pupils.'[95]). Though
this integration of pronunciation into educational methodology
will be discussed in more detail in Chapter 6, the fact that the
emergent educational system was also to embrace these norm and
deviation paradigms of accent difference is clearly not irrelevant at
this stage. 'Talking proper', as we will see, was to be an educational desideratum too, and the pronouncing dictionary not immaterial to its encouragement.

As Fasold stresses, authors of grammars and usage books
naturally have an impact on language use only 'to the extent their
work is consulted';[96] the extensive evidence of their deployment,

[92] Ibid. 206.
[93] D. Booth, *The Principles of English Grammar* (London, 1837), 11.
[94] See p. 303.
[95] Privy Council Committee on Education, *Extracts from the Reports of Her
Majesty's Inspectors of Schools* (London, 1852), 192.
[96] R. Fasold, *The Sociolinguistics of Society* (Oxford, 1984), 253.

in both public and private forms, over the nineteenth century does nevertheless, in a variety of ways, combine to suggest that their influence was in fact far from minimal, at least in terms of emphasizing the 'proper' notions of correctness, even if not (in real terms) of achieving the national accent for all which many, as we have seen, endeavoured to provide. By the end of the nineteenth century, John Walker had, for example, almost become a household name, so that manuals of etiquette could refer to those obsessed with linguistic propriety as trying to 'out-Walker Walker',[97] and even Dickens could allude to Walker's dictionary in *Dombey and Son* as being part of the preferred reading of Miss Blimber (' "If my recollection serves me," said Miss Blimber, breaking off, "the word analysis, as opposed to synthesis, is thus defined by Walker . . . *Now* you know what analysis is, Dombey" ').[98] He had in effect become one of the icons of the age, commonly referred to as 'Elocution Walker', just as Johnson had come to be labelled 'Dictionary Johnson' in the public mind. Contemporary references to Walker's influence in this sphere are thus frequent, spanning a range from the relatively objective to the downright eulogistic. For Russel in 1801, the *Critical Pronouncing Dictionary* which constituted the most important of Walker's publications was no less than 'a glorious monument of human genius, manifesting, to his contemporaries and to posterity, a happy combination of persevering industry with extensive erudition'. It would, as he asserts with little sense of his own hyperbole, 'perpetuate his name with more erudition, and more venerable regard, than if he had amassed stones and mortar to a greater degree of elevation and circumference equal to the pyramids of Egypt'.[99] Long after Walker's death in 1807, the same commendations continue; as Peter Nuttall, for instance, declares in 1873, 'the name of WALKER, as one of our earliest orthoepists, is known and duly appreciated wherever the English language is spoken'.[100] Such praise testifies to the enthusiasm generated towards issues of linguistic control with little room

---

[97] *Society Small Talk. Or What to Say and When to Say It*, 2nd edn. (London, 1880), 116: 'The peculiar manner in which certain people pronounce certain words under the impression that the doing so is fine and fashionable, is in itself the height of vulgarity . . . They in a way endeavour to out-Walker Walker.'

[98] C. Dickens, *Dombey and Son* (London, 1848), ed. A. Horsman (Oxford, 1974), 184.

[99] Russel, *Multum in Parvo*, 57.

[100] P. A. Nuttall, *Walker's Pronouncing Dictionary of the English Language*, 4th edn. (London, 1873), p. iii.

for doubt. Even Alexander Ellis, from a vantage point intentionally within the new (and more objective) descriptivism of the later nineteenth century, commends Walker's activities and influence in this sphere, in spite of his criticisms of the fallible assumptions of authority which Walker (and other writers) had so frequently taken upon themselves: 'Walker has done good and hard work; he has laid down rules, and hence given definite assertions to be considered, and he has undoubtedly materially influenced thousands of people who looked upon him as an authority.'[101]

From his own vantage-point in America, the lexicographer Noah Webster had, even by the late eighteenth century, been amazed at such English veneration (and obeisance) towards these self-appointed arbiters of linguistic authority. Describing the rise of 'individuals, who dictate to a nation the rules of speaking, with the same imperiousness as a tyrant gives orders to his vassals', he marvelled at the servility which could result: 'strange as it may appear, even well-bred people and scholars, often surrender their right of private judgement to these literary governors. The *ipse dixit* of a Johnson, a Garrick, or a Sheridan, has the force of law, and to contradict it is rebellion.'[102] James Boswell for one, in spite of Johnson's reassurances that his accent was 'not offensive', had indeed surrendered his own 'right of private judgement' in precisely this way to Sheridan himself (as well as to Mr Love of Drury Lane). Just as Sheridan's course of lectures had expounded the ways in which 'the attainment [of the London standard] is ardently desired by an infinite number of individuals',[103] so therefore did Boswell take personal lessons from Sheridan in a stated attempt to 'improve' his own native tone.[104] The evidence of other individuals reveals the operation of similar processes of sensitization, corroborating the ways in which, as William Cockin had stressed in 1775, 'it appears . . . that works of this nature may at least be as much service in teaching us to perceive as to execute'.[105] Sir Christopher Sykes in 1778, for example, thus earnestly sought a tutor for his offspring who would be qualified to eradicate their

---

[101] Ellis, *Early English Pronunciation*, ii. 629.
[102] N. Webster, *Dissertations on the English Language* (Boston, Mass., 1789), 167–8.
[103] Sheridan, *Course of Lectures*, 30.
[104] Boswell, *Life of Johnson*, ii. 159.
[105] W. Cockin, *The Art of Delivering Written Language* (London, 1775), p. ix.

regional accent, a mode of speech increasingly being seen as incompatible with any pretensions to status. He too desired 'improvement' in these respects; as he wrote to the Reverend Cleaver: 'the person who has hitherto had the instruction of my children is going into another line of life, indeed he is no loss as he has done them all the good he is capable of, which was to teach them to read English though but ill'. His quest was instead for 'any young man you think fit to succeed him', the one specification being that he 'can correct their Yorkshire tone'.[106] The letters of Maria Edgeworth similarly expose her own increasing awareness of features which, for earlier writers such as Swift, had not been interpreted either as 'error' or as unacceptable. Edgeworth, in contrast, comments on the linguistic 'problems' she faced in her visit to Liverpool, the old connotative dichotomies between capital and the rest of the country evidently having been enhanced in line with the newly normative views on that 'disgrace' which the use of regional markers could bring in its wake. As she concludes of Mr Roscoe of Allerton Hall, 'a strong provincial accent . . . destroys all idea of elegance'.[107] 'Ridicule' must surely attend the use of 'broad Yorkshire or Somersetshire in the drawing room',[108] averred Mrs Elizabeth Montagu at the end of the eighteenth century, betraying a similar awareness of the shift in language attitudes in her conviction that this conjunction was clearly incompatible.

Certainly thousands of people each year flocked to the lectures of Walker and Sheridan as they individually toured the country, expounding their theories on the new elegancies of speech. Mrs Sheridan in 1762, for example, affirmed the popularity of her husband's lectures with pride:

The Course of Lectures which Mr Sheridan is now reading in the city is attended in a manner which shows the people more warm and earnest on the subject than can well be conceived; his auditory seldom consisting of less than five hundred people, and this is the utmost the hall will contain; many have been disappointed for want of room, and he is strenuously solicited to repeat the Course again immediately in the same

---

[106] Sledmere MSS, Sir Christopher Sykes's Letter Book, 1775–90, Sykes to Revd W. Cleaver, 15 Sept. 1778; cited in F. M. L. Thompson, *English Landed Society in the Nineteenth Century* (London, 1963), 135.

[107] Maria Edgeworth, *Letters From England, 1813–1844*, ed. C. Colvin (Oxford, 1971), 7.

[108] Cited in W. Matthews, *Cockney Past and Present: A Short History of the Dialect of London* (London, 1972), 222.

place. This I believe he will comply with, though he is to give another Course next month at Spring Gardens.[109]

Lest this be interpreted as being merely the evidence of wifely partiality, Watkins in 1817 provides additional confirmation of such success: 'Incredible as it may seem, the fact is certain, that he had upwards of sixteen hundred subscribers, at a guinea each, besides occasional visitors, which, with the advantage arising from the publication of the course, at half-a-guinea in boards, must have rendered his emoluments very considerable.'[110] Walker too received considerable commendation for his lectures, even being invited to give private seminars on elocution to the Heads of Houses and assorted Fellows in the University of Oxford following his more general lectures there; as he noted in his *Elements of Elocution* of 1781: 'Having had the honour, a few years ago, to give public lectures in English Pronunciation at the University of Oxford, I was some time afterwards invited by several of the Heads of Houses to give private lectures on the Art of Reading, in their respective colleges.'[111]

Journals of the day also reinforced corresponding emphases for their own readers, devoting considerable space and attention to debating the rival claims of different modes of pronunciation, as well as the rival merits of different pronouncing dictionaries. The *Critical Review* in 1796, for instance, commends the potential efficacy of William Smith's pronouncing dictionary of 1795 in terms which effortlessly reinforce the propagated links between 'talking proper', and the social mobility that might result:

we have seen an eminent lawyer getting rid almost entirely of his Northern accents, and thus making his way to the highest post in his profession: and we can take upon ourselves to say, that, with equal care, the rest of his countrymen, and the inhabitants of Ireland, might be brought nearly upon a level with the best speakers in the metropolis.

As this indicates, these issues were deemed relevant for Scotland as well; a 'Northern accent', as the sub-text of this review reveals, could impede social progress and professional advance. This too was a localized marker to be regarded as unacceptable within the emergent ideologies of 'standard' speech and its embedded social

---

[109] Cited in Benzie, *Dublin Orator*, 27–8.
[110] J. Watkins (ed.), *Memoirs of R. B. Sheridan* (London, 1817), 79.
[111] J. Walker, *Elements of Elocution* (London, 1781), a4^r.

values; like many other writers, Walker was helpfully to provide a separate section in his own dictionaries in order to aid 'the Natives of SCOTLAND' in 'attaining a just Pronunciation of English' and the same is proffered the 'Natives of IRELAND'. Sheridan himself was, of course, Irish, while Johnston, Buchanan, Elphinston, and Smith were Scots; as their comments indicate all too frequently, such provenance was to be no excuse for the failure to modify speech habits in the direction of 'standard' norms, especially since guidance on these subjects was becoming so readily available.

As Sylvester Douglas (Lord Glenbervie), another Scot, reveals in his own *Treatise on the Provincial Dialect of Scotland* (with its subtitle 'being an attempt to assist persons of that country in discovering and correcting the defects of their pronunciation and expression'), language attitudes and attendant ideologies of a standard did indeed seem to exert equal influence over Britain as a whole. 'By a provincial dialect is understood, not strictly the dialect peculiar to any particular province or district', he explained, 'but rather that of a whole country or district where the common language is spoken with a barbarous and classical impurity'; therefore 'it matters not whether there subsists any political connection between such district and that in which the classical idiom prevails'.[112] In such terms 'the idiom peculiar to Scotland' was to be constructed as 'a provincial and vicious dialect of English', particularly open to the issues of correction and the hegemonies of England in linguistic as well as political ways.[113] Images of language and disadvantage, so habitual within prescriptive discourses of the late eighteenth and nineteenth centuries, were hence to apply equally to the Scots ('there are I believe few natives of North-Britain, who have had occasion either to visit or reside in this country, that have not learned by experience the disadvantages which accompany their idiom and pronunciation'[114]). Notions of a 'standard', founded on English models and accompanying perceptions of the 'classical purity' of London, as Douglas illustrates, can equally infuse popular attitudes and value-judgements towards accent in Scotland and Ireland as well as provincial England; these language varieties too were, seemingly effortlessly, to be assimilated within the assumptions of norm and deviation so

---

[112] S. Douglas, *A Treatise on the Provincial Dialect of Scotland* (1779), ed. C. Jones (Edinburgh, 1991), 97.
[113] Ibid. 99.   [114] Ibid.

central to the prescriptive and standardizing ethos. The prevalence of such conceptions would undoubtedly have lent additional impetus to Boswell's own desire for 'improvement' in the accents he himself employed.

In real terms it was, of course, precisely this education in 'perception' and language attitudes, as William Cockin had realized early on, which was to have the most far-reaching effects as ideologies of a 'standard' (and their concomitant beliefs in the values which the 'best' language might suggest) did indeed gradually come to affect people's attitudes to 'talking proper' on a scale which almost matched the images of linguistic convergence so persuasively urged by writers within the prescriptive tradition. It is clearly this which lies behind the patterns of sensitization so ably illustrated by Mrs Montagu and Maria Edgeworth, by Boswell or Sir Christopher Sykes, and indeed behind the undoubted popularity of sixpenny manuals such as *Hard Words Made Easy, Mind Your H's and Take Care of Your R's,* or *How to Shine in Society* which were published in such abundance throughout the nineteenth century (texts which moreover explicitly addressed such messages to those in the middle and the lower sections of society too). Supply in such instances is not only generated by demand, but it acts equally as an index to the changing sensibilities of the age, and to the dissemination of the ideology of standardization—the belief in the need to conform—even if not, in actual fact, being able to attest the degree of conformity in itself. It is in such terms that the diffusion of these ideas is most significant.

Ideas of a 'standard' in this sense were to prove remarkably powerful, and certainly those images of national harmony dependent upon, and to be generated by, the shared and uniform accent for all remain evocative, being invoked at regular intervals throughout the nineteenth century (notably in the context of education as we shall see in Chapter 6). Newman in 1869 still, for example, chooses to depict England in terms of an alliance of national honour and linguistic reform which is markedly familiar from texts of a century before: England is 'a nation which desires to eliminate vulgar provincial pronunciation, to educate and refine its people'. By doing so, it will 'get rid of plebeianism, and fuse the orders of society into harmony'.[115] Precisely as in Sheridan's

[115] F. W. Newman, *Orthoëpy: Or, a Simple Mode of Accenting English* (London, 1869), 16.

own aspirations for standardization and its social consequences, a non-localized accent is portrayed in terms which still superficially adhere to egalitarian principles of 'improvement' in line with these specifically social sensibilities towards speech; 'provincial' pronunciation is, in such terms, inherently 'vulgar' and hence an unaccountable marker of the 'plebeian', a marker of negative status which must be eradicated for the good of all.

Such naïve beliefs in the benefits of linguistic paternalism were in reality, however, to prove largely misguided, a fact all too evident in the value-judgements Newman employs in describing (or perhaps rather proscribing) these linguistic variations of the later nineteenth century. As one system of 'odious distinctions', in Sheridan's words, was changed, another was of course gradually to arise in its place, a shift which is already marked in the language adopted by Edgeworth and Sykes, or by Boswell and Mrs Montagu in the sensitivities they evinced towards the spoken word. Recognition of a 'standard' brings not only a sense of a 'non-standard' but a 'sub-standard' too, here construed in terms of lack of 'elegance', or imputations of 'ridicule', and its associated images of disadvantage. As this suggests, the non-localized (and 'superior') accent which Sheridan and others had advocated as an instrument of egalitarianism was to become not a marker of the 'harmony' desired but instead one of the most potent social symbols in existence, proclaiming not 'the place of a man's birth' in the terms of Sheridan's original criticism, but instead his social level.

It was to take Noah Webster, outside England, to state most clearly the potentially disadvantageous social side-effects which these notions of a spoken standard, as well as differential access to its norms, might indeed have. Resistant, as already indicated, to the mantle of authority which so many writers on the language assume, Webster goes on to expose with ease the ostensible altruism and misplaced egalitarianism of prescriptive ideology in this context. Though, like Sheridan, he does acknowledge that in the ideal world 'a sameness of pronunciation is of considerable consequence in a political view',[116] in the real one, as he also contends, the outcome is likely to be somewhat different. The introduction of standards of 'good' speech, especially when described by means of differential social values, was far more likely to foster than to

[116] Webster, *Dissertations*, 19.

dispel the existing asymmetries of society. It would in effect provide new sets of inequalities rather than the harmony Sheridan (and others) had initially proclaimed. As Webster rightly stresses:

While all men are on a footing and no singularities are accounted vulgar and ridiculous, every man enjoys perfect liberty. But when a particular set of men, in exalted stations, undertake to say 'we are the standards of propriety and elegance, and if all men do not conform to our practice, they shall be accounted vulgar and ignorant,' they take a very great liberty with the rules of the language and the rights of civility.[117]

Webster tellingly exposes the dangers evident within the values and value-judgements which, in Britain, had so often come to surround these pressures for conformity in terms of speech. Even Sheridan's professed altruism is, as we have seen, phrased in language which equates only one variety of English with 'good' speakers, and the others with 'disgrace', 'vulgarity', or aesthetic demerit: 'Would it not contribute much to the ease and pleasure of society, . . . if all gentlemen in public meetings, or private company, should be able to express their thoughts . . . with an utterance so regulated, as not to give pain to the understanding, or offence to the ears of their auditors?', he asks in defence of a national accent in 1781.[118] The sub-text of norm and deviation, fundamental to prescriptive ideology, is all too clear in such claims and both Edgeworth and Mrs Montagu reveal the consequences of these ideas. As Webster realized, articulating preconceptions of this order in the authority of printed texts was much more likely to strengthen than diminish any system of subjective inequalities already in existence. 'An attempt to fix a standard on the practice of any particular class of people is highly absurd' as well as 'unjust', he adds in further condemnation from his own, more objective, vantage-point in America.[119]

The 'perfect liberty' analysed by Webster, and employed as a linguistic ideal by Sheridan and others, could in reality rest only in the descriptive acknowledgement that all varieties of the language are equal, and that the same equality extends to their speakers. Though a staple of modern descriptive comment on language and linguistic variation, perceptions of this order were, however, rarely forthcoming in the late eighteenth century, and

---

[117] Ibid. 24–5.   [118] Sheridan, *Rhetorical Grammar*, p. xv.
[119] Webster, *Dissertations*, 25.

indeed for much of the nineteenth too. In contrast, formalizing one accent as 'better', and all others as indicative of 'disgrace', was inevitably to be inimical to 'equality' of any kind. Prescriptive ideology in these terms, in spite of its professed egalitarianism, instead merely reinforces notions of the cultural hegemony of one social group above others, offering, as in Milroy's critique of notions of prestige in accounts of linguistic change, 'a conceptualization of sociolinguistic space that is unidimensional—a space in which the élite groups set the tone in language, dress and other cultural matters, and in which lower groups strive to imitate their lead'.[120] Such paradigms are fundamental to much prescriptive writing, underlying the frequent persuasion exerted upon readers to emulate their 'betters' in linguistic terms, and similarly to divorce their accents (and accompanying socio-linguistic identities) from the 'vulgar'. One way of speaking is, in consequence, invariably privileged above all others and the fictions of 'empowerment' proffered by Sheridan and others in this context rest only in assimilation to this one variety, not in recognition of the validity of other modes of speech. Entirely in keeping with ideologies of a standard, the aim is, of course, to displace heteroglossia with monoglossia, and existing variation with a 'norm' which is, as we have seen, frequently phrased in social terms which themselves rely on images of language and disadvantage fundamentally alien to the issues of equality otherwise so enthusiastically proclaimed. Webster in 1789 thus exposes with particular clarity the weaknesses within the notions of linguistic 'liberty' which were regularly, and at times paradoxically, advanced in the drive to disseminate non-localized norms of speech. Outside the utopian visions of writers such as Sheridan in which the workings of prescriptive ideology in the form of a non-localized accent served to unify rather than divide the nation, reality was instead to intrude with a vengeance. Though a non-localized accent did indeed gradually appear, it was to remain redolent of the 'best' speakers, and, in such terms, was to act merely as a further marker of social distinction for those who succeeded in assimilating to its norms.

As this indicates, norms of correctness, regardless of how widely they are propagated, will rarely tell the whole story and that this

---

[120] J. Milroy, 'Social Network and Prestige Arguments in Sociolinguistics', in K. Bolton and H. Kwok (eds.), *Sociolinguistics Today: International Perspectives* (London, 1992), 147.

is so should not, in itself, be surprising. Even taking a simple pragmatic approach, for example, it is clear that should writers in the prescriptive tradition have been in the fortunate position of being directly able to impose upon the language of their readers the non-localized norms which they prescribed, there would necessarily still have remained vast sections of the population who, by virtue of their illiteracy, would have been immune to their dictates. Pronouncing dictionaries and the mass of other publications devoted to the norms of speech were open books only to those who could read, and though estimations of literacy over the nineteenth century vary considerably, it seems reasonable to assume, with Altick, that it could not by any means have exceeded half the population at the beginning. As Altick adds moreover, even generalized estimates of this kind tell us nothing of the *quality* of literacy which such figures represent.[121] The ability to read a simple chap-book would scarcely guarantee enough facility to cope with the elevated prose of a Sheridan or a Walker in their declarations of the need for national norms of speech. Even though increased access to education over the nineteenth century meant that levels of literacy were gradually to rise, Sheridan's solution to the localized divisions of accent nevertheless continues to manifest a certain naïvety in the face of social reality in the late eighteenth and nineteenth centuries. 'If a method of acquiring a just pronunciation by books, as well as conversation, were established, the acquisition would not be circumscribed within such narrow bounds, but would lie open to all British subjects wherever born',[122] he somewhat optimistically declared.

Even if these problems of equal access to this information were somehow to be resolved, it would not necessarily encourage the uniform adoption of that 'best' accent which Sheridan and others prescribed. Accent functions in reality as a social symbol which is, in a number of ways, far more complex than these earlier accounts of 'good' and 'bad' language tend to suggest, and its differences indicate far more than social status (or otherwise) in the voices of that London élite which were held up as an example for general use. It also, for example, functions as a marker of group membership and as a signal of solidarity, able to operate within the range of social groupings in society, signalling patterns of inclusion and

---

[121] Altick, *English Common Reader*, 170.   [122] Sheridan, *Dissertation*, 18.

exclusion, of 'belonging' and 'outsiders' which by no means operate solely with reference to speakers of the so-called 'best' English. In such terms, the 'talking proper' of one speaker may well be another speaker's 'talking posh' and a marker of affectation and pretension; not everyone will by any means desire to assimilate to the norms specified as 'best', irrespective of the number of social and intellectual virtues with which such variants are theoretically imbued. Society is not unidimensional, even if prescriptive texts tended to assume it was; forms indicative of regional location, and of lower status groups too, have, as modern sociolinguistic study has often pointed out, their own prestige and their own role within the functioning of group relationships and social networks. Similarly, accent loyalty can and will impede uniform change in the direction of norms proffered as the most prestigious, as the continued absence of a non-localized accent for all of course reveals.

William Labov's twentieth-century researches in the island of Martha's Vineyard, Massachusetts, aptly illustrate, for example, the ways in which the issues of identity which speakers may wish to assert by means of the language they adopt will by no means always be those of the theoretically most statusful groups in society. Documenting the increasing use of centralized enunciations of the diphthongs in words such as *rise, house* (the use of /əɪ/ and /əʊ/ rather than /aɪ/ and /aʊ/) Labov clearly reveals the more emblematic roles which accent (and individual variables) can play within a speech community. Such centralized sounds being closely associated with the rural Chilmark fishermen of the island (the descendants of the original Yankee settlers), assimilation in these contexts, as Labov contends, tends to take on the social meanings of indigenousness and of 'belonging'. These connotative values contrast markedly with the non-centralized (and overtly more 'statusful') variants employed by the tourists from the mainland who, each summer, invade the island, outnumbering the islanders themselves. In these terms, adopting the use of centralization is aligned with a positive view of island identity; as Labov states: 'When a man says [rəɪt] or [həʊs], he is unconsciously establishing the fact that he belongs to the island; that he is one of the natives to whom the island really belongs.'[123] This sound change in progress is moreover away from overtly recognized norms, acting instead in

---

[123] W. Labov, *Sociolinguistic Patterns* (Oxford, 1978), 36.

response to social pressures on a local rather than a national level and clearly indicating that the direction of linguistic change can and does run counter to the forms used by élite groups in society, a fact which exposes another fiction (or fallacy) within those accounts of linguistic convergence which were so regularly manipulated within the prescriptive tradition.

As this suggests, it is therefore heterogeneity rather than homogeneity, pluralism rather than the monolithic which in real terms will mark linguistic usage in a multi-dimensional society. This, rather than uniformity, is the normal state of language and, as language history reveals, all the prescription in the world will not necessarily effect any change, nor will it bring that national uniformity of usage which its advocates in the late eighteenth and nineteenth centuries had hoped for. Language instead, especially in its spoken forms, varies regionally, socially, and contextually as speakers modify aspects of their linguistic behaviour in keeping with the demands of register or style, formality or its converse. There are, in these terms, few absolutes in language as it is really used, though they proliferate in the schema of prescriptive texts and indeed in language attitudes too. Even a simple examination of prescriptive grammar is able to reveal the truth of this for though Lowth, for example, *pace* Walker, had 'gravely vindicated the rights of analogy',[124] revealing grammatical error in what had previously been acceptable, the common targets of prescriptive censure which resulted, such as the split infinitive or the preposition in final position, were nevertheless not eradicated. Their usage still persists, albeit, especially in the written language, hemmed around with notions that they are somehow 'not quite right' or are, in some way, 'incorrect'. Similarly, proscriptions devoted to constructions such as *different to/different from* have not resulted in the invariability which eighteenth- and nineteenth-century patterns of prescription intended; both are, to the continued disgust of pedants, still used, though again their use is often infringed with the notion that one is somehow 'better' than the other. In more formal (and especially written) circumstances, it is this 'correct' use of language to which speakers can accordingly attempt to incline, while disregarding such assumed proprieties in their ordinary speech.

---

[124] Walker, *Critical Pronouncing Dictionary*, 1st edn. (1791), p. iii.

The same precepts apply equally in terms of accent. The prescriptive principles espoused by Sheridan and others in their attempts to raise the linguistic 'consciousness' in terms of speech act as a concise index to the assimilation of pronunciation within the concerns of codification, and its own motivations to 'correct' the language. As we shall see, just as Lowth formalized a range of grammatical shibboleths to good effect, at least with reference to what people think about language, even if not in terms of what they actually do (especially in less formal situations), so were writers on the spoken word to foster a similar set of markers whereby 'good' and 'bad' might be determined, and a sense of a national standard of speech set up on 'proper', and ruled, foundations. Modern self-evaluation tests reveal the legacy of these ideas, regularly evincing people's responsiveness to notions of 'correct' English, even if such features are not consistently implemented in their ordinary speech; as the sociolinguist Peter Trudgill's data on linguistic usage in twentieth-century Norwich make clear,[125] speakers can be very aware of the 'proper' variants of speech such as the presence of [h], or not 'dropping the 'g'' in words such as *walking* (variants which rise to prominence as indices of 'correctness' over the course of the late eighteenth and nineteenth centuries) while not necessarily adopting these forms in their ordinary usage. Similarly, self-evaluation tests (in which speakers are asked to evaluate their own speech) tend to reveal the same results. As Wardaugh confirms, 'such tests seem to tap what speakers believe are the norms that operate in society', exposing language attitudes with more clarity than they do the actual usage of the speakers concerned.[126]

Sheridan's initial aims had, of course, been to change and to inform habits of mind together with habits of speech, to raise the 'consciousness' as well as to point out 'error' and to specify norms. It was, in the end, the former which was ultimately created with most success: 'consciousness', an 'idea in the mind', a set of beliefs surrounding the emerging and non-localized 'received pronunciation' which in themselves were often at some remove from linguistic reality, especially as far as the majority of the population were concerned. It is, for example, notions of this order which

---

[125] P. Trudgill, *The Social Stratification of English in Norwich* (Cambridge, 1974).
[126] R. Wardaugh, *An Introduction to Sociolinguistics* (Oxford, 1986), 195.

lie beneath the growing belief that it is possible to speak English 'without an accent', an equation which perhaps reveals more clearly than any other the norm and deviation frameworks which were so commonly engaged in this context; to speak English 'with an accent' (although it is, in reality, a linguistic impossibility to speak it without one) served as a marker of deviation from a perceived, and idealized, norm. As pronunciation increasingly became a national status symbol, if not a symbol of the national harmony originally envisaged, it was convergence of this kind, in terms of belief if not always of behaviour, which was most successful. 'The common standard dialect is that in which all marks of a particular place and residence are lost, and nothing appears to indicate any other habits of intercourse than with the well-bred and well-informed, wherever they may be found',[127] stated Smart in 1836, confirming (and encoding) this shift in perception in general terms.

Attitudes to /h/-usage, perhaps prime among the emerging set of non-localized features of speech, can hence display a corresponding bias in accounts of its use, as in this comment by Leach in 1881, who clearly envisages all 'good' speakers as invariably [h]-full (the non-localized norm), and all 'bad' ones as [h]-less. He maps simple equations of 'standard' or otherwise on to the patterns which result: 'As the chemist employs a compound of sulphur in order to decide whether a substance belongs to the group of higher or baser metals, so does society apply the H-test to unknown individuals, and group them according to their comportment under the ordeal.'[128]

In the real and quantitative terms of linguistics, such notions are again myths, highly effective in the ideology of standardization and its binary absolutes, but not borne out to the same extent in its processes where speakers of all social groups will instead use varying percentages of [h] or [Ø] in response to the situational variables of formality, or the speaker variables of status, gender, or age. In their more formal language, for example, speakers regularly tend to use higher frequencies of the variants perceived as being most 'statusful', responding in such patterns of style-shifting to normative pressures above levels of conscious social

---

[127] B. H. Smart, *Walker Remodelled. A New Critical Pronouncing Dictionary* (London, 1836), §178.
[128] A. Leach, *The Letter H. Past, Present, and Future* (London, 1881), 11.

awareness. In more informal styles, conversely, such frequencies diminish. While language itself will therefore commonly evince these complex patterns of co-variation, ideologies of standardization will, instead manifest patterns of binary absolutes: 'good', 'bad', 'right', 'wrong', 'prestigious', 'vulgar', '[h]-fullness', '[h]-lessness', and it is these in which people tend to believe, in spite of all empirical evidence to the contrary. It is in such terms, as in those adopted by Leach, that national norms (and stereotypes) of speech as well as speaker did indeed commonly come to exist, triggering remarkably homogeneous reactions all over the country, even if the heterogeneities of actual usage did remain to a larger extent.

The true sense of a 'standard' is, as a result, perhaps best understood in the terms selected by Milroy and Milroy: 'an idea in the mind rather than a reality—a set of abstract norms to which actual usage will conform to a greater or lesser extent.'[129] Whereas ordinary users of the language will therefore regularly give credence to the idea of inviolable norms of 'good' usage (often discrediting their own habitual linguistic behaviour in the process and thereby overtly subscribing to the notions of an absolute standard on the lines preferred by Sheridan so long ago), in the real world language will vary, as already indicated, in rather more complex ways. Even Received Pronunciation (RP), contrary to much popular belief, is far from monolithic and, as one would expect, it too favours heterogeneity above the ideals of uniformity so regularly propagated over the course of the eighteenth and nineteenth centuries. The evident dichotomy which can therefore exist between patterns of usage and *attitudes* to usage clarifies what can be seen as the skewed operation of standardization as process and ideology, as well as illuminating more precisely the nature of that prescriptive legacy of the eighteenth and nineteenth centuries. As Milroy and Milroy affirm, it was in fact these more ideological aspects of standardization which were to be most widely established over the course of the eighteenth century, creating the extensive awareness of a set of notions governing 'good' and 'bad' usage, together with corresponding assumptions about 'standard', 'substandard', and

---

[129] J. Milroy and L. Milroy, *Authority in Language: Investigating Language Prescription and Standardization* (London, 1985), 23.

'non-standard', to which, as they add, 'nearly every speaker now subscribes in principle.'[130] It is precisely this set of differences which, at the end of the nineteenth century, Henry Sweet was also, with particular acuity, to stress as relevant as he sought to expose the fictions and the facts which had come to surround a spoken standard by that time. 'Remember that language exists only in the individual, and that such a phrase as "standard English pronunciation" expresses only an abstraction', he exhorted his readers in 1890.[131] In spite of such correctives, fictions of a standard in other more absolute terms have of course continued to prevail, still informing the ideologies of 'talking proper' and, in the nineteenth century, proving equally pervasive in the realms of popular attitudes to speech as well as in works on language themselves.

What is, in effect, created by such preoccupations is a national speech community on the (more abstract) lines of that discussed by the modern sociolinguist William Labov: 'The speech community is not defined by any marked agreement in the use of language elements, so much as by participation in a set of shared norms [which] may be observed in overt types of evaluative behaviour.'[132] It is the hegemonic role of the standard which thus tends to be most apparent. As John Barrell has noted in this context: 'the language of Britain . . . was seen and was used as a means of impressing on the inhabitants of the country the idea of their unity, while at the same time it could be used (as it still is, of course), as a means of confirming . . . the divisions it pretended to heal.'[133] That this is so is, as we will see, all too prominent in the language used of and about the nuances of that 'proper' speech which was ideally to be adopted by all. Social stigma, social prejudice, the 'homogenizing aspirations for gentility' discussed by Stone and Stone,[134] the social insecurities of the middling sections of society all form recurrent frames of reference within these attempted delineations of 'good' against 'bad' English. Whether manifested in passive or active terms, perception of the norms of speech, and of the embedded social values which these contain, was gradually

---

[130] Ibid. 36.   [131] H. Sweet, *A Primer of Phonetics* (London, 1890), 3.

[132] Labov, *Sociolinguistic Patterns*, 120–1.

[133] J. Barrell, *English Literature in History 1730–80: An Equal Wide Survey* (London, 1983), 111.

[134] L. S. Stone and J. C. F. Stone, *An Open Elite? England 1540–1800* (Oxford, 1984); see p. 83.

to change, as non-localized patterns founded in emulation of London forms of speech were increasingly recognized as the standard to be attained, and paradigms of exclusion (and exclusivity) were, in turn, increasingly predicated upon the ways that one chose to speak.

2

Images of Accent: Prescription, Pronunciation, and the Elegant Speaker

'A STANDARD is that by which we ascertain the value of things of the same kind; so a standard weight is that by which we try the justness of all other weights',[1] wrote the author and divine, William Enfield, in his treatise on language in 1809. In popular (as well as prescriptive) perceptions, a standard variety of pronunciation was similarly to incorporate evaluative mechanisms of this order, though the relevant values were rarely to be those of language alone. Notions of 'elegance', 'propriety', 'politeness', and 'refinement' are regularly ascribed to its use, as well as extended to its users. Images of 'class' and 'status', 'vulgarity' or 'incorrectness' frequently surround the act of speech. Evaluation, in contexts such as these, tends to take on the nature of social response, fusing with the prejudices and preconceptions of society in its own notions of 'good' and 'bad', 'right' and 'wrong'.

In their drive to raise the linguistic consciousness in terms of accent, the appeals of Sheridan and others have perhaps already revealed that what correspondingly tends to emerge is not that 'doctrine of appropriate usage' which characterizes more objective and descriptive accounts of language in the twentieth century, but instead what can be seen as the 'doctrine of subjective inequality'. This, as Hudson points out, trades not on objective criteria of linguistic inequality founded on, for example, the absence of appropriate communication skills or discoursal responses, but operates instead in terms of language attitudes, on what 'people *think* about each other's speech'. As he adds:

In some societies (but by no means all) people are credited with different amounts of intelligence, friendliness and other virtues according to the way they speak, although such a judgement based on speech may be

---

[1] W. Enfield, *A Familiar Treatise on Rhetoric* (London, 1809), 5.

wrong. Consequently, whatever virtues are highly valued, some speakers are thought to have more of them than they really have, simply because they have the right way of speaking, and others are thought to have less because their speech conveys the wrong impression.[2]

It is this principle which lies behind the use of subjective reaction tests in modern sociolinguistic studies. Initially developed by social psychologists, such tests prove remarkably informative about socio-linguistic stereotypes in the speech community, and the ways in which, as Hudson notes, speakers are willing to 'use the speech of others as a clue to non-linguistic information about them, such as their social background and even personality traits like toughness or intelligence'.[3] In the attitudes to speech (and speakers) which such studies therefore reveal, RP users of 'proper' English are, for instance, commonly credited with greater levels of intelligence, authority, and self-confidence, whereas speakers with rural accents are conversely assumed to be more friendly, more sympathetic, and more good-natured, as well as less authoritative. It is equally principles and stereotypes of this order which writers in the late eighteenth and nineteenth centuries were to attempt to codify in terms of the standardizing ideology, making explicit perceived affiliations of accent and power (or powerlessness) and willingly specifying the aesthetic and intellectual affinities which given accents, and even individual sounds, might be assumed to possess. Such notions of subjective inequality inform the impulses both to codify, and to conform to, the canons of 'talking proper', and eighteenth- and nineteenth-century accounts of accent discuss the repercussions of such attitudes with little sense of reserve.

'Vulgarity', for example, materializes as a highly effective epithet of prescriptive censure, regularly applied in the intent to eliminate pronunciations deemed improper. Though not unknown before in the application of appropriate linguistic tenets (John Hart, as we have seen, writes his *Orthographie* with the intent of enabling the 'rude countrie Englishman' to gain knowledge of the 'better' English of the day), the emphasis and tenor of later comments again differ significantly. 'Let him who would polish his pronunciation be very attentive to these remarks', warned the grammarian P. Walkden Fogg, for example, in 1796 in his directives on the art of 'good' enunciation: 'without abiding by the regular sound of

---

[2] R. A. Hudson, *Sociolinguistics* (Cambridge, 1980), 169.   [3] Ibid. 202.

letters, ... his discourse will appear vulgar.'[4] Accent is overtly manipulated as an image of the speaker's inner qualities, value-judgements such as these readily being employed in order to encourage the convergent behaviour desired. To be 'vulgar' was, in Walker's terms, to be 'plebeian, suiting the lower people ... mean, low', and the gloss he provides for 'mean' makes the pejorative intent still clearer: 'wanting dignity, of low rank or birth; low-minded, base, despicable; low in the degree of any property, low in worth'. As Holmberg affirms, vulgarity was, in such ways, to be a major prescriptive weapon, readily being applied to variants regarded with disfavour within prescriptive tenets of correctness.[5] Not for nothing does Walker proclaim that he is the first writer to include the word 'vulgarism' in the lexicographical context of the dictionary: 'This word is in no dictionary that I have met with, but seems sufficiently authorised both in writing and conversation to entitle it to a place in a repository of the English language.'[6]

With reference to the spoken language, such attitudes become almost a commonplace of comment on pronunciation. It is, for example, pronunciation which 'distinguishes the educated reader and speaker from the vulgar and uneducated one',[7] as Vandenhoff stressed in 1862. Henry Alford two years later condemns [h]-dropping in precisely the same terms: 'a vulgarism ... common throughout England to persons of low breeding and inferior education'.[8] 'A person who uses vulgarisms will make but little way in good circles', *Talking and Debating* similarly averred,[9] giving ample details of the social consequences which might ensue. Language, as such comments indicate, was regularly to be described, and perhaps more particularly, proscribed in terms of its attendant social meanings and the correlations proclaimed to hold between variant and social value.

Paradigms of 'beauty' and 'ugliness' make their due appearance too, further amplifying these resonances of the standard ideology for the spoken word. Johnston points out the '*grating* sounds' of

---

[4] P. Walkden Fogg, *Elementa Anglicana; or, the Principles of English Grammar* (Stockport, 1796), ii. 169.

[5] B. Holmberg, *On the Concept of Standard English and the History of Modern English Pronunciation* (Lund, 1964), 35.

[6] J. Walker, *Critical Pronouncing Dictionary*, 4th edn. (1806), note under the word *vulgarism*.

[7] G. Vandenhoff, *The Lady's Reader* (London, 1862), 22.

[8] Alford, *A Plea for the Queen's English*, 40.   [9] *Talking and Debating*, 15.

provincial discourse for the edification of his readers; more 'elegant' equivalents such as those used in the intentionally invariant (and metropolitan) 'standard' are, he recommends, to be adopted in their stead.[10] Likewise, for Buchanan, forms that deviate from the standard he attempts to document, and in turn disseminate, are not only 'rough' and 'unpleasant', but also 'vicious', with all its eighteenth-century connotations of the 'depravity of manners' specified by Dr Johnson.[11] The aesthetic appeal of the 'standard' itself receives corresponding emphasis in ways which are designed to appeal to the aural as well as social sensibilities of speakers. Whereas for Douglas provincial articulations are liable to be 'ludicrous' as well as 'awkward', the 'best' speech of the capital is redolent of polish and of ease.[12] In a parallel way, Murdoch emphasizes the desirability, as well as the 'politeness', of one variety above others, focusing on its role as 'an essential part of a genteel and liberal education'.[13] Validating notions of the 'inherent value' of this one form of English, such often-iterated statements simultaneously confirm the perceived subordinacy of other modes of speech, as well as revealing the foundations of a number of long-standing cultural stereotypes about accent and identity.

Just as in modern English the 'cultivated voice' emerges as a popular collocation for the nuances of 'talking proper', so do texts in the eighteenth and nineteenth centuries explicitly endorse these more emblematic roles of accent. Culture, signifying both style of life and style of mind, is presented as an integral aspect of the 'received' standard of speech delineated by such writers: Benjamin Smart, for instance, an elocutionist and prolific writer on pronunciation, develops the binary oppositions favoured by the prescriptive tradition into a series of contrasts specifically founded upon an idealization of the 'cultivated speaker' set against the manifest improprieties of the 'vulgar' one: 'The cultivated speaker employs a definite number of sounds which he utters with precision, distinctness, and in their proper places; the vulgar speaker misapplies the sounds, mars or alters them.'[14] Glossed by Walker in 1791 as 'the art of improvement and melioration', 'cultivation'

---

[10] Johnston, *Pronouncing and Spelling Dictionary*, p. v.
[11] J. Buchanan, *Linguae Britannicae Vera Pronunciatio* (London, 1757), p. xx n.
[12] Douglas, *Treatise on the Provincial Dialect of Scotland*, 99.
[13] Walker, *Critical Pronouncing Dictionary*, ed. Murdoch (1809), p. i.
[14] B. H. Smart, *A Practical Grammar of English Pronunciation* (London, 1810), 9.

of this order was naturally to exclude the provincial where words were spoken in a way untainted, and hence 'unimproved', by the 'rational' dictates of prescriptivism. 'Mere provincialisms have no place in cultivated speech', as an 1885 *Handbook of Pronunciation* proclaimed,[15] specifying still further—in an extension of Darwinianism—that since it is language which differentiates man as superior to other species, so it can only be the best language, and particularly the 'best' accent, which makes plain in him the realization of this superior potential:

Language is the chief of those attainments which distinguish man from the lower animals. The perfection and grace with which one speaks his mother tongue, is justly regarded as an index of his culture and associations. We instinctively gauge the cultivation of men by their pronunciation, as well as by their spelling and grammar.[16]

Phyfe makes the same equations even clearer, if something of a closed circle: 'Since cultivated people are, in general, presumed to speak accurately, accuracy in pronunciation comes naturally to be regarded as a sign of culture, and there is, therefore, a tendency to imitate the pronunciation of the cultured classes.'[17] In a book aimed, as the title-page indicates, at schools and colleges as well as being intended for private use, such value-judgements are enshrined as facts to be learnt and, in turn, implemented. As Phyfe asserts still more categorically: accent 'is the best *prima-facie* evidence of general culture. On this account it appeals to all.' It alone forms 'the stepping stones to a more liberal culture'.[18]

Irrespective of the facts of educational background or estimations of IQ, speakers were therefore, on such subjective foundations, regularly to be judged as 'ignorant' or 'illiterate', 'educated' or 'uninformed'. Such stereotypes can still, of course, prove pervasive in popular attitudes to accent, as indeed can corresponding ones of the 'educated accent', the superficialities of articulation being, in relevant formulations, interpreted as an image of intellect, and indeed as a sign of intelligence itself. Subjective reaction tests in modern sociolinguistic studies again supply ample evidence of the continuing (if mistaken) operation of such evaluative systems, but the printed texts of the late eighteenth and nineteenth centuries are, if anything, still more overt in their

[15] L. Sherman, *A Handbook of Pronunciation* (London, 1885), p. iv.
[16] Ibid., p. iii.   [17] Phyfe, *How Should I Pronounce?*, 13.   [18] Ibid., p. v.

accounts of the affinities assumed to pertain to speech in this way. 'Language, both oral and written, is an exponent of the condition of the mind; when mean and inappropriate it infers [*sic*] that the habits of life and the condition of mind are equally mean and uncultivated' stated, for example, the Reverend D. Williams in 1850.[19] 'It is certain that nothing marks more quickly a person's mental and social status than his practice in this regard', averred Phyfe of the 'best' accent which he too advocates for general adoption.[20] 'If bad spelling is generally the sign of an *imperfect* education, certainly nothing more shows the want of education or of good association than incorrect pronunciation, and there is nothing more difficult to avoid being noticed or to disguise', the author of *Common Blunders in Speaking and Reading* similarly set forth.[21] 'Manner' and not 'matter' was, it seemed, to be accorded the primary role in such notions of intellectual ability, as well as of social refinement, a correlation already evident in Douglas's observations in the late eighteenth century: 'In the pulpit, at the bar, or in parliament, a provincial phrase sullies the lustre of the brightest eloquence, and the most forcible reasoning loses half its effect when disguised in the awkwardness of provincial dress.'[22]

Such evaluative patterns, as Bloomfield later indicated in 1927, rest on the central premiss that an ignorant person simply does not know the correct forms of language. Rather than taking account of the more complex socio-symbolic roles played by accent in terms of group membership and social solidarity with other formations in a multi-dimensional society, the assumption is not that speakers may simply prefer (as in Martha's Vineyard)[23] to diverge from those features deemed 'correct' in the wider speech community. Instead, popular interpretations rely on notions that 'in the process of education, one learns the correct forms and, by practice and an effort of will ("careful speaking") acquires the habit of using them. If one associates with ignorant speakers, or relaxes the effort of will ("careless speaking"), one will lapse into the incorrect forms.'[24] Though obviously flawed as a linguistic

[19] Williams, *Composition*, 5.   [20] Phyfe, *How Should I Pronounce?*, p. v.
[21] C. Hartley, *Everyone's Handbook of Common Blunders in Speaking and Reading* (London, 1897), preface.
[22] Douglas, *Treatise on the Provincial Dialect of Scotland*, 99.
[23] See pp. 52–3.
[24] L. Bloomfield, 'Literate and Illiterate Speech', *American Speech*, 2 (1927), 432.

model, such notions tend nevertheless to be effective, at least in terms of language attitudes, often still leading speakers to devalue their own speech forms in preference to these variants deemed more redolent of 'educated' status, regardless of the levels of education which, in reality, they themselves may have attained.

Such issues of course all pertain to that ideology of standardization which, as we have seen in Chapter 1, was consciously and deliberately inculcated in terms of 'talking proper'. Images of culture, education, intelligence, or vulgarity tend to emerge as a direct consequence of such preoccupations, embedded in the set of beliefs by which this aspect of standardization can be recognized, and providing an additional index by which its evolution can be traced. The fostering of sensibilities of this order documents, in other words, the patterns of discrimination which evolve towards variations in speech previously regarded more with acceptance than abhorrence, evincing notions of stigma which are articulated in social as well as linguistic terms. It similarly reveals the operation of a set of socio-cultural stereotypes (the 'lady', the 'gentleman', the 'parvenu', the 'Cockney', the 'aspiring middle class') to which we will return, but which are significant in both prescriptive and sociolinguistic terms. Stereotypes are, for example, often fundamental to language attitudes and to their study, acting, as J. C. Wells confirms, as 'simplified and standardized conceptions of kinds of people, conceptions which we share with other members of our speech community'.[25] Similarly, as the sociolinguist Roger Bell notes in this context, prescriptive rules can offer much of interest to the sociolinguist for they 'embody formulations of attitudes to language use which, even if ignored in practice by users, are indicators of social views of "correctness" that influence such behaviours as stereotyping and hypercorrection: both important variables in style-shifting'.[26] Language attitudes such as these are, as a result, naturally informative in their own right, playing on notions of identity (in both positive and negative terms) which can achieve wide diffusion throughout society. They can in addition, as Fasold rightly stresses, be 'even more valuable as a tool in illuminating the social importance of language'.[27]

The fact that social meanings were conveyed, either inadvertently

[25] J. C. Wells, *Accents of English* (Cambridge, 1982), i. 29.
[26] R. T. Bell, *Sociolinguistics: Goals, Approaches and Problems* (London, 1976), 90.
[27] Fasold, *Sociolinguistics of Society*, 158.

or intentionally, by the modes of speech employed is, as the range of comments already cited has indicated, brought into considerable prominence in much of the writing on pronunciation which appeared from the late eighteenth century onwards. As Sheridan noted of the localized standard which he sought to diffuse as a non-localized norm, since this was so closely associated with the speech of the 'best' society in London, it operated as a social testimony, 'a sort of proof that a person has kept good company'. Capable of being 'acquired only by conversing with people in polite life', it is, he states, 'on that account sought after by all, who wish to be considered as fashionable people, or members of the beau monde'.[28] Whereas Puttenham and Cooper had earlier been content simply to describe enunciation (and the fluctuations which marked its use), Sheridan was therefore to draw extensively on the specifically social meanings of 'talking proper', given prominence time and time again in an age seemingly fascinated by prescriptive ideology and the growing sense that accent could operate as a prime vehicle for social identity. Similarly, though Cooper had a section in his seventeenth-century *English Teacher* devoted to 'Barbarous Speaking', this is, for example, merely a list setting forth enunciations of various words incompatible with the 'best dialect', such as *chimly* for *chimney*, *dud* for *did*. It does not, as does Smart's later account of 'barbarous speaking' in 1810, present them in terms of a system of social alignments expressly designed to appeal to the social sensibilities (and linguistic insecurities) of his readers:

There are two pronunciations even in London, that of the well-bred, and that of the vulgar; and the difference does not consist merely in the various manner of pronouncing particular words, but often with the latter in a corruption of fundamental sounds. In short, it is owing to the one being cultivated, and the other neglected. The cultivated speaker employs a definite number of sounds which he utters with precision, distinctness, and in their proper places; the vulgar speaker misapplies the sounds, mars or alters them.[29]

Smart's polarization of the differentials of breeding and birth sets up paradigms of accent and advantage, or conversely disadvantage, which are fundamentally alien to the accounts of speech provided by Cooper and his contemporaries in the seventeenth

---

[28] Sheridan, *Course of Lectures*, 30.   [29] Smart, *Practical Grammar*, 9.

century (though they are entirely typical, in a number of ways, of those in the late eighteenth and nineteenth centuries). The shifts in attitude are in fact marked. As William Enfield, author of the highly popular *Speaker*, specified: 'these faults [of provincial enunciation], and all others of the same nature, must be corrected in the speech of a gentleman, who is supposed to have seen too much of the world, to retain the peculiarities of the district in which he was born.'[30]

Aligning social exclusivity with the exclusion of regional markers from speech, both Enfield and Sheridan, as well as Smart, give voice to the socially normative ways in which the attempted standardization of the spoken language, and specifically of pronunciation, was to be carried out. Retaining marks of the regional was deemed deleterious to gentlemanly (and superior) status, just as assimilation of the characteristics of the 'best' London speech was, in turn, to suggest inclusion in the ranks of the 'received'. Within the framework of much prescriptive writing, and the attitudes to the language which it encodes, each utterance becomes, in effect, an act of identity, locating the user within social space by means of the variables employed. In such terms, a non-localized accent was promoted as a marker not only of linguistic purity but of social precedence, a correlation which was firmly established by the mid-nineteenth century: ladies and gentlemen, as *How to Shine in Society* affirms for its own aspiring readers, were to be recognized by their 'purity of accent' which 'belongs to no city or district'.[31] 'Behind every norm there is a value', states Downes[32] and in such conceptions, social and linguistic hegemony were to operate in parallel, validating selected aspects of élite culture alone in ways which, as many writers stress, had no little appeal for a society frequently characterized—as by Forster in 1767—by the 'perpetual restless ambition in each of the inferior ranks to raise themselves to the level of those immediately above them'.[33] The author and social reformer Samuel Smiles made the same point for the nineteenth century: from this point of view, English society was, it seemed, unremittingly inspired by 'the constant struggle

---

[30] W. Enfield, *The Speaker: or, Miscellaneous Pieces, Selected from the best English writers. To which is prefixed An Essay on elocution* (London, 1774), a2ʳ.

[31] *How to Shine in Society*, 20.   [32] Downes, *Language in Society*, 215.

[33] N. Forster, *An Enquiry into the Present High Price of Provisions* (London, 1767), 41; cited in McKendrick, *et al.*, *Birth of Consumer Society*, 11.

and pressure for seats in the front of the social amphitheatre'. Statements of this order are common within contemporary accounts of this period; in these terms, 'talking proper' was also to emerge as a significant social ambition, its newly encoded shibboleths imaging forth the boundaries of acceptability and its converse, as well as the stated cultural hegemonies of the 'best' society.

Social (and linguistic) distinction were thus regularly presented in terms of the London standard alone, entirely irrespective of the actual facts of rank and the linguistic habits of the higher echelons of society (for even the gentry, as we have seen, were in reality by no means immune from those charges of social 'disgrace' attending upon the use of regional markers in speech). As the anonymous author of *Observations Respectfully Addressed to the Nobility and Gentry* had, for example, noted in 1836, though 'correct pronunciation . . . is what we expect to find . . . in all polite society', the realities of parlance indeed often diverged from this ideal, especially for those who found themselves obliged to reside for any space of time outside London: 'a residence of any period in the country, will often vitiate the enunciation: a kind of fulness, or we may say, a coarseness and vulgarity of tone, is acquired, especially in youth, which is extremely difficult to eradicate.'[34] In spite of the differences which in real terms could therefore pertain from these idealized norms, principles of emulation, ambition, and upward convergence, in terms of status as well as speech style, were nevertheless fostered by many writers on the language, as images of social ambition were likewise assimilated into that prescriptive drive to sensitize speakers to the social sub-texts conveyed within their words.

Images of social mobility are, for instance, often explicitly made to surround the specifications for convergent behaviour in speech; as W. H. Savage stressed in 1833, the ability to use 'correct' rather than 'incorrect' language was itself to be 'the talisman that will enforce admiration or beget contempt; that will produce esteem or preclude friendship; that will bar the door or make portals fly open'.[35] Attention to accent was vital, so the new canon went, in the course of any social metamorphosis, a reminder frequently

---

[34] *Observations Respectfully Addressed to the Nobility and Gentry on the Existing Importance of the Art and Study of Oratory* (London, 1836), 19–20.
[35] W. H. Savage, *The Vulgarisms and Improprieties of the English Language* (London, 1833), pp. iv–v.

issued in the context of that other prevalent stereotype of the nineteenth century, that of the 'new rich'.³⁶ *Talking and Debating*, as we have seen, made the same point; pronunciation in itself was to be the 'passport to new circles of acquaintance'.³⁷ As *Vulgarities of English Corrected* (1826) similarly noted, here with reference to [h]-dropping:

> This is a very common mistake among many who have, by industry or good fortune, risen above their original station and prospects, and therefore imagine, very mistakingly, that they are entitled to take their place with the well bred and the well educated. They may do so, without doubt, on the influence of their money or property, but they will infallibly expose themselves to be laughed at and ridiculed, by those whose reading and education enable them to see their low expressions, vulgar pronunciations, and continual blunders in grammar.³⁸

Texts such as *Hints on Etiquette and the Usages of Society*, a work which went through nineteen editions in five years, reinforce the same message. Though social mobility was by no means rare in nineteenth-century society, in the stated terms of prescriptive ideology and the hegemonies of the 'best' English which it came to express, it is made clear that in order to secure the intended rise in social level, appropriate advances must be made in manners as well as material possessions:

> in a mercantile country like England, people are continually rising in the world. Shopkeepers become merchants, and mechanics manufacturers; with the possession of wealth they acquire a taste for the luxuries of life, expensive furniture, and gorgeous plate; also numberless superfluities, with the use of which they are only imperfectly acquainted. But although their capacities for enjoyment increase, it rarely occurs that the polish of their manners keeps pace with the rapidity of their advancement: such persons are often painfully reminded that wealth alone is insufficient to protect them from the mortification which a limited acquaintance with society will entail upon the ambitious.³⁹

Such comments of course resolutely maintain the view that society is unilinear rather than pluralistic, perceiving (and pre-scribing) only one model for emulation in both social and linguis-tic senses; from this often-endorsed perspective, differences were

---

³⁶ See also pp. 124–29.   ³⁷ *Talking and Debating*, 15.
³⁸ *Vulgarities of Speech Corrected* (London, 1826), 40.
³⁹ *Hints on Etiquette and the Usages of Society* (London, 1836), 10–11.

necessarily promoted as flaws and emulation (and, in linguistic terms, convergence) was presented as the obvious consequence. It was thus the acquisition of these less tangible assets which, in prevailing ideologies of social and linguistic thinking, was often deemed to be the more significant. As Bagehot proclaimed: 'There is no country where a "poor devil of a millionnaire is so ill off as in England!" ' Further encoding these perceptions that 'money alone—money *pur et simple*—will not buy "London Society" ',[40] he too emphasized that the economic alone was to be adjudged inadequate in confirming social advance. As in the images of accent already discussed, it was 'manner' rather than 'matter' (especially in terms of language) which was regularly brought to the fore in contemporary accounts of the social constructs of superiority; 'the wealthy man, great in his accumulation of riches, if he be not in possession of knowledge sufficient to command respect, and if he speak ungrammatically, is not considered a gentleman',[41] Marcus Davis therefore also asserts. Or as a later manual of etiquette makes plain in a similar discourse on the significance of manners: 'The proverb which warns us against judging by appearances can never have much weight in a civilised community. There, appearance is inevitably the index of character. First impressions must, in nine times out of ten, be formed from it, and that is a consideration of so much importance that no-one can afford to disregard it.'[42]

Language, as this indicates, was to be deployed as a prime signifier of the social divide, imaging forth social identity, whether real or intended. This too was to act as a marker of the 'two nations' and, just as Gaskell, Dickens, and Disraeli chose to explore such differences in fictional works such as *North and South*, *Hard Times*, or *Sybil*, so was language, and specifically accent, perceived as dealing with precisely the same thing. Disraeli comments on the 'two nations . . . who are formed by a different breeding, are fed by a different food, are ordered by different manners'.[43] Newman articulates parallel divisions of social space with reference to the spoken word, urging the inception of educational remedy in this context in another plea for national harmony and

[40] W. Bagehot, *The English Constitution* (London, 1867), 120.
[41] M. Davis, *Everybody's Business* (London, 1865), 16–17.
[42] *Modern Etiquette in Public and Private* (London, 1888), 39.
[43] B. Disraeli, *Sybil; or, the Two Nations* (London, 1845), i. 149.

non-localized speech: 'The earliest business of the primary teacher is Elocution, not Grammar. He should teach pure correct sounds, and cultivate both ear and tongue. The national importance of this is great. Coarse, plebian utterance, sticking to men through life, splits the nation into two castes.'[44]

As in their original application distinguishing the Gileadites from the Ephraimites (Judges 12: 5–6), so were the shibboleths documented during the eighteenth and nineteenth centuries to serve as distinguishing markers of different social groupings and different social stereotypes. It was, however, 'class' and not ethnicity which commonly came to operate as the basis of these divisions. 'The lower classes of people cannot be expected to devote much time to the study of their native language' wrote the anonymous author of *Errors of Pronunciation* in 1817, justifying the need for the manual he supplies in order to remedy such deficiencies.[45] 'The language of the highest classes . . . is now looked upon as the standard of English pronunciation', R. G. Graham affirmed in 1869.[46] Or as Alfred Leach commented of the role of /h/, the most popular of all the shibboleths given voice during this time, 'H, in speech, is an unmistakable mark of class distinction in England, as every person soon discovers'.[47] Language is 'an instrument of communication as well as ex-communication',[48] while a 'standard', as modern sociolinguistic studies have stressed, is above all a social institution, standardization a form 'of social behaviour towards language'.[49] Both these aspects are common in the range of comments addressed to speakers of English over the nineteenth century. While social comment seems at times inseparable from the linguistic sensibilities which Sheridan and others had early striven to inculcate, issues of acceptability frequently engage with notions of social stigma in order to enhance corresponding proscriptions in terms of sound. Affiliations with élite culture (and the 'upper class') conversely appear in accounts of enunciations deemed more

---

[44] Newman, *Orthoëpy*, 22–3.

[45] *Errors of Pronunciation and Improper Expressions* (London, 1817), p. iv.

[46] G. F. Graham, *A Book About Words* (London, 1869), 156.

[47] Leach, *The Letter H*, 10.

[48] P. J. Waller, 'Democracy and Dialect, Speech and Class', in id. (ed.) *Politics and Social Change in Modern Britain: Essays Presented to A. F. Thompson* (Brighton, 1987), 2.

[49] Downes, *Language in Society*, 34.

'correct' as notions of 'identity politics' are manipulated to apparently good effect. Popular cultural constructs such as the 'lady' or the 'gentleman'[50] are in these terms to be recognized by their superior proprieties in the forms of speech, while other, more derogatory social labels are applied to those who deviate from its stated norms. As Michael Shapiro has noted, 'every society is involved, to some degree in identity politics, with separating people into groups with identities which frequently form a hierarchy of worthiness'.[51] In the late eighteenth and nineteenth centuries, however, a period marked by no little change in the context of the social order and the social labels prominent within it, such processes are perhaps engaged upon with a fervour which is more marked than otherwise, especially given this conjunction with the shifting sensibilities of prescriptivism and the standard ideology in itself. The end result is, of course, perceptible in the correlations (then and now) so often assumed to hold true between accent and class, whether, as Leach indicates, in terms of the 'lower class' speakers who drop their [h]s, or those higher in the social hierarchy who are assumed to retain theirs. Accent, in the grammars, dictionaries, and manuals of linguistic etiquette published in such abundance over the nineteenth century, becomes a prominent symbol of a stratified society, which was itself undergoing a number of changes in its prevalent notions of social identity.

As Gareth Stedman-Jones confirms, 'changes in the use of language can often indicate important turning points in social history'.[52] Certainly, in terms of semantics alone, it is evident that both 'accent' and 'class' shifted their boundaries over the eighteenth and nineteenth centuries. Accent, for example, had earlier primarily signified position of stress within articulations of a word, a sense illustrated in Isaac Watts's *Art of Reading and Writing English* of 1721: 'The Accent is a Peculiar Stress or Tone of Sound that the Voice Lays upon any Syllable.' Its later meaning, in which it signifies primarily pronunciation, is illustrated by William Cobbett in 1819 in a typically iconoclastic asseveration against the prevailing tide of thought: 'children will pronounce as their fathers and

---

[50] See Ch. 4.
[51] M. Shapiro, 'A Political Approach to Language Purism', in B. H. Jernudd and M. J. Shapiro (eds.), *The Politics of Language Purism* (Berlin, 1989), 22.
[52] G. Stedman-Jones, *Outcast London* (Oxford, 1971), p. v.

mothers pronounce . . . speakers whose approbation is worth having will pay little attention to the accent'.[53] 'Class' too extends its meanings, and notions of social level, previously phrased in terms of 'rank' and 'interest', the 'assumptions of inherited hierarchy and unequal birth' described by Geoffrey Hughes in his own study of language and social development,[54] were gradually to be joined by an alternative set of social definitions based instead around these nuances of 'class'.

Examining such diachronic transformations within the meanings and use of words, Raymond Williams, for example, stresses that relevant semantic shifts in this context 'belong essentially to the period between 1770 and 1840, which is also the period of the Industrial Revolution, and its decisive reorganization of society'.[55] The conjunction of these changes becomes almost a commonplace of historical comment on the period; 'the birth of a new class society', states Harold Perkin in 1969, was one of 'the most profound and far-reaching consequences of the Industrial Revolution'.[56] Asa Briggs similarly endorses the ways in which the industrial revolution came to constitute a revolution not merely of technical innovation and activity, but also of social thinking itself.[57] Indeed, as the population doubled, and then trebled, as a largely agrarian social order became instead one marked by the urban and commercial, as railways extended the potential for geographical mobility at a hitherto unexpected rate, and as a new set of white-collar and professional occupations came into being, a new system of advantages, and, conversely, of inequalities, did in a number of ways come to displace those which had previously pertained.

In this context, it was commonly the scale of these changes which was seen as most significant; though society had of course by no means been static in the years before the mid-eighteenth

---

[53] W. Cobbett, *A Grammar of the English Language in a Series of Letters* (London, 1819), 15. The first edn. of Cobbett's *Grammar* was published in New York in 1818; the first English edn. was published in London in the following year. All citations are from the latter. See also pp. 88–9.

[54] G. Hughes, *Words in Time: A Social History of the English Vocabulary* (Oxford, 1988), 6.

[55] R. Williams, *Keywords: A Vocabulary of Culture and Society* (London, 1976), 61.

[56] H. Perkin, *The Origins of Modern English Society 1780–1880* (London, 1969), 176.

[57] A. Briggs, *The Age of Improvement* (London, 1960), 65.

century, it had not witnessed large-scale changes such as those which accompanied the Industrial Revolution. Likewise, while vertical mobility was both acknowledged and recognized as a social phenomenon before this date, it is the number and nature of the shifts in social level which is most striking, serving to create perceptions (and associated stereotypes) not only of the 'new rich', but also of a new, and extensive middle section of society. In such terms, society was to conceive, recognize, and signal the nuances of social status in significantly different ways; 'class' emerges as a popular social label and, as we have seen, attitudes to accent were not to be entirely immaterial in this respect, frequently being linked to the issues of mobility and self-help which likewise appear as prevalent constructs in social thinking over this time. Moreover, as Björn Jernudd notes, 'It is in periods of transition . . . that puristic responses [to language] are especially likely to arise',[58] a comment which certainly takes on enhanced validity if one considers the sensitization towards the spoken word which became prominent over the late eighteenth and nineteenth centuries.

In terms of semantics, the differences between 'class' and 'rank' are, in fact, often given as being fundamental to these transitions and their associated issues of mobility. Commenting on 'the fixed, invariable, external rules of distinction of rank, which create no jealousy, since they are held to be accidental', Samuel Johnson, for example, sets forth those traditional perceptions in which social organization in England had been seen as something stable rather than fluid, determined by birth rather than by the possibilities of individual endeavour. 'Subordination tends greatly to human happiness', he stated. 'Contentions for superiority [are] very dangerous . . . all civilised nations have settled it upon a plain invariable principle. A man is born to hereditary rank; or his being appointed to certain offices, gives him a certain rank.'[59] A perpetual struggle for precedence would, he warned Boswell, result from the demise of such rules. 'Class', on the other hand, seemed to offer potential for the creation rather than merely the inheritance of social location, contributing to that 'struggle for precedence', as well as those 'contentions for superiority' which duly appear in contemporary comment on the period.[60] 'Class', originally applied

---

[58] B. H. Jernudd, 'The Texture of Language Purism: An Introduction', in Jernudd and Shapiro (eds.) *Politics of Language Purism*, 3.
[59] Boswell, *Life of Johnson*, i. 442.   [60] Williams, *Keywords*, 61.

as a generic term for any grouping, comes instead to signify a
particular view of social formation, one in which social position
was not necessarily determined by birth. Though such lexical
transitions are not in any way neat or well defined, with users of
the language tending to adhere to older senses alongside the
adoption of new ones throughout the nineteenth century, what
is particularly striking is the clear emergence of a specific set of
terminology relating to this new conception of social identity.
'Class' became a prominent designation under which opinions
about society, and its members, were organized by writers of
the time. 'Middle-class', working-class', 'upper-class', 'class-
consciousness, 'class-distinctions', 'class-feelings' ('class-interests'
and 'class-superiority' in Mill), together with 'class-education' and
'class-barrier', among others, bear witness to the lexical expansion
arising from this shift in social thinking.[61] Its social sense legitimized in *OED* from 1773 (but actually in existence for some time
before),[62] 'class' thus seemed to offer, as Penny Corfield has noted,
'a new vocabulary and conceptual framework for . . . the interpretation of society'.[63] It became not only a way of perceiving, but
of behaving, and equally, as we have seen, of speaking, and though
the term 'class dialect' does not appear, according to *OED*, before
1901 (the first citation for its use is in Greenough and Kittredge's
Words and Their Ways), the deliberate inculcation of a form of
speech conceived in terms of relationships to the social hierarchy
clearly existed long before this date.

Nevertheless, 'writing about social class in England', as Ian
Bradley has remarked, 'is rather like talking about food in France
or discussing industrial efficiency with the Japanese. Because it
functions as a national obsession, it is a risky and even a presump-
tuous enterprise which is beset with pitfalls and dangers'.[64] Prime
amongst these is, in fact, the definition of 'class' itself, for though

[61] Attested respectively from 1830, 1816, 1826, 1887, 1841, 1839, 1848, 1859,
1868, and 1889 in *OED*.
[62] See e.g. J. Nelson, *An Essay on the Government of Children* (London, 1753):
'Every nation has its Custom of dividing the People into Classes. Were we to
divide the People, we might run it to an Infinity: to avoid Confusion therefore, I
will select five Classes; *viz* the Nobility, the Gentry, the genteel Trades . . . the
common Trades, and the Peasantry.' Cited in P. Corfield, 'Class by Name and
Number in Eighteenth-Century Britain', *History*, 72 (1987), 38.
[63] Corfield, 'Class by Name and Number', 39.
[64] I. Bradley, *The English Middle Classes Are Alive and Kicking* (London, 1982), 7.

its ramifications were easily assumed as social labels in eighteenth-
and nineteenth-century texts, it is important to be aware of what,
precisely, is being signified by the choice of such appellations.
Class, as both historians and sociologists have stressed, is formally
an economic determinant alone: 'an economic grouping depending
on the value of a person's labour and his share of property'.[65]
Economic considerations are therefore conventionally of primary
importance in establishing class formation. Marx's proletariat and
bourgeoisie, the 'masters and men' of Gaskell's *North and South*,
Disraeli's 'two nations . . . who are formed by a different breeding,
are fed by a different food, are ordered by different manners' can
all be seen to encode the economic realities of social difference in
nineteenth-century society.[66] 'In a progressive civilisation, wealth
is the only means of class-distinction', Lord Valentine, in *Sybil*, is
informed.[67]

Such interpretations prove problematic in a number of ways,
and not least in terms of those correlations between accent and
class which have often endured as an equally prominent aspect of
this 'national obsession'. As texts such as *Vulgarities of Speech
Corrected*, *Hints on Etiquette*, or Marcus Davis's *Everybody's Business* have already indicated in this context, wealth, though it may
indeed be a means by which class membership may be formally
assigned, does not, and did not, always confer in equal measure
that status, or social honour, that might be thought to go with it.
'In the final analysis objective social stratification may be unattainable', May notes: 'for in a large part a person's class is what
he believes it to be and, more importantly, what others accept it
to be'.[68] The difference felt to pertain between respective stereotypes of the 'self-made' and the 'gentleman' throughout the
nineteenth century provides, for example, a case in point. Without
instruction in those other symbols of social honour associated
with elevated status, not least of them the use of /h/, the 'vulgar
rich', as Kington-Oliphant stressed, irrespective of the amount of
property they might possess, could not and would not be accorded
acceptability. It was this circumstance which rendered remedial
education in the proprieties of language highly important. 'Many

---

[65] T. May, *An Economic and Social History of Britain 1760–1970* (New York,
1987), 43.
[66] *Sybil*, i. 149.   [67] Ibid. ii. 203.
[68] May, *Economic and Social History of Britain*, 43.

a needy scholar might turn an honest penny by offering himself
as an instructor of the vulgar rich in the pronunciation of the fatal
letter', Kington-Oliphant notes of /h/-usage and the 'new rich' in
this context.[69] W. D. Rubenstein offers similar corroboration for
this perception in his own (rather more empirical) study of the
'new men of wealth' in nineteenth-century society. He points out
that, in reality, 'for the self-made man, there was an unbridgeable
gap of behaviour, attitude, and accent (and often of more formal
characteristics like religion) between the old aristocracy and the
nouveaux riches'; as he adds, 'no amount of land purchase would
affect [this]'.[70] A large amount of entrepreneurial fortune was
expended in acquisitions of this kind—Samuel Whitbread bought
Bodwell Park in 1751, and Woolmers a few years later, Matthew
Boulton bought Tew Park, and Albert Brassey Heythrop House,
the Peels bought Drayton Manor, Wedgwood built Etruria and
Barleston Hall, and Richard Arkwright's descendants accumu-
lated estates so that his four surviving grandsons, for example,
owned property in Derbyshire, Leicestershire, Essex, and Here-
ford. Nevertheless, as the social historians Stone and Stone
likewise affirm, even this was not necessarily to be adequate to
award the benefits of complete social acceptability: 'no amount of
land purchase would confer social acceptability upon a man whose
wealth was obtained in sordid ways, whose origins were obscure,
whose manners and accent were demonstrably vulgar, and whose
religion might well be non-conformist.'[71] Money may certainly
secure much, but, as many were to emphasize, it did not automatically provide control of those other, often more intangible
markers which may have superior powers of conferring—and signifying—respectability, or membership of the genteel. As Kington-
Oliphant, Rubenstein, and Stone and Stone all agree moreover,
language regularly impinged upon the allocation of social values.
It was refinements of speech which, they stress, were to be seen
as an increasingly vital acquisition among the other attributes of
the socially mobile.

As comments such as these indicate, it seems clear that prevalent
notions of the importance of accent and its correlations with the
issues of 'class' did not, in real terms, align quite as well as their

[69] T. Kington-Oliphant, *The Sources of Standard English* (London, 1873), 333.
[70] W. D. Rubenstein, 'New Men of Wealth and the Purchase of Land in Nineteenth-Century England', *Past and Present*, 92 (1981), 140.
[71] Stone and Stone, *An Open Élite?*, 207.

conventional stereotypes suggest. The economic could be disregarded in favour of other indicators of social standing and social
origin; the enunciation of /h/ could proclaim social origins in ways
which transcended the import of property and possessions. As a
result, though notions of social level are formally accorded in
terms of 'class' on economic grounds, they are, in reality, often
influenced by a wider set of behavioural norms and expectations,
perhaps foremost among which is assimilation to designated 'styles
of life', and to the markers seen as characteristic of particular
social groupings. Amongst these, styles of speaking were likewise
not to be immaterial. Just as Disraeli's comment on the 'two
nations' has indicated, notions of social difference rest therefore
on far more than mere matters of finance, especially in terms of
popular perception. 'Formed by a different breeding, . . . fed by a
different food, . . . ordered by different manners', people are
regularly aligned into social groupings on grounds such as these,
irrespective of their pecuniary level.

This evident disjunction between indices of economic standing
and these other, less concrete, indicators of social position is, of
course, by no means confined to the past. Ivor Morrish makes
plain with reference to the twentieth century that 'a docker may
earn more than a schoolmaster but this does not necessarily put
both of them in the same class—indeed, none of them would
claim to be in the same class',[72] and the resulting recognition of
group relationships in terms of shared norms and patterns of
behaviour rather than simply in terms of shared financial parition
is, in fact, much in evidence in nineteenth-century comment too.
The Economist, for example, though overtly making use of 'class'
terminology in 1857 in order to describe observed changes in society
('society is tending more and more to spread into classes—and
not merely classes, but localised classes, class colonies'),[73] nevertheless prefers to account for these changes with reference to
social patterns and affinities which are fundamentally distinct from
those which might be assumed on the basis of the purely financial:

There is a much deeper social principle involved in the present increasing
tendency to class colonies. It is the disposition to associate with equals
—in some measure with those who have similar practical *interests*, in still

---

[72] I. Morrish, *The Sociology of Education*, 2nd edn. (London, 1978), 123.
[73] Cited in D. Smith, *Conflict and Compromise: Class Formation in English Society
1830–1914* (London, 1982), 15.

greater measure with those who have similar tastes and culture, most of all with those with whom we judge ourselves on a moral equality, whatever our real standard might be.[74]

Similarly though Leach, as we have seen, willingly adopts the language of 'class' in order to discuss the solecism of [h]-dropping and its role as social marker ('H, in speech, is an unmistakable mark of class distinction in England, as every person soon discovers'), it is clear that it is by no means the merely economic signifiers of social identity which are relevant here. Indeed, as he confirms, though financial advantage may enable the purchase of superior clothes, any illusions of social standing (or superiority) thereby created may be rapidly dispelled once a person begins to speak:

I remarked upon this to an English gentleman, an officer, who replied— 'It's the greatest blessing in the world, a sure protection against cads. You meet a fellow who is well-dressed, behaves himself decently enough, and yet you don't know exactly what to make of him; but get him talking, and if he trips upon his H's that settles the question. He's a chap you'd better be shy of.'[75]

Marshall makes the same point in her own work on occupation and the social order in nineteenth-century society: 'The struggling clerk, who earned less than the expert fine cotton spinner, underlined this superiority by his dress, his speech, and his manners. These, and not his income, were what distinguished him from the working class.'[76] Social affinities based on markers of 'style of life' rather than upon parities of income, or indeed capital, thus function as the matrix in which notions of social cohesion or division within the community (including those of language) are to be enacted. The relevant terms are, in effect, those of 'status', not of 'class', and this difference is, in a number of ways, important in our conceptions of the role of accent as social symbol over this time.

Though 'class' and 'status' are, to an extent, interrelated, their differentiation rests in the economic emphasis of the former as a means of social definition, in contrast to the priority given to social habits, social manners, 'way of life' (amongst which language forms a composite part) by the latter. It is this contrast which can, for example, be used in the interpretation of Marcus Davis's comment on the importance of 'grammaticality' above

---

[74] Ibid.   [75] Leach, *The Letter H*, 10–11.
[76] Marshall, *Industrial England*, 96–7.

wealth for the 'gentleman' ('the wealthy man, great in his accumulation of riches, if he be not in possession of knowledge sufficient to command respect, and if he speak ungrammatically, is not considered a gentleman'), as well as in Leach's observations about the superior import of [h] in conversational discourse. The separation of the two as social constructs stems from the work of Max Weber who, recognizing that a simple one-to-one correspondence between economic and social standing did not, in fact, appear to be borne out by the working, and indeed thinking, of society, suggested instead the necessity of discriminating the economic ('class'), social ('status'), and political ('party') factors within social organization. Pointing out, precisely in line with those nineteenth-century attitudes already discussed, that mere economic power is by no means a recognized base of social honour,[77] Weber gives expression to the complexities which can attend perceptions of social station. Status, if not class, was firmly determined on the evaluative basis of a set of external symbols such as education, dress, manners, and language, all of which serve to establish a group's behavioural norms, its salient markers of identity and belonging, or in Weber's terms, its 'social honour'. The presence of certain factors, or the absence of others, hence delineate patterns of inclusion within the organization of society, conferring, or indeed withholding membership of the various status groups of society. It was command of these attributes which was, in essence, to define position, prestige, and 'social honour' in ways more subtle, and succinct, than those enabled by mere financial clout

With reference to language, and these escalating preoccupations with its role in social manners, social habits (and, indeed, social honour), such criteria of status, though they are admittedly vaguer in some ways than those based on class, do nevertheless seem to offer a perspective which is potentially useful. It is, for instance, clear that accent in the nineteenth century, as in the twentieth, came to correlate closely with status rather than class *per se* in structured patterns of co-variation which still hold true. In other words, though its correlations with 'class' have come to be something of a cliché in comment on language in England, it is in fact *status* in which such patterns fundamentally reside. Lesley

---

[77] M. Weber, 'Class, Status, Party', in R. S. Neale (ed.), *History and Class: Essential Readings in Theory and Interpretation* (Oxford, 1983), 57.

Milroy's analysis of sociolinguistic method in the twentieth century bears out this conclusion ('It appears then that the important variable which sociolinguists usually characterise as *class* is more specifically an evaluative one—status'[78]) and the letters, journals, newspapers, as well as texts on the language of the late eighteenth century and afterwards provide earlier confirmation of this fact. Accent emerges as an external signal which is unambiguously able to suggest social honour or its absence, and to extend similar patterns of evaluation to speaker as well as speech, predicating attendant issues of exclusion and exclusivity as it does so.

In Thomas Sheridan's work therefore, the 'disgrace' attending accents localized outside London is, at least theoretically, inimical to high social standing—a badge of dishonour—while the respect conferred by conformity to the 'best' London styles of speech acts as a marker (of status not of 'class') which will command the requisite esteem and admiration: 'a sort of proof that a person has kept good company', as Sheridan declares. Precisely in line with other symbols of social honour, attitudes to accent variation tend to function in socially evaluative ways of this kind, and are detailed in the late eighteenth and nineteenth centuries perhaps with more clarity, and greater explicitness, in the workings and dissemination of prescriptive ideology than any other marker of social identity. 'Respect', 'esteem', 'honour', and appropriate antonyms, as well as incontestable assertions of 'good', 'bad', 'right', 'wrong', and the favourite epithets of 'vulgar' and 'polite', proliferate within ostensibly linguistic descriptions, as pronunciation is specifically delineated in terms of its effects on the social affections, and the indices of standing which may thereby be exposed. As the author of *How to Shine in Society* underlined, for example, 'what advantages has the talent of conversation for he who aspires to honour and esteem, or wishes in short to rise in the world?',[79] specifying equally that conversational skills alone were as nothing if coupled with phonemic impropriety.

Command of a non-localized accent was, in such ways, deemed to symbolize much more than mere articulatory control, assimilation to its defining features overtly being integrated with contemporary

---

[78] L. Milroy, *Observing and Analysing Natural Language: A Critical Account of Sociolinguistic Method* (Oxford, 1987), 32.
[79] *How to Shine in Society*, 9.

issues of mobility, status, and success. Sensitization to the value of accent, just as in Sheridan's original conceptions of its role, thus proceeds simultaneously in terms of its status values too and within a few decades, as we have seen, such links were inseparable, embedded in the changing social fabric, and shifting social organization, of a newly industrialized society. Conformity, emulation (of the 'proper' models), and notions of improvement, all precepts in line with the codifying ethos of the age, were regularly presented as important linguistic tenets to be adhered to in the quest to signify status and the finer nuances of identity.

Fashion too played its allotted role. As Weber himself notes, the differentiations which operate in terms of status within society 'evolve in such a way as to make for strict submission to the fashion that is dominant at a given time in society'.[80] Prescriptive preferences for a non-localized accent, presented as a defining symbol of the 'gentleman' by Enfield in 1774, were hence gradually also assimilated into the canons of fashionable behaviour, though fashion in this instance was definitively 'high' rather than 'low', reflecting 'society' in its metropolitan senses rather than society as a whole. Redolent of familiarity with the 'best' speech of London, such speech patterns were adjudged to exert an obvious appeal, conformity to them stressed not only in the dictates of prescriptive texts, but also in literature, works on etiquette, and in popular journals as the true markers of the statusful and 'polite'. It is the absence of such markers which is, for example, presented as the factor which denies Gladstone, among others, membership of such ranks: 'Gladstone has too much of the Northern accent to be strictly gentlemanly', as Sir William Hardman commented.[81]

As texts such as *How to Shine in Society* or *How to Speak with Propriety* combine to suggest, however, more significant overall, and ultimately pervading much more of society than the élite integration of the successful few (and the linguistic standards ostensibly required of them), was the rather more widespread assimilation to notions of the gentry in cultural terms which was, in a number of ways, also taking place over the eighteenth and nineteenth centuries. 'Those who [fill] the higher ranks of life, are naturally regarded as patterns, by which the rest of the world are

[80] Neale, *History and Class*, 63; see also pp. 120–3.
[81] Sir William Hardman, *Papers*, ed. S. M. Ellis (London, 1925), i. 219.

to be fashioned', the religious (and educational) writer Hannah
More had noted in her *Thoughts on the Importance of the Manners
of the Great to General Society*.[82] Though More herself did not believe
in emulation as an adjunct to social mobility, there were, it seemed,
to be many who did; evident in the imitation of manners and
habits, of styles of behaving, dressing, and, of course, of speaking,
the statusful proprieties of the gentry classes did in a number of
ways appear to influence attitudes to social norms and behavioural
ideals across far wider sections of society than might initially be
assumed. Notions of the attempted cultural assimilations resulting
from such tendencies are, for instance, readily detected in the
'consumer revolution', documented as a significant accompaniment
to the social and industrial upheavals of the time by Neil
McKendrick; as he confirms, 'in imitation of the rich the middle
ranks spent more frenziedly than ever before, and in imitation of
them the rest of society joined in as best they might—and the best
was unprecedented in the importance of the effect on aggregate
demand'.[83] Clothes, fashions for both house and person, possessions of all kinds came to signify each step in intended social
advancement, a lesson which was, for example, well learnt by the
Veneerings and their own conspicuous consumption in Dickens's
Our Mutual Friend.

Cobbett, amongst others, criticized imitative behaviour of this
order with vehemence when he encountered it in his *Rural Rides*
('I daresay it had been *Squire* Charrington and the *Miss* Char-
ringtons; and not plain Master Charrington and his son Hodge and
his daughter Betty Charrington, all of whom the accursed system
had transmuted into a species of mock gentlefolk'). George Eliot
ventured similar censure upon behaviour she too clearly regarded
as pretension:

In our day . . . we can hardly enter the least imposing farm-house without
finding a bad piano in the 'drawing-room', and some old annuals, dis-
posed with a symmetrical imitation of negligence, on the table; though
the daughters may still drop their *h*'s, their vowels are studiously narrow;
and it is only in very primitive regions that they will consent to sit in a

---

[82] H. More, *Thoughts on the Importance of the Manners of the Great to General
Society* (London, 1788), 2.
[83] McKendrick *et al.*, *Birth of Consumer Society*, 11.

covered vehicle without springs, which was once thought an advance in luxury on the pillion.[84]

As contemporary comment thus reveals, this 'culture of gentility' could extend far beyond the stereotypes of the 'new rich', influencing not only the upper, but also the middle and even at times the lower sections of the social hierarchy. These, Stone and Stone confirm, 'instead of resenting [their social superiors], . . . eagerly sought to imitate them, aspiring to gentility by copying the education, manners, and behaviour of the gentry'.[85] It was 'homogenizing aspirations for gentility' of this order which, in real terms, were also to contribute to extending the appeal of 'talking proper' (and accompanying sociolinguistic attitudes) outside that largely localized élite which initially had had access to its forms. Discussed by Cobbett in terms of the 'constant anxiety to make a *show* not warranted by the reality' and by Stone and Stone in terms of a 'psychological cohesion' leading to the widespread emulation of typical signifiers of superior status (the use of boarding schools, the role of leisure as social symbol) among the middle classes,[86] this naturally had its linguistic repercussions too. 'You may talk of the tyranny of Nero and Tiberius; but the real tyranny is the tyranny of your next-door neighbour', wrote Bagehot in the mid-nineteenth century. 'Public opinion is a permeating influence, and it exacts obedience to itself; it requires us to think other men's thoughts, to speak other men's words, to follow other men's habits.'[87]

It is circumstances of this kind which seem to have led to the marked popularity of texts which claimed to set forth the dicta of phonemic propriety, trading on (and further diffusing) ideologies of a standard as they did so. As Alexander Ellis had observed, 'real communication between class and class is impossible', a fact which provided a seemingly insurmountable barrier to the acquisition of 'proper' accents by the masses. Largely denied direct

---

[84] G. Eliot, 'The Natural History of German Life', first pub. in *Westminster Review*, 66 (July 1856), 51–79, repr. in Eliot, *Essays*, ed. T. Pinney (London, 1963), 273–4.

[85] Stone and Stone, *An Open Élite?*, 409.

[86] Ibid. 409. See also pp. 161–3.

[87] W. Bagehot, 'The Character of Sir Robert Peel', in id., *Works*, ed. F. Morgan (Hartford, 1891), iii. 3–4.

communication, therefore, the consequences of this are exemplified not only in the flood of pronouncing dictionaries which, as already indicated, were published over the nineteenth century, but also in the continued demand for works on specific sounds, above all perhaps on the correct use of /h/: *Harry Hawkins' H Book*, *Mind Your H's and Take Care of Your R's*, *Poor Letter H*, and *The Letter H. Past, Present, and Future*, were all published and reprinted numerous times over this period. Accent, a social marker which, as such texts stressed, was able to suggest respectability by its cadences, and status by its tones, was thus explicitly fused with principles of imitative cohesion; the burgeoning white-collar and professional sections of society apparently endorsed its norms enthusiastically if contemporary comment is to be believed. Certainly discussions of /h/, as we will see, regularly stress the assimilatory endeavours of the middle sections of society in this area, neatly paralleling twentieth-century evidence on that hypercorrection often perceptible in lower-status groups in their more careful speech.[88]

As W. P. Robinson affirms, speech may indeed 'reveal preferred identity as much as real identity'; as he adds in this context: 'once . . . distinctive features are exposed, people aspiring to a certain identity may be able to incorporate them in their speech'.[89] The normative specifications of pronunciation which, as we will see, tended to expose distinctive features of this order with particular clarity from the late eighteenth century onwards were, as a result, presented as highly useful, especially for the new non-manual workers of the time. By such means, 'preferred identity' might be realized—at least when required. 'We create our 'rules' so as to resemble as closely as possible those of the groups with which from time to time we want to identify' wrote LePage in 1980[90] and the same processes may again be assumed to work equally well for the nineteenth century, similarly motivating the

[88] Trudgill's researches in Norwich have, for example, regularly revealed patterns of variation in which variants perceived as more 'statusful' in the wider speech community appear with far greater frequency than one might expect in the formal speech of members of the lower middle class. Hypercorrection, the over-extension of a particular linguistic usage in the attempt to emulate others, is, as he and a variety of other linguists have concluded, a common phenomenon in such contexts.

[89] W. P. Robinson, *Language and Social Behaviour* (London, 1972), 72.

[90] R. LePage, 'Projection, Focusing, Diffusion', *York Papers in Linguistics*, 9 (1980), 15.

shift towards (and away from) stated variables depending on the contexts in which speakers might find themselves. Certainly those intent on professional mobility were often openly exhorted to remember such 'rules' in their linguistic behaviour: 'The perusal and profit of the ledger should be preceded, accompanied, or at least followed, by a little study of grammar', *P's and Q's*, with its subtitle *Grammatical Hints for the Million*, directs.[91] Due emphasis is given to the fact that the use of language may complement, or confound, any newly gained social advantage for the aspiring clerk and speaking 'with care and attention to grammatical proprieties, such as proper aspiration' is presented as essential. Phonemic cause and social effect in this circumstance are made particularly clear:

Boys and girls may, and very often do, rise above their original level in society, and doing so they should be prepared to adorn the new station they may fill . . . Want of education sadly mars what talent, or labour, or money, or comparative accident may help to make; and if the men, or women, be not themselves aware of the defect, their children, friends, and relatives, have often painfully to feel it.[92]

If the issues of social status and cultural assimilation were not in themselves to exert sufficient persuasion upon the speaker to amend existing improprieties of speech, the notion of social shame was, as this illustrates, to be deployed in their stead. Convergent behaviour, in terms of social, cultural, and linguistic norms, was to be decisively promoted as the aim for all in search of true propriety, all aspects which likewise manipulate those fictions of empowerment which are so common within the standard ideology. One way of 'talking proper' was privileged above all others in many contemporary attitudes to the language, and in time this came to be regarded as perhaps the salient marker of privilege in itself, capable of implying not only superiorities of standing and of knowledge but, more significantly, also being assumed to convey those attendant values of power and authority which (in subjective reactions to its use) were likewise often assumed to be embedded in its forms.

Works such as *P's and Q's* therefore tended to voice explicit appeals to ambitions to signify possession of the 'manner' proper to the popular social constructs of 'gentleman' or 'lady', not least

---

[91] Hon. Henry H., *P's and Q's*, 78 n.   [92] Ibid.

since it was behaviour, rather than ancestry or lineage, which was increasingly regarded as the defining characteristic of these social icons. Walker's 1791 definition of a 'lady' ('a woman of high rank') was, for example, increasingly superseded, as the nineteenth century advanced, by definitions in which manners again assume prominence: 'a term of complaisance; applied to almost any well-dressed woman, but appropriately to one of refined manners and education', as the lexicographer John Ogilvie notes in 1870.[93] Semantic transformations of a similar kind are perceptible in the connotations of 'gentleman' too: 'a man of birth, a man of extraction' glosses Walker. Though these resonances remain ('every man above the rank of yeoman, comprehending noblemen' as Ogilvie correspondingly adds in 1870) its *'highest sense'* is somewhat different: 'in the *highest sense*, the term *gentleman* signifies a man of strict integrity and honour, of self-respect, and intellectual refinement, as well as refined manners and good breeding.'[94] Like the semantic shifts perceptible in 'accent', and indeed in 'class' too, these particular changes in meaning indicate the processes of semantic extension, whereby these social labels assumed much wider currency in social terms than had hitherto been the case, undergoing accompanying processes of 'devaluation' as they did so. ' "You mustn't say 'gentlemen' nowadays," ' as Mrs Swanton admonishes Elfride in Thomas Hardy's *A Pair of Blue Eyes* (1873): ' "We have handed over 'gentlemen' to the lower middle classes, where the word is still to be heard at tradesmen's balls and provincial tea-parties, I believe." '

Hardy's account of the shifting semantic contexts of this word indicates with some precision the processes of emulation and assimilation which were, in a variety of ways, taking place, and not only of course within semantic space. Manuals on how to attain the markers of 'gentleman' or 'lady' abound; as *Advice to a Young Gentleman on Entering Society* (1839) specified in this context: 'There are certain arbitrary peculiarities of manner, speech, language, taste, &c. which mark the high-born and high-bred. These should be observed and had.'[95] The role of manners in marking social identity is made still more evident by the author's

---

[93] J. Ogilvie, *The Comprehensive English Pronouncing Dictionary* (London, 1870), definition of the word *lady*.

[94] Ibid., definition of the word *gentleman*.

[95] *Advice to a Young Gentleman on Entering Society* (London, 1839), 77.

subsequent comment: 'they are the signs-manual of good-breeding by which gentlemen recognize each other wherever they meet.' The central tenet, in essence, again rested on the recognition that given information on the right symbols of social status and 'style of life', of which speech was, as we have seen, the most immediate in its effects, their readers could themselves suggest a standing higher than they actually possessed, command a propriety which would in turn command respect. It is these 'arbitrary peculiarities of speech' which are explicitly proffered within the tenets which this, and similar works, endorse.

Imitative cohesion, as set out in handbooks of this kind, hence becomes the art of social illusion, and the examples (and exemplars) given in this context are clear and to the point. 'No one could imagine Lord John . . . issuing his orders to the channel fleet with the accent of a Cockney; or John Campbell, Duke of Argyll, admonishing a postman on the effects of mountain dew with the accent of a citizen of Inverary', as *How to Shine in Society* warned.[96] Cultural assimilation is, in these particular workings of prescriptive ideology, made inseparable from linguistic assimilation, and its pressures are persuasive; by modifications of accent, and familiarity with this particular 'signs-manual', the resonances of gentility could unambiguously be imaged forth. Whether using the accents of lower-class London, or the 'provincial' tones of Scotland, the detrimental effects on perceptions of one's social standing (as well as upon those other subjective associations already discussed) was to be the same. Language was embedded in assumptions of social difference and disadvantage, and although this may be unfair, as Marcus Davis indicates, it was also in many ways to seem irremediable by the later nineteenth century: 'Why is an ill-dressed man, in labourer's apparel treated with *contumely* even in courts of justice . . . Because they are totally unacquainted with that branch of knowledge that gives to man a tower of defence . . . They have not that command of language which imparts confidence, not only to assert our rights but defend them.'[97] The relevant maxim to be drawn from this was, as Davis asserts in the opening words of his book, that 'It is EVERYBODY'S BUSINESS to speak; and if it is EVERYBODY'S BUSINESS to speak, it is worth EVERYBODY'S while to speak correctly.'[98]

[96] *How to Shine in Society*, 20.
[97] Davis, *Everybody's Business*, 18.   [98] Ibid. 1.

Few, asserted Phyfe, were to be entirely immune from this
equation, whether in terms of the attitudes they held towards
linguistic usage, or the linguistic habits which they in turn endeavoured to adopt. Accent, he stressed, 'appeals to all, since
there is no one so wholly indifferent to the estimate formed of his
social position, and who, in consequence, would not cultivate
those arts that are at once the criteria of social standing and the
stepping stones to a more liberal culture.'[99] It was, as this indicates, the 'cultivated' voice which was widely perceived as the true
mirror of the 'cultured' speaker, where 'culture' itself served as
a synonym for the privileged and polite: 'a good orthoepy', as
Savage indicated, 'will never fail of producing impressions in
your favour'[100] and indeed, as modern subjective reaction tests
continue to affirm, how one spoke could, it seemed, be of more
importance at times than what one said, linguistic 'manners' in-
fringing upon the images of power and authority conveyed by the
'right' sort of speech. It is a transition illustrated particularly well
in the various editions of William Cobbett's own *Grammar of the
English Language*, originally published in England in 1819. Addressing his text to 'soldiers, sailors, apprentices, and ploughboys',
Cobbett, like Sheridan, had presented the knowledge of linguistic
propriety as an indispensable acquisition: 'in no situation, which
calls on a man to place his thoughts on paper, can the possession
of it fail to be a source of self-congratulation, or the want of it a
cause of mortification and sorrow.'[101] Unlike Sheridan however,
Cobbett presented grammar rather than accent as of foremost
importance in this context. Resolutely maintaining older views
such as those endorsed by Joseph Priestley in his own assumption
that pronunciation is 'a matter of decoration only', Cobbett
similarly stated that 'children will pronounce as their fathers and
mothers pronounce; and if, in common conversation, or in
speeches, the matter be good and judiciously arranged, the facts
clearly stated . . . the words well chosen and properly placed, hearers
whose approbation is worth having will pay very little attention to
the accent.'[102]

Cobbett's son James, however, born in 1803 and growing up in
a significantly different linguistic and cultural climate, presents a
somewhat different emphasis in his 1866 edition of his father's

[99] Phyfe, *How Should I Pronounce?*, p. v.
[100] Savage, *Vulgarisms and Improprieties*, p. v.
[101] Cobbett, *Grammar of the English Language*, 9.   [102] Ibid. 15.

work. Clearly feeling it incumbent upon him to redress any earlier textual imbalances, he adds a new chapter headed 'Pronunciation: Certain Common Forms Pointed Out and Corrected'. Cobbett senior's precept that '*pronunciation* is learnt as birds learn to chirp and sing' so that, consequently, it 'ought not to occupy much of your attention'[103] is as a result reinterpreted in accordance with tenets more typical of the 1860s. Cobbett junior instead adds: 'That shows the importance of attending to children's ways of speaking while they are at an early age.'[104] Both father and son comment on the facts of variation in pronunciation, but it is the differences in attitude which are more striking than any similarities arising from the shared subject matter. 'The differences [in pronunciation] are of very little real consequence . . . though the Scotch say *coorn*, the Londoners *cawn*, and the Hampshire folk *carn*, we all know they *mean* to say *corn*' wrote William in 1819.[105] 'Many of these terms are of constant use, and the mispronouncing of some of them is particularly offensive' amended his son in 1866.[106]

James Cobbett can, in a number of ways, be seen as an exemplar of that consciousness of accent and its social values which Sheridan and others had deliberately attempted to raise. He willingly concurs with the notions of inherent value and aesthetic demerit which are, as we have seen, staples of the standard ideology, endorsing the importance of linguistic convergence in terms his father would have abhorred. He is of course, in this, merely a product of his age; that reorientation of attitudes so marked over the nineteenth century in terms of attitudes to language and notions of phonetic propriety in particular, naturally also infuses the precepts he provides. Such attitudes, and their diffusion, were exploited in literature as in life and authors, likewise embedded in these resonances of prescriptive ideology, trade in parallel ways on the images of accent and the social signals which had come to be almost inseparable from the acts of enunciation thereby involved. 'Consciousness' of this order hence receives an additional correlate in its working out within the fictional world, as authors too, as we

---

[103] Ibid.
[104] J. Cobbett, *A Grammar of the English Language in a Series of Letters. With an Additional Chapter on Pronunciation by James Paul Cobbett* (London, 1866), 242.
[105] Cobbett, *Grammar of the English Language*, 15.
[106] J. Cobbett, *Grammar of the English Language: With an Additional Chapter*, 247. See also L. C. Mugglestone, 'Cobbett's *Grammar*; William, James Paul, and the Politics of Prescriptivism', forthcoming in *Review of English Studies*.

shall see, proved themselves to be equally receptive to the repercussions of a 'standard' and to the change in attitudes which had ensued.[107]

It is, however, perhaps useful at this point to shift our focus to the actualities of speech in the late eighteenth and nineteenth centuries in order to illustrate the deployment of these issues with reference to a number of the features which, in various ways, were to be particularly characteristic of images of accent and acceptability at this time. One of the most prominent topics for discussion in works on language, for example, was the way in which the *a* before voiceless fricatives in words such as *fast*, *bath*, or *last* should be pronounced. Its realization as a long [ɑ:] (as in modern southern enunciations of *fast*) now, of course, functions as one of the primary markers of a non-localized 'standard', or RP, accent and, although its transformation to this salient feature of 'talking proper' is now seemingly secure, it is perhaps salutary to remember that this was by no means so well established in the late eighteenth century. Using [ɑ:] was in fact, for much of the nineteenth century, instead quite likely to damn the speaker, in the words of various critics of the language, as 'inaccurate', 'vulgar' or 'uneducated'. Questions of social and linguistic acceptability are, as in the images of accent already discussed, overtly made to surround this change in progress, writers on the language adopting, with considerable vigour, opposing positions in which they embraced the propriety of using the short or long, front or retracted, sounds of *a* in words such as *bath*, *task*, or *fast*. Prescriptive methodology, in this as in all else, was willingly to draw on the various social stereotypes prominent in contemporary comment and the opportunities which they offered for praise or blame.

Walker, for example, emphasized to his by no means inconsiderable audiences that to use the lengthened [ɑ:] was the preserve of 'inaccurate speakers, chiefly among the vulgar', and he added, with the full force of emotive zeal, 'every correct ear would be disgusted at giving the *a* in these words the full long sound of the *a* in *father*'.[108] The use of the short [æ] is, conversely, 'elegant', 'accurate' and 'precise', the social nuances of refinement being heavily weighted in its favour. Other writers, however, endorse

---

[107] See also Ch. 5.
[108] J. Walker, *Critical Pronouncing Dictionary*, 2nd edn. (1797), §163.

other views and William Smith and Stephen Jones in (respectively) 1795 and 1798 select instead the proscribed [ɑ:] as their own preferred variant. As Jones comments, 'Mr. Walker . . . seems to have employed [the lengthened sound of *a*] with too much timidity . . . encouraging a mincing modern affectation, and departing from the genuine euphonical pronunciation of our language.'[109] Smith in turn comes in for censure from Walker himself for this choice, as debates on the articulation of this group of words evolved into a highly partisan affair: 'In this work he [Smith] departs frequently from my judgment, and particularly in the pronunciation of the letter *a* . . . that this was the sound formerly, is highly probable from its being still the sound given to it by the vulgar, who are generally the last to alter the common pronunciation.'[110] The debate continued through much of the nineteenth century, Smart in 1836 trading overtly on that heightened consciousness towards the social meanings of speech, and advising his readers to avoid vulgarities such as the lengthened *a* in their enunciation should they wish to convey overtones of the polite rather than the merely improper.

As Downes notes, fundamentally 'a language change involves a change in norms',[111] and in the conflicting claims of individual writers and speakers at this time about the 'proper' use of *a*, this is precisely what can be seen to be in operation. The change, however, comes to involve not only linguistic norms but social ones too in the rhetoric commonly employed as, with habitual ease, writers sought to appeal to the social (and status) insecurities of their readers. 'Of the propriety or impropriety of this, a well-educated ear is the best judge', Walker remarks on the use of [æ], deploying familiar paradigms of knowledge and ignorance; 'well-educated ears are now averse to this pronunciation', stresses Smart more explicitly.[112] Though the use of a lengthened sound is in fact attested from the late seventeenth century, appearing first in the work of Cooper in 1687,[113] throughout the late eighteenth and nineteenth centuries it is nevertheless often depicted as the preserve of the 'vulgar', the 'ignorant', or the socially unacceptable.

---

[109] S. Jones, *Sheridan Improved. A General Pronouncing and Explanatory Dictionary of the English Language*, 3rd edn. (London, 1798), p. ii.
[110] Walker, *Critical Pronouncing Dictionary*, 2nd edn. (1797), §79 n.
[111] Downes, *Language in Society*, 214.   [112] Smart, *Practical Grammar*, 99.
[113] Cooper, *The English Teacher*, 34.

Overtly labelled in such negative ways, it is therefore proscribed in terms of social as well as linguistic shibboleths, regularly being affiliated, in addition, to 'Cockney' usage, the strongly negative values of this social stereotype being assumed to act as sufficient dissuasion for any speaker.

In reality of course, and outside the binary schemes favoured by writers on the language, both short and long sounds were used, even within that 'good' speech which Walker and others attempted to portray. Prescriptive methodology, habitually intolerant of optional variability in language, will, however, sanction only one mode of pronunciation as 'correct', and in this context it often chose to do so by utilizing socially constructed appeals which laid bare selected social meanings in speech. Accent and its role in revealing, or indeed concealing, social identity, comes to form the sub-text of such descriptions, texts such as *Common Blunders in Speaking and How to Avoid Them* deliberately emphasizing both social and aesthetic values in their prescriptive attempts to control the direction of change: 'do not pronounce the words *ask, lance, plaster,* as if spelt *arsk, larnce, plarster.* Such a style of pronunciation is offensive and grating to the ear.'[114] Particularly interesting are the repercussions that such prescriptive propaganda can be seen to have, both in terms of linguistic behaviour and language attitudes.

Novelists, for example, readily come to trade on these common perceptions of stigma, allocating forms such as *farst* and *larff* to characters located in the lower spheres of life, and thus further encoding (and diffusing) the ideologies of a standard in this context for their readers: 'parsty' says Barkis in *David Copperfield,* 'larst' says Andrew Peak, Godwin Peak's consummately Cockney uncle in Gissing's *Born in Exile.*[115] Real speakers too, according to contemporary comment, were by no means immune to dicta which so emphatically stressed 'elegance' in the avoidance of the longer sounds of *a* in articulations of *path* and other similar words. The phililogist and lexicographer John Longmuir, writing in 1864, notes in his own account of pronunciation that though variation between [ɑː] and [æ] was still apparent, it was the latter which dominated for careful speakers concerned with the maintenance

---

[114] *Common Blunders in Speaking and How to Avoid Them* (London, 1884), 9.
[115] See also Ch. 5.

of 'correctness' and 'proper' speech. This was moreover seen as being sanctioned in particular by Walker's superior apprehensions in matters of phonetic nicety. As Longmuir observes: 'the high character of Walker, and the increasing dislike of anything resembling a drawl in speaking, gave currency to the change . . . Walker's extreme short sound of . . . *pass*, like *passive*, is now generally adopted as the proper sound.'[116]

Still more striking is the evidence which suggests that while the social correlates so liberally accorded to these realizations seem to have led certain speakers to endeavour to adopt the use of [æ] exclusively, they also seem to have led to the creation of an artificial and compromise 'middle sound', intermediate between [æ] and [ɑ:], adopted by particularly careful speakers, and, as we may imagine, in contexts of greater formality. Longmuir notes, for example, that 'there is a disposition among literary men and public speakers to unite on some *intermediate* sound between the entire broadness of the *a* in *father*, and the narrowness of the *a* in *fat* . . . In this way, they guard against that undue prolongation of the *a* which offended Walker'.[117] Alexander Ellis too confirms this predilection, isolating the use of an intermediate and 'delicate' sound, which is deliberately adopted by 'refined' speakers in preference to realizations in [ɑ:] 'which they consider too "broad" ', and to those in [æ] which were deemed too 'mincing'.[118] It was this, in the evidence of Ellis and many other writers on the language, which apparently became the preserve of the speech-conscious and intentionally correct, who, submitting to the ideologies of standard norms wielded by Walker and others, attempted to respond by shifting their own language habits in favour of this compromise realization, and hence, at least in terms of prescriptive theory, avoiding the stigmas of 'vulgarity', 'ignorance', and 'impropriety'.

Ellis's further specification of co-variation in this context, detailing a correlation of such variants not only with status but also with gender will be discussed in a later chapter.[119] What is clear, however, even from this brief survey is the fact that notions of accent and identity, articulated in prescriptive texts and a staple of the standardizing ideology, did not seem to operate in a vacuum.

---

[116] J. Longmuir, *Walker and Webster Combined in a Dictionary of the English Language* (London, 1864), §6.
[117] Ibid.   [118] Ellis, *Early English Pronunciation*, ii. 593.
[119] See pp. 196–9.

For those sensitive to the shades of sociolinguistic symbolism so deftly manipulated in ostensibly objective accounts of language use, the use of the correct speaker as a social ideal could, and seemingly did, lead to attempts to change hitherto accepted patterns of pronunciation even within variants of a single phoneme, and particularly in the more formal registers of the language (the language of 'public speakers and literary men' as Longmuir notes) when speakers tend to be at their most aware, and hence often more receptive to the norms of correctness propagated within the wider speech community.

As Greenbaum has noted, the fundamental premiss behind patterns of prescription of this kind (as well as responses to them) relies on the notion that 'correct performance marks the user as a responsible member of society', while 'incorrect performance is viewed as contributing to the decay of the language'.[120] Issues of authority (and its requisite projection) are, as in those subjective reaction tests already discussed,[121] again involved in the language attitudes which result; with reference to the prescriptions and proscriptions surrounding the 'proper' enunciation of *a*, directives on this particular head were, it seems, hence regularly to be assimilated. As late as the first decade of the twentieth century the phonetician Walker Ripman still observes that 'it is sometimes found that precise speakers, through an excessive desire to avoid any suspicion of Cockney leanings in their speech, substitute [a] for [ɑ], saying, for instance, [faːðə] in place of [fɑːðə]'.[122] As this suggests, it evidently took some time to dispel the connotative legacies of the eighteenth and nineteenth centuries for this particular detail of speech.

Like the 'naice' speakers of the twentieth century, it was, however, especially those who apparently felt themselves open to the suspicion of vulgarity, or who aspired to a refinement which they did not in fact possess, who seemed most of all to assume such 'correct' forms in their speech, being precisely akin in this to the lower-middle-class speakers documented in the sociolinguistic surveys of Peter Trudgill or William Labov. These, as already indicated, similarly hypercorrect in their use of variants perceived as most statusful, revealing marked levels of linguistic insecurity

---

[120] S. Greenbaum, *Good English and the Grammarian* (London, 1988), 33.
[121] See pp. 58–9.
[122] W. Ripman, *The Sounds of Spoken English* (London, 1906), 55.

in their attitudes towards their own linguistic usage, as well as in their willingness to approximate more closely to the stated norms of 'proper' language in their more formal speech. It was of course speakers of this order who were explicitly targeted by the writers of the sixpenny manuals such as *Hard Words Made Easy* (1855) and *Mind Your H's and Take Care of Your R's* (1866) with their own recommendations to those seeking to make their way in the social order to 'Avoid a too broad or too slender pronunciation of the vowel *a*, in words such as *glass* . . . Some persons vulgarly pronounce the *a* in such words, as if written *ar* and others mince it so as to rhyme it with *stand* . . . Equally avoid the extremes of vulgarity and affectation.'[123] Speakers more secure in their sociolinguistic identities would hardly have been tempted by the titles of these works, nor would they have formed part of their by no means inconsiderable readership.

Nevertheless, in spite of all these specifications for attempted cultural cohesion by means of speech, it was, in the end, not to be this 'middle' variant, or even [æ], but instead the theoretically 'vulgar' [ɑː] which stabilized as one of the dominant markers of RP, a hallmark, paradoxically, of that most 'elegant' speech which Walker and others had sought to define (at least in part) by the very fact of its exclusion. The interactions of language, society, prescriptive tenets, and the sociolinguistic sensibilities of speakers are in such ways much more complex than might at first be assumed. In real terms, for example, the use of [ɑː], recorded first, as we have seen, in the late seventeenth century, remained as a variant realization throughout the eighteenth and nineteenth centuries, gradually extending its use and distribution at the expense of [æ], though its diffusion throughout relevant environments was never complete.[124] The censure which it received in terms of the standard ideology over this time is in many ways therefore merely a reaction to an observable change in progress in a language in which stability was revered and, as we have seen, the rights of codification were regularly asserted above those of 'custom' or usage.[125] As the anonymous author of *Vulgarisms and Other Errors*

---

[123] C. W. Smith, *Mind Your H's and Take Care of Your R's* (London, 1866), 34.

[124] *Asp, lass, mass*, for example, although satisfying the requisite phonological conditions, nevertheless all have [æ] in RP (though [ɑː] for the latter is recorded in conservative Catholic usage). By analogy, *pasta* is now wavering between [æ] and [ɑː].

[125] See pp. 24–5.

of Speech averred on the subject of linguistic change, for example, 'it is not innovation that is reprehensible, but innovation without good cause, and, worst of all, innovation for innovations's sake'.[126] Using [ɑ:] rather than the long-established [æ] was, in such terms, likely to be proscribed as precisely such 'unnecessary' innovation, though the fact that similar patterns of usage were in evidence in lower-class London speech seems to have given extra point to those notions of correctness and social value prioritized in relevant prescriptive propaganda. 'Vulgarity' was rightly perceived as the most powerful weapon for its attempted control, though the very nature of this linguistic change and its diffusion inevitably confronts another prescriptive fiction of 'proper' language; as this makes plain, though prescriptive writings on the language almost invariably present élite models of enunciation as the ideal for emulation for the rest of society, paradoxically the real direction of linguistic change can instead regularly run counter to such precepts. As countless sociolinguistic studies have revealed, the nexus of change, and the innovating groups in society, are usually to be found in lower rather than higher echelons; the fear of the 'other' in both social and linguistic terms hence motivates prescriptive denunciations of change which are in fact still to be found today, as in that set of attitudes surrounding late-twentieth-century reactions to 'Estuary English' and its own assumed shibboleths of speech.[127]

As this particular sound change in the nineteenth century thus illustrates, though prevalent attitudes to language will not necessarily affect the ultimate progress of a linguistic change (just as the modern cries of 'degeneration' surrounding the semantic shifts in words such as *aggravate* or *gay* will in no way prevent their advance), they can nevertheless prove pervasive in terms of popular notions of correctness. In such ways, just as in the twentieth century those most conscious of the perceived merits of correctness will endeavour to modify their usage accordingly, resolutely avoiding *aggravate* in the sense of 'to annoy', so did their nineteenth-century counterparts presumably try, with equal resolution, to avoid [ɑ:], especially in the more formal contexts of speech

---

[126] *Vulgarisms and Other Errors of Speech* (London, 1868), p. iv.

[127] Estuary English, first described in 1984 in the *Times Educational Supplement*, is usually characterized as a 'classless' blend of RP and 'Cockney', spoken in the area around London and the Thames valley and marked by a range of 'proscribed' (though common) articulations such as the glottal stop or the use of /t, d/ deletion.

when speakers are particularly on their guard. Such patterns present us yet again with the disjunction between the operation of standardization as a process and as an ideology; it is of course the latter, and not the former, which generates these beliefs in the set of 'right' and 'wrong' enunciations in this context, and which in turn leads to the effective dissemination of a number of sociolinguistic stereotypes over the course of the nineteenth century (the 'vulgar' use of [ɑː], the 'refined' use of its 'middle' equivalent). The actual processes of standardization may thus be at some removes from the idealized and often binary oppositions of the prescriptive tradition, evident here in the fact that a range of variants is still apparent over the country in relevant words, as well as in that the one variant which has emerged as a non-localized 'standard pronunciation feature' ([pɑːə], [bɑːɒ] for *path, bath*), is not the one endorsed by the majority of nineteenth-century observers.

Other changes in progress, perhaps predictably, reveal similar patterns, though they can in addition illuminate other aspects of those prescriptive fictions which were so often deployed in the aim to create the 'plain and permanent standard of pronunciation' advocated by Sheridan and others. Another particularly prevalent image within writing on the language, and attitudes to its use, is, for example, that of the 'elegant' speaker, set out perhaps most effectively by Johnson in his own dictum that 'for pronunciation the best general rule is, to consider those as the most elegant speakers who deviate least from the written words'.[128] Though one of the few comments on pronunciation in his dictionary of 1755, this precept was nevertheless recognized as important, embracing as it did linguistic ideals in which written and spoken language, grapheme and phoneme, were in harmony. It evolved into a concise definition of 'elegant' speech and was, as a result, often cited, influencing popular notions of propriety in works such as the *Grammar* of Lindley Murray, a text which went through thirty-four editions by 1821, and which, without reservation, endorsed the view that 'it is a good rule, with respect to pronunciation, to adhere to the written words, unless custom has clearly decided otherwise'.[129] The grammars of countless other writers provided similar echoes: 'Dr. Johnson judiciously ... remarks that "For

---

[128] Johnson, *Dictionary*, a2ᵛ i.
[129] L. Murray, *English Grammar Adapted to the Different Classes of Learners*, 5th edn. (York, 1799), 13.

pronunciation the best rule is, to consider those as the most
elegant speakers, who deviate least from the *written* words" ' wrote
Lewis Brittain in 1788.[130] 'Dr Johnson's Dictionary may be consulted with great advantage. He says, and very justly too, "that
they are the most elegant speakers who deviate least from the
written sound" ', wrote Thomas Carpenter in 1825.[131] Time and
time again, the authority of Johnson's own words was used to
confirm notions of the superior authority of grapheme above
phoneme.

Johnson, of course, merely gave influential voice to a common
assumption about the relationship of spoken and written languages:
that graphemes were primary, and phonemes secondary seemed
for many to be borne out by the greater perfection and stability
of the former, against the flux and instability which the latter still
evinced. Moreover, as Stubbs has pointed out, though the spoken
word is accorded clear linguistic primacy, in popular thinking it is
instead its written equivalent which assumes a social (and cultural)
priority which is far from insignificant,[132] especially when knowledge of this order was itself often seen as an index of social
standing. It was 'literate speakers' who, in the thinking of the day,
reflected such superior knowledge in their speech. 'Illiterate ones',
as Johnson also noted, revealed merely ignorance: 'we now observe
those who cannot read to catch sounds imperfectly, and utter them
negligently.'[133]

Notions of 'literate speech' on these lines came to influence
materially common opinions on correct speech, not least in the
context of the shibboleth of [h]-dropping which was, as already
indicated, also being encoded over this time. It is, however, the
'dropped *r*' which will now occupy our attention, since this too
exemplifies in many ways the interactions of prescriptive ideology,
literate speech, and those socio-symbolic values which were never
far from issues of phonemic propriety during the nineteenth century. As with 'h' ([h]), for example, the 'dropping' or vocalization
of 'r' ([r]) in words such as *car* [kɑ:], and *chart* [tʃɑ:t], where it

---

[130] L. Brittain, *Rudiments of English Grammar* (Louvain, 1788), A1ᵛ.
[131] T. Carpenter, *The School Speaker* (London, 1825), p. vi.
[132] M. Stubbs, *Language and Literacy: The Sociolinguistics of Reading and Writing*
(London, 1980), 29.
[133] Johnson, *Dictionary*, A2ʳ.

is no longer pronounced post-vocalically in RP or approximations to it,[134] involves the apparent loss of a 'letter'. Still worse, from contemporary points of view, it involved the creation of a number of homophones such as *lord* and *laud*, *lorn* and *lawn*, as words which had hitherto been distinct were, by means of this vocalization, rendered identical in sound, though in spelling they naturally remained distinct. Given typical prescriptive sensibilities on this score (Newman in 1878, for example, directed heavy censure towards the 'assimilating and trait-destroying tendencies of slovenly speech'),[135] this presented a situation guaranteed to arouse attack, and socially constructed epithets were applied accordingly to those who revealed such 'carelessness' and 'negligence' in their speech. Many writers (and speakers) in turn seemed to cultivate an ostrich-like mentality, resolutely refusing to acknowledge that such a change had taken place, or that, if it had, it had done so only in the most vulgar of surroundings.

As with a number of other features of eighteenth- and nineteenth-century pronunciation, notions of the social distribution of linguistic items were to be manipulated to particularly good effect, stated correlations of accent and 'class' encoding potent social and linguistic stereotypes which did not pass unremarked. In the chosen paradigms of prescriptive texts, it is the 'vulgar', the 'Cockney', the 'lower classes', and the 'illiterate' who vocalize [r], while the 'elegant', the 'polished', and the 'educated' retain its use in the precision of their careful, and literate, speech. 'Poor Letter R' is even, in the hands of a 'Robert Ruskin Rogers', made to publish his own eloquent appeal on the subject of his use and abuse, his first-person address drawing out the pathos of his situation— regularly neglected, forgotten, and abandoned in the pronunciation of words:

Let me appeal to your good nature and fellow-feeling, under the insults and indignities to which I am continually exposed . . . In public assemblies and in private societies, I am frequently wounded by the ignorance of my *character* and claims so commonly betrayed.[136]

---

[134] Rhotic accents (those which retain the /r/) are still present in Scotland and Ireland, whereas variable rhoticity can still mark (lower-status) accents in e.g. north-west England.

[135] F. W. Newman, 'The English Language as Spoken and Written', *Contemporary Review*, 31 (1878), 702.

[136] R. R. Rogers, *Poor Letter R, Its Use and Abuse* (London, 1855), 14–15.

Attitudes to the loss of [r] again exemplify the divergence which
can occur between linguistic fact and fiction. In reality, its vocalization in these positions had been attested since the mid-eighteenth
century, its absence rather than its presence being more typical of
the emergent RP of the nineteenth century. Nevertheless, theoretical criteria of acceptability rarely sanctioned this development,
and the fictions of social identity attached to its use remained
remarkably powerful if contemporary accounts are to be believed.
'Cockney', a term of abuse regularly applied to many linguistic
sins of the age, is given particular emphasis in condemnatory
accounts of the loss of [r], its absence thus being deliberately
associated with a social sub-stratum characterized by convictions
of its complete social, and linguistic, unacceptability: both Hill in
1821 and Smart in 1836, for example, link the loss of [r] to the
'provincialists' and the Cockney 'vulgar' of the 'metropolis',
deliberately utilizing the connotative values of these epithets in the
proscriptions they endeavour to enforce. The repercussions of this
equation intervened even in the realms of poetry, and rhymes
which traded on the use of aural rather than visual correspondences
in this context were as a result often proscribed as 'Cockney
rhymes', in spite of their evident validity to ear if not to eye.[137]
Thomas Hood the younger, in a section of his text devoted to the
aspiring poet, hence felt driven to exhort 'the writer of verse to
examine his rhymes carefully': 'see that they chime to an educated
ear. Such atrocities as "morn" and "dawn", . . . "fought" and
"sort", are fatal to the success of verse. They stamp it with vulgarity,
as surely as the dropping of "h" stamps a speaker.'[138]

Such rhymes were, in the ideology of the time, 'Cockney',
untenable within the sanctity of verse, a fact, or fiction, likewise
made plain by J. E. Carpenter in 1868: 'In a young author's first
volume I found "Italy" made to rhyme with "bitterly". Now
"Iterly," in the mouth of a public speaker, would condemn him
as a thorough Cockney. "Armies" with "calm is", is another of
this same writer's cockney rhymes.'[139] It was stigmas of this sort
which were used to hound Keats, whose rhymes of *thorns/fawns*,
and *thoughts/sorts* contravened popular notions of correctness of

---

[137] See L. C. Mugglestone, 'The Fallacy of the Cockney Rhyme: From Keats
and Earlier to Auden', *Review of English Studies*, NS 42 (1991), 57–66.
[138] T. Hood, *The Wakefield Spelling Book* (London, 1868), 44.
[139] J. E. Carpenter, *Handbook of Poetry* (London, 1868), 12.

precisely this kind, even if they did agree with the realities of linguistic usage at the time. Keats's use of aural rather than visual authority in his poetry was, however, typically to bring censure rather than praise. John Lockhart, writing in *Blackwood's Edinburgh Magazine*, thus deploys notions of 'literate speech' in a form of literary criticism which readily reveals the operations of social as well as linguistic prejudice (as well as further confirming the wider impact of language attitudes outside the confines of the prescriptive tradition itself). Keats is, on such grounds, 'an uneducated and flimsy stripling'. He is 'without logic enough to analyse a single idea, or imagination enough to form one original image'. More fundamentally, he is also '[without] learning enough to distinguish between the written language of Englishmen and the spoken jargon of Cockneys'.[140] Keats is, in effect, 'illiterate', ignoring the authority of graphemes in the phonemic correspondences he employs.

What is perhaps most striking is the very pervasiveness of this idea, so that it comes to form a recurrent element in descriptions of Keats's linguistic and poetic failings. Gerard Manley Hopkins in 1880, for example, still avers: 'there is one thing that Keats's authority can never excuse, and that is rhyming open vowels to silent *r*s, as *higher* to *Thalia*: as long as the *r* is pronounced by anybody, and it is by a good many yet, the feeling that it is there makes this rhyme most offensive, not indeed to the ear, but to the mind.'[141]

Such comments again reveal most clearly the ways in which the ideology of standardization could command an extensive subscription to its norms; the presence of [r], promoted as part of 'correct' speech, was 'standard', all else 'substandard'. Hopkins effectively points up the disjunction which results from such beliefs in his acknowledgement that rhymes of this order offend the mind rather than the ear, contravening perceptions of linguistic usage, rather than linguistic usage itself. As this indicates, speakers could, in effect, recognize the discrepancy between ideologies of a standard and its processes, though the dominance of common value-judgements in

[140] J. G. Lockhart, 'On the Cockney School of Poetry No. IV', *Blackwood's Edinburgh Magazine*, 3 (1818), 520, 521.
[141] G. M. Hopkins, letter to R. W. Dixon (22 Dec. 1880), in Abbot (ed.), *The Correspondence of Gerard Manley Hopkins and Richard Watkins Dixon* (London, 1935), 37.

these contexts would paradoxically lead them to adhere to the former above the latter. It is of course this which is most significant in attitudes to the loss of [r]; as Hopkins confirms, the combined claims of education, and the associated fictions of literate speech, were to suggest to many that they still heard, or at least they thought they ought to hear, the retention of [r] in 'good' speech, even though theory and practice in this respect were usually to be at odds. Tennyson, for example, boldly asserted his own conformity with prescriptive sensibilities on this score in his statement that 'I would sooner lose a pretty thought than enshrine it in such rhymes as "Eudora" "before her", "vista" "sister" ',[142] but rhymes such as *thorns/yawns*, or *drawn/lawn/thorn* can nevertheless be detected in his verse.[143] Given his habitual sensitivities towards the subject of accent, it is unsurprising that Gissing reacts in the same way: 'What a fearful rhyme I came across the other day, in Keats's verses on Indolence. With *farce* he positively rhymes *grass*. Ye heavens!'[144]

Principle and practice, ideology and process again diverge, and the standard norms overtly subscribed to can in reality be abandoned when the speaker, or writer, is off their guard. As the writer (and founder member of the Philological Society), Edwin Guest, noted of this phenomenon in 1838, 'many who insist upon its pronunciation, drop it, immediately their attention is diverted, or their vigilance relaxed',[145] and this fact applies both to poets and to ordinary users of the language. Distinctions between *laud* and *lord* are, as Ellis confirms in 1869, entirely theoretical, a product of 'careful speakers when they are thinking particularly of what they are saying'.[146] In the early twentieth century, the philologist and lexicographer Henry Wyld was still making resolute attempts to instil a sense of linguistic reality into this debate, revealing the pervasive and long-term influence of language attitudes in this

---

[142] Cited in O. Jespersen, *A. Modern English Grammar on Historical Principles* (London and Copenhagen, 1909), i. §13.23.

[143] A. Lord Tennyson, *The Druid's Prophecies* (1827), ll.26–8; *Recollections of the Arabian Nights* (1830), ll.100, 103, and 106. For examples in other eighteenth- and nineteenth-century poets, see Mugglestone, 'The Fallacy of the Cockney Rhyme', 64–5.

[144] Letter to Algernon Gissing, 23 Sept. 1883, in *The Collected Letters of George Gissing*, ii: *1881–1885*, ed. P. F. Mattheisen, A. C. Young, P. Coustillas (Ohio, OH, 1991), 161.

[145] E. Guest, *A History of English Rhythms* (London, 1838), i. 313.

[146] Ellis, *Early English Pronunciation*, ii. 603.

respect: '[Ordinary speakers] even go to the length of pretending that they can hear a difference between such pairs as *horse–hoarse*, *Parma–palmer*, *kernel–colonel* . . . Of course, a distinction can easily be made; pronunciation can be faked to any extent. The point is that in ordinary educated English speech in the South, there is no difference between the above pairs.'[147]

Such notions of 'literate speech' as manipulated within the precepts of the standard ideology do, as a result, seem to have led many nineteenth-century speakers, especially amongst those whose acquisition of educated rank was relatively recent, to attempt to retain [r] in their speech. Like the 'middle sounds' of *a* already discussed, its use in time becomes a marker of the speech-conscious, or of the intentionally 'elegant' in Johnson's terms, who endeavoured (at least when concentrating on proprieties of this order in their more formal speech) to reflect the distinctions of the written language in line with such popular attitudes to correctness. Over the course of the nineteenth century, such recurrent patterns lead in fact to what might be recognized as the phenomenon of the 'hyperliterate speaker', a social and linguistic stereotype associated in contemporary comment with public speakers, as well as associated stereotypes of the 'newly rich' and aspiring in the middle sections of society. The anonymous author of *Hard Words Made Easy* hence notes in terms of [r]: 'Some of our public speakers, who push accuracy of utterance beyond a wholesome limit, get the habit of trilling the *r* so much that one would think that they wished to be thought unlettered Scotch or Irish peasants'[148] Sedulous attention to graphemes above phonemes (and to the theoretical rhoticity of the 'best' speech) could, as this reveals, be pushed too far, and this fact, in novels and journals as well as in popular comment on language, is made into a further distinguishing marker of the intentionally, but not actually, 'genteel'. John Earle in 1871 comments on spelling pronunciations of *Derby* and *clerk* 'which many persons, especially of that class which is beginning to claim educated rank, now pronounce literally'.[149] Geoffry Hill similarly draws attention to the over-use of [h] among the middle sections of society:

[147] H. C. Wyld, *The Historical Study of the Mother Tongue* (London, 1906), 16.
[148] *Hard Words Made Easy* (London, 1855), 4.
[149] J. Earle, *The Philology of the English Tongue* (London, 1871), 146.

It is not as a rule the very poor who introduce h's, but the small shopkeeper and the villager who reads at home in the evening instead of going to the public-house. They are slightly better educated than many of those with whom they associate, and naturally wish to make their superiority evident; for some reason they adopt this plan of doing so.[150]

It was of course precisely these patterns which George Eliot had made use of in her own linguistic characterization of, for example, Mr Casson, landlord of the Donnithorne Arms and erstwhile butler of Donnithorne Chase, in *Adam Bede*: ' "They're cur'ous talkers i' this country, sir; the gentry's hard work to hunderstand 'em. I was brought hup among the gentry, sir, an' got the turn o' their tongue when I was a bye." '[151] Other novelists too picked up and reinforced these features (and accompanying language attitudes), often depicting this striving for phonemic correctness and graphemic correspondence in various characters located at the outer edges of respectability. In the wider context, however, it is important to recognize that this trend towards spelling pronunciations was in fact to gather a far greater momentum, leading to a general shift in the pronunciation of many words such as *falcon*, *forehead*, and *waistcoat*,[152] a topic to which we shall later return, revealing as it does the ultimate dissemination of the ideals of literate speech into the facts rather than the fictions of usage.

Notions of the 'elegant' and 'literate' speaker, and their workings within eighteenth- and nineteenth-century writing (and thinking) on language can of course be found in many other forms, governing the notions of impropriety generated about the loss of contrast between words such as *witch* and *which*,[153] or about the 'proper' way in which the final syllables of *walking* or *talking* should be pronounced.[154] It provides an image of the workings of prescriptive methodology which was often central to contemporary attitudes towards language, as well as significant within the evaluative responses of which they were, as we have seen, regularly formed.

[150] G. Hill, *The Aspirate* (London, 1902), 43.
[151] G. Eliot, *Adam Bede* (London, 1859), i. 20.
[152] *Falcon* < OFr. *faucon, falcun* was, in the 18th c., pronounced without the [l], being transcribed]faw'kn[by Walker in 1791. By 1825, however, the appeal of graphemic logic was beginning to shift notions of acceptability; Samuel Oliver notes 'Walker pronounces *falcon fawkn*, an ordinary but a vicious sound' (1825), 287 n. 3. By the end of the 19th c., enunciations with [l] were common. *Forehead* and *waistcoat* had habitual pronunciations as [fɒrɪd], [wɛskət] respectively.
[153] See pp. 225–9.   [154] See pp. 150–5.

Like ideologies of a standard, prescriptivism too operates best as an attitude of mind, a set of beliefs about language and language use, and in terms of linguistic history it cannot be ignored, diffused as it was far beyond those who simply wrote on the language and articulated its stated norms. Even these, however, were often merely ordinary speakers of the language, untrained observers, many of whom simply record their own attitudes and evaluations in ways which, as we have seen, are far removed from the comments of professional linguists in the twentieth century. Schoolmasters, actors, vicars, and ordinary individuals all ventured to write on accent during this period. Walker was himself originally an actor as well as an elocutionist, Douglas had a significant legal, political, and administrative career from which the concerns of language were, at least professionally, far removed. Yet, in his leisure hours, he penned his *Treatise on the Provincial Dialect of Scotland* for those 'whose language has already been in a great degree refined from the provincial dross, by frequenting English company, and studying the great masters of the English tongue in their writings'. Such writers, as Eagleson stresses, were themselves part of the popular culture they document, 'grassroot witnesses to changes in progress' and grassroot witnesses to changes in attitude too.[155] It is this that such writers reveal so well and where a large part of their value lies. In their stated correlations with the speaker variables of status or gender, they set forth with particular clarity the social pressures which accrued around notions of 'talking proper', to which they themselves are subject and which they themselves endorse.

Though their evidence can tend therefore to be subjective rather than objective, readily deploying, as we have seen, popular social stereotypes in favour of empirical research, it can nevertheless be illuminating, offering a mass of detail on those images and associations which had come to surround attitudes to accent, as well as sound changes in progress. Varying in ability from the writers who legitimately attempt to engage with the nuances of sounds and the emerging sense of a phonetic science (Thomas Batchelor, the elocutionist Alexander Bell, Alexander Ellis, and a variety of other writers might here be enumerated by virtue of the particular

---

[155] R. D. Eagleson, 'Sociolinguistic Reflections on Acceptability', in S. Greenbaum (ed.), *Acceptability in Language* (The Hague, 1977), 64.

acuity of their comments, for example) to those who merely adhered to the prescriptive commonplace, it is thus the collective voice of these writers which can be most significant. Through the patterns of contradictions and conceptions which emerge, and through the loaded language by which current realizations are described, they often reveal a fairly precise picture of the state of the language, and the state of language attitudes, throughout the late eighteenth and nineteenth centuries. As Manfred Görlach confirms, 'gaps in the historical sources prevent us from reconstructing gradual shifts of pronunciation to the extent that is desirable (and necessary) in Labov's view',[156] but the sheer mass of data of all kinds available over this time does tend to give clear sense of which issues were regarded as important, as well as suggesting in broader lines the patterns of variation (both social and linguistic) within which such patterns might be placed. It is, of course, only by their agency that the rise of a 'standard' accent in any sense can be documented over this period.

[156] M. Görlach, *Introduction to Early Modern English* (Cambridge, 1991), 62.

3

/h/ and Other Symbols of the Social Divide

THE use of [h], in modern English, has become one of the principal signals of social identity, its presence in initial positions associated almost inevitably with the 'educated' and 'polite', while its loss commonly triggers popular connotations of the 'vulgar', the 'ignorant', and the 'lower class'. Surrounded by social values, and attendant value-judgements, the dropping of [h], as J. C. Wells has pointed out, now operates as 'the single most powerful pronunciation shibboleth in England',[1] a ready marker of social difference, a symbol of the social divide. In literature and language alike, sensitization to the social distribution of linguistic items has, with particular frequency, attached itself to patterns of [h]-usage, its presence (in the right place) suggesting familiarity with conventional proprieties of speech,[2] while its absence has come to function as a prime diacritic of the linguistically and socially unacceptable. Such patterns often figure significantly in modern literature, so that characters delineated in terms of their rustic location, rudimentary education, or membership of the lower classes all tend to have speech marked by strategic omission of [h]: ' "It's your ladyship's own 'ut" ', says Mellors to Lady Chatterley, for example. ' "I don't in the least want to turn you out of your hut" ', says Lady Chatterley to Mellors.[3] On such differences turns the social distance between them, the gamekeeper and the lady.

The inability to use [h] in line with such now prevalent notions of correctness has, in this way, evolved as a convenient form of

---

[1] Wells, *Accents of English*, i. 254.

[2] The use of [h] does not occur invariably in all syllable-initial positions even in RP. Form words of frequent occurrence, such as *have, had, her, his* will, for example, often have zero-realization of [h] as a result of use in positions of weak stress within the sentence. Word internal stress can also play a similar role, governing the use of traditionally [h]-less forms in words such as *historical, hysterical*, in constructions such as *an historical play* /ən ɪs'tɒrɪkl pleɪ/, the weak stress of the first syllable tending to lead to the non-realization of [h].

[3] D. H. Lawrence, *Lady Chatterley's Lover* (Florence, 1928), 110–11.

social shorthand, regularly signified in literature by graphemic deviation from the expected forms of the text. Using '*and*' and not *hand*, or, as Mellors does, '*ut* and not *hut*, has come to suggest a whole complex of social meanings, founded upon popular conceptions of 'talking proper'. Such associations are not confined to the twentieth century. The phonetician Henry Sweet in 1890 similarly comments on the role of [h] as 'an almost infallible test of education and refinement',[4] and Alexander Ellis, another characteristically objective observer, noted earlier in 1869 that 'at the present day great strictness in pronouncing *h* is demanded as a test of education and position in society'.[5] Assumptions of culture, status, and education seem almost inseparable from its use, the relevant evaluative paradigms, as these comments suggest, being all too readily extended to speaker as well as speech. Even encyclopedias in the late nineteenth century stressed its role in determining, and assigning, social status, enumerating details of 'proper' usage in this context among the other facts offered for the erudition of readers. 'The correct pronunciation of this difficult letter is one of the most delicate tests of good breeding' as the new edition of *Chambers's Encyclopaedia* admonished in 1888,[6] devoting an entire section to descriptions of its use.

In the past, just as in the present, it might therefore seem that attitudes to /h/ had always embraced these correlations with status and social standing with habitual readiness. In the late nineteenth century, /h/ was, as Kington-Oliphant emphasizes, the 'fatal letter',[7] with the consequences of its use and misuse potentially momentous in the search for social acceptability. Standing as it does as a near-tangible manifestation of the 'two nations' theme, writers such as Dickens, Gaskell, and Gissing employ patterns of <h>-presence and absence in ways which are familiar from the Lawrence text already mentioned; 'struggles with the h-fiend' hence mark the social progress of Richard Mutimer, the working-class hero of Gissing's novel *Demos*,[8] while Gaskell's *North and South* similarly explores the social and linguistic stereotypes associated

---

[4] H. Sweet, *Handbook of Phonetics* (Oxford, 1877), 195.
[5] Ellis, *Early English Pronunciation*, i. 221.
[6] *Chambers's Encyclopaedia. A Dictionary of Useful Knowledge* (London, 1888), v. 492.
[7] Kington-Oliphant, *Sources of Standard English*, i. 333.
[8] G. Gissing, *Demos. A Story of English Socialism* (London, 1886), i. 115.

with its use, not least of which are those surrounding the 'new rich' of the Industrial Revolution. Edith, for example, immediately expects linguistic infelicities in this respect once Mr Thornton, the Darkshire mill-owner, arrives in London: 'I asked [Henry] if he was a man one would be ashamed of; and he replied, "Not if you have any sense in you, my little sister." So I suppose he is able to sound his *h*'s, which is not a common Darkshire accomplishment.'[9]

Edith's immediate equation of social shame with lack of facility in the use of /h/ epitomizes particularly clearly the social values and social assumptions with which its presence was, and is, imbued. Nineteenth-century authors wield consummate skill in its deployment in socially sensitive ways, and writers on the language, especially by the second half of the nineteenth century, write eloquently on the social consequences which follow its 'abuse'. Their vehement proclamations, and the very abundance of prescription and proscription on this head, indeed make it tempting to assume that such a situation had always existed. This assumption would, however, be mistaken, for the rise of /h/ as social symbol does not antedate the eighteenth century, and, more specifically, it becomes prominent only towards its end. Transformations within the role of /h/ accompany, in other words, those wider transformations then taking place in English society and, in particular, within thinking about the nuances of accent as a social as well as a linguistic phenomenon. That rise to social prominence which is so marked in attitudes to the presence and absence of [h] is therefore, in a number of ways, inseparable from the shifting social contexts of the time, in which, as we have seen, attitudes to language could and did manifest more than strictly philological interest.

Early attitudes to [h], for example, accorded most importance to its role in differentiating words such as *hill/ill*, or *hand/and*, rather than to any ability it possessed for the social differentiation of speakers. The latter is not mentioned. Still earlier comments regularly dispute whether [h] could be granted the status of a 'letter' or, in modern terms, a sound at all. From such apparent unconcern nevertheless arose the shibboleth of the 'dropped [h]' and its attendant social stigma. A study of its rise into social as well as phonemic significance serves, as a result, to exemplify with particular

---

[9] Mrs Gaskell, *North and South* (London, 1855), ed. A. Easson (Oxford, 1973), 428.

clarity many of the issues which came to surround the ideals of 'talking proper' in the late eighteenth century and afterwards. The forces of respectability and emulation, the patterns of cultural and social cohesion, the social (and linguistic) stereotypes of the 'lady' and the 'gentleman', or the Cockney and the parvenu, were all to have their correlates in the use, and misuse, of /h/.

Before looking in more detail at the patterns which came into existence in the late eighteenth and nineteenth centuries, it is, however, necessary to begin with a brief overview of far earlier developments of this sound in English, since it is in such remote beginnings that a number of significant points concerning the use of /h/ lie. Its early history is, for example, by no means simple. Given aspiration in initial positions in Old English, patterns of use were rendered more complex by the Norman Conquest and the resulting influx of French loan words in which the grapheme <h>, as in *honour, hour,* and *honest,* was silent. The phoneme /h/ (and often, as a result, the grapheme too) had in fact early been lost in Anglo-Norman, and loan-words such as *herb, heir, host* regularly appeared in English in [h]-less (and <h>-less) forms. *Erbe* (MnE *herb*) deriving from OF *erbe* and, in turn, Lat. *herba*, and *ost* (MnE *host*) deriving from OF *ost* and, in turn, Lat. *hostem*, were duly incorporated into English along with many similar words. The fact that the relevant Latin antecedents of such words contained <h> was, however, often to lead to the respelling of loan-words of this order. *Herb* was often spelled with non-phonetic <h> by 1475, *honor, honur, honour* were all increasingly frequent spellings in Middle English; *heir*, from OF *eir, heyr*, often appeared as *eyr, ayre*, and *here*.[10]

The end result of such developments was of course to complicate considerably the hitherto relatively simple patterns of <h> and /h/ correspondence in English. It led in effect to a situation in which the grapheme <h> could be realized as [h] in native words, such as *hand, horse, house*, or conversely, in the pronunciation of loan words such as *horrible, humour*, it could, and did, appear as [Ø], that is, without any realization at all. In other words, French loans regularly 'dropped their [h]s', and at some date, such habits seem to have been extended into native words as well, though the

---

[10] Such etymological remodelling was not, however, exempt from error, and words such as *hermit* and *hostage* derive in fact from etymologically <h>-less forms, Lat. *erēmita* and OF *ostage*.

exact timing of this development is a matter of some dispute. Roger Lass, for example, argues for a process beginning in the eleventh century,[11] J. C. Wells for one after the colonial conquest of America, a nation in which, as he rightly asserts, [h]-dropping is unknown.[12] Medieval manuscripts certainly display considerable variation in their use of <h>, a fact often attributed to French scribal habits, though this interpretation has, probably rightly, been contested. As James Milroy notes of such patterns in early Middle English: 'the *prima facie* evidence for [h]-dropping continues well into EModE—long after there can be any suspicion of direct Anglo-Norman influence . . . All this evidence suggests strongly that (h) has been a *variable* in English for many centuries.'[13] In the absence of direct comment, however, it remains difficult, if not in fact impossible, to ascertain with precision the onset and history of [h]-dropping in native words.

Some certain evidence for a date earlier than that advocated by Wells is nevertheless presented by the *Welsh Hymn*, a text dated around 1450. By means of its patterns of alliteration, this is able to provide conclusive proof that [h] was silent in metrically stressed words such as *hands* and *hight*. Northern writers on pronunciation moreover, such as R. Brown in *The English-School Reformed* (1700), also attest similar patterns in their own speech, Brown describing zero-realization of [h] in stressed words such as *hand*, *heart*, as well as in unstressed *his*.[14] This survey, although based on such disparate evidence does, however, make it clear that habits of dropping [h]s had certainly developed in some, if not all, varieties of English before the advent of the late eighteenth century. By this date therefore, the phenomenon itself was not new, though the increasing presence of adverse comment on this situation, apparent from the second half of the eighteenth century onwards, may indeed have been so.

Of course, the previous absence of such overt sensitization can merely be seen as the reflection of those more tolerant attitudes to variation which are, as we have seen, characteristic of comment

---

[11] R. Lass, *The Shape of English* (London, 1987), 96.

[12] Wells, *Accents of English*, i. 255.

[13] J. Milroy, *Linguistic Variation and Change: On the Historical Sociolinguistics of English* (Oxford, 1992), 142.

[14] Form words of frequent occurrence, such as *have*, *has*, regularly occurring in positions of weak stress within the sentence, will, as already indicated, normally 'drop their [h]s' in the usage of all speakers.

on language before the mid- to late eighteenth century. Whereas the new prescriptive rigour of the latter tended to polarize variant pronunciations into 'correct' and 'incorrect', issuing prescriptions and proscriptions accordingly, the very absence of such habits of thought before this date in terms of /h/ is, for instance, made particularly clear by writers such as William Laughton. Author of *A Practical Grammar of the* English *Tongue*, Laughton simply states of /h/ in 1739 that 'tho' it be sometimes silent, so are many other Consonants, in particular Positions'.[15] No further comment is deemed necessary, and certainly no social correlations are either observed or made. Any discussion specifically received by /h/ was in fact rather more likely to concern its (frequently contested) right to claim the very status of 'letter', or, in modern terminology, that of phoneme. 'H . . . hath no particular formation, neither does it make any sound of it self, but a bare *aspiration* . . . whether it ought to be call'd a letter or not . . . let everyone enjoy his own opinion', Christopher Cooper, for example, had written in 1687[16] and such classificatory uncertainties were not limited to the seventeenth century. In 1748 the grammarian Benjamin Martin is still able to note of his fellows that 'it is very surprising to find grammarians disputing whether this be a letter or not, when at the same time it would be ridiculous to dispute it being a distinct sound'.[17] Adducing minimal pair structures (*ear/hear, art/hart*) as evidence, he demonstrates the phonemic status to which /h/ was, in his opinion, unreservedly entitled: 'witness the words ear, art, arm, ill, &c. which by prefixing H, become heat, hart, harm, hill, quite different words and sounds from the former'.[18]

Far from being the 'fatal letter' of Kington-Oliphant's nineteenth-century conceptions, the fact that the status of /h/ as 'letter' has to be repeatedly questioned and affirmed in this way reveals with little room for doubt that its use in the earlier part of the eighteenth century (and before) can hardly have been invested with those social values which later came to be so commonplace in comment on language and propriety. The transition, both in terms of comment on /h/ and its attendant connotations, seems instead to come decisively with the second half of the eighteenth century, as

---

[15] W. Laughton, *A Practical Grammar of the* English *Tongue* (London, 1739), 31–2.
[16] Cooper, *The English Teacher*, 21.
[17] B. Martin, *Institutions of Language* (London, 1748), 20.   [18] Ibid.

accent is incorporated into the prescriptive consciousness, and the renewed interest in elocution forces a new awareness of the ideals of speech. Fashion, and a heightened responsiveness to the role of external markers in assigning social status (real or intended) was also to play its part. Thomas Sheridan, the writer who had so persuasively urged the cultivation of the linguistic consciousness in terms of accent in 1762 is, appropriately, the first to record this new and corresponding sensitization to the loss of [h]. Articulated within his larger tribute to the social values of speech, and his exhortations on the need for new sensibilities towards its use, the omission of [h] is rapidly incorporated into the prevailing prescriptive framework, with all its specifications of desired norms, undesirable deviation, and of the social consequences which pertained to both.

Perfectly expressing the normative ideals of the age, Sheridan, as we have seen, berates the dulled linguistic consciousness which then still existed in terms of pronunciation.[19] Perception was apparently equally blunt in terms of [h]. Providing the necessary 'information' to expose the errors of older habits, as well as to inculcate the adoption of new ones ('consciousness cannot exert itself when barred up by habit'), Sheridan, as expected, readily adopts the appropriate rhetoric of prescription in this context. Striving to inspire awareness of the non-localized norms proper to a 'standard' and national language, he goes on to provide the first information in which the long-standing variations in the use of /h/ are placed explicitly within those normative frameworks which were later to become so familiar. As he states: 'There is one defect which more generally prevails in the counties than any other, and indeed is gaining ground among the politer part of the world, I mean the omission of the aspirate in many words by some, and in most by others.'[20] The selected terms are manifestly those of acceptability and unacceptability, in which [h]-dropping is a 'defect' and an error, regardless of its stated prevalence. The fact that its use is apparently common even among the 'polite' is similarly disregarded. As in Robert Lowth's dictates on the flat adverb,[21] the heterogeneities of usage are intentionally to be discarded in favour of a monolithic and corrected norm. Though [h]-dropping is therefore self-evidently part of the 'best' speech which Sheridan intends as

---

[19] See pp. 18–22.   [20] Sheridan, *Course of Lectures*, 34.   [21] See p. 11.

the basis of his standard, previously established 'custom' can be no sanction for continued 'incorrectness' in this matter. Sheridan's further comments make this plain: 'I have met with but few speakers in the course of my experience, and those only in the most correct speakers . . . of persons who have not been guilty of omitting the aspirate from some words, or giving it faintly in others.'[22]

Sheridan's text skilfully manipulates the prescriptive tenor of the age. According to this account therefore, the theoretically 'correct' usage of [h], in which it was pronounced rather than being dropped, was indeed rare, but it was this very rarity which was to be prized, evincing as it did the superior facilities of a small group of people able to wield the aspirate with ease, and without incurring the 'guilt' accorded to those who fail in this respect. The connotative values of this description are unmistakable, and through the four succeeding editions of *A Course of Lectures on Elocution*, as well as in Sheridan's numerous personal appearances on his lecture tours and readings, their appeal was not to be forgotten. The presence of [h] became an important element within that ideology of a 'standard' (and its associated non-localized norms) then growing up around pronunciation.

The desired standard, as we have seen, was above all to be a sociolect, and, more specifically, one propagated in terms of the 'polite'. Sheridan in 1781 asserts as a general truth, for example, that '*False* and *provincial* accents are to be guarded against, or corrected. The manner of pronouncing which is usual among people of *education*, who are natives of the *metropolis*, is, in every country, the *standard*.'[23] The patterns of italicization he adopts make the salient points clear, setting up familiar oppositions between 'provincial' and 'metropolis', and 'educated' and 'false'. In all of these, the use of [h] comes to figure highly, its absence signifying (at least within the schema adopted by manuals of etiquette, linguistic fashion, and of course prescriptive texts) a conspicuous unfamiliarity with élite culture and the stated proprieties of good London speech, whether by dint of residence within the provinces, or a social location outside the polite. Sheridan's recommendations in his *Lectures* for ways in which to achieve the conformity and correctness he deemed essential ('the best method of curing this

---

[22] Sheridan, *Course of Lectures*, 35.   [23] Sheridan, *Rhetorical Grammar*, 176–7.

will be to read over frequently all words beginning with the letter
H . . . in the dictionary, and push them out with the full force of
the breath'[24]) were rapidly to be joined by other comments which
incorporated a new and more deliberate sense of social prescription
within their stated tenets.

James Elphinston's *Propriety Ascertained in her Picture* (1786), a
text which aimed to describe 'good' pronunciation and the means
by which to achieve it, made, as its title suggests, frequent reference
to the social values coming to surround the spoken word. His
comments on [h] accordingly reveal not only a new concern for
'correctness' on the lines set down by Sheridan, but also make
plain an increasingly explicit sense of social 'lowliness' and 'impropriety' associated with conceptions of its loss. Elphinston's
comment (in his own reformed, and intentionally phonetic, spelling
system) that 'Dhey dhat think *uman, umor,* and dhe like, look too
umbel, may innocently indulge the seeming aspiration' can thus be
used to adduce a specifically social sensitivity coming to surround
the loss of [h].[25] Words such as *human, humour,* and *humble* (as
well as *herb, hospital, hostler, hotel*) had, of course, by dint of their
non-native origins, traditionally been pronounced without [h], a
fact recorded by, amongst others, Walker, Johnson, and Sheridan.
Elphinston, however, seems to reveal a change in the way people
viewed such forms, the non-appearance of [h] in such words
coming to suggest not the expected continuities with the past, but
instead affiliations with a social status (or absence of it) which
people would perhaps prefer not to own. As he indicates, spelling
such words in his reformed orthography without the <h>, as indeed
would be needful if the realities of pronunciation were to be
truthfully indicated, was a practice that some people might feel dis-
inclined to adopt. Omitting the <h> was laden with suggestions
of apparent *umbleness* which, as its semantic alignments imply,
was capable of denoting not only 'lack of arrogance, pride, and
immodesty', as in Walker's definition of 1791, but, equally, lack
of status: 'low, not high, not great' as Walker's dictionary also
explains. In this Elphinston read his audience well, and generations of future speakers were, as we will see, to restore the [h] in
this (and similar) words in keeping with such perceptions.

---

[24] Sheridan, *Course of Lectures*, 35.
[25] J. Elphinston, *Propriety Ascertained in her Picture* (London, 1786), 15.

Elphinston's comments on these particular connotations therefore already bring to the forefront, in 1786, a clear sense of the
social meanings which were to be involved in the use of [h].
Within a few decades prescriptive writing was almost uniformly
endorsing the peculiar propriety of pronouncing [h] in terms which
trade overtly on the socio-cultural associations which its presence
(and absence) could variously comport. Its omission is 'vulgar',
according to Smart in 1810, associated with the lower orders in
London. According to Thomas Batchelor in 1809, its loss par-
takes of parallel associations of low status, and is a feature marked
among the 'peasantry' in Bedfordshire who, in this as in their
other infelicities of speech, are to be regarded as 'depraved'.[26] At
this date, however, the use of [h] tends to appear as merely one
of a list of pronunciations deemed significant in 'talking proper'.
By the 1850s, in contrast, its role had consolidated still further so
that it alone regularly assumes pre-eminence amongst a range of
stated markers of the 'educated' and 'refined'. By the 1860s, the
resulting patterns of linguistic prejudice, voiced in social terms,
and explicitly endowed with social repercussions, are particularly
widespread, though they are perhaps stated most clearly in Mr
Podsnap's dicta on this head in *Our Mutual Friend*. Expounding
on the subject of these nineteenth-century sensitivities to the use
of [h] to the Frenchman (whose habitual articulations in the novel
unfortunately preclude its use), its social affiliations are unambiguously aligned with the stratified usages of a class society:

'Ah! Of a Orse?' inquired the foreign gentleman.
'We call it Horse', said Mr Podsnap, with forbearance. 'In England,
Angleterre, England, We Aspirate the "H" and We Say "Horse". Only
our Lower Classes Say "Orse"!'[27]

Though the lexis used again outwardly specifies 'class', it is nevertheless evident from other comments that relevant correlations, as
already indicated, were to work more fundamentally in terms of
status.
The heightened emphasis being placed on the articulation of
[h], both in social and linguistic terms, was in fact increasingly to

[26] T. Batchelor, *An Orthoëpical Analysis of the English Language*, including *An
Orthoëpical Analysis of the Dialect of Bedfordshire* (London, 1809), ed. A. Zettersten,
Lund Studies in English, 45 (Lund, 1974), 111.
[27] *Our Mutual Friend* (London, 1865), i. 100.

lead to the sense that it should in fact appear whenever and wherever <h> was manifest in the spelling. 'What can reflect more on a person's reputation for learning, than to find him unable to pronounce with propriety and elocution?'[28] as the schoolmaster and orthoepist James Buchanan had early commented in 1757, setting out the paradigms of knowledge and ignorance which could accrue around the spoken word. Popular appreciations of linguistic propriety by the nineteenth century indeed tended to confirm or confound reputation for learning on the basis of such habits of [h]-usage: the loss of [h] is 'a mark of inferior education . . . calculated to produce a great prejudice against the offender in all persons of refinement', George Vandenhoff declared in his *Lady's Reader* of 1862.[29] 'Nothing so surely stamps a man as below the mark in intelligence, self-respect, and energy, as this unfortunate habit', stated Alford two years later,[30] making specific the extension of these evaluations from education to intellectual capacity in itself. As in those canons of 'literate speech' discussed in Chapter 2,[31] the visual authority of words was to be adopted as a ready guide to phonemic propriety in this context. Grapheme was to function as 'educated' authority for phoneme, and 'social humility' and indeed inferiority (or 'lowness' as Elphinston indicates) was potentially to be suggested by those who failed in this respect. While 'literate speakers', at least in terms of the prevailing prescriptive ideology, thus made plain the facts of their superior education by matching grapheme with appropriate sound, or <h> with [h] in their speech, so therefore did the non-appearance of [h] take on the values not only of the 'lower class', but also of the 'uneducated', the 'uncultured', and the 'illiterate', those who dropped an [h] because they were unaware of the presence of <h> in the spelling. The pressures which such fictions of speech exerted were considerable, and the marked extension of spelling pronunciations in words in which zero-realization (or non-pronunciation) of [h] had hitherto been acceptable, if not *de rigueur*, acts as a concise index of their effectiveness. By the end of the nineteenth century, only *heir, honest, honour,* and *hour* (and derivatives) remained [h]-less, social sensitivity to its presence having succeeded in redressing centuries of custom with regard to *herb* and *humble, hospital, human,* and

[28] Buchanan, *Linguae Britannicae*, p. vii.
[29] Vandenhoff, *The Lady's Reader*, 16.
[30] Alford, *A Plea for the Queen's English*, 40.   [31] See pp. 97–102.

humour, for example, all of which now contain [h] as well as <h> in England—though not, incidentally, in America where the 'perfect liberty' advocated by Webster has,[32] it seems, ensured continuity with historical rather than orthographical precedent. *Herb* still retains its [h]-less realizations throughout General American, and the American South preserves similar forms for *humble*. In England on the other hand, even traditionally [h]-less native words such as *forehead* and *neighbourhood*, traditionally /fɒrɪd/ and /neɪbərʌd/ (and still attested by Murray in *OED i* in these forms) were eventually to succumb to this general trend; in the twentieth century *hotel* too is joining this list.[33]

Such notions of literate speech were not, of course, the only elements of that prescriptive armoury to be mobilized as deterrents against the omission of [h] where sanctioned by habit rather than orthoepical dictate. Walker, for example, censures [h]-loss as a 'vice' of the Cockneys,[34] thereby trading very effectively in his resulting proscriptions on a social symbolism long connected with Cockney 'ignorance' as much as with their low status in the capital.[35] Lindley Murray too capitalized on these stated shibboleths of the 'ignorant', stressing the import of [h]-loss as an indubitable signifier of lack of education. Urging remedial activity in this area for the many users of his *Grammar*, he develops in particular the need for increased vigilance on the part of teachers, making explicit the role of [h] as an integral part of the emergent and specifically 'educated' standard accent:

From the . . . negligence of tutors, and the inattention of pupils, it has happened, that many persons have become almost incapable of acquiring its just and full pronunciation. It is therefore incumbent on teachers, to be particularly careful to inculcate a clear and distinct utterance of this sound, on all proper occasions.[36]

Reprinted numerous times, and widely used as a school book of high repute, Murray's *Grammar* was by no means insignificant in the dissemination of new ideals of phonemic propriety, especially

---

[32] See pp. 47–8.
[33] As S. Ramsaran noted in 1989: 'In the case of *hotel* . . . an /h/-less form is fairly widespread, e.g. *an hotel*, though the pronunciation with initial /h/ is commoner.' A. C. Gimson, *An Introduction to the Pronunciation of English*, 4th edn., rev. S. Ramsaran (London, 1989), 193.
[34] J. Walker, *A Rhetorical Grammar* (London, 1781), 16.
[35] See also pp. 99–102.   [36] Murray, *English Grammar*, 11.

when combined with the barrage of information and attack coming from a variety of other sources. Educational methods, for instance, were often to adopt Murray's principles without reservation, so that throughout the century directions for the assessment of teaching prowess regularly came to comprise assessment of the use of /h/, in teacher as well as pupils. *The Elementary School Manager* by M. Rice-Wiggin and A. Perceval Graves thus includes the following in its directives for establishing the success of a reading lesson in school, formalizing notions of the 'educated' accent in the implementations of the standard ideology which they endorse:

Is every mistake promptly noticed by the teacher, and is his notice anticipated by putting out of hands on the part of the scholars to show that they, too, have observed the mistake? In particular, are mistakes such as *emphasis, punctuation,* and *aspirates* noticed and corrected with even the youngest children?[37]

The ability to read well, as this suggests, was frequently deemed to include the oral proprieties of enunciation, as well as the comprehension of graphic symbols on the page. Rendering <h> as [Ø] instead of the 'proper' [h] was, as a result, to be treated in many educational textbooks under the heading of 'Defective Intelligence',[38] a label which further indicates the perceived alliances of manner and matter, pronunciation and IQ which had come into being in this context by the middle of the nineteenth century. To drop an [h] was, in prevailing social and linguistic stereotypes, to be 'uneducated', and was hence untenable in either teacher or pupil. As a result, though pedagogical tenets of this order were later criticized, it was nevertheless common in many schools throughout the nineteenth century for children to be penalized just as much for dropping an [h] as for mistaking a word altogether; both, as we will see in Chapter 6, were regarded as fundamental errors. Her Majesty's Inspectors of Schools tended on the whole to agree. Correct management of this phoneme was a clear witness of the efficacy of correct teaching practice in a school, as Mr Nevill Cream affirmed in his inspector's report for 1861:

[37] A. Perceval Graves and M. Rice-Wiggin, *The Elementary School Manager* (London, 1879), 116.
[38] See p. 300.

Inferior teachers . . . tell me it is useless to try and teach the children to do so [pronounce [h]]; that the parents at home unteach, by their conversation, whatever is taught at school; that it is provincial, and make a great many other excuses. On the other hand, a good teacher says nothing, but sets to work; and the next year every child, from the oldest to the youngest, pronounces the *h* with correctness.[39]

As such comments indicate, educational fashion was at times also to be constructed in terms of that sensitization to speech which had come to form a composite part of the standardizing ideology in the nineteenth century; it too regularly saw and depicted /h/ as one of its hallmarks of success or failure. It is, however, outside rather than inside the schoolroom that 'fashion' of this order may be assumed to hold greatest sway, and though education was clearly not immune from its dictates, the awareness (and influence) of fashion in the wider frameworks of society was, in fact, to be recognized as particularly significant. Specific details of speech were frequently encompassed by its rulings, and in turn within the legitimate spheres of influence it assumed.

Attitudes to language, as William Cramp stressed in 1838, could indeed be markedly responsive to fashionable example: 'The orthography and pronunciation of today, though perfectly consistent with analogy, may be denounced as vulgar and inaccurate tomorrow, if a popular character chance to deviate from established usage.'[40] Though an observation characterized by a certain amount of hyperbole, it does seem to be borne out by the comments of other writers on the language. William Smith, for instance, had noted even in the late eighteenth century that the preferred realization of /a/ in words such as *fast, path* in the short [æ] by the actress Sarah Siddons certainly appeared to have given additional impetus to that shift away from the longer and retracted [ɑ:] which he himself favoured: 'In almost all the words which are the subject of the foregoing notes, the pronunciation of Mssrs. Sheridan and Walker is daily gaining ground from its being adopted by the best Actress, which this, or any age produced.'[41] Weber in his own discussions of social formation was also to highlight the role of

---

[39] Cited in R. Robinson, *A Manual of Method and Organisation. Adapted to the Primary Schools of Great Britain, Ireland, and the Colonies* (London, 1863), 3 n.

[40] W. Cramp, *The Philosophy of Language* (London, 1838), 8.

[41] W. Smith, *An Attempt to Render the Pronunciation of the English Language More Easy* (London, 1795), 8 n. See also p. 91.

fashion, noting, in his account of the evaluative patterns common within perceptions of the nuances of status, that 'above all, this differentiation evolves in such a way as to make for strict submission to the fashion that is dominant at a given time in society'.[42]

Fashion was notably to impinge upon the role of [h] as a perceived status-marker, and those notions of 'submission' which Weber introduces in this context (or, in linguistic terms, convergence) were to be equally important, not least in terms of the cultural hegemonies frequently manipulated within much prescriptive writing. As *Etiquette for Ladies and Gentlemen*, published in 1839, asserted: 'society has its "grammar", as language has; and the rules of that grammar *must* be learnt, either orally or from reading'.[43] In such terms therefore, the presence of /h/ was to figure significantly in the grammar of both language and society, a signifier in both of acceptability, and due decorum. Relevant fashion was, however, deemed to be synonymous with London fashion alone and its accompanying notions of a metropolitan élite; it is, as we have seen, the London 'standard' which Sheridan, Smart, and others attempted to prescribe for general use, perpetrating images of a unidimensionality in social space which do not, of course, conform to reality and to the complexities of society *in toto*. It was, nevertheless, the undeniably élitist overtones of London fashion, and of the 'best' society, which surface most regularly in this context within prescriptive propaganda and its accompanying ideologies. Manuals of etiquette too willingly endorsed the same paradigms for their readers, again fostering selected images of imitative cohesion. The anonymous *Etiquette for All* of 1861, specifying the need to gain 'a polite and refined manner in our social intercourse', hence emphasized that London fashion was to reign supreme: 'Fashion is omnipotent with the generality of mankind ... he who would mix with his kind with pleasure to himself and those whose society he seeks, must obey her sway and submit to her laws.'[44] Six years later *The Laws and Bye-Laws of Good Society* decisively commented on the role of /h/ in this respect: 'The omission or the importation of the aspirate in the wrong place is a sure sign of defective training. It grates on the ear with peculiar harshness, and is utterly out of keeping with

---

[42] Neale, *History and Class*, 63.
[43] *Etiquette for Ladies and Gentlemen* (London, 1839), 10.
[44] *Etiquette for All* (London, 1861), 6.

pretensions to being considered *bien élevé*.'[45] Similarly, Smart included a section in his *Walker Remodelled* of 1836 entitled 'Hints for Londonizing a Rustic Utterance', noting that 'a man displaying [a rustic accent] must have a huge portion of natural talent or acquired science, who surmounts the prejudice it creates'.[46] Fashion, and the assumed deference to its propagated norms, in such ways tended to enhance that emphasis being placed on linguistic conformity to the London 'standard' (as well as its needful dissemination) by writers such as Sheridan and Smart, Walker and Knowles. Just as McKendrick documents the eagerness with which provincial patrons awaited the arrival of the newest styles from the capital, commenting on the rapid diffusion of imitations of the latest fashion,[47] so too did a certain receptivity to metropolitan styles of speech tend to operate, at least in terms of language attitudes (and the proprieties then assumed in the 'best' speech), even if they were not invariably to be borne out in the execution of ordinary conversation. As the self-styled I. S. L. notes in *Fashion in Language* (1906), by the end of the nineteenth century this 'correct' use of [h] was, in many ways, to be recognized as the very keystone of linguistic fashion. 'Certainly no one who wishes to follow the fashion can neglect it', he adjured.[48]

In the frameworks adopted by handbooks of social advice, by magazines and journals, in literary texts and in the numerous penny manuals addressed specifically to instruction in 'correct' pronunciation (and, of course, in prescriptive works themselves), the 'neglect' of [h] was indeed 'unfashionable', as well as 'rustic' and 'provincial', with all the negative status connotations which these epithets contain. Smart's 'well-bred' speaker was to be found, and emulated, in polite London society, while Batchelor's 1809 account of the 'depraved' pronunciation of Bedfordshire rests on differences seen as deviations from fashionable London norms, the use of /h/ being a means of differentiating 'polite' and 'peasantry' in his stated terms. Dickens makes use of similar oppositions; depicting the nuances of Peggotty's accent only once in the first chapter of *David Copperfield*, the displacements of <h> which

---

[45] F. W. R. and Lord Charles X., *The Laws and Bye-Laws of Good Society. A Code of Modern Etiquette* (London, 1867), 19.
[46] Smart, *Walker Remodelled*, §178.
[47] See McKendrick *et al.*, *Birth of a Consumer Society*, ch. II.
[48] I. S. L., *Fashion in Language* (London, 1906), 13.

this involves convey the facts of her social location without further comment being necessary: ' "there's the sea; and the boats and ships; and the fishermen; and the beach; and Am to play with—." Peggotty meant her nephew Ham, . . . but she spoke of him as a morsel of English Grammar.'[49] It is, in such comments, all too clear that Peggotty's linguistic mannerisms betray familiarity with provincial Yarmouth rather than the London *bon ton*. By the mid-nineteenth century, [h] is regularly selected as the foremost marker of the emergent (and non-localized) RP, and notions of fashion, status, and also education, all exhorted subscription to its norms.

Elocution masters, members of another white-collar (and itself highly fashionable) profession which saw a notable expansion in its numbers over this time, also blazoned forth their abilities in this context. 'Misplaced aspirate', as well as lisping, stuttering, stammering, and monotony 'permanently cured', stated Charles Hartley, self-styled Professor of Elocution, in an advertisement appended to one of his own books on the correction of linguistic error. As Hartley's specification of 'remedy' indicates moreover, notions of the impropriety of the 'misplaced aspirate' were readily subsumed within those metaphors of the 'sick language' which also feature highly in prescriptive accounts of language use in this period. 'Faults in articulation, early contracted, are suffered to gain strength by habit, and to grow so inveterate by time, as to be incurable', as Sheridan had written, for example, of the evidently debilitated state of speech in the late eighteenth century.[50] 'Nothing is so infectious as a vicious accent or vulgar manner', the author of *Good Society. A Complete Manual of Manners* later discoursed in 1869,[51] revealing the continuity of these ideas within the linguistic sensibilities of the nineteenth century. As Thomas indicates in his own later analysis of such patterns, 'purists are keen to see themselves as physicians administering to the body of language',[52] curing, purging, and, in time, healing its infections. Certainly texts on English pronunciation, centring on the drive for a spoken standard over the eighteenth and nineteenth centuries, often adopted such modes of thinking and representation in their tenets on this

---

[49] C. Dickens, *David Copperfield* (London, 1850), ed. N. Burgis (Oxford, 1981), 22.
[50] Sheridan, *Course of Lectures*, 36.
[51] *Good Society. A Complete Manual of Manners* (London, 1869), 91.
[52] G. Thomas, *Linguistic Purism* (London, 1991), 22.

head: dropping an [h] was a 'weakness' for which 'remedy' was necessary. It was this that the prescriptive tradition sought to supply in such abundance.

That these appeals in terms of [h] struck home was not, however, simply attributable to such descriptions of its absence as a 'defect' for which elocution could offer a 'cure'. Comment on the social unacceptability of its loss tended in addition to draw on a knowledge of popular social stereotypes, and the proscriptive persuasions which these too could exert to apparently good effect. Whereas, as Sheridan had indicated in 1762, familiarity with London norms of speech signified equally a familiarity with 'good company', and Walker had similarly traded on the appeal of the 'polite', unfamiliarity with the newly codified proprieties of [h]-usage came to signify a range of social meanings often presented as necessarily incompatible with the social aspirations and ambitions of many speakers of English. That well-established tendency of linguistic fashion to emphasize 'manner' when estimating 'matter', and to deploy external symbols as signifiers of internal worth and value, was in these terms often to compound the importance given to 'correct' enunciations of [h].

One particularly common pattern of comment, for example, is discernible around the social (and linguistic) stereotypes of the 'new rich', and the 'self-made-man'. Popular images of the 'self-made' indeed often relied on a social satire dependent for its effects on the perceived combination of lavish wealth with a total absence of the niceties of manner and breeding which denote the socially acceptable. In such ways, the stigma of trade was to have its linguistic correlates too, and notions of the 'vulgar' develop specific semantic overtones in this context, 'vulgarian', for example, coming most frequently to denote a 'rich person of vulgar manners' over the course of the nineteenth century. ' "Did you not marry a low creature—a vulgarian—a tradesman's daughter?" ' as *OED* records in illustration, citing Bulwer Lytton's *My Novel* of 1853. The result was a social, cultural, and linguistic stereotyping of notions of the parvenu, a word which was itself introduced into the lexicon only from the beginning of the nineteenth century: 'an upstart, or one newly risen into notice', glosses Ogilvie in his dictionary of 1870. In consequence, just as the correct use of [h] was depicted as one of the distinguishing marks of the 'gentleman', so conversely was its misapplication, and particularly its over-use, often to be presented as a marker of the 'would-be gentleman', and of those who sought social cohesion with the established élite by patterns of strategic, and somewhat over-enthusiastic emulation. In such terms (at least within these prevalent socio-cultural stereotypes), the use of [h] was regarded as a prime distinguishing shibboleth; whereas the enunciation of the word *shibboleth* itself (as 'sibboleth') had enabled the Gileadites to recognize the Ephraimites, so by means of [h], or rather by its loss, were the newly rich equally to be found out. Within much prescriptive writing, even though the 'best' speakers had themselves been more frequently marked by its absence in the late eighteenth century, by the middle of the nineteenth century it was this which was commonly to take pride of place in the hegemonic manipulations of 'talking proper' which proliferated. In the popular mythology which results, just as the 'gentlemanly treatment' of [h] characterized those with hereditary social honour,[53] so therefore were the aspiring and newly rich seen as being inevitably betrayed by their linguistic infelicities in this respect.

Poor Letter H, a sixpenny manual devoted entirely to the pronunciation of [h] and its social importance, hence directs pointed satire at the social presumption and phonetic ignorance of the parvenu: 'We must, however, protest against the barbarity of a rich nobody, who having, perhaps, more money than wit, built himself a large mansion, and dubbed it his *habbey*.'[54] *Punch* was likewise to reinforce the prevailing ideology in similar terms, the family of the Spangle-Lacquers, in spite of their superficial polish, unfailingly revealing their status as 'vulgar rich' by their linguistic mannerisms and affectation. Over-sensitized to the use of [h] by the reams of contemporary comment which stressed its role as pre-eminent social marker, the new rich, in these popular stereotypes, were thus to display marked traces of their social origins in their speech. Like the lower middle class in William Labov's sociolinguistic researches in New York,[55] they are, for example, depicted as hypercorrecting in their use of variables imbued with overt status, and, in turn, as over-using [h] out of all proportion to accepted proprieties. As the empirical researches into the linguistic behaviour of such socially insecure groups in the twentieth

---

[53] Hon. Henry H., *Poor Letter H*, 40th edn. (1866), p. iv.   [54] Ibid. 35.
[55] W. Labov, *The Social Stratification of English in New York City* (Washington, 1966).

century suggest, however, it is not entirely unfeasible that a grain of truth may indeed be present behind the linguistic scapegoating of the new rich in this specific instance. Peter Trudgill's research in Norwich, for example, reveals regular patterns of hypercorrection by groups insecure within the social hierarchy, so that, in their more formal speech, they use with markedly greater frequency variants (such indeed as [h]) which are regarded as statusful in the wider speech community. Bearing in mind Bell's 'uniformation principle' ('the linguistic processes taking place around us are the same as those which have operated to produce the historical record of the language')[56] or the implications brought out by Labov in his own discussions of the validity of using the present to explain the past, it is not inconceivable that something of the same patterns should again hold true, especially given the high levels of overt comment surrounding /h/ and its social values during the nineteenth century, a situation guaranteed to foster the linguistic (and status) anxieties of many speakers. Moreover, as sociolinguistic data similarly confirm,[57] social mobility in itself is, in a number of ways, particularly linked to linguistic modifications of this kind, a finding which suggests that those who are upwardly mobile are indeed somewhat more likely to respond to those norms promoted as prestigious.

Be that as it may, it is, however, more than clear that the author of *Poor Letter H* chooses to ridicule explicitly the folly of the 'rich nobody' in these terms, mocking by his wordplay the over-use of [h] where its presence was unwarranted by the orthography (as in *abbey*), as well as its reckless omission elsewhere: 'he would persist in saying that the *habbey* was his *'obby'*.[58] The parvenu, in such terms, emerges as a crystallization of the 'illiterate speaker', his social elevation refused sanction on the grounds of these markers of 'ignorance' rather than 'knowledge' which continue to litter his speech. Such perceptions again point up the disjunctions between 'class' and 'status' in the context of language; in spite of the acquisition of a '(h)abbey', the two self-evidently do not run in

---

[56] Bell, *Sociolinguistics*, 188.

[57] See W. Labov, 'The Effect of Social Mobility on Speech Behaviour', *International Journal of American Linguistics*, 33 (1967), 58–75. ('The most striking finding . . . is that a group of speakers with a past history of social mobility is more apt to resemble the next highest socioeconomic group in their linguistic behaviour than the one with which they are currently associated.')

[58] Hon. Henry H., *Poor Letter H*, 40th edn. (1866), 35.

parallel. Language still images forth his social origins, and status insecurities. Kington-Oliphant in 1873 makes exactly the same point, further encoding this particular stereotype. The loss of [h] is 'a hideous barbarism' of which the self-made are unduly fond,[59] and even given the role of political representation, 'their hopes of Parliamentary renown are often nipped in the bud by the speaker's unlucky tendency to "throw himself upon the 'ouse" '.[60] It is in ways such as these that /h/ takes on its role as the 'fatal letter'; no mere phoneme, its use was deemed to form one of the most powerful social and linguistic barriers in nineteenth-century society. Irrespective of material gain, the new rich were, in conceptions such as these, necessarily to be educated in its 'proper' use if, in any sense, they were to merit the élite acceptability desired. The remedial endeavours of impecunious scholars are thus commended by Kington-Oliphant himself in a contract to be based upon the due exchange of social knowledge for the rich but ignorant, with financial reward for the wise but poor. As he urges: 'Many a needy scholar might turn an honest penny by offering himself as an instructor of the vulgar rich in the pronunciation of the fatal letter.'[61]

Of course, stereotypes are not reality, though they do, as already indicated, tend to play a key role in the evaluation of speech and hence in the workings of language attitudes. Negative sensitization to the variant in question does, however, as modern studies in sociolinguistics reveal, tend to be enhanced by its stated or perceived affiliation to certain social groups; it is this which, for example, lies behind the similar stigmatization (and stereotyping) of the 'toity-toid' enunciations (of 'thirty-third') which mark notions of the New York accent in America, hence informing collective language attitudes in a parallel way, regardless of the actual linguistic habits of New Yorkers and the more complex patterns of variation which they will, in reality, exhibit. In the nineteenth century, it is clear that the 'new rich' were popularly selected as just such another stereotype in which notions of exclusion and exclusivity in terms of social and linguistic values could readily be predicated, though that the actual new rich were not completely immune to such

---

[59] Kington-Oliphant, *Sources of Standard English*, i. 333.
[60] Ibid.   [61] Ibid.

assimilatory pressures is, in fact, revealed in the habitual patterns of social cohesion which relevant families could enact. As Coleman has stressed, though entrepreneurs themselves tended to devote most attention to consolidating business rather than social opportunities, the sons, and especially the grandsons of such dynasties tended instead to partake of the requisite social transformations to secure acceptability, commonly being sent to established public schools, and being encouraged, in turn, to shed the nuances of accent which might mark their social origins in ways which are precisely parallel to the stereotypes generated within the prescriptive tradition. As a result, as one writer noted in the *Bradford Observer* in 1870: 'I see around me many manufacturers of the old school, men who speak in the dialect and have disdain for gloves.' Yet these, he added: 'curiously enough, send their sons to be educated at the Universities, where they emerge gloriously incapacitated for business in many instances.'[62] Those who did succeed in their industrial and financial expansions at this time were, in other words, not to be entirely immune from the cultural hegemonies and social proprieties often stated as requisite for members of the 'best' society—taking note of their niceties if not for themselves, then for their families and descendants. This explains the desire of the engineer Matthew Boulton (James Watt's partner) for his grandson to be sent to Eton, rather than to the academy at Birmingham which he had himself attended. By such means, he stressed, 'a vicious pronunciation and vulgar dialect' might be countered and avoided, as indeed would any associated socio-cultural stereotypes, including those of the 'new rich' and the parvenu.[63]

Accent, often conceived of in contemporary metaphors as a passport, securing entry not to other countries but to other social spheres ('the talisman that will . . . bar the door or make portals fly open', as Savage notes),[64] receives therefore perhaps its clearest correlates in the resulting attitudes to the use of /h/ and its vital role in securing, or impeding, social advance. It too naturally became part of the ideology of self-help (that 'masterpiece of propaganda . . . by which a middle-class ideal was spread throughout the whole of

---

[62] *Bradford Observer*, 9 June 1870; cited in E. M. Sigsworth, *Black Dyke Mills* (Liverpool, 1958), 72–3.
[63] Cited in D. G. Coleman, 'Gentlemen and Players', *Economic History Review*, 26 (1973), 105.
[64] Savage, *Vulgarisms and Improprieties*, pp. iv–v.

society' as May notes)[65] propagated so effectively by Samuel Smiles; just as Smiles had commended the endeavours of Richard Arkwright sitting down to learn grammar at the age of 50, so too did texts such as *Plain Living and High Thinking. Practical Self Culture* (1880), *Getting on in the World; or, Hints on Success in Life* (1877), or *The Secret of Success; or, How to Get on in the World* (1870) endorse the same paradigms. In an age 'bent on mutual improvement', as the anonymous author of *Talking and Debating* (1856) pointed out,[66] relevant amelioration in this respect was moreover to suggest, and promise, far more than mere articulatory prowess. Given control over the phonetic niceties required in polite life, 'we feel a just pride in having subdued some of the roughnesses that beset our moral life, and of having acquired in their stead the polish that bespeaks refinement'.[67] Contrasting greatly with the cursory attention afforded it by Johnson a century before,[68] the use of [h] had, by the 1850s, consolidated in the popular imagination as a prime symbol of precisely that 'polish' which *Talking and Debating* describes. Its loss denotes the 'roughness' that the intentionally respectable should tame, whilst its presence constitutes an external symbol seen as emblematic of the refined and internal 'moral life'. As such texts indicate moreover, though Kington-Oliphant seems to have envisaged supply of, and demand for, instruction in /h/-usage only in terms of the entrepreneurial parvenu, in reality the striking popularity of manuals devoted to instruction in the proprieties of [h] can only be explained by the fact of the massed ranks of the 'middling sort', and their own widespread awareness of the socio-symbolic aspects of language. It is, for example, these who are the intended audiences of the sixpenny manuals on 'talking proper' or the manuals of etiquette which sought to disseminate the stated proprieties of élite culture to those without such knowledge. As the author of *Hints on Etiquette and the Usages of Society* affirms, 'this is not written for those *who do* but for those who do *not know what is proper*, comprising a large portion of highly respectable and estimable people, who have had

---

[65] May, *Economic and Social History of Britain*, 206.
[66] *Talking and Debating*, 4.   [67] Ibid.
[68] Johnson, *Dictionary*, a2ʳ: '*H* is a note of aspiration and shows that the following vowel must be pronounced with a strong emission of the breath, as *hat*, *horse*. It seldom, perhaps never, begins any but the first syllable.' See also L. C. Mugglestone, 'Samuel Johnson and the Use of /h/', *Notes and Queries*, 243 (1989), 431–3.

no opportunity of becoming acquainted with the usages of the (so termed) best society'.[69]

Works such as *Harry Hawkins' H Book* or *Poor Letter H*, for example, went into many editions, the latter being reprinted three times in 1854 alone, while the former went through two editions in as many years. *Mind Your H's and Take Care of Your R's* was similarly popular, and demand was such that books of accompanying exercises were swiftly devised to supplement the main text, a means by which the 'vulgar', whether rich or otherwise, might monitor their conformity to a linguistic norm presented as integral to good standing in the eyes of the world. Just as with the pronouncing dictionaries discussed in Chapter 1, it was practical and conscientious application which was depicted as the route to success. In such terms, just as the enthusiasm for self-improvement is accurately reflected in the 55,000 copies of *Self-Help* sold within five years of publication, or the favour with which Chambers's *Popular Educator* was received, so is the craving for correctness in terms of /h/ embodied in the extensive sections on its 'correct' use demanded, and provided, in editions of *The Family Herald*,[70] or, more particularly, in the popularity of *Poor Letter H. Its Use and Abuse*, a manual of pronunciation purportedly written by /h/ itself, and of which well over 43,000 copies had been produced by the mid-1860s.

The fortieth edition of *Poor Letter H* in fact appeared in 1866, and its preface opened with a due exclamation of surprise that yet another edition of this work had been deemed necessary:

What! issue another edition of Poor Letter H ... ! Yea, verily; for the circulation of forty thousand have been but as drops poured into the mighty tide of human life, whereon float hundreds of thousands who don't know an H from an A; and who, when meeting with the one or the other, make the most frightful and cruel mistakes with these poor innocent sufferers.[71]

---

[69] *Hints on Etiquette and the Usages of Society*, 5.

[70] The *Family Herald* contains, for example, the following 'Humble Petition of the Letter *H* to the Inhabitants of London and its Environs': 'The memorial of your unfortunate petitioner humbly showeth, that although conspicuous in heraldry, entitled to the first place in honour, and remarkable in holiness, yet he has been, by many of you, most injuriously treated; spoiled in health, driven from home, and refused a place, not only in your house, but in every home, hut, or hamlet, within your controul. You refuse your petitioner help, and cut him off also from hope, the last resource of the unfortunate, both here and hereafter...' (6 July 1844), 143.

[71] Hon. Henry H., *Poor Letter H*, 40th edn. p. iii.

As the title indicates, the tone adopted is that of pathos, emanating from the unjustly abused; /h/, given his full name as the 'Hon. Henry H.' (and described as 'very aristocratic in . . . birth and connections'),[72] is anthropomorphized, his title duly indicating the degree of status which has accrued around him and which he has, in turn, come to represent. The text presents a personal appeal from him to the 'million' who, in spite of the efforts of education and the schoolmaster, still commit 'the great social literary evil of aspirating wrongly'.[73] 'Million', in a typical nineteenth-century collocation, is intended to signify 'the multitude, the bulk of the nation', a specification of readership and utility which again reveals the joint claims of language and nation in the drive to disseminate a standard of 'good' usage throughout the land. *Poor Letter H* thus plays heavily on the notions of the ridicule and social shame which must always attend errors in this context, giving countless examples of the embarrassing slips which can result from infelicity in the use of [h]: 'I have heard a person, who was very well dressed, and looked like a lady, ask a gentleman who was sitting by her, if he knew whether Lord Murray had left any *H*eir behind him:- the gentleman almost blushed, and I thought stopped a little, to see whether the lady meant a *Son* or a *Hare*.'[74] More than mere embarrassment, *Poor Letter H* openly exploits the ways in which misuse of /h/ was, in prevailing attitudes to correctness, capable of revealing more concisely than any other sign the facts of a social origin which the speaker may have hoped to have left behind. In the instance given above, for example, the 'person' has the superficial and visual appearance of a 'lady', yet, by the misuse of [h] which follows, is revealed as a mere pretender to ladylikeness. The true 'gentleman' almost blushes at the shibboleth she commits. In spite of her appearance, the speaker is therefore evidently no 'lady' in the full sense of the term—or at least as it pertained, as we shall see in Chapter 4, to yet another popular social stereotype with its own behavioural norms and ideals.

Ridicule, both social and linguistic, most obviously attends the unintentional homophones created by the misapplication, or indeed lack of application, of [h], and instances of the ambiguities thus caused abound in the pages of this little book: accounts of orders to servants to reheat dishes of meat, given in the form of ''eat it and bring it up again when it was a little otter',[75] anecdotes

---

[72] Ibid., p. v.   [73] Ibid., p. iv.   [74] Ibid. 16–17.   [75] Ibid. 26.

in which, in 'a respectable music shop', a lady is requested to "*um* the *h*air' after which, as Henry H. recalls, 'it was very hard to control the risible faculties',[76] or tales of recently recovered 'gentlemen' who, upon being congratulated upon their improved state of health, give the following response: ' "Thank you", said the gentleman; "the doctor says that I shall now do very well, but I must take care not to *eat* myself." '[77] The central tenet manifest in each of these examples only reinforces the doctrine of correctness surrounding /h/, and the social meanings and social repercussions which it had come to hold, as well as manipulating to no little effect common prescriptive targets directed at words which, though distinct in their orthographical realizations, are rendered identical in speech. This in itself, as we will see, was to inspire a consummate fear of mergers as a species of linguistic change; as attitudes to the loss of [r] have already revealed, the homophones which resulted from this change (*ma, mar, pa, par, stalk, stork*) were regarded as particularly emblematic of 'slovenliness', and hence particularly deserving of censure. The same premises come into operation in the case of [h]-dropping too, where the failure to make distinctions manifest in the written language (*air/hair, ire/hire*) is deployed as yet another signifier of the 'illiterate' speaker, with all the sociocultural connotations which this conveys. All these were to combine in pressuring speakers to redress their own habits of 'negligence' in this matter.

Addressing the vowels (likewise anthropomorphized in this text), the Hon. Henry H. hence pleads for further vigilance in this sphere as a means of avoiding not only his own humiliation (arising from such frequent neglect), but also that more pertinent social humiliation and absence of status which will certainly befall speakers who persist in making such unfortunate mistakes: 'I have written to you, my little Vowels, to see if you and I together cannot do something to stop the mockeries we receive, and also to prevent the thousands who mock us, no doubt unintentionally, from being themselves laughed at and thought nothing of.'[78] Nevertheless, if, as the Hon. Henry H. asserts, social humiliation and 'being thought nothing of' inevitably come to those who fail in this respect, so conversely is the promise of social honour explicitly held out to those who strive towards and achieve propriety in these terms: 'If

---

[76] Ibid. 24.   [77] Ibid. 25.   [78] Ibid. 27.

my good friends, *the Million*, would try to remember . . . and speak
out H . . . a great many of our readers and speakers, and I think
some of our preachers too, would cut a far better figure in public
and in society than they now do.'[79]
Works such as *Poor Letter H*, written in an accessible manner,
and delineating the socio-symbolic portents of /h/ in a tone marked
more by its bluntness than by any assumed or euphemistic restraint,
were hence particularly effective in securing wide dissemination
for those normative tenets which had come to be inseparable from
its use. Its price (a mere sixpence) would likewise have facilitated
purchase by many in the middle and lower ranks of society, serving
equally to inculcate a consciousness of /h/ of which even Sheridan
would have been proud. Its title page alone, with a cartoon illustrating in graphic terms the solecism of [h]-dropping, as well as
the ensuing embarrassment (see Fig. 3.1) would alone have been
enough to make the intended point.

Other popular works in the second half of the century were to
employ analogous methods to achieve the same result. *Harry
Hawkins' H Book*, for example, works by the similarly comic deployment of the unfortunate Harry's mistakes in the course of his
phonemic education, so that, hastening to inform his Aunt Hannah
of the egg laid by his hen, he declares 'Oh aunt *anna* . . . my *en
as ad* another *hegg* . . . I've put it in an *at* box in the *en ouse*'.[80] Dependent as they are on graphemic deviation as a sign of phonemic
impropriety, such misspellings gradually decrease in frequency as
the tale advances, and as Harry matures into a 'literate speaker'
of the first order, triumphing over the infelicities in this respect
which had so beset his youth. Granted his early wish (' "Aunt
anna", said poor Harry, "I wish I *ad* a book full of H's; I would
read it over and over again and again, till I got quite used to
saying them" '), we proceed through the tales of 'The Hawk',
'The Hairy Ape' and such delights as 'Humphrey Hobb's Huge
Hog', in all of which the H's are capitalized for the benefit of
those readers industriously mirroring Harry's progress. It is, of
course, a story with a Happy end:

Harry has learned to aspirate His H's. By the time Aunt Hannah Had
written all these stories for little Harry, He Had indeed begun to improve

[79] Ibid. 39.
[80] E. A. S. Eccles, *Harry Hawkins' H Book* (London, 1879), 6–7.

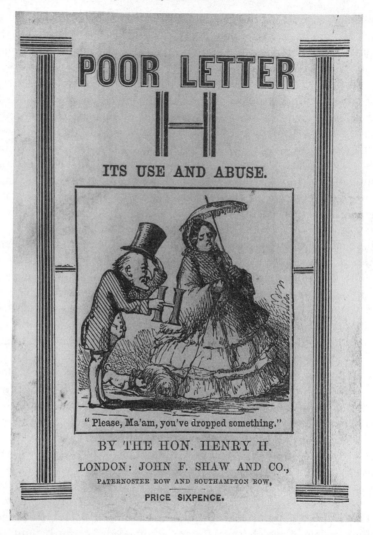

FIG. 3.1. The title-page of *Poor Letter H. Its Use and Abuse*

in pronouncing His H's. He continued to read a part of His H book out loud every day for some time longer; and wHen He was eleven years old, and His Aunt Hannah and Mr. Hungerford both thought Him old enough to go to Hazleden Grammar School, He was able to learn Hic, Haec, Hoc, without any difficulty.[81]

[81] Ibid. 45–6.

Other writers too commended the efficacy of this book in the ways in which it provided appropriate remedy and instruction in the use of /h/. As Alfred Leach in his own work on this topic noted: 'this little book cannot be too warmly commended as a practical and amusing method of learning to aspirate'. He encouraged his own readers to 'put their aspirative faculties to a crucial test, by reading aloud the story of "The Hairy Ape" ', just as Harry Hawkins himself had done.[82]

'Literacy' and 'illiteracy', and fictions of them in speech, are, as we have seen, particularly important in this context, the visual authority of <h>, as in the prominence accorded to it in *Harry Hawkins' H Book*, often being used to sanction, if not in fact demand, the corresponding presence of [h]. Stereotypes of the 'elegant' and 'literate' speaker do not, however, inform only manuals of usage such as *Harry Hawkins' H Book* or indeed C. W. Smith's *Mind Your H's and Take Care of Your R's*. Still more prevalent, and potentially of equal if not indeed of greater influence in this respect were, however, the conventions used to represent speech in eighteenth- and nineteenth-century literature, intentionally marking, as they do, gradations in the social hierarchy by frequent recourse to notions of 'literate speech', and its converse. Though this will be discussed in greater detail in Chapter 5, a preliminary investigation of the socio-symbolic potential of the written word, and of its graphemic deviations, within representations of fictional spoken discourse is nevertheless illuminating at this point. In the context of that gradual and social sensitization to the phenomenon of [h]-dropping, literary works can in fact provide a parallel, and at times highly useful source of evidence on the shift in attitudes surrounding its use, as strategic misspellings involving <h> develop into one of the prime signifiers of status within the novel.

Using written texts as evidence for spoken change is, of course, in general beset with problems, especially since, given the limitations of the English alphabet, a mere twenty-six graphemes must suffice for the representation of forty-four phonemes. Mimesis in this respect is clearly impossible, and few authors, dramatists, or poets tried or indeed wished to give completely accurate transcriptions of speech within their works. George Bernard Shaw's venture at doing this for Eliza's (Cockney) pronunciation in *Pygmalion* is, for example, abandoned after a few lines: 'Here, with apologies,

[82] Leach, *The Letter H*, 44 n.

this desperate attempt to represent her dialect without a phonetic alphabet must be abandoned as unintelligible outside London.'[83] George Eliot earlier experienced similar difficulties with her own endeavours to be true to the sound of words in *Adam Bede*: 'my inclination to be as close as I could to the rendering of dialect, both in words and spelling, was constantly checked by the artistic duty of being generally intelligible.'[84] Clearly at best a compromise is achieved, blending linguistic reality and artistic demands in the depiction of speech. Though there may indeed be certain hazards of this order of which it is well to be aware, literature is still capable of offering evidence of value, and this is perhaps especially true in terms of /h/, since its grapho-phonemic correspondences are, on the whole, more straightforward than are, for example, those involving vowels and vocalic change. Above all, literature, like language itself, is embedded in a social milieu and a social context which cannot readily be ignored; as Roger Fowler has rightly stressed, it must itself be seen as 'a kind of discourse, a language activity within social structure like other forms of discourse'.[85] In this light, it would certainly seem mistaken to suggest that literary texts, in the fictions of speech which they generate, as in the cultural and social contexts in which their characters move, are entirely autonomous creations, formed without reference to outside social influences, attitudes, and assumptions.

The patterns used to represent speech in the novel can therefore be seen in many ways as tending to encode prevalent opinions and suppositions towards, and about, the role of language as social signifier. As such, the attitudes which they present towards variation, to social norms of speech, and to corresponding notions of 'deviation' can all offer illuminating parallels for that evidence already considered on the rise of /h/ as social symbol. Novels of the eighteenth and nineteenth centuries, for example, commonly reflect contemporary notions of social prejudice and social praise in abundance. The representation of speech by significant patterns of respelling, as well as in the form of direct comments about accent, thus in turn functioned as a major way by which many authors chose to convey social sub-texts of this order, deliberately

---

[83] G. B. Shaw, *Androcles and the Lion, Pygmalion, Overruled* (London, 1916), 107.
[84] Letter to Walter Skeat, 1872, George Eliot, *Letters*, ed. G. S. Haight (London, 1954–6), ix. 39.
[85] R. Fowler, *Literature as Social Discourse* (London, 1981), 7.

manipulating the accidentals of their texts in order to signify social differences important in the larger structures of their work. Patterns of /h/-usage offered a ready means by which to do this, particularly since the grapheme <h> is able to stand as a relatively clear signifier of the presence of [h]; ' "I should have thought that there would hardly be such a thing as a Methodist to be found round here" ' says the unknown (but evidently 'educated') traveller in the opening of *Adam Bede*, manifesting perfect felicity in his use of <h> (and hence, we are to understand, [h]). Patterns of its equally significant absence can be indicated by the liberal use of the apostrophe, or, in earlier texts, by the simple fact of <h>-omission: ' "He'll be comin' of hage this 'ay-'arvest" ', as the traveller is in turn informed by Mr Casson. Dickens's lower-class characters are, correspondingly, often depicted as being seemingly incapable of pronouncing *hand* other than as *and*, *hungry* other than as *ungry*, or, conversely, *under* other than as *hunder*. Such systematic patterns are, in real terms, fictions just as much as the characters themselves. As the philologist Otto Jespersen has pertinently remarked on these literary habits of representing [h]-usage by the mid-nineteenth century, 'many novelists would have us believe, that people who drop their aspirates place false aspirates before every vowel that should have no [h]; such systematic perversion is not, however, in human nature'.[86] Novelists, equally embedded in the workings of prescriptive ideology and its repercussions, tend therefore to provide another source of information on the social stereotypes associated with speech and its social symbolic variations. In the actualities of linguistic usage, on the other hand, patterns of variation would necessarily be far more complex, based not on simple oppositions of [h]-absence for 'lower-class', and [h]-presence for the 'upper', but (as is indicated in modern sociolinguistic studies) on quantitative variations of 'presence and absence' and paradigms worked out in terms of 'more or less' instead of these favoured (but unrealistic) absolutes.[87]

The literary awareness of the value of <h> or <'> as socially significant diacritics in novels of the mid-nineteenth century does

---

[86] Jespersen, *A Modern English Grammar*, i. 379.

[87] Trudgill, in *The Social Stratification of English in Norwich*, for example, gives statistical patterns for the use of /h/ in Norwich in which the percentage of its use is the most significant factor, members of what he labels the 'middle middle class' dropping it 6% of the time, the lower middle class 14% of the time, the upper working class 40% of the time, and the middle working class 59% of the time.

nevertheless bear clear witness to a sensitization and shift in attitudes to the use of /h/ which is, in many ways, parallel to that
attested in contemporary manuals of etiquette, pronunciation, and
elocution. Just like works on language, the novels, poetry, and
drama of the age attest the dominance of /h/ as social symbol.
Moreover, they can also offer additional evidence of its rise into
such a role, as well as clarifying still further those fictions of
'literate speech', and attendant socio-cultural stereotypes, which
came to surround its use.

The differentiated use of the grapheme <h> as a stylistic marker
in literary works begins in fact in the middle decades of the
eighteenth century, antedating by some years those first explicit
comments on its attendant social proprieties which are to be found
in Thomas Sheridan's *Course of Lectures on Elocution* in 1762. The
beginnings of this stylistic tradition, however, are tentative, early
examples of the deliberate displacement of <h> offering little
promise of that heightened role it was later to assume. It merely
appears as one of a range of devices used to characterize the
uneducated user of language, such indeed as the eponymous hero
of Henry Fielding's *Jonathan Wild*. Published in 1743, Fielding's
novel can be used to illustrate with particular clarity the inception
of those traditions of <h>-usage which were later to become so
dominant in fictional form. In a letter 'which we challenge all the
Beaus of our Time to equal either in Matter or Spelling', Wild's
epistolary endeavours produce the following: 'I sollemly purtest,
that, of all the Butys in the unaversal Glob, there is none kabable
of hateracting my IIs like you. Corts and Pallaces would be to me
Deserts without your Kumpany.'[88] As this reveals, visual and
graphemic deviation function as the primary means of linguistic
satire, forms such as 'pallaces' or 'corts' or 'kumpany' being used
to generate a powerful impression of the non-standard within, and
in spite of, Wild's attempts at eloquence. Of course such forms
are, in actual fact, no more distinct from the currently acceptable
pronunciations than are their more usual graphemic structures.
The success of this technique, however, depends not on the fidelity
which may or may not exist between the written and spoken
forms selected, but instead on the clear perception of notions of
norm and deviation which are offered to the reader.

[88] H. Fielding, *The Life of Mr. Jonathan Wild* (London, 1743), 227.

Wild's role is as a prototype of the 'illiterate speaker' who, as Dr Johnson was later to observe, 'catches sounds imperfectly and utters them negligently'.[89] Wild's letter to Miss Tishy, revealing widespread ignorance of the conventional canons of good spelling, offers instead a form of 'eye dialect' or approximate transcription, which is capable of suggesting not only ignorance, but also something of the sounds used in speech. Though far from accurate as transcriptions go, the selection of the form *hateracting* (for *attracting*) is nevertheless of interest, foregrounding not only an extra (and paragogic) syllable, but also a superfluous initial <h>, and suggesting a realization akin to those later habitually adopted in prevalent stereotypes of the 'new rich'. In an era in which graphemes were popularly taken as 'proper' signifiers for the presence of phonemes (an equation aided by the semantic ambiguities of the term 'letter' in itself),[90] the use of <h> in this way can be interpreted to imply the presence of initial aspiration where none is sanctioned, either by the conventional orthography, or by those 'elegant' speakers who abide by it in their speech.

What is also clear is the muted significance such forms have at that particular point in time, deviations involving <h> (and hence [h]) being well in a minority among the range of other devices employed. Similarly restricted use of this feature also marks Smollett's early work. *The Adventures of Peregrine Pickle* of 1751, for example, contains another 'illiterate' missive resembling, in its chosen techniques, that allocated to Wild by Fielding. Mrs Hornbeck, a former oyster-wench liberally endowed with all the social connotations which this label might be assumed to convey, communicates with Peregrine during his travels in France to inform him of her location: ' "I lotch at the *hottail de may* . . . ware I shall be at the windore, if in kais you will be so good as to pass that way at sicks a cloak in the heavening". '[91] Again, relevant deviations can be seen to depend not on the dropping of <h> (prime in later texts) but instead on its unwarranted presence in *heavening* (for *evening*) and *hottail* (for *hotel*), examples which suggest distributional

---

[89] Johnson, *Dictionary*, Preface A2ʳ.

[90] As Ogilvie indicates in 1870, 'letter' was, in contemporary linguistic usage, often to signify sound as well as symbol: 'a mark or character written, printed, engraved . . . ; used as the representative of a sound . . . an articulation of the human organs of speech.'

[91] T. Smollett, *The Adventures of Peregrine Pickle* (London, 1751), ii. 52.

patterns not only at odds with conventional spelling but also with expected enunciations. The comedy in both, however, turns fundamentally not on the fact of such graphemic (and underlying phonetic) deviation in itself, but also on the puns thereby generated with other semantically disparate, but graphically analogous, words: *heaven* in the first instance, *hot* and *tail* in the second. Nevertheless, such occurrences, though already proving useful as diacritics of status, again form a clear minority.

By the time of Smollett's last novel, *The Expedition of Humphry Clinker*, published twenty years later in 1771, this distribution is, however, undergoing a significant pattern of change. A novel in which Smollett utilized a notably extensive range of graphological deviation, *Humphry Clinker* offers a striking selection of visual improprieties by which deficiencies of education, or nuances of social and regional location, are to be indicated. The aim is, it must be admitted, scarcely one of verisimilitude in terms of linguistic truth and mannerism. Clinker himself, for example, though brought up in a workhouse, invariably has diction devoid of the orthographical idiosyncrasies (and attendant phonemic implications) such as we might perhaps have expected. Win Jenkins, the Welsh maidservant, does have language characterized by a striking range of syntactic and semantic, as well as graphemic deviations, but by no means all of these can specifically be attributed to her stated provenance.

Nevertheless, Smollett's depiction, and more specifically his selection, of Win's linguistic habits is interesting. A maidservant, she unites the fact of subordinate social status with an intentionally comic confusion in terms of conventional linguistic proprieties. Malapropisms and homophonic substitutions proliferate in her letters, as she selects *syllabubs* instead of *syllables* and employs *ware* instead of *wear*, *bare* instead of *bear*, or *infection* instead of *affection*. It is perhaps therefore not surprising that the use, and misuse, of <h> should also be so prominent in Smollett's chosen representations of Win's idiolect. Comically creating new homophones for words which, at least in their habitual enunciations, are quite distinct, *animals* are rendered as *honeymills*,[92] *pious* as *pyehouse*,[93] and her epistles are sent from *Haddingborough*[94] (as well as *Addingborough*)[95] rather than from their actual address in Edinburgh.

[92] Id., *The Expedition of Humphry Clinker* (London, 1771), i. 229.
[93] Ibid. ii. 83.   [94] Ibid. ii. 226.   [95] Ibid. ii. 228.

Win's evident uncertainties on the use of <h> (and /h/) are further compounded in forms attesting its deletion when it should in fact be present; she writes with compassion of Lydia Melford's sensibilities ('I doubt her pore art is too tinder'),[96] and of the collapse of her own pretensions to style ('I thoft as how there was no arm in going to a play at Newcastle, with my hair dressed in the Parish fashion').[97] Such linguistic improprieties confirm Win's role as a more advanced type of the 'illiterate speaker' such as we have already encountered in Jonathan Wild. More than this, however, they also serve to stress the sense of social unacceptability which [h]-loss was coming to denote in the changing linguistic consciousness of the day. The fact that Tabitha Bramble, Win's mistress, shares her maid's every linguistic idiosyncrasy with one exception, that of [h]-usage, renders its connotative meanings clear. Linguistic and intellectual satire are directed equally at the foibles and fallacies of both, but it is the use of <h> which provides a clear marker of their social differentiation, and their respective roles as mistress and maid.

This development of <h>, and its absence, as convenient diacritics of social status in literary works thus parallels the beginnings of comment on its role as a determiner of linguistic propriety (or otherwise) in works directed specifically towards comment on the language. Moreover, just as later writers on pronunciation were increasingly to stress their heightened sense of its utility as social symbol, so were later literary works to intensify the prominence accorded its displacement. By the 1840s the absence of <h>, although rarely deployed in entirely systematic ways, had become an almost inevitable accompaniment to the speech of lower-class characters. Dickens, for example, makes full use of it to establish social distance and social differentiation in his novels. Sam Weller, Mrs MacStinger in *Dombey and Son*, the urchin thieves of *Oliver Twist* (though not of course Oliver himself, by virtue of his own status as hero),[98] as well as the rich cast of Cockney figures who habitually inhabit Dickens's works, are all in some measure united by their preference for this sociolinguistic marker, and by the associated graphemic deviations which feature in depictions of their speech. Heroines, heroes, and the upper and middle classes are, conversely, largely exempt from such representations, a dichotomy

---

[96] Ibid. iii. 68.   [97] Ibid. ii. 225.   [98] See p. 222.

which strengthened prevailing stereotypes in which those given the benefit of birth and breeding outside the lower social spheres never in any circumstance condescended to drop an [h]. In the contrastive usages of, say, Mrs Crupp, David's London landlady in *David Copperfield* and those of his aunt, Betsey Trotwood, or between the disguised Lady Dedlock and Jo, the crossing sweeper in *Bleak House*, the linguistic antecedents of Mellors and Lady Chatterley are, at least in this matter, clear. ' "Hush! Speak in a whisper! . . . Did he look, when he was living, so very ill and poor?" ', says Lady Dedlock to Jo, ' "this is the public 'ouse where I was took to" ', says Jo.[99] The ease with which the recognition of norm and intended deviation could be achieved in literary form undoubtedly ensured the popularity of patterns of <h>-usage in such works. Their connotative values clear, the minute a character was made to say *'ere* rather than *here* or *hup* rather than *up*, one immediately knew that one was dealing with a member of a class below the middle ranks, or at least with one whose origins were 'low'. The usage of <h>, not only in Dickens, but in Thackeray, Gissing, Gaskell, George Eliot, Charles Reade, and virtually any other novelist who made the attempt to delineate accent, is made to signify social inferiority with surpassing regularity.

Such differential patterns of propriety in language could, however, also be employed to more subtle ends within the novel, capable not only of the broad depiction of social difference, but equally, in skilful hands, of enhancing thematic and narrative concerns beyond the portrayal of simple social stereotypes. Dickens's *Great Expectations* provides a case in point, the use of <h> acting as a complex diacritic of social status, social mobility, and of the increasing social distance between Pip and Joe. Both are, in the beginning, equals as well as allies against the Ram-paging of Mrs Joe. Joe, though uneducated and illiterate, is loved and respected by the youthful Pip for his consummate goodness, and 'tender simplicity'. Pip, before his introduction to Satis House, looks up to Joe in uncomplicated admiration and esteem, so that after the history which Joe gives of his early and troubled life, Pip concludes:

Young as I was, I believe that I dated a new admiration of Joe from that night. We were equals afterwards, as we had been before; but, afterwards at quiet times when I sat looking at Joe and thinking about him, I had

[99] C. Dickens, *Bleak House* (London, 1853), 1. 237–8.

a new sensation of feeling conscious that I was looking up to Joe in my heart.[100]

No social shame about Joe's lowly occupation as blacksmith diminishes Pip's respect, nor do the abundant examples of Joe's linguistic 'ignorance', including, naturally enough, that concerning the correct positioning of /h/: ' "I never was so much surprised in all my life—couldn't credit my own ed—to tell the truth, hardly believed it *were* my own ed" ', Joe, for instance, asserts, amply illustrating his difficulties.[101] Indeed, Pip's own first efforts in the domain of written English reveal that he too (at least at first) shared Joe's distributional indecision on this matter. His missive to Joe, inscribed as they both sat at the fireside one winter's evening, begins: 'MI DEER JO i OPE U R KRWITE WELL i OPE i SHAL SON B HABELL 4 2 TEEDGE U JO.'[102] Pip's approximate versions of *hope* and *able* unambiguously indicate his social affinities in this context.

Linguistic self-consciousness, applied to himself as well as to Joe, comes only with Pip's first visit to Satis House, and with Estella's estimation of him as 'a common labouring boy'. Presented with a brusque introduction to social awareness and its linguistic correlates (' "He calls the knaves, Jacks, this boy!" said Estella with disdain'),[103] Pip undergoes a rapid education into the niceties of social class and its possibilities for social shame. Estella's methods of education into the sensibilities of status are, in this, far more effective than the haphazard teaching practices of Mrs Wopsle's school:

I took the opportunity of being alone in the court-yard to look at my coarse hands and my common boots. My opinion of those accessories was not favourable. They had never troubled me before, but they troubled me now, as vulgar appendages. I determined to ask Joe why he had ever taught me to call those picture-cards, Jacks, which ought to be called knaves. I wished Joe had been rather more genteelly brought up, and then I should have been so too.[104]

Pip's new consciousness of correctness and its converse in terms of external markers acts as a refrain in the early part of the novel. 'Shame', linguistic and social, is contracted like a disease, and the initial revelation of his 'great expectations', comes as a release

---

[100] Id., *Great Expectations* (London, 1861), i. 103–4.   [101] Ibid. i. 98.
[102] Ibid.   [103] Ibid. i. 126.   [104] Ibid. i. 130.

from a social environment, and a social contact, which Pip now sees as degrading. Moving to London in the next stage of his social education, that of becoming a 'gentleman', Pip seeks knowledge to remedy his previous ignorance of manners. By the time of Joe's first visit to him in the city, he is already affecting incomprehension at Joe's realizations of Miss Havisham's name and its unfortunate initial aspirate:

'Next day, Sir', said Joe, looking at me as if I were a long way off, 'having cleaned myself, I go and see Miss A.'
'Miss A., Joe? Miss Havisham?'
'Which I say, Sir', replied Joe, with an air of legal formality, as if he were making his will, 'Miss A., or otherways Havisham.'[105]

Both socially and linguistically, as well as geographically, Pip is indeed now a long way off, and his comments prove it, his changed attitudes to Joe, and to Joe's pronunciation, betraying strong convictions of social inequality which override the old and easy harmonies of his youth. As this indicates, an awareness of such attitudes towards /h/, perhaps even more than to its actual use, can in such ways function as an additional and useful index of Pip's social advance, and accompanying moral regression, in the first half of the book. More obvious as a literary focus, however, and of far greater weight in terms of characterization are the habits of strategic [h]-dropping adopted by that consummate hypocrite, Uriah Heep, in Dickens's earlier novel, *David Copperfield*.

The often-professed 'umbleness of Uriah Heep forms one of the most memorable leitmotifs of character used in Dickens's novels, the word *humble*, and its derivatives, being used with remarkable profusion in almost each and every conversation in which Heep engages. Humility is adopted, at least overtly, as the dominant element in his personal creed, and its lexical presence almost invariably accompanies his own (and his mother's) attempts at self-definition:

'I am well aware that I am the umblest person going', said Uriah Heep, modestly; '. . . My mother is likewise a very umble person. We live in a numble abode, Master Copperfield, but have much to be thankful for. My father's former calling was umble. He was a sexton.'[106]

---

[105] Ibid. ii. 134.   [106] *David Copperfield*, 200.

Such servile litanies emphasize, as Heep intends, the fact of his obsequious lowliness. They do this, however, not only by means of his measured repetitions, but also, more interestingly from our point of view, by means of the habits of [h]-dropping which Heep assumes. Iterations of humility in this way inevitably also become iterations of [h]-dropping, for, though *humble* is a loan word (deriving from OF *umble, humble*), and hence originally [h]-less in English,[107] attitudes to this distribution were, over the nineteenth century, in the process of changing. In its role as one of the most salient markers of absence of status, Uriah's preference for the dropped [h] thus aptly reinforces the pose which he so assiduously adopts.

No other visual and graphemic deviations are made to disfigure his speech, giving <h>, and its absence, an uncontested prominence in Heep's idiolect. In this context, its socio-symbolic properties are paramount in its interpretation and use. No ordinary 'illiterate speaker' such as those we have encountered before, Heep's linguistic infelicities take on something of deliberation in his strategic adoption of [h]-loss. Just as Mr Casson in Eliot's *Adam Bede* adopts more [h]s than are strictly necessary in his attempts to suggest identity with the gentry (' "I daresay he'd think me a hodd talker, as you Loamshire folks allays does hany wonn as talks the right language" '),[108] so does Uriah Heep shed them with equal enthusiasm in order to convey the opposite—an apparently unassuming identity with the lowest of the low. ' "The ouse that I am stopping at—a sort of private hotel and boarding ouse, Master Copperfield, near the New River ed—will have gone to bed these two hours" ', as he tells David, inveigling his way into stopping with him for the night,[109] and further demonstrating his linguistic abasement with facility.

Heep's paradoxical pride in the very fact of his humility is paralleled by his equally paradoxical status as an educated man who assiduously cultivates his knowledge alongside this use of such stereotypical markers of the 'ignorant', 'uneducated', and lowly. When David first encounters him, Heep is, for example, applying himself with all due care to the study of 'Tidd's Practice' in the

---

[107] See p. 110.   [108] G. Eliot, *Adam Bede*, ii. 324. See also p. 104.
[109] *David Copperfield*, 327.

self-avowed aim of 'improving my legal knowledge'; nevertheless, all ambitions of advance are strenuously denied. 'Too umble' ever to become Mr Wickfield's partner (at least so Uriah, at this stage, asserts), he manifests a similar horror at ideas of linguistic self-aggrandizement. David's offer to educate him in Latin is hence refused on the predictable grounds of Uriah's all-encompassing 'umbleness:

'Oh, indeed you must excuse me, Master Copperfield! I am greatly obliged, and I should like it of all things, I assure you; but I am far too umble. There are people enough to tread on me in my lowly state, without my doing outrage to their feelings by possessing learning. Learning ain't for me. A person like myself had better not aspire. If he is to get on in life, he must get on umbly, Master Copperfield.'[110]

A knowledge of Latin was of course traditionally part of the liberal education of the 'gentleman', a marker of status which conveyed meanings of social superiority as effectively as did certain nuances of dress, or, equally, of language. Uriah's determination to disavow its benefits is entirely characteristic of his personality, or at least of those aspects of it which he so diligently promotes. As he stresses, 'a person like myself had better not aspire', and his denial of aspiration is deployed in the novel with typical Dickensian wit, his repudiation of ambition effectively being mirrored in his language as Heep denies his aspirates for all they are worth. He follows his father's doctrine of humility (' "People like to be above you", says father, "keep yourself down" '),[111] quite literally to the letter: ' "I won't provoke my betters with knowledge, thank you, I'm too umble" ',[112] as he informs David in response. ' "Your elth and appiness" ', he toasts him later in the book; 'art', 'arsh', 'ealth', and 'appy' act as Heep's preferred versions of *heart*, *harsh*, *health*, and *happy*, and in affirming (although covertly) his own intentions towards Agnes Wickfield, the same markers, and their role in assigning social distance, make their habitual appearance: ' "Agnes Wickfield is, I am safe to say, the divinest of her sex . . . To be her father is a proud distinction, but to be her usband" ', runs his abruptly truncated commendation.[113] Heep's refusal to acquire knowledge above his station thus encompasses, with some deliberation, not only the use of Latin but also the correct positioning of /h/, together with its statusful social meanings.

---

[110] Ibid. 218.   [111] Ibid. 491.   [112] Ibid. 218.   [113] Ibid. 292.

All his humility is, of course, only assumed for outward show.
Heep is ultimately exposed for what he is, an 'incarnate hypocrite'
as Traddles declares, a swindler and a cheat, a liar and fraud, who
has used his stated monopoly of the humble virtues to gain an equal
hold in the realms of vice, most notably as they concern control
of Mr Wickfield's business. His mask of humility abandoned,
Heep's true self is revealed. Arrogance and pride displace his
disguise of meekness, assumed authority (instead of 'umbleness')
tempers his speech: ' "You always were a puppy with a proud
stomach, from you first coming here; and you envy me my rise,
do you?" ', he tells David.[114] ' "None of your plots against me; I'll
counterplot you! Micawber, you be off. I'll talk to you presently" ',
he continues. Heep's new discourse is marked by command, and
a sense of that power which he has in reality wielded for so long:
' "Think twice, you, Micawber, if you don't want to be crushed.
I recommend you to take yourself off, and be talked to presently,
you fool!" ', ' "You hold your tongue, mother, least said, soonest
mended!" '[115] As David rightly remarks, ' "there is a sudden change
in this fellow, in more respects than the extraordinary one of him
speaking the truth" '.[116] This change moreover extends to his use
of [h]. His pose of humility forgotten as he is brought to bay,
Heep, in his anger, manifests a new ability for control, not only
in terms of that assumed over other people, but also over the use
of [h]: ' "Miss Trotwood, you had better stop this; or I'll stop
your husband shorter than will be pleasant to you.... Miss
Wickfield, if you have any love for your father, you had better not
join that gang.... Now, come! I have got some of you under the
harrow. Think twice, before it goes over you." '[117] *Have, husband,
harrow, had* no longer pose problems. The use of [h], long described
in contemporary writings on language as an effective symbol of
power and position, here makes full appearance, as the 'old trick'
of humility is entirely dropped, together with its markers, linguistic
as well as social.

Heep's role as linguistic hypocrite as well as fraudulent power-
monger does work to show in some measure the uses to which
contemporary sensitization to /h/, and to its social values, could
be put outside the maintenance and perpetuation of mere social
stereotypes. Dickens's control of linguistic nuance is masterly,

[114] Ibid. 639.   [115] Ibid. 640.   [116] Ibid. 639.   [117] Ibid. 640.

though his fusion of both phonemic and semantic meaning within Heep's habitual asseverations of 'umble' standing is here perhaps particularly worthy of note.

Already in 1786, Elphinston had commented on the growing tendency to add [h] to realizations of *humble* (and its derivatives) amongst those who feared that articulations with its absence might suggest more than was, in fact, intended.[118] By the 1850s, this transition was nearing completion, as [h]-full realizations of *humble* became ever more the norm, and [h]-less ones, in spite of their traditional validity within the language, were increasingly allied, in their connotative associations, with the statusless and 'low'. Nevertheless, as *David Copperfield* was published, contemporary comment on [h] and its 'proper' pronunciation still betrayed some hesitation on this matter: Smart's *Walker Remodelled* of 1846, noted, for example: 'In some pronouncing dictionaries *herb* and *hospital* are included among the words whose initial *h* is silent; but the *h* may be aspirated in these and their derivatives without the least offence to polite ears; and even in *humble* and *humour*, the sounding of the *h* is a fault, if a fault, far less grating than it would be in *heir*, *honest*, and the other words stated above.'[119] As this indicates, that increasing tendency to sound [h] wherever <h> appeared in the spelling had led to its use in many words where it had formerly been silent. Confirming the acceptability of this process, Smart makes it clear that its extension to *humble* (and *humour*) was also well under way. This vacillation was, in many ways, rather effectively resolved, at least within the popular mind, by Dickens's own selection of 'umbleness' as an integral element of Uriah's linguistic and moral disguise. Using *umble* and not *humble* was afterwards far too often associated with the name of Heep, as his infamy came to extend even here. Castigating those who still adhere to the 'bad habit' of [h]-less realizations of this word, Alford in 1864 hence comments: 'it is difficult to believe that this pronunciation can long survive the satire of Dickens's in David Copperfield.'[120] Leach in 1881 was still more specific, as well as laudatory on the subject of Dickens's achievements in this respect:

The H of *Humble* has of recent years been reinstated in public favour by the late Mr Charles Dickens, whose 'Uriah Heep' remains a warning to

---

[118] See p. 115. [119] B. H. Smart, *Walker Remodelled*, §56 n.
[120] Alford, *A Plea for the Queen's English*, 54.

evil-doers and H-droppers. It would be a boon to all speakers of English if a series of 'Uriah's' could contrive to eliminate every otiose H from the language.[121]

By the late 1860s, traditional patterns of norm and deviation had, as a result, largely shifted in this context, so that Longmuir in 1864 stresses the 'increasing tendency to sound the *h* in these words',[122] and the book of exercises designed to accompany Charles Smith's *Mind Your H's and Take Care of Your R's* of 1866 devotes a special section to words with 'formerly silent *h*' amongst which *humble* (and derivatives) occupy a prominent place. By the end of the century its traditionally [h]-less enunciation had passed into history, though that of *honour* and *heir, hour, honest* and *hotel* still remained. As Hill commented in 1902: 'there is a marked tendency at present to decrease the number of such words [in which [h] is silent], but the restoration of the 'h' is sometimes quickened by circumstances; thus the sarcasm of Dickens and the contemptible character of Uriah Heep have caused the 'h' to reappear in "*umble*' much sooner than in "*ospital*."[123]

Literary deployment of /h/ as social signifier has, of course, continued to the present day, language attitudes towards its absence having, since the mid-nineteenth century, remained remarkably constant. Usually adopted for the 'vulgar' and the 'lower class', it acts, then as now, as a readily comprehensible signal of the socially unacceptable, the only difference now being, in literary terms, the establishment of the apostrophe as a regular diacritic of its absence. Used sporadically in this function by compositors in Dickens's time, its use was gradually consolidated until by the end of the century it had emerged as an easily recognizable signal of the intentionally deviant in terms of speech. Gissing's novels of this period illustrate its action well, so that, in *Born in Exile*, for example, its presence litters the speech of Godwin Peak's Uncle Andrew, drawing attention to features deemed unacceptable: ' "I've been tellin' Jowey, Grace, as I 'ope he may turn out such another as Godwin 'ere. 'E'll go to Collige, will Jowey. Godwin, jest arst the bo-oy a question or two, will you? 'E ain't been doin' bad at 'is school. Jest put 'im through 'is pyces, as yer may sye." '[124] Patterns of

---

[121] Leach, *The Letter H*, 57–8.
[122] Longmuir, *Walker and Webster Combined*, p. xii.
[123] Hill, *The Aspirate*, 37.   [124] *Born in Exile*, i. 127.

apostrophe presence and absence thus work contrastively among characters to differentiate them in terms of language and of status, its dense application here unambiguously conveying the facts of Andrew Peak's cockney standing. Loss of [h] is marked seven times in five lines, a characteristic of the 'hateful voice' depicted. Apostrophes in Godwin's own 'proper' speech conversely figure only in entirely grammatical relations, marking not ignorant omission, but instead the function of the possessive, or legitimate contractions such as 'can't'.

The apostrophe emerges as the marker, in visual terms, of the 'dropped letter', bearing witness once more to popular equations of grapheme and phoneme in the notions of visual propriety commonly adopted in texts. A parallel process is evident in the increased attention paid to another 'dropped letter' over this time, that of <g> in words such as *walking*. Realizations of *ing* in present participle forms such as *walking*, now 'standard' in [ɪŋ], had in fact traditionally been 'without the 'g' in [ɪn]. In phonetic terms, the difference is merely that between use of the alveolar nasal [n] and that of the velar nasal [ŋ]. In social terms, however, the connotative values surrounding each came to mean much more, and, like the use of [h], the selection of [ɪn] or [ɪŋ] was in time to embody precise stratifications on the social scale for those sensitized to their use. Such sensitization, as for patterns of [h]-usage, does not antedate the mid-eighteenth century; Swift, in lines 415–16 of 'Verses on the Death of Dr Swift', written in 1731, for example, happily rhymes *doing* and *ruin*: 'Envy hath owned it was his doing | To save that helpless land from ruin.' Still later Crabbe in his *Poetical Epistles* rhymes *Delight in* and *fighting*[125] and other examples attesting such equivalence can easily be found. With the second half of the eighteenth century, however, and with that increased attention being paid to accent, to conceptions of its norms, and, importantly, to its attempted 'correction', things gradually began to change. Prescriptive sensibilities are, in this context, first perceptible in the works of writers such as the grammarian and educational writer John Rice, whose *Introduction to the Art of Reading*

---

[125] G. Crabbe, *The Complete Poetical Works*, i: *Poetical Epistles I. From the Devil. An Epistle General*, eds. N. Dalrymple-Champneys and A. Pollard, (Oxford, 1988), p. 82, ll. 123–4: 'While you, of a Nation I take such Delight in | Are inferior in Fraud, tho' you beat them at fighting' (written soon after Crabbe came to London in April 1780).

with Energy and Propriety of 1765 also introduces a new sense of propriety to this hitherto acceptable pronunciation. The use of [ɪn] is, he admits, 'taught in many of Our Grammars' but custom is, as ever, to be no sanction in the face of newly perceived error: '[It is] a vicious and indistinct Method of Pronunciation, and ought to be avoided; as by these Means, *hearing* may possibly be mistaken for *herein*, *looking* for *look in*, *getting* for *get in*; and yet this Mode of Pronunciation is taught in many of our Grammars.'[126] The dictates of reason are asserted above those of custom, informing the objections made; 'dropping the g' generates homophones which are unwarranted by the orthography, and, at least in the stated terms, leads therefore to ambiguity. Of course, in reality, the long-established correspondence of forms such as *looking* for *look in* made confusion unlikely, as indeed did the differing contexts and constructions in which they were employed. Nevertheless, the objection is made and 'graphemic logic', as for /h/ and <h>, was eventually to win the day, aided by those widespread connotations of knowledge versus ignorance which commonly attended the use of 'literate speech' or its converse. By 1791 Walker is already asserting, with all his influence, the importance of the correct use of [ɪŋ] rather than [ɪn] as a marker of status by the 'best speakers', though at this stage words such as *singing* and *ringing* are still, for reasons of euphony, given as exempt from its use. Words containing the morpheme {ing} are, as Walker notes, 'frequently a cause of embarrassment to speakers who desire to pronounce correctly', and he recommends due observance of the 'proper' patterns: 'a repetition of the ringing sound in successive syllables would have a very bad effect on the ear; and therefore, instead of *singing*, *bringing*, and *flinging*, our best speakers are heard to pronounce *sing-in*, *bring-in*, and *fling-in*.'[127] Batchelor in 1809 reveals similar preferences; whereas the use of [ɪn] elsewhere is necessarily a marker of the 'illiterate' speaker, 'when the sound *ng* . . . occurs twice in succession, as in *singing*, an *n* is always used . . . as it prevents a monotonous sound'.[128] Smart's *Walker Remodelled*, however, later remodels this particular tenet too in line with the extension of such fashionable principles of correctness; no exceptions from

---

[126] J. Rice, *An Introduction to the Art of Reading with Energy and Propriety* (London, 1765), 50 n.
[127] Walker, *Critical Pronouncing Dictionary*, 1st edn. (1791), §410.
[128] Batchelor, *An Orthoëpical Analysis*, 105.

the 'logical' and general rule are allowed. By 1836 [ɪn] is therefore, at least in theory, restricted to the 'vulgar' and statusless, whereas [ɪŋ] marks the 'polite' and intentionally statusful. Another symbol of the social divide has come into being.

The reality, however, tended as always to be a little less simple than that suggested by the prescriptive, and popular, fictions which were generated in abundance by such writers. The use of [ɪn] did indeed gain all the negative connotations such writers had averred, and literary works, with plentiful use of apostrophes to mark omission, reinforced them still further, making plain its status as 'deviation' against an intended norm with <g>. Dickens in *Little Dorrit*, for example, chooses to pick out the inferior social status of Mrs Bangham, charwoman and ex-prisoner of the Marshalsea, by such means: ' "What between the buryin' ground, the grocer's, the waggonstables, and the paunch trade, the Marshalsea flies get very large." '[129] Mr Peggotty's linguistic affiliations to the lower classes in *David Copperfield* are similarly marked: ' "You're a wonderin' what that's fur, sir! Well, it's fur our little Em'ly. . . . when I'm here at the hour as she's a comin' home, I puts the light in the winder." '[130] Nor was Dickens alone in the use of these habitual markers, but, as for /h/, Gissing, Gaskell, Thackeray, Eliot, Reade, together with a multitude of others, share in these conventions by which the linguistic habits of the other half of the two nations were to be delineated. From its beginnings in the polite usage of the mid-eighteenth century, the use of <in'> had, a century later, emerged as a well-attested linguistic stereotype of the 'vulgar' and the lower class.

Literature too makes ample use, for comic purposes, of the patterns of hypercorrection which arise in response to the propagation of a new prestige norm. Just as the linguistically insecure were often to attempt to assert a status they did not in reality possess by means of the superabundance of [h]s they were prepared to wield, so too were the uneducated, and the socially and linguistically aspiring, depicted as endeavouring to add 'dropped g's' where appropriate, and equally, of course, where inappropriate. Thackeray's *Vanity Fair* provides clear examples of this mechanism in action in the speech of Joseph Sedley's valet. Described as 'the most

---

[129] C. Dickens, *Little Dorrit* (London, 1857), ed. H. P. Sucksmith (Oxford, 1979), 62.

[130] *David Copperfield*, 383.

solemn and correct of gentlemen', his language nevertheless displays habitual patterns of displacement as far as those two status markers [ŋ] and [h] are concerned: ' "Mr Sedley was uncommon wild last night, sir", he whispered in confidence to Osborne, as the latter mounted the stair. "He wanted to fight the 'ackney-coachman, sir. The Capting was obliged to bring him up stairs in his harms." '[131] Iterations of *Capting* rather than *captain* (and *harms* rather than *arms*) are in such ways used to mark the social inferior, whose excessive zeal leads him to attempt to use such forms, while his knowledge is inadequate to enable him to do so in accordance with the 'proper' models of speech. The same process is evident in the linguistic forms allocated by Thackeray to Blenkinsop, the Sedley's housekeeper: ' "Pinner says she's always about your trinket-box and drawers . . . and she's sure she's put your white ribbing into her box." '[132] The substitution of *ribbing* for *ribbon* is again made to act as a clear diacritic of lower social status. A range of similar confusions based on [ɪn] and [ɪŋ] in fact seem to have been common according to the evidence available, as speakers apparently endeavoured to conform to new notions of linguistic (and social) prestige, replacing [ɪn] with [ɪŋ] as they did so. As such examples illustrate, however, the enthusiasm for such exchanges could be somewhat excessive, generating the 'correct' use of [ɪŋ] not only in the present participle or verbal noun, but also in many other words in which the final unstressed syllable could be realized as [ɪn]. Jo in *Bleak House*, for example, receives a *sovring* rather than a *sovereign* /sɒvrɪn/, and Thomas Bilder, the zoo keeper in Bram Stoker's *Dracula* (1897), makes similar use of *garding* for *garden*, *certing* for *certain*. In the nineteenth century, *lupings*, *childring*, and *kitchings* are all attested. The 'chicking' revered by Maggy in *Little Dorrit* is also to be seen under this head as, illustrating popular phonemic confusions in her placements of [ŋ], she adds the <g>, as well as dropping it elsewhere. As with those earlier comments on hypercorrections involving /h/, some caution is, however, to be recommended before accepting these stereotypes as in any way representing a straightforward depiction of the truth.

In spite of such well-attested stereotypes of speech therefore, problems (at least in terms of attendant connotative values) do

---

[131] W. M. Thackeray, *Vanity Fair, A Novel Without a Hero* (London, 1848), 51.
[132] Ibid. 55.

emerge, and particularly with the recognition that the use of [ɪn] served equally well as a stereotype to denote the linguistic habits of the extreme upper class, and the massed ranks of those who engage, with all their 'dropped g's', in the pursuits of *huntin'*, *shootin'*, and *fishin'*. Disturbing the prescriptive paradigms set up by contemporary writers on the language, a consideration of reality instead exposed the social fictions manipulated in orthoepical attempts to regularize and correct the language. The highest echelons of those 'best speakers' drawn up by Walker as a norm to be emulated and admired were in fact to show a marked preference for realizations in [ɪn] rather than the 'correct' [ɪŋ]. Secure in their well-established status, and with no need to seek social or linguistic advice from the many manuals of etiquette which proffered it to any available audience, such speakers were moreover to remain largely immune from prescriptive control and popular sensibilities, a pattern similarly reinforced in modern sociolinguistic work where groups stable within the social hierarchy are indeed less likely to conform to normative pressures from outside. In the nineteenth century, such speakers were often castigated for this refusal to conform to the norms which, in theory if not in practice, they themselves were supposed to epitomize. Gwynne, for example, in 1879 regretfully admits that such pronunciations are 'prevalent among even the best educated people of England' and he goes on to admonish those who perpetuate this error for the bad examples which they set: 'This is . . . a greater blemish, where we have a right to look for perfection, than the peculiarities of the provinces in those who reside there.'[133] This coexistence of the same pronunciation in the extremes of society, in hyperlect as much as basilect, nevertheless endured throughout the century, [ɪn] functioning as a marker of the lower classes and of rusticity, and yet simultaneously signifying 'the peculiar accent . . . of aristocracy', as Galsworthy phrased it in his descriptions of Mrs Dennant in *The Island Pharisees* (1904).[134] As Ross, however, notes in his account of the U and non-U of language, this anomaly was to be brought into line in the early decades of the twentieth century: 'It [ɪn] certainly survived into the 'twenties but, even then, sounded

---

[133] P. Gwynne, *A Word to the Wise*, 2nd edn. (London, 1879), 60.
[134] J. Galsworthy, *The Island Pharisees* (London, 1904), 190.

silly and affected unless used by the very old U. Now it exists only as a joke, usually made by the non-U against the U.'[135] Providing a fairly close parallel to the shifts in thinking and social value which surround /h/, eighteenth- and nineteenth-century attitudes to [ɪn] and [ɪŋ] do likewise manifest a similar rise to prominence in prescriptive comment and popular proprieties, leading in time to a reorientation in habits of speech, at least for those concerned about the social meanings imparted by the choice of such forms. Certainly by the end of the nineteenth century it is clear that the use of /ɪŋ/ is itself one of the 'standard pronunciation features' to be expected in the non-localized norms regarded as 'correct', whilst speakers of U-RP (and indeed adoptive RP in the late nineteenth century) could, in addition, maintain their own non-localized norms of [ɪn], a stereotype which still of course lingers on in that collocation of *huntin'*, *shootin'*, *and fishin'*. Prevalent attitudes to the use of [ɪn] and [ɪŋ] throughout the nineteenth century do not entirely conceal, however, the fictions, both social and linguistic, which commonly lurk behind pronunciations promoted as overtly symbolic of social divisions. Popularly depicted as a binary opposition between 'illiterate' [ɪn] and 'literate' [ɪŋ] in another common contrast of 'knowledge' versus 'ignorance', the actual situation was, of course, more complex. The facts of variation rule out such simple alignments, and distributions of [ɪn] and [ɪŋ] would in again real terms have fallen not into such simple and absolute patterns of presence or absence, but (as for (h)) instead more complex ones of presence *and* absence, the respective percentages of each being stratified alongside social variables such as status and style, context or gender.

Such 'dropped letters' did not, of course, provide the only vehicles for social sensitization to the use of individual variants in speech, though they were undeniably prominent in the barrage of prescriptive and popular comment on language which appeared throughout the late eighteenth and nineteenth centuries. Sounds which, at least according to the conventional orthography, could have no validity in the 'best' speech were likewise often to be isolated as being similarly deviant; the phenomenon known as 'intrusive [r]' provides a particularly good example in this context,

---

[135] A. S. C. Ross, *How to Pronounce It* (London, 1970), 16.

especially since the same (negative) attitudes towards its use can, in the late twentieth century, still be discerned—regardless of the linguistic and social fictions on which they rest.

The development of intrusive [r] is, in fact, closely linked to the vocalization or loss of [r] in final position, by which means words such as *ma* and *mar*, as we have seen, hence become identical, both being articulated (in the non-localized accents of 'proper' speech) as /mɑ:/. In connected speech, however, a word like *mar*, if followed by another word beginning with a vowel, will in fact see its [r] retained, a feature known as 'linking [r]'. As a result, whilst a construction such as *far from* will be sounded as /fɑ: frəm/, *far away* will instead be pronounced /fɑ:r əweɪ/. This also happens word internally in similar circumstances, so that alternations such as *fear fearing* /fɪə fɪərɪŋ/ are also common. The use of linking [r], in other words, operates as a sandhi phenomenon, being used to obviate hiatus between different sounds and thereby securing a smoother transition between two adjacent vowel sounds in these particular conditions. Intrusive [r] develops analogically, and its use is exactly parallel to that of the inoffensive linking [r]. It appears in identical phonetic environments, such as after /ɑ:/ and /ɔ:/ (as in *catarrh* and *law*) and especially after /ə/, as in *Laura*, and it is this which leads to the commonly stigmatized forms such as the interposed [r] sound in constructions such as *law of the land* (/lɔ:r əv ðə lænd/), or, word internally, to articulations of *drawing room* as /drɔ:rɪŋ ru:m/. From a phonetic point of view, words such as *fear* and *idea* are identical in their closing sounds (/fɪə, aɪdɪə/, and it is thus entirely natural that they should behave in an identical way in connected speech: *fear of* /fɪər əv/, *idea of* /aɪdɪər əv/. From a prescriptive point of view, however, the orthographical disparities evident within their written forms were often to make the use of the latter (though not the former) entirely untenable within popular conceptions of 'proper' English.

Characteristic manifestations of the presence of intrusive [r] are, in consequence, often severely condemned. Smart enumerates it among his catalogue of the features which define the 'vulgar' as opposed to the well-bred speaker, noting of the former: 'He annexes the sound *r* to the vowel sound denoted by *aw*, in *jaw, paw, saw*'.[136] His idealized 'well-bred' counterpart has no such 'flaw', instead

---

[136] B. H. Smart, *A Grammar of English Sounds* (London, 1812), p. xxv.

exhibiting a perfect correlation of spoken and written forms, even in unaccented syllables. Alford in 1864 similarly strives to eliminate intrusive [r] from educated speech, equating it on levels of 'incorrectness' with that other great social shibboleth, the loss of [h]; it too is 'enough to make the hair of any one but a well-seasoned Cockney stand on end'.[137] Even Alexander Ellis, intentionally located within the newly descriptive rigour of late-nineteenth-century linguistics, shares in these patterns of proscription, and the language of subjective inequality rather than objective observation features highly in his comments. Intrusive [r] is 'a non-permissive trill' and 'the very height of vulgarity';[138] it marks the 'uneducated' ('there also exists a great tendency among all educated speakers to introduce an (r) . . . as [in] *drawing, sawing*'),[139] and, of course, the 'illiterate'. As he states, 'illiterate speakers—those who either do not know how to spell, or ignore the rules of spelling in their speech—usually interpose an (r) between any back vowel, as (a, A, ɑ) and a subsequent vowel.'[140]

Nor does that other great stereotype, the 'Cockney', remain absent from the proscriptive persuasions intentionally exerted upon speakers of the language in these texts. In 1870, intrusive [r] is still being given as 'insufferably vulgar', and as a prime 'characteristic of cockney breeding, as *Maidarill* (for Maida Hill)—not unpardonable in an omnibus conductor, and *Victoriarour Queen*—quite unpardonable in an educated gentleman'.[141] Notions of status and affiliations with the social hierarchy are, as this indicates, readily manipulated by the standardizing ideology in this as in other contexts, again erecting an idealized 'best' form of the language employed by those higher in the social order (which is in turn presented for due emulation) and an erroneous, and 'illiterate' flawed form of English, which is to be corrected in favour of this propagated norm.

In real terms, on the other hand, this dividing chasm between 'educated' and 'uneducated' speakers was a prescriptive fiction, just as much as were those censorious (and socially motivated) comments directed towards the loss of [r] itself in these positions.

---

[137] Alford, *A Plea for the Queen's English*, 50.
[138] A. J. Ellis, 'Tenth Annual Address of the President to the Philological Society', *Transactions of the Philological Society* (1881), 317.
[139] Id., *Early English Pronunciation*, ii. 603.   [140] Ibid. i. 201.
[141] J. Hullah, *The Cultivation of the Speaking Voice* (Oxford, 1870), 53–4.

As Sweet noted, with some frustration, of contemporary attitudes to intrusive [r]: 'I know as a fact that most educated speakers of Southern English insert an *r* in *idea(r) of, India(r) Office* etc. in rapid speech, and I know that this habit, so far from dying out, is spreading to the Midlands; and yet they all obstinately deny it.'[142] Its use was in fact widespread—James Lecky transcribes it in his notes of the speech of 'eminent preachers and University professors' in the 1880s[143]—and it is clear that even those who traditionally exemplified notions of RP and its non-localized norms featured it in their everyday speech, even if (as Sweet suggests) perhaps endeavouring to avoid it in their more formal registers. Its rôle as a theoretical shibboleth has, however, remained no less powerful in some ways for this lack of any objective validation. It is, for example, regularly made the subject of twentieth-century manifestations of the 'complaint tradition' in the columns of the daily newspapers where it still appears as a stated (and stigmatized) marker of the social divide. Language attitudes, as this indicates, can remain remarkably constant, even in the face of linguistic reality. In terms of the standard ideology therefore, intrusive [r] is not a feature of the 'best English', even though speakers of mainstream RP do in fact naturally make use of it where circumstances require. Speakers of adoptive RP on the other hand (i.e. those who did not use this accent as children) tend to avoid it, clearly being subject in this to the manipulations of the standard ideology and its theoretical notions of correctness. As Wells notes,[144] such speakers tend to have little control over the more 'informal' characteristics of this mode of speech, so that the assimilations, elisions, and other contextual modifications which occur in this as in any other accent are avoided owing to some preconception (conscious or unconscious) that such features are, in some way, incompatible with the 'best' speech which RP must surely represent and indeed embody. Intrusive [r] too comes under this heading. 'In native-speaker RP it is usual to use sandhi [r] in the appropriate places, in the environments where it is 'intrusive' (unhistorical, not corresponding to the spelling) just as in those where it is not', Wells confirms of twentieth-century RP, and the same may

---

[142] H. Sweet, *A Primer of Spoken English* (Oxford, 1890), viii.
[143] J. Lecky, *Phonetic Journal*, 27 Feb. 1886; cited in Jespersen, *Modern English Grammar*, i. §13.42.
[144] Wells, *Accents of English* (Cambridge, 1982), ii. 284.

be assumed for its antecedents in the nineteenth century.[145] In contrast, as he adds, 'the speech-conscious tend to regard intrusive [r] as incorrect, and hence attempt to avoid it . . . the typical outcome is the suppression of most sandhi /r/s'. In such ways, modern speakers of adoptive RP can be regarded as the heirs of that proscriptive censure proffered so liberally in this context over the course of the nineteenth century, as well as illustrating (here in the empirical terms of modern linguistics) the legacy of language attitudes, and the effects that these notions of stigmatization and of shibboleths can indeed have upon those sensitive to their appeal.

[145] Ibid.

4

Ladylike Accents and the Feminine Proprieties of Speech

THE 'lady', and her masculine counterpart in social status, the 'gentleman', combined to exert a profound influence on notions of propriety, behaviour, and 'correctness' throughout the late eighteenth and nineteenth centuries, the cultural hegemony of such stereotypes being reinforced, as many social historians have noted, by a strong association with contemporary ideals of refinement. Seen as epitomizing a standard of life which encompassed manners as well as morals, their role, Charlotte Yonge stresses, was deservedly that of the exemplar; ladies and gentlemen were to be recognized by their 'high-bred bearing, and grace of manner', by their 'code of honour, courtesy, and natural power of conforming to it'.[1] 'It is this', she adds, 'which proscribes all the meaner faults, by simply regarding them as impossible in gentleman or lady, such, we mean, as listening at doors, looking into letters, . . . and likewise all struggles for place, rude and rough speech and manner'.[2]

Propriety and impropriety often being assigned in line with conformity to such idealized social roles, conceptions of the 'proper' lady, and the gentleman, regularly came to act in socially normative ways for those sensitive to their appeal, inspiring, for example, further aspects of that 'cultural cohesion' documented by Stone and Stone.[3] As J. F. C. Harrison has noted in *Early Victorian Britain*, 'the concept of gentility functioned as an agency of social discipline',[4] regularly informing, in this context, selected specifications of speech as well as of behaviour. The spirit of emulation which was apparently evinced by dint of such popular attitudes to the nuances of conduct provoked a steady stream of comment. Drawing on other prevalent social images, for example, Macaulay expostulated on the seemingly relentless ambition of the middle classes:

---

[1] C. M. Yonge, *Womankind* (London, 1878), 28.
[2] Ibid. 28–9.   [3] See p. 83.
[4] J. F. C. Harrison, *Early Victorian Britain 1832–1851* (London, 1971), 126.

'The curse of England is the obstinate determination of the middle classes to make their sons what they call gentlemen.'[5] Samuel Smiles, with some dislike, described the popularity of these more superficial aspects of 'self-help' in similar terms: 'There is an ambition to bring up boys as gentlemen, or rather 'genteel' men; though the result frequently is only to make them gents.'[6] Just as 'boys' were to become 'gentlemen', so, as Mrs Ellis noted in another account of the cultural hegemonies exerted by these notions of an élite, were 'girls' to be 'young ladies'—often irrespective of the actual walks of life they were to occupy:

Amongst the changes introduced by modern taste, it is not the least striking, that all the daughters of tradespeople, when sent to school, are no longer girls, but young ladies. The linen-draper whose worthy consort occupies her daily post behind the counter, receives her child from Mrs Montagu's establishment—a young lady. At the same elegant and expensive seminary, music and Italian are taught to Hannah Smith, whose father deals in Yarmouth Herrings; and there is the butcher's daughter, too, perhaps the most ladylike of them all.[7]

Such metamorphoses in terms of social labels (and accompanying notions of identity) were not confined merely to children. On the contrary, according to contemporary documentation, this social education in the requisite acquirements of polite life could, it seemed, begin at any time of life; both George Eliot and William Cobbett, as has already been indicated, devoted no little censure to the pretensions affected by farmers and their families in these respects.[8] Giving more direct illustration of such patterns, Thomas Raybould, for example, a Staffordshire manufacturer of scythes and spades, was to write the following letter to his wife in 1789, instructing her in the ladylike proprieties he felt to be suitable for their avowedly genteel life: 'Don't suffer Mary Mogg to sit at table with you to drink tea, as it does certainly let you down very much, as it is a very odd affair if you cannot look upon yourself as a gentlewoman, and let her sit at the ironing table. If your mother

[5] Macaulay, *Life and Letters*, ed. G. O. Trevelyan (London, 1878), i. 338; letter to his sister Hannah, 14 Oct. 1833.
[6] S. Smiles, *Self-Help: With Illustrations of Conduct and Perseverence* (London, 1859), ed. A. Briggs (London, 1958), 290.
[7] S. S. Ellis, *The Women of England, Their Social Duties, and Domestic Habits* 3rd edn. (London, 1839), 107.
[8] See pp. 82–3.

suffers such things, it is what no gentlewoman does, therefore you must not.'[9] Raybould's specifications stress the import, and dissemination, of the cultural construct of gentility and its behavioral norms. His income at that time comprised only around £100 a year, but assimilation to the conventions of 'gentle' living was, nevertheless, not to be neglected. His wife's role was to divorce herself from her social inferiors, 'never to carry a basket to work as long as you are my wife', and to behave, in other words, as a lady of leisure. She was to 'look upon herself as a gentlewoman' ('a woman of birth above the vulgar, a woman well-descended' as John Walker glossed in 1791). The adoption of associated markers of 'ladylike' propriety was in this, of course, not entirely divorced from Raybould's perceptions of his own status. Artisans had wives who worked; 'gentlemen' did not.

Such attitudes were not uncommon, and amongst the middle ranks of society a widespread shift gradually took place in the roles and occupations seen as suitable for these reconstructed 'ladies' of the household. They were frequently to be 'dismissed from the dairy, the confectionary [*sic*], the store-room, the still-room, the poultry-yard, the kitchen-garden, and the orchard', Margaretta Grey noted in her diary in 1853.[10] Resulting conceptions of feminine propriety came to dictate proficiency, not in these traditional occupations of home-baking or brewing, but instead in the leisured arts and 'accomplishments', those external signifiers of the genteel over which 'ladies', of whatever rank, were to have command. Such wasteful redundancy (and social pretension) was vehemently criticized by Cobbett, and Grey herself was hardly less muted in the condemnation she accorded this phenomenon: 'A lady, to be such, must be a mere lady, and nothing else. She must not work for profit, or engage in any occupation that money can command . . . what I remonstrate against is the negative forms of employment, the wasting of energy, the crippling of talent under false ideas of station, propriety, and refinement.'[11]

Even by the end of the eighteenth century, as Mary Poovey has confirmed, the stereotype of the 'Proper Lady' who resulted from

---

[9] Lambeth Palace, Court of Arches MSS, Process Book D 1793, fo. 69; cited in Stone and Stone, *An Open Elite?*, 410.
[10] Recorded by her niece, Josephine Butler, in *Memoir of John Grey of Dilston* (Edinburgh, 1894), 288 n.
[11] Ibid.

such reorientations 'was a familiar household companion',[12] and the 'refinement, 'propriety', 'modesty', 'delicacy', and 'virtue' presented as salient parts within her make-up dominated conceptions of femininity. These propagated norms were widespread, diffusing idealized abstractions of behaviour to which, as again for language, actual behaviour will of course tend to conform only to a greater or lesser extent. Even women located lower in the social hierarchy were, however, not to be entirely immune from the pressures which ensued. Though forced by necessity to work, they were, as Janet Murray points out, 'often judged by the same standards of angelic, sheltered femininity as middle-class and upper-class women'.[13] Notions of perfect womanhood thus tended to dominate ideals of female behaviour, deportment, and decorum throughout society, and they were in turn encoded and reinforced in the many manuals of conduct and etiquette produced to this end. Likewise, penny magazines such as the *Family Herald*, or the popular novels of writers such as Rosa Nouchette Carey, Mrs Craik, Rhoda Broughton, or Charlotte Yonge regularly held up for emulation the standards of behaviour, and the accompanying standards of language, which were deemed to characterize this social icon. As Mrs Craik averred, 'the nameless graces of ladyhood' must necessarily comprise 'the quiet dignity of speech and mien' just as much as 'the repose of perfect self-possession'.[14]

Language, perhaps predictably, plays an integral role in the social and cultural definitions of the 'lady' which emerge over the course of the nineteenth century, as indeed it does in corresponding ones of the gentleman. Commonly placed on a moral pedestal in Victorian eulogies ('from the very susceptibility of her nature, woman is to be more virtuous than man', as *Woman's Worth* stressed in 1847),[15] the lady, as we shall see, was to occupy a linguistic pedestal too, ideally revealing, and reflecting, similar virtues in her speech. In some senses, the 'gentleman' is of course also made to

---

[12] M. Poovey, *The Proper Lady and the Woman Writer: Ideology as Style in the Works of Mary Wollstonecraft, Mary Shelley, and Jane Austen* (Chicago, Ill., 1984), 3.

[13] J. H. Murray, *Strong-Minded Women, and Other Lost Voices from Nineteenth-Century England* (London, 1982), 170.

[14] Mrs D. M. Craik, 'Parson Garland's Daughter', in id., *Two Marriages* (London, 1881), 228.

[15] *Woman's Worth: Or Hints to Raise the Female Character*, 2nd edn. (London, 1847), 3.

share in this paradigmatic function. Endowed with a super-abundance of internal as well as external merits, he is, for example, additionally characterized by his total command of the 'best' (and non-localized) markers of speech: 'Purity of accent is the grand distinctive feature of a gentleman', as the author of *How to Shine in Society* declared.[16] The manipulation of notions of accent and identity in such socially specific ways is by no means rare, and with reference to the 'gentleman', his dress, his language, his pronunciation, even his gloves, were all regularly seen as being liberally endowed with social meanings suggestive of this matchless status. *What Shall We Do With Tom?*, a manual of advice for parents, which readily proffers the answer 'make him a gentleman', hence notes:

It is said that in dress the true gentleman is distinguished by faultless linen, and by accurately-fitting gloves. And in education he is distinguished by his unfailing self-possession and by good spelling . . . he ought never to trip into the vulgarism of mispronouncing his words. They are the faultless linen and the accurately-fitting gloves; the little things that carry with them the 'ring' of true gentility.[17]

The gentleman might be duly distinguished by his perfection in such matters; the lady, however, if she was fully to justify her right to such an appellation, was to excel still further. In the set of attitudes and ideals which come to dominate in thinking in this area, whereas high standards of behaviour and virtue will necessarily distinguish the gentleman, still higher ones must mark the woman who intends to assume, and indeed to convey, her truly gentle standing. *Good Society. A Complete Manual of Manners* unhesitatingly gives expression to this belief: 'Granted that truthfulness, gracefulness, considerateness, unselfishness, are essential to the breeding of a true gentleman, how infinitely more they must be to the breeding of a true lady!'.[18] Or as *The Woman's Book* 'containing everything a woman ought to know' later affirms, ' "Manners makyth Man" and woman too, for if good manners are so essential to man, are they not then indispensable to woman, whose great object in life is to please?'[19]

Paragons in such moral spheres, 'true ladies', so the thinking

---

[16] *How to Shine in Society*, 20.
[17] R. Brewer, *What Shall We Do With Tom? Or, Hints to Parents and Others About School* (London, 1866), 75.
[18] *Good Society*, 49.
[19] F. B. Jack, *The Woman's Book* (London, 1911), 325.

went, must eclipse their male counterparts still further in those delicate nuances of breeding which are carried, and conveyed, by manner, etiquette, and, from the point of view of this book, by language. Compliance with the established tenets of feminine conduct is presented as imperative, associated prescriptions (and proscriptions) appearing not as options but as laws: 'it is absolutely essential that a lady should conform strictly to the usages and rules of society', *Take My Advice* contends, for 'what in a gentleman would be a venial offence against good taste and good breeding, would bring ridicule upon a lady moving in the same circles.'[20] Nor indeed should the imputation of 'ridicule' be underestimated in this context. As Fanny Burney avowed in her diary: 'I would a thousand times rather forfeit my character as a writer than risk ridicule or censure as a female.'[21] "In [the woman] . . . all the minor observances of etiquette are absolutely indispensable', *Good Society* similarly avers,[22] stating as axiomatic that '[the lady] must be even more on her guard than a man in all those niceties of speech, look, and manner, which are the especial and indispensable credentials of good breeding'.[23]

Within the contemporary stereotypes which result, the Proper Lady thus tends to be endowed with a heightened awareness of all that was deemed requisite to perfect propriety and decorum of behaviour; any lapses from such elevated standards were, as this indicates, to be viewed with some severity. Woman, in such ideal manifestations, was to act as guide and censor, her influence immeasurable in ensuring the elevated tone demanded in 'good' society. As *Woman's Worth* expounds, for example: 'how much must the refinement, manners, and habits of society depend upon them! . . . there is nothing, whether it be in temper, manner, or speech, which she cannot restrain.'[24] Regularly constructed as a guardian of morals, woman was equally to guard 'manners' too, censuring the indecorous and impolite, the 'vulgar' and the 'improper': 'the female sex is invested with the power of giving a form and colouring to the manners of the age', as Miss Hatfield observed in 1803.[25] Such responsibilities were not to be abdicated

[20] *Take My Advice* (London, 1872), 309.
[21] Madame D'Arblay, *Diary and Letters*, ed. C. Barrett (London, 1876), i. 102; cited in F. Burney, *Evelina*, ed. E. A. Bloom (Oxford, 1968), p. xx n. 1.
[22] *Good Society*, 49.   [23] Ibid.   [24] *Woman's Worth*, 50–1.
[25] Miss Hatfield, *Letters on the Importance of the Female Sex. With Observations on their Manners and Education* (London, 1803), 70.

lightly. In all things, including of course language too, conformity to these canons of the 'proper' and 'ladylike' was to be presented as of particular moment. A woman was 'brought up to consider custom and opinion her sovereign ruler' commented John Stuart Mill in his discourse upon their subjection and Mrs Ellis offered similar affirmation in this context in her own book on *The Women of England*: 'the dread of being censured or condemned, exercises, I am inclined to think, a far more extensive influence over [woman's] habits and her feeling. Any deviation from the fashionable mode of dress, or from the established usages of polite life, presents an appalling difficulty to a woman of ordinary mind brought up under the tutelage of what is called the world.' As she adds with some insistence, 'She cannot—positively cannot—dare not—will not do anything that the world has pronounced unlady-like.'[26]

In these terms, distinctions of gender were readily to impart different criteria of acceptability for language and behaviour. Conformity, as Mrs Ellis makes clear, was, for example, to be equated above all with 'ladylike' correctness, a parallel extended with some facility into the use of language and considerations of its own allotted role in setting forth the nuances of ladylike demeanour. Status, propriety, purity, and refinement were all values which, it seemed, were embedded in the ways one spoke; as in those notions of subjective inequality already discussed, their stated affiliations formed a central tenet in many of the texts proffered for specifically female instruction. Propriety, for example, itself a cardinal virtue within descriptions (and prescriptions) of ideal femininity, was a quality regularly deemed to encompass details of language. *Girls and Their Ways. By One Who Knows Them* asserts the undisputed value of propriety as a guide to all aspects of female behaviour: not only in terms of their 'dress and demeanour', but also in their 'speech', the intended female readership is instructed to 'study the highest propriety, and the strictest reserve'.[27] *The Young Housekeeper* of 1869 emphasizes similar dictates: 'You should be quite as anxious to *talk* with propriety as you are to think, work, sing, paint or write according to the most correct rules.'[28] Impinging on virtually every facet of feminine ideology, propriety was the rule by which ladylike behaviour might

---

[26] Ellis, *The Women of England*, 309–10.
[27] *Girls and Their Ways. By One Who Knows Them* (London, 1881), 71.
[28] *The Young Housekeeper* (London, 1869), 8.

be judged, being, as Hannah More had early affirmed, 'to a woman what the great Roman critic says action is to an orator; it is the first, the second, the third, requisite . . . the criterion of true taste, right principle, and genuine feeling.'[29] As texts such as *How to Speak with Propriety* indicate, however, it was seen equally as a common desideratum in speech throughout the late eighteenth and nineteenth centuries, a standard by which the 'proper' use of language was to be appraised, and speakers in turn evaluated.

Language, and specifically spoken language, was as a result frequently stipulated as a salient feature of female propriety in itself. Mentioned in both *Girls and Their Ways* and *The Young Housekeeper*, for example, its use was presented as an external virtue able to signify the true breeding which alone befits the lady, imaging forth interior virtue by means of its own exterior refinements. George Vandenhoff makes this particularly clear in *The Lady's Reader*, a work devoted to that vocal elegance often seen as requisite for proper womanhood. 'Grace of speech' is commended highly. Rendering a woman more attractive (as the opening statement of the book asserts), it is given as fundamental in ladylike conduct: 'no lady's manner', Vandenhoff insists, 'can be said to be completely *comme il faut* if her utterance, in ordinary conversation, be defective or inelegant'.[30] Social propriety, in the thinking of the day, was therefore to be met, and matched, with corresponding proprieties of language. Above all, accent, a feature so important to first impressions, must be carefully controlled. Stating that he writes 'without exaggeration', Vandenhoff insists upon the value of enunciation in all assessments of ladylike identity: 'correctness and grace of utterance are requisite distinctions of a lady's conversation'; for her, 'a slovenly style of speech' forms 'as great a blemish as inelegant and ungrammatical language'.[31] For true femininity, he adds, appealing to Cordelia's nineteenth-century counterparts, there should be 'no instrument more sweet than the voice of woman'.[32]

Such notions of 'elegance' form recurrent terms of commendation in Vandenhoff's account of the phonemic perfection deemed vital for the 'lady', just as they do in Johnson's own commendations of the 'best speakers' of the mid-eighteenth century.[33]

---

[29] H. More, *Strictures on the Modern System of Female Education* (London, 1799), ii. 6–7.
[30] Vandenhoff, *The Lady's Reader*, 1.   [31] Ibid. 2.
[32] Ibid. 3; see also pp. 173–5.   [33] See p. 97.

Defined in Walker's *Critical Pronouncing Dictionary* as 'the beauty of propriety', its appropriateness in this context was obvious, though it is perhaps made still clearer by the fact that 'ladylike' itself is, in the same work, glossed as 'soft, delicate, elegant'. Ladylike speech was thus by definition both 'proper' and 'elegant' and, as we have seen, proper and elegant language was, in turn, to be fairly unambiguously located in those non-localized norms of a 'standard', in conformity to them, and in the marked affiliations with social status which they had also come to convey over the course of the nineteenth century. For the 'lady', as Vandenhoff declares, 'the speaking of her native language with purity and elegance of pronunciation, in an agreeable tone of voice' is the marker which alone will communicate to her auditors 'the *prestige* of refinement and high breeding'.[34] It is this at which she is advised to aim, and which is set out for her instruction in *The Lady's Reader*, just as it is in a plethora of other books, magazines, and journals produced at this time.

Such terms make the cultural and socio-symbolic correlates of speech clear: in line with their role as guardians of manners and of morals, exemplary ladies must, so these convictions went, find exemplary accents, located in the 'polite' rather than in the 'provincial', and in that emerging non-localized norm of speech later to be formalised as RP. That often asserted 'disgrace' surrounding the use of 'dialect' was in such ways to take on stronger reverberations within the corresponding definitions of feminine nicety. 'Her accent is not provincial', as *Etiquette for Ladies and Gentlemen* decreed in 1839 of the markers by which the 'lady' was to be identified.[35] Such tenets came to form the foundation of an evident intersection between those ideologies of a standard already discussed, and equally prevalent ideologies of the feminine and the ladylike. A marriage of ideas attended with no little degree of success, it was moreover to be aided immeasurably by this compatibility of the terms employed. Propriety and impropriety, as we have already seen, form integral elements of that prescriptive lexis whereby regional accents (and proscribed variants) were condemned, constituting a topic on which the authors of both *How to Speak with Propriety* and *How to Shine in Society* discourse at length. Purity also, a cardinal virtue for the female sex, is likewise

---

[34] Vandenhoff, *The Lady's Reader*, 1.
[35] *Etiquette for Ladies and Gentlemen*, 45.

endowed with distinctive applications within notions of non-localized accents and their rightful dominance. 'Purity of accent', as *How to Shine in Society* confirms, is that which 'belongs to no city or district',[36] and Smart (along with many others writers) readily engages in binary oppositions of 'pure' and 'impure' which are neatly mapped on to non-localized norms of accent based in the 'best speech' of London, in contradistinction to 'impurities' deemed intrinsic to the 'provincial'. Logically therefore, pure ladies must speak only with the purest accents, as Vandenhoff affirms. 'A lady's accents must be pure, her tones sweet', corroborates Mrs Sangster in her *Hours with Girls*.[37] The Young Lady's Book of 1876 endorses this still further, fusing cultural and linguistic stereotypes alike in its assertions that one of the primary duties which the 'young ladies' of the title are to assume lies in their very defence of English itself from 'impurity', an aim facilitated by that exemplary purity of language which 'ladies' must adopt at all times, and in all forms of language which they use.[38] Given common conceptions of the wider values of female purity ('gently, imperceptibly, but most certainly, will she imbue with her own purity and beneficence the atmosphere in which she moves', as *The Young Lady's Book* of 1829 proclaimed),[39] the same affiliations form the sub-text of attitudes towards the language of the Proper Lady. Imperceptibly, but certainly, was she to impose standards of usage upon her auditors by her own exemplary proprieties of phoneme and of phrase.

'Refinement' was usefully to partake of this same duality of reference. Its connotations, as Walker specifies, being those of 'improvement in elegance or purity', notions of 'refinement' likewise found a natural home in both popular and prescriptive attitudes to the values necessary within correct standards of speech. Accent in *Talking and Debating* (1856) is that which can evince familiarity (or otherwise) with 'refined circles'.[40] As *Behaviour: A Manual of Morals and Manners* attests, 'the first and highest of human accomplishments is a clear, distinct, well-modulated speech', an attribute which is located in 'a refined and elegant way of speaking', or in

---

[36] *How to Shine in Society*, 20.
[37] Mrs M. Sangster, *Hours With Girls* (London, 1882), 79.
[38] Mrs H. Mackarness, *The Young Lady's Book* (London, 1876), 121.
[39] *The Young Lady's Book. A Manual of Elegant Recreations, Exercises, and Pursuits* (London, 1829), 23–4.
[40] *Talking and Debating*, 4.

other words, in an accent free from the imputations of impropriety, vulgarism, or the provincial.[41] Important therefore as a general desideratum in 'proper' speech, the presence of 'refinement' is again presented as still more vital in associated conceptions of feminine identity and behaviour, a view often expressed in works directed towards both language and conduct. *Etiquette, Social Ethics, and the Courtesies of Society*, the title of which exemplifies common equations made in the nineteenth century between manners and morals, hence combines gender, status, and language in the imperatives it issued to its female readers. Cautioned to 'remember your standing as gentlewomen' at all times, they are similarly not allowed to forget that they must 'never approve a mean action, nor speak an unrefined word'.[42] Any inadvertent breach of such prescribed standards was likely to bring in its wake consequences which were potentially momentous. As the author adjures, 'the least want of refinement in conversation lowers a woman, ay, and for ever'.[43]

Evidently integral to notions of feminine status, the presence of refinement is endowed with still greater value in this context by Charlotte Yonge. Admitting that in real terms refinement is 'just as much a Christian grace in a man as in a woman', Yonge is nevertheless strikingly explicit on the subject of its differential import in constructions of gender and identity. Of equal significance in terms of 'Christian grace' it might indeed be, but refinement occupies a far higher order for woman against man, for without it, she adds, 'he is not such a hateful unsexed creature . . . as a woman is'.[44] 'True womanhood' being 'unsexed' by being unrefined, the linguistic correlates of this cultural ideal thus in turn receive due emphasis in Yonge's work. The '*lowest* standard for a lady' must include 'correct pronunciation', she specifies, noting further that such 'correct English' is in itself to be understood as 'a mark of real refinement of mind and cultivation'.[45]

Such attitudes make very clear the affinities of language, mind, and gender which were commonly endorsed over the course of the nineteenth century. Since the lady, at least within these iterations of popular mythology, was supposedly endowed with sensibilities more delicate than those of the common order (as *Advice to*

---

[41] T. L. Nichols, *Behaviour: A Manual of Manners and Morals* (London, 1874), 59.
[42] *Etiquette, Social Ethics, and the Courtesies of Society* (London, 1834), 38.
[43] Ibid.   [44] *Womankind*, 172.   [45] Ibid. 73–4.

Governesses, for example, notes of the future female charges of its readers, 'their sense of right and wrong will be more refined', and they will, as a result, 'be called upon to hold up an higher standard of purity and excellence, endeavouring to engage every one within their reach to rally round it'),[46] their use of language was naturally to be placed in these same exemplary paradigms, likewise subject to heightened sensitivities towards issues of 'right' and 'wrong', 'good' and 'bad', as well as to those emblematic properties of 'purity', 'refinement', and 'propriety' already discussed. The 'consciousness' of good pronunciation so early advocated by Sheridan was, in frequently constructed appeals of this order, hence to reach even higher levels of recommendation and prescriptions for due convergence. These attitudes explain in some measure the exaggerated reactions which can attend absence of conformity in this respect, a convention well illustrated in fictional form in Hardy's *The Mayor of Casterbridge*, where Elizabeth-Jane's occasional use of dialect induces outrage in her father, given his own new social construction as 'gentleman' rather than hay-trusser:

'Bide where ye be', he echoed sharply. 'Good God, are you only fit to carry wash to a pig-trough, that ye use such words as those?'
She reddened with shame and sadness.
'I meant, "Stay where you are", father', she said, in a low, humble voice. 'I ought to have been more careful.'[47]

'Marks of the beast to the truly genteel', such terms as 'bide' for 'stay', or 'greggles' for 'wild hyacinths', are of course incompatible with the ladylike status, and accompanying sensibilities, which Henchard aims to impose upon his daughter. Capable of belying this new identity, they are accordingly proscribed, as indeed is the similar use of the regional as opposed to the 'refined' for Margaret Hale in Gaskell's *North and South*. As her mother reprimands: ' "Margaret, don't get to use these horrid Milton words. 'Slack of work': it is a provincialism . . . it has a very vulgar sound and I don't want to hear you using it." '[48]
True ladies were supposed to know better, and slang, infelicities of tone and phrase, as well, of course, as mispronunciations of various kinds, were all popularly construed as indicating lower,

---

[46] *Advice to Governesses* (London, 1827), p. v.
[47] T. Hardy, *The Mayor of Casterbridge* (London, 1886), i. 246.
[48] *North and South*, 237.

and less refined, levels of sensitivity than those expected of this perfect femininity.[49] Guardians of the moral right and wrong, ladies were thus also to assume the role of guardians of the language; as *The Young Lady's Book* of 1876 reveals, for example, they themselves were to form the direct heirs (or heiresses) of John Walker and Samuel Johnson. The spirits of the latter being actively summoned to provide the proper inspiration ('Shades of Johnson and Walker! arise and defend the poor ill-used English language'), it is into the hands of young ladies that their canons of correctness against 'slovenly utterance' must now pass. As the writer eloquently appeals, 'will not our young ladies stand up for their own mother tongue and, by speaking it in its purity, redeem its lost character?'.[50] Linguistic responsibility is by such means conferred upon the lady in the exemplary use of the spoken language by which she is to be recognized, and, in turn, defined.

In the prevailing tenets of true womanhood, this in effect comes to constitute a charge entrusted to them from childhood as texts such as *Girls and Their Ways* suggest. Provided with a parallel volume, *Boys and Their Ways. By One Who Knows Them*, the differences between the two provide still more evidence on nineteenth-century gender differentiation and the role of language (and language attitudes) within it. A section dealing with 'The Girl in her Leisure Hours' hence notes: 'The arrangement of the voice, . . . the just emphasis, the skilful inflection, the distinct articulation, the accurate pronunciation: these are graces to be acquired by careful study and constant practice.'[51] The corresponding section treating the 'leisure hours' of boys mentions instead the interest to be found in the study of botany, geology, chemistry, or music. Linguistic nicety only intrudes upon mention of conversation to be addressed to women, the boy 'in his mother's presence' being directed to 'subdue

---

[49] See e.g. the 'unfeigned astonishment' with which, in R. N. Carey's *Not Like Other Girls* (London, 1884), Mrs Challoner regards her youngest daughter, Dulce, merely because she has betrayed feminine linguistic proprieties in using the Christian name of one of their (male) friends. Though Dulce explains in self-defence that ' "I am only repeating Miss Drummond's words—she said "Archie" ', Mrs Challoner is not appeased: ' "But, my dear, there was no need to be so literal", returned Mrs Challoner reprovingly; for she was a gentlewoman of the old school, and nothing grieved her more than slipshod English, or any idiom or idiocy of modern parlance in the mouths of her bright young daughters; to speak of any young man . . . without the ceremonious prefix was a hideous misdemeanour in her eyes.' (ii. 124).

[50] Mackarness, *The Young Lady's Book*, 121.

[51] *Girls and Their Ways*, 25.

his voice and lay aside his rough manners', while to his sister he must likewise be 'gentle and polished in his language.'[52] Such social norms and their attendant absolutes belong of course to the realm of stereotype rather than to reality *per se*. As already indicated, they encode prevalent cultural images and ideals of behaviour, offering constructions of gender and identity which, though conventional and even formulaic in their dictates, can nevertheless be of importance. Stereotypes of this order are 'interesting as clues to our *ideology* of femininity and sex difference', as Deborah Cameron has pointed out in *The Feminist Critique of Language*,[53] and indeed they do convey with particular explicitness the cultural as well as linguistic pressures which were commonly exerted on eighteenth- and nineteenth-century females from their earliest years. Intruded into magazines, into manuals of housekeeping, into contemporary literature, and even into education, as much as into those works more expressly directed towards prescription of 'ladylike' conduct, such attitudes and ideals secured wide dissemination.

Women, as Wollstonecraft observed, 'must be educated, in great degree, by the opinions and manners of the society they live in'.[54] As maiden, wife, and even mother, the use of 'proper' language was to form a central part of this specifically female education, issues of 'identity politics' and associated socio-cultural attitudes impinging to no little extent upon these particular aspects of the opinions and manners of society. The voice, for example, presented as a particularly prominent element within those external signals by which notions of identity were to be conveyed to the outside world, received marked attention within the norms presented for the erudition of girls. Even divorced from its associated specifications of accent, it emerges as a recurrent topos in depictions of the truly feminine and, as for Cordelia, commendations liberally accrue around that 'voice ever soft, gentle, and low'. 'Our girls should seek to cultivate a low voice, "that excellent thing in woman"', *Girls and Their Ways* remarks.[55] 'Remember in conversation that a voice "gentle and low" is, above all extraneous accomplishments,

---

[52] *Boys and Their Ways. By One Who Knows Them* (London, 1880), 14.
[53] D. Cameron (ed.), *The Feminist Critique of Language: A Reader* (London, 1990), 24.
[54] M. Wollstonecraft, *A Vindication of the Rights of Women* (London, 1792), in *The Works of Mary Wollstonecraft*, ed. J. Todd and M. Butler (London, 1989), v. 90.
[55] *Girls and Their Ways*, 70.

"an excellent thing in woman" ', *Good Society. A Complete Manual of Manners* verifies, delineating further the peculiarly statusful properties of this acquisition: 'There is a certain distinct but subdued tone of voice which is peculiar only to persons of the best breeding. It is better to err by the use of too low than too loud a tone.'[56] The 'careful repressive influence' which Charlotte Yonge so commends in female education clearly takes on additional values in such contexts, and, as *The Habits of Good Society. A Handbook of Etiquette for Ladies and Gentlemen* makes plain, all natural properties of vocal pitch and volume must in fact be curbed in 'proper' ladylike speech. The lady's address 'should be polite and gentle', but it was given as of still greater significance that her words 'should be gently spoken, . . . the voice loud enough to be caught easily, but always in an undertone to the power of voice allotted by nature'.[57]

Affiliations with perceived status are of course overtly manipulated in such maxims on 'talking proper'. The use of a loud voice, standing as it does outside the stated canons of acceptability, was often regarded as manifesting obvious deficiencies in ladylike status as well as in ladylike sensibility; it is, as *Etiquette for the Ladies* asserts, 'utterly plebeian'. On such grounds, as the author continues with a marked lack of moderation, it is 'repulsive in a lady'.[58] *Hints to Governesses* makes much the same point, aligning propriety and pronunciation in another account of the essential management of the voice. Reiterating the value of Cordelia as feminine exemplar in terms of language, the voice 'ever soft | gentle and low, an excellent thing in woman.' (*King Lear*, v. iii. 270–1) is extolled for use on all occasions, even when in reprimand: 'A gentle reproof in a soft tone of voice will be found most effectual.—Loud, angry tones are extremely unladylike, and degrading.'[59] Submissive enunciation is therefore the ideal at which all ladies, and would-be ladies, are to aim, and the hallmark by which they will in turn be known; 'one can always tell a lady by her voice and laugh', *Etiquette for Ladies and Gentlemen* proclaims, 'neither . . . will ever be loud or coarse, but soft, low, and nicely modulated. Shakespeare's

---

[56] *Good Society*, 99.
[57] *The Habits of Good Society. A Handbook of Etiquette for Ladies and Gentlemen* (London, 1859), 265.
[58] *Etiquette for the Ladies* (London, 1837), 19.
[59] *Hints to Governesses. By One of Themselves* (London, 1856), 17.

unfailing taste tells you that—"A low voice is an excellent thing in women".'[60] Comments such as these are, of course, all further manifestations of the role which the voice plays within nineteenth-century feminine ideology. It is moreover, as Graddol and Swann in the twentieth century confirm, of no little import within wider ideologies of gender and their associated manifestations: 'through its pervasiveness in both public and intimate encounters', they point out, '[the voice] constantly establishes a difference between the sexes'. It is, as a result, 'likely to perform an important ideological role'.[61] Its dominance within contemporary images of femininity in the nineteenth century certainly would not lead one to dispute such assertions, and various aspects of its 'proper' use regularly make an appearance in other accounts of the gender roles which the nineteenth-century woman was expected to fulfil to the best of her capacities.

The significance of elocution and vocal training for women in the eighteenth and nineteenth centuries is, for instance, commonly presented in the framework of the social roles which they will later adopt. As wives, as mothers, or simply in the bosom of their own families, the correct management of the voice was frequently depicted as an asset incontestable in the values it would confer. Vandenhoff was notably eulogistic in this context, exalting its role in contemporary constructions of femininity. 'Is there any acquirement more domestic, more peculiarly feminine?' he demanded in a question entirely rhetorical within his text.[62] Certainly, the specifically 'domestic' applications of this ability did reinforce its perceived relevance in female education and training, and reading aloud was envisaged as a sphere in which the vocal proprieties of women could be employed to the enjoyment of all, adding immeasurably to the comforts of the home. Vandenhoff continues his eulogy on elocution, femininity, and the necessary acquisition of the 'standard accent' in precisely this strain: 'HOME, the domestic circle, is the legitimate scene of a woman's accomplishments; and an attainment which can add the charms of intellectual entertainment to the other attractions of her fireside, is certainly worthy of particular attention in a system of female education.'[63]

[60] *Etiquette for Ladies and Gentlemen*, 26.
[61] D. Graddol and J. Swann, *Gender Voices* (Oxford, 1989), 142.
[62] Vandenhoff, *The Lady's Reader*, 2–3.   [63] Ibid. 3.

Other writers advocated the importance of correct elocution in similar terms. *The Young Lady's Book* in 1876 unreservedly endorsed the precept that 'a woman who reads aloud really well holds a power of pleasing difficult to over-estimate, since it is an every-day accomplishment, and eminently suited to home life',[64] while *Girls and Their Ways* emphasized how 'graceful' was this accomplishment, not least since, in the hands (or perhaps rather voices) of its female readers, it was capable of 'investing the winter evening with a new charm'. 'Accurate pronunciation' is therefore to be acquired by 'careful study and constant practice', so that such additional and especially feminine charms may captivate the domestic circle.[65] A glowing picture is envisaged of the result to be expected from command of this indispensable accomplishment: 'What a depth of significance is given to a fine passage by a skilful reader; what lights and shades she indicates in it; how she conveys the sentiment, the feeling to the heart and mind of the reader.'[66]

Mrs Beeton too, that very icon of the home and its management, was likewise to endorse such sentiments in her own exposition of the duties of the mistress of the house, pointing out how 'delightful' was this feminine recreation of reading aloud,[67] but the reality corresponding to such idyllic representations was not always so congenial. Florence Nightingale, for one, viewed the elocutionary endeavours which could occupy whole evenings as a source of tedium rather than entertainment, deeming them 'the most miserable exercise of the human intellect'.[68] Harriet Martineau presented a similarly discouraged impression in *Deerbrook* where a typical evening in the Greys' household is accompanied by the reading out of forty pages of the latest novel from the 'Society'. Not without their critics therefore, such occupations did nevertheless form another pastime at which women were expected to excel, a skill by which they could enhance still further the pleasures of home. Reading well, and with the 'correct' accent, became another aspect of that vocal propriety depicted as essential, encoded in educational precepts as well as manuals of conduct as a sign in

---

[64] Mackarness, *The Young Lady's Book*, 45.
[65] *Girls and Their Ways*, 25.   [66] Ibid.
[67] 'Nothing is more delightful to the feminine members of a family, than the reading aloud of some good standard work or amusing publication', I. Beeton, *Beeton's Book of Household Management* (London, 1861), 17.
[68] F. Nightingale, *Cassandra* (1852); cited in Murray, *Strong-Minded Women*, 91.

itself of 'educated' status. As Vandenhoff notes on the opening page of his *Lady's Reader*, 'the speaking of her native language with purity and elegance of pronunciation' and with 'an agreeable tone of voice' will, for the lady, constitute 'the distinguishing marks of a good education'.

The home was naturally perhaps the most central aspect of feminine ideology and proper womanhood in the nineteenth century, iterated alike in images of the 'angel of the house' which so influenced idealized Victorian conceptions of woman's rightful role, as well as in the many manuals of conduct devoted to these shared issues of gender, language, and education. 'Let what will be said of the pleasures of society, there is after all "no place like home" ', as *Woman's Worth* announced to its readers, stressing that here, and here alone, might woman be seen in her 'true and proper station'.[69] Such comments were commonplace; 'Home has justly been called "her empire", and it is certain that to her it is a hallowed circle, in which she may diffuse the greatest earthly happiness, or inflict the most positive misery', stated *The Young Lady's Book* in a similar strain.[70] Education should therefore also rightly tend to this end, a precept of course already evident in the emphasis placed on elocution for enhancing the joys of domestic life.

Female education, as Mrs Ellis indicated,[71] was in consequence often to be subject to some notable deficiencies. As many writers noted, it seemed to provide a grounding in manner rather than matter, in show rather than substance. Rosamond Vincy in *Middle-march* is educated in how to get into (and out of) a carriage, Margaret Sherwin in Wilkie Collins's *Basil* receives 'a drawing-room-deportment day once every week—the girls taught how to enter a room and leave a room with dignity and ease'. Such pro-mised acquirements are lauded on many a prospectus for 'genteel' ladies' establishments outside as well as inside the realms of fiction; 'to make the daughters of England what is called accomplished, seems to be the principal object aimed at', as *Woman's Worth* asserted of that 'ornamental' education all too often offered to girls.[72] Dancing, singing, foreign languages, deportment, all formed staples of the nineteenth-century female syllabus, whether in terms

---

[69] *Woman's Worth*, 99. [70] *The Young Lady's Book*, 23.
[71] See p. 161. [72] *Woman's Worth*, 11.

of boarding-school education, genteel seminaries, or the governess employed at home. 'To render them as superficially attractive, and showily accomplished, as they could possibly be made without present trouble or discomfort to themselves' was generally the aim, as Anne Brontë noted in her (fictionalized) account of her own experiences as a governess in *Agnes Grey*. While for the boys in her charge she was to 'get the greatest possible quantity of Latin grammar and Valpy's Delectus into their heads, in order to fit them for school', for the girls she was instead to 'instruct, refine, and polish',[73] instilling the requisite sense of external decorum and exemplary conduct. As expected, this particular orientation of pre-occupations again tends to have its own repercussions in the context of language.

Knowledge of phonemes and propriety of enunciation is, as a result, frequently commended as a most desirable acquisition for the young female. James Buchanan in *The British Grammar*, for example, early recommends that 'in every Boarding-School where there are ladies of rank' there should be the attendance of 'Proper Masters', this specification being made, however, primarily so that such 'ladies' may be taught 'to read with an accurate pronunciation' as well as 'to write their own language grammatically'.[74] Graham endorses a similar point of view in 1837; 'the art of reading and speaking with propriety' was to be regarded as a prime 'department of ornamental education' facilitating 'a certain established standard of elegance'.[75] As *Woman's Worth* exhorted its own readers: 'if such pains are worth taking in learning how to sing, it would surely be worth learning how to speak; the latter is far more useful than the former, and, at the same time, far more pleasing.'[76] This was, as *The Young Lady's Book* of 1876 stressed, 'a topic of no small importance in the education of girls',[77] enhancing, as it did, their attractiveness, as well as facilitating the harmonies of the home, and forming an external signifier of refinement of no small value. 'Correct pronunciation' was indeed to be regarded as 'the first and highest of human accomplishments', *Behaviour: A Manual of Manners and Morals* emphasized;[78] as Drew added in *The*

---

[73] A. Brontë, *Agnes Grey* (London, 1847), ed. H. Marsden and R. Inglesfield (Oxford, 1988), 64.
[74] J. Buchanan, *The British Grammar* (London, 1762), p. xxxi.
[75] J. C. Graham, *Principles of Elocution* (Edinburgh, 1837), 9.
[76] *Woman's Worth*, 72–3.   [77] Mackarness, *The Young Lady's Book*, 45.
[78] Nichols, *Behaviour*, 59.

Elocutionist Annual for 1889, this, in particular, 'gave the finishing touch to a good education', rendering 'a woman far better fitted to shine in society'.[79] Bell's *Ladies' Elocutionist* and his *Elocutionary Manual* were hence frequently commended for the study of young ladies, and deficiencies in the use of /h/ or /ŋ/ are, as we shall see, depicted in no uncertain terms as detracting from that 'purity' and 'delicacy' which should be mirrored in their speech. Vandenhoff's *The Lady's Reader*, for example, stressed the particular importance of 'accomplishment' in this respect. The absence of /h/ being construed as 'a gross vulgarism in speech', as well as 'a mark of inferior education', this, he states, undoubtedly arouses 'great prejudice' towards the speaker as well as to what is spoken. As expected, such proscriptions operate with even greater rigour for the 'lady; for her the dropping of [h] is, in consequence, 'a fatal blot in ordinary conversation', and a trait which 'no care, no labour, can be too great to eradicate'.[80] Other works on feminine conduct endorse the need for similar exertion on the part of their readers, drawing on notions of social shame or blunted sensibility in the context of those who offend in such ways. As *Private Education; Or a Practical Plan for the Studies of Young Ladies* notes: 'The manner of expressing yourself should be particularly attended to as well as your pronunciation. How would it sound at your own table if you should say "Will you take a little *air?*" for hare. "Do you ride on *orseback* for horseback?".[81] The social sub-text in such advice is, as this indicates, suggested fairly unambiguously.

The prevalence of this particular set of language attitudes is, like those relating to the proprieties of /h/ or /r/, similarly embedded in literary contexts as authors revealed themselves (as we shall further see in Chapter 5) notably responsive to the socio-cultural symbolism which language could import as well as to the gendered assumptions which may surround its 'proper' use. It is, for example, precisely this educational focus (and that doctrine of the superficial within it) which Dickens satirizes with such skill in *Little Dorrit* in the person of Mrs General. Employed after the renewed rise to fortune of the Dorrits, her guiding principle is 'the formation

---

[79] E. Drew, *The Elocutionist Annual for 1889* (London, 1889), 125.
[80] Vandenhoff, *The Lady's Reader*, 16–17.
[81] *Private Education; Or a Practical Plan for the Studies of Young Ladies*, 3rd edn. (London, 1816), 280–1.

of a surface' upon those given to her for instruction, a process
rendered peculiarly visual by dint of Dickens's metaphorical skills
('In that formation process of hers, she dipped the smallest of
brushes into the largest of pots, and varnished the surface of every
object that came under consideration.')[82] Language too was, of
course, to be included within these operations as Mrs General,
'the Fair Varnisher', likewise attempts to give a similar sheen to
the linguistic accomplishments of the young ladies in her charge.

Possessing herself the 'low soft voice' so beloved of works on
feminine conduct, Mrs General is an able tutor in the linguistic
niceties which can enhance appearance. Fanny Dorrit's idioms
are, for example, rephrased in line with greater feminine propriety,
so that 'tumbled over' (' "they would not have been recalled to
our remembrance . . . if Uncle hadn't accidentally tumbled over
the subject" ') becomes instead 'inadvertently lighted upon' (' "My
dear, what a curious phrase . . . Would not inadvertently lighted
upon, or accidentally referred to, be better?" ').[83] However, it is in
Mrs General's strictures to Amy on the terms by which her pa-
ternal parent is to be addressed that the inclusion of norms of
language within these attitudes to 'proper' and feminine appearance
is best exemplified. Incorporating not only advice on the lexical
preferences which are more becoming to true decorum, but also
commending certain phonemes above others on account of the
appearance thereby given to the lips, Mrs General is most precise
on this subject:

'Papa is a preferable mode of address', observed Mrs General. 'Father is
rather vulgar, my dear. The word Papa, besides, gives a very pretty form
to the lips. Papa, potatoes, poultry, prunes, and prism, are all very good
words for the lips: especially prunes and prism. You will find it serviceable,
in the formation of a demeanour, if you sometimes say to yourself in
company—on entering a room, for instance—Papa, potatoes, poultry,
prunes and prism, prunes and prism.'[84]

The use of *papa* is hence extolled, not because it is a better expression of filial regard, but instead by virtue of its inaugural phoneme,
a bilabial plosive which gives a becoming pout to the lips in its
articulation, entirely suitable, of course, for the appearance of a
young lady as she enters a room.

The single-minded focus on manners at the expense of morals

---

[82] *Little Dorrit*, 438–9.   [83] Ibid. 467).   [84] Ibid. 461–2.

which is so evident in Mrs General's educational maxims does of course betray the spirit of exaggeration. Nevertheless, criticisms of such inverted principles as manifested in fact rather than fiction abound in contemporary comment. As Dorothy Marshall has commented, fiction can, in some ways, be 'a better guide to the norm than fact'. As she adds, 'whereas the historian is faced by the endless variety of the individual, the novelist tends to reflect the contemporary image';[85] as we have already seen, authors are indeed equally aware of this sense of a 'norm', and attendant attitudes, in ways which can by highly illuminating.[86] Dickens's talents are certainly acute in this respect, and though heavily ironic, his portrait of Mrs General in *Little Dorrit* embodies in concrete form the familiar equations made between accomplishments and education in the teaching of girls, as well as the role which language commonly assumed in both.

Even in real terms, the arts of speech were therefore often to form salient aspects of the conduct set down for women, and manuals on female education did not hesitate to endorse their import, or the need for their acquisition. Such sentiments were, for instance, endorsed by Mrs Montagu, the 'authoress and leader of society' as she is described in the *Dictionary of National Biography*, with reference to her own nieces. 'The most accomplished lady he ever saw', according to her husband's cousin (as well as being 'an honour to her sex, country and family'), Mrs Montagu commends her sister's decision to send them away to a boarding-school on the grounds that, though 'what girls learn at these schools is trifling, . . . they unlearn what would be of great disservice —a provincial dialect, which is extreamly ungenteel'.[87] Almost a century later, the same preoccupations with 'talking like a lady' in the education of girls could, however, still be detected, assimilated even within the educational reforms of Frances Mary Buss.

Headmistress (and founder) of the Frances Mary Buss School (later the North London Collegiate School) and founder also, in 1870, of the Camden School, Buss's methods were, in many ways, often regarded as embodying the improvements in educational opportunities which were becoming available for girls in the latter part of the century. Nevertheless, even she was not to neglect the

[85] Marshall, *Industrial England*, 61.   [86] See pp. 136 ff.
[87] J. Doran, *A Lady of the Last Century* (London, 1873), 181.

voice, or its importance in feminine education. As Sarah Burstall,
who attended Camden School in the 1870s, confirms, the syllabus
in 1874 continued to include a marked emphasis on 'excellent
English . . . with speech-training and the study of poetry', just as
it was still 'considered correct to have dancing lessons'.[88] As this
indicates, the old legacy of accomplishments and elocution for
girls could linger on even in the more enlightened educational
regimes of the late nineteenth century, tempered to an extent,
however, by the importance gradually being given to science,
algebra, and geometry as newly appropriate aspects of female
knowledge. Nevertheless throughout the century, as this indicates,
female education could explicitly reinforce both that ideology of
a standard already discussed and, in its marked gender divides of
subject and appropriate instruction, inculcate ideals of 'talking
proper' which are also often presented as fundamental within prevailing ideologies of feminine propriety. Education, as we will see
in Chapter 6, could in fact be markedly responsive to these issues
of a 'standard' so widely propagated over the nineteenth century.
As this suggests, the specifically feminine aspects of associated
beliefs were to receive due notice too.

Language, however, could also assume equal, if not greater,
prominence in the other social roles which women were to assume
within the home, first that of wife, and secondly that of mother.
In both of these, according to contemporary comment, ladylike
felicities of 'proper' language were by no means to be unimportant. The role of wife was, for example, frequently presented in
the biblical guise of the helpmeet. 'I believe—as entirely as any
other truth which has been from the beginning—that woman was
created as a help-meet to man', maintained Charlotte Yonge in
Womankind.[89] 'That she might be a help meet for man, was the
intention of the Almighty in forming woman', *Woman's Worth*
similarly affirmed: 'she is made a being who can think, and feel,
and reflect,—a being who can assist in his affairs—who can smooth
the rugged brow of care, can cheer through the toil and strengthen
in the task.'[90] Her education before marriage was therefore, at
least ideally, also to be directed to these particular ends, a conception which is perhaps expressed with greatest clarity by *Woman:*

---

[88] S. A. Burstall, *Retrospect and Prospect: Sixty Years of Women's Education* (1933);
cited in Murray, *Strong-Minded Women*, 232.
[89] *Womankind*, 9–10.   [90] *Woman's Worth*, 18.

As She Is, And As She Should Be, a text published in two volumes in 1835. As the author rhetorically demands, 'What *is* the destination of women? . . . They compose one half of the species, and arc destined to constitute the happiness of the other half; they are to be wives and mothers;—in a word, they were created for the *domestic* comfort and felicity of man. Their education, then, must be *relative to man!*'[91] Readily answering his own question, the anonymous author thus sets forth a canon of female behaviour (and indeed education) which was in fact to be frequently endorsed. Home, for instance, is regularly presented not only as woman's rightful place, but also as the abode of her greatest influence, for good or ill. Upon this influence moreover, and upon her rightful discharge of such responsibility, depends the behaviour of man himself. 'As a man carries with him through the world those same habits and feelings he has gathered in his Home—and as these habits and feelings are principally derived from the influence of woman', we are informed, 'woman in performing her Home-duties takes a vast share in the concerns of the community.'[92]

This equation was effortlessly extended into domains of language too, as the 'good' wife was in turn depicted as linguistic as well as moral exemplar, able to inculcate the 'proper' and non-localized standards of speech in her children (a subject to which we will return), as well as to aid, or indeed abet, her husband's social progress by her own use of language. Mrs Valentine, preceptress of *The Young Woman's Book* of 1878, provides both general and specific illustration of the apparent truth of such maxims within the joint concerns of feminine and linguistic ideology. Self-improvement in terms of language is, for instance, presented as a significant aspect of the wifely role itself, part of that love, honour, and obedience which should characterize female behaviour in the married state. As Mrs Valentine duly stresses, in an era of much social mobility 'when a man may rise from the station of a working mechanic to that of a *millionaire*', women ought be just as aware of their responsibilities to their husbands in this respect as they were in all others.[93] Denied the means of achieving such mobility independently (as Wollstonecraft declared, 'the only way women can rise in the world [is] by marriage'), women were instead

[91] *Woman: As She Is, And As She Should Be* (London, 1835), i. 252.
[92] *Woman's Worth*, 100.
[93] Mrs C. Valentine, *The Young Woman's Book* (London, 1878), 235.

required to aid and foster that of their husbands. Their own
language, and the status implications it could convey, was in turn
to be regarded as by no means immaterial to his success. Gissing,
of course, in *New Grub Street*, graphically depicts the shame of a
man whose wife's linguistic failings continually manifest the social
gulf between them, Mrs Yule rarely being allowed to talk to her
child, for fear of any 'contamination' which might result:

From the first it was Yule's dread lest Marian should be infected with her
mother's faults of speech and behaviour. He would scarcely permit his
wife to talk to the child. At the earliest possible moment Marian was sent
to a day-school . . . any sacrifice of money to insure her growing up with
the tongue and manners of a lady. It can scarcely have been a light trial
to the mother to know that contact with her was regarded as her child's
greatest danger; but in her humility and her love for Marian she offered
no resistance. And so it came to pass that one day the little girl, hearing
her mother make some flagrant grammatical error, turned to the other
parent and asked gravely: 'Why doesn't mother speak as properly as we
do?' Well, that is one of the results of such marriages.[94]

Mrs Valentine too spells out the linguistic responsibilities which
marriage should bring. Detailing the ways in which a wife's speech
should enhance her husband's status, she gives as a general guide
the maxim: 'It is required of all wives to cultivate themselves as
much as may be, in order to be fitted for any position.' By such
self-education in the requisite proprieties of speech, however, as Mrs
Valentine did not fail to observe, women were by no means neglec-
ting their own interests: 'A young woman who teaches herself to
speak and write properly has taken a step upwards in the world,
and is sure to benefit by it.'[95] Emphasizing the heightened anguish
caused, in such conceptions, by mispronunciation in the female
sex ('What can be more distressing than to hear bad English
spoken and words mispronounced by people, who by a very little
trouble might speak like ladies?'),[96] Mrs Valentine's lessons in this
context are to be endorsed still further by the use of pertinent
example, as she proceeds to narrate the tale of a woman who
shamed her husband, and dishonoured his status, by the continued use of articulatory (and social) solecisms such as these:

We remember hearing of a lady who by her husband's high character and
industry had been placed in a good position, putting the poor man to

[94] *New Grub Street* (1891), i. 170–1.
[95] Mrs Valentine, *The Young Woman's Book*, 235.   [96] Ibid.

evident shame by her foolish and ignorant mistakes—such as 'I was a-sayin' to Villiam today that I 'ate 'ock, it gives me an nedache'.[97]

Provided with this negative exemplar of the failed helpmeet, it is all too clear that 'proper' wifely duty includes, and indeed demands, knowledge of those linguistic proprieties which befit the status of one's husband, lest, like 'poor Villiam', he is to be demeaned by such unladylike infelicities in his spouse. The spectre of such marital embarrassment, complete here with its range of 'ignorant' markers (amongst which [h]-loss is all too conspicuous appearing as it does in *ate*, *'ock*, and *nedache*), is held up in warning, the utility of a pronouncing dictionary subsequently being recommended for all those who are, as a result, rendered 'anxious for self-culture'.[98]

Other texts mirror the same preoccupations and the same ideological bias in the beliefs and ideals endorsed. *The Young Housekeeper*, for example, issuing detailed directions to the woman newly married, similarly includes a section on the 'proprieties of speech' which are to be regarded as compatible with this new social role. This enumerates a selection of female linguistic stereotypes ('the young housekeeper' of the title is to have speech 'neither too loud nor too low', and a 'loquacious propensity' is to be avoided),[99] as well as emphasizing the importance of being 'correct in accent'. It gives, for example, the stringent recommendation: 'learn when to use and when to omit the aspirate *h*. This is an indispensable mark of a good education.'[100] The consequences attendant upon lack of wifely application in this respect are, however, nowhere brought out more clearly than in Hill's own book on *The Aspirate*.

Discussing the ways in which [h]-dropping was habitually attended with marked social stigma and disgrace in the nineteenth century, Hill provides one of the most complete accounts of its role in assigning the social values of impropriety, inferior status, and inadequate refinement. 'The modern English', as he notes, 'have given a fictitious importance to the letter by making the correct use of it a mark by which refined and educated people may be differentiated from those that are not.'[101] Seen as concisely establishing affinities of breeding and cultivation, its importance inside, as well as outside, the marital condition is given equal prominence is Hill's text. In marriage, spouses must, he

[97] Ibid.   [98] Ibid. 243.   [99] *The Young Housekeeper*, 8.
[100] Ibid.   [101] Hill, *The Aspirate*, 5.

states with some rigour, be compatible in terms of [h]-usage just as in their other tastes and habits. 'When a question about h's arises between husband and wife', he points out, 'forgiveness on either side is most difficult.'[102] Thus presented as a source of manifest discord between prospective partners, its effects were such as should not be underestimated; the 'Proper Wife', like the 'Proper Lady', was to be responsive to issues of correctness on this matter. Hill, 'without fear of contradiction', offers a general rule on this head: 'So important indeed is the question of the use of h's in England, . . . that no marriage should take place between persons whose ideas on this subject do not agree.'[103]

Like Mrs Valentine, Hill is armed with appropriate examples with which to illustrate the dire effects of the failure to heed such advice. His references are, however, rather more specific, drawing on the 'Clitheroe Abduction case':

Our readers may remember that one of the grievances felt by the wife against the husband in the Clitheroe Abduction case was that he accused her of dropping her h's. 'On sitting down to dinner', said the lady, according to the *Lancashire Evening Post,* 'an incident occurred which affected me greatly, coming as it did so immediately after the marriage. I made some observation to Mr. Jackson, when he suddenly said. "Where are your h's?" I felt very much incensed, but I said nothing, though I thought it a very strange beginning.'[104]

Leading as it did to such unfortunate consequences, Hill's maxim on the importance of perfect congruity in patterns of [h]-usage and its role in securing conjugal bliss scarcely needed to be made clearer.

Reinforcing the advice given by the anonymous H. W. H. in *How to Choose a Wife* ('Perpetual nausea and disgust will be your doom if you marry a vulgar and uncultivated woman'),[105] the emphasis placed on perfect linguistic propriety as yet another aspect of wifely duty merely reiterates those heightened pressures to conform to the highest models of behaviour which were constantly imposed on women by these iterations of feminine ideology and the prescriptive dicta which they frequently incorporated. *Matrimony: Or, What Married Life Is, and How to Make the Best of It,* a text which went through two editions within its first year

---

[102] Ibid. 13–14.   [103] Ibid. 13.   [104] Ibid. 14–15.
[105] H. W. H., *How to Choose a Wife* (London, 1854), 51.

of publication, offers advice markedly similar in kind, devoting chapter 3 to the principle that 'Marriages should be Equal in Elocution'. The central precept endorsed here is that 'equality gives pleasure, inequality pain', but again the greatest attention is directed to the shame, embarrassment, and anguish of the husband who must needs endure the mangled articulations, and infelicitous syntax of his wife:

Suppose the husband to be the better educated and the more refined. In this case, he is almost sure to find his wife's domestic arrangements far below his standard of taste; hence his eye is offended. Her language too is characterised by grammatical blunders in arrangement, pronunciation, and the improper use of words; hence his ear is offended. Whilst painfully feeling his situation in this respect, he kindly and earnestly endeavours to raise up his wife to his own standard. In some rare cases, he succeeds in a good measure; but we believe in the majority of cases, it is a complete failure.[106]

The depiction of this unfortunate circumstance continues on a note of pathos surpassing even that invoked by the Hon. Henry H. in lamenting his own use and abuse. 'In case of failure', as the (male) author continues, 'the only alternative is, that he must be constantly finding fault, or in silent and gloomy despair, move on every week, day, and hour, all his life severely tried and hampered with the natural and necessary results of an unequal education.'[107] Wives, mend your speech, is of course again the relevant maxim which was endorsed.

Within these particular manifestations of the standard ideology, similar pressures were frequently also to be imposed on the nineteenth-century woman in her role as a mother, not least since it was from her own use of language that the child would learn its first words. Her role as guardian of 'proper' language could, in such instances, assume even greater value, influencing the diffusion of the 'best' (or 'worst') language in itself. Writers commonly stressed the total receptivity of the child to the standards set by the mother, whether in word or in deed. 'The first days of humanity are under woman's guidance', *Woman's Worth* affirmed: 'impressions are then formed never to be obliterated—the young mind

---

[106] J. Maynard, *Matrimony: Or, What Married Life Is, and How to Make the Best of It,* 2nd edn. (London, 1866), 98–9.
[107] Ibid. 99.

is then as pliable as wax, and will receive any form or stamp. The bent of future character is formed in childhood—early habits, early impressions, are never entirely obliterated.'[108] Given such strictures, the responsibilities of the mother in terms of precept and example were rarely represented as negligible: 'What influence may not a mother exert? She is a pattern which her children are constantly striving to imitate; her actions are made the models of theirs.'[109]

Her accents too were to be placed within these same paradigms, and if she had not already rendered them 'pure' and 'correct' in her role as proper 'helpmeet' for her husband, it was more than ever necessary for the mother to master such needful proprieties of speech for the benefit of her offspring. *The Mother's Home Book* offers plentiful advice on this head, urging the mother to improve her speech and to act, in effect, as articulatory instructress (and an agent of standardization) for her children:

It is decidedly the duty of the mother to pronounce every word she utters distinctly, and in a proper tone, carefully avoiding, and strictly forbidding, the mis-pronunciation of any word. To accomplish this end more surely, the mother ought to speak in such a manner as will give the child the opportunity of observing the motion of her mouth, as well as hearing the sound of her voice.[110]

Other comments are similarly clear and to the point, endorsing yet again the ways in which woman's role was, as the author of *Woman: What She Is and What She Should Be* had professed, simply 'relative to man'. As Farquhar declared in this context, 'woman is ever moulding the future man', and it was for this reason that the 'tones of her voice' were to be important: they will, he added, 'have given a stamp, before infancy is past, to his character, which after years may deepen, but seldom, if ever, obliterate'.[111] Sub-texts of guilt, responsibility, and the need for perfect conformity to the canons of 'good' speech, are again all too obvious. Many other texts were eloquent in a similar strain: 'the mother is an educator of God's own appointment',[112] proclaimed *The Popular Educator*, stressing that, in consequence, the

[108] *Woman's Worth*, 21.   [109] Ibid., 28–9.
[110] *The Mother's Home Book* (London, 1879), 199.
[111] B. A. Farquhar, *Female Education* (London, 1851), 4.
[112] *The Popular Educator* (London, 1864), 175.

purity, refinement, and propriety urged upon her from her own earliest years would necessarily find true meaning in the creation of the appropriate linguistic environment for the education of her child in the nuances of 'standard' speech. Even the phonetician Walter Ripman, in spite of his claims as a scientist of language, saw this as a means by which the standard variety of speech would, in all its purity, be properly imparted to the young in the twentieth century too. The superior sensibilities of women to the social values of speech would take on unquestioned utility in this respect. Girls, he notes, are 'particularly appreciative of the social advantages of good speech, and quick to copy the models supplied by their mistresses'; this facility was of undoubted value since 'in their turn, especially as mothers . . . , they carry on the work of imparting good speech'.[113] As in the comments of *The Young Lady's Book*, women were, in the earlier years of this century, evidently still to be regarded as the guardians of language in matters of phonological as well as lexical nicety. Just as in nineteenth-century texts, the same preconceptions (and attendant stereotypes) endure: 'the exquisitely feminine duties of the nursery', as Rosa Nouchette Carey articulated in one of her novels, were in such senses often deemed to include the inculcation of non-localized norms of speech, the advantages of which were clearly insuperable: 'What an advantage to parents to have their little ones brought into the earliest contact with refined speech and cultivated manners—their infant ears not inoculated with barbarous English'.[114]

The most detailed exposition of this ideal, however, comes not in fiction but in *The Young Mother*, a text produced by the Religious Tract Society in 1857. It sets forth with precision the articulatory niceties which the 'good' mother must impart, as well as laying due emphasis on that propriety which will thereby of course also be transmitted:

A sensible mother will uniformly make it a principle never to teach anything that will have to be unlearned. Hence . . . she will take care to pronounce every word distinctly and in a proper tone; and, especially when the child is learning to articulate, she will so speak as to give him an opportunity of observing the motion of her mouth as well as hearing the sound of her voice. Those who have not had experience in the early teaching of children,

---

[113] W. Ripman, *English Phonetics* (London, 1931), 7.
[114] *Not Like Other Girls*, i. 130.

can scarcely imagine how much this will obviate difficulties, and assist in forming the habit of reading with correctness and propriety.[115]

The elocutionary precepts absorbed by the woman herself in her youth are in such ways to be rendered into practical skills, as, with due care, she is to impart the nuances of 'talking proper', and, in effect, to 'standardize' the accent of the child from the moment of his (or indeed her) first words. 'The first lesson which a child should be taught, is how to articulate correctly', as *The Mother's Home Book* added,[116] stressing the ways in which the mother was to watch not only her own words (in line with the manifold tenets of propriety, social as well as linguistic) but also those of her child. Mispronunciations suffered to go uncorrected at this stage would later prove ineradicable. It was the mother's clear duty to correct, to refine, and to perfect. Moreover, any breaches of such duty would later be all too apparent, just as the negligent failings of mothers in the past were still evinced in the problems which so many continued to face over the articulation of [h]. This too was to be the mother's fault: 'The habit of incorrect and careless speaking may, in innumerable instances, be traced to the errors of childhood being unchecked, or, in truth, not being pointed out as errors at all. The non-aspiration of the letter *h*, or its aspiration in the wrong place, is one of the most prominent of these defects.'[117] Giving a list of other articulatory oversights on the part of mothers of the past, the author adds for the benefit of those of the present: 'all faults of this kind ought to be at once discouraged, and some penalty attached to a repetition of them.' Whether this penalty is to be imposed on mother, or on child, is not, however, made clear.

If possible, *The Popular Educator* went still further in these respects, recommending attendance in the nursery of a cultivated English home for each and every aspirant speaker of 'proper' English. The supervision of a mother versed in these true proprieties of speech is thus envisaged as the one sure means to escape the taints and errors which otherwise might, all too easily, affect modes of speech:

Of all teachers of English grammar the best is a well-educated English mother. Hence it is evident that a nursery in a cultivated English home, is the best school of English grammar. As a matter of fact, it is in such

---

[115] *The Young Mother* (London, 1857), 165.
[116] *The Mother's Home Book*, 198. [117] Ibid. 202–3.

schools that, among the upper classes of the country, the young learn to speak correct English from their earliest days. Were all English children trained in such schools, the language would be everywhere well, and grammatically spoken. Consequently, could we place our students in cultivated nurseries, they would soon speak and write their mother tongue with correctness and propriety.[118]

Being only a manual of self-help, such a solution is unfortunately not possible for the readers of *The Popular Educator*, though it does, however, promise the next best thing in its endeavours to 'bring forth and set before them in a living and organic form the spoken language of such nurseries'.

Women's linguistic responsibilities were as a result not slight. Popular stereotypes of them as wives, as mothers, as ladies, and simply as females in their own right indeed presented behavioural norms and expectations which exacted conformity to the highest models in terms of speech and especially in terms of accent. Ideologies of 'talking proper' and corresponding ones of 'proper' femininity tended, as this illustrates, to exhibit a remarkable harmony, the former regularly being used to enhance prescriptions (and proscriptions) within the latter. A marker of the truly feminine, such precepts were not disregarded lightly, and though the New Woman of the latter parts of the century attempted to escape such shackles, popular attitudes to language and to behaviour depicted her conduct as deviating from the norms of true womanhood, and from that delicacy of language by which it should be characterized. That independence from the formal notions of propriety endorsed by this alternative social construct was, of course, necessarily to be constructed as 'other'; espousing alternative ideological strategies, the 'New Woman' evidently posed a threat to the established behavioural norms and ideals (including those of language), and her manifestations were accordingly stigmatized in a variety of ways. Gissing's short story 'Comrades in Arms' can, for example, be taken as representative in this context, with its effective depiction of the 'anti-feminine' Miss Childerstone, a journalist, portrayed as gradually 'growing less feminine' in both language and manners: 'She turned to the waiter, "Roast mutton—potatoes—bread. And—soda-water" . . . "Thanks, old man; I am better acquainted with my needs than you are".'[119]

---

[118] *The Popular Educator*, 175.
[119] G. Gissing, *Human Odds and Ends. Stories and Sketches* (London, 1898), 2.

More typical representations of the feminine tradition in the guise of 'propriety' or 'respectability' nevertheless tended to continue unabated, the leader in the magazine the *Lady* in February 1893, for example, still exuding congratulation on the sheer abundance of those rules which, for women, demand conformity and which can in turn be used as markers of their 'proper' and undeviating identity:

> It is a good thing for everyone that there are rules by which Society, now that it has become so vast and complicated a machine, is held together and enabled to work smoothly and easily . . . it changes very fast and you must keep up with it or you will stand out and no gentlewoman wants to attract observation or comment or she is not a gentlewoman.[120]

Given the prevalence and longevity of language attitudes in these particular cultural conceptions, it is as a result perhaps hardly surprising that works aiming to set forth the canons of propriety (linguistic and otherwise) for the benefit of a female audience seem to have achieved notable popularity; *Etiquette for the Ladies*, in its fourth edition in 1837, had, by 1846, reached a total of a further twenty-nine editions. New and popular periodicals such as the *Englishwoman's Magazine*, or the *Lady's Companion and Monthly Magazine* fulfilled the same function, supplying that advice on the social niceties depicted as necessary for the woman in her various social roles as wife or spinster, schoolgirl, and mother. Nor, given this abundance of information on such 'proper' behaviour, is it entirely unexpected that a number of writers attest, with equal consistency, the existence of heightened female sensitivities in this respect. *Etiquette for Ladies and Gentlemen* depicts women as 'more susceptible of external polish than Man is', and develops this idea in specifically linguistic, albeit generalized, terms: 'She is imitative in a great degree, and speedily catches the tone and manner of the people with whom she associates.'[121] *The Manners of the Aristocracy* likewise stresses the superior responsiveness of women in this context: 'women acknowledge more readily than men that universal passport to consideration—perfect manners.' Advice proffered for their improvement is apparently readily

[120] Cited in L. Davidoff, *The Best Circles: Society Etiquette and the Season* (London, 1973), 66.
[121] *Etiquette for Ladies and Gentlemen*, 10.

accepted, and acted upon: 'women are quicker in profiting by the hints contained in such volumes, and are less likely to be led astray by any errors they may contain.'[122] The *Family Herald* in 1844 offered similar certainties to its readers: 'Young ladies learn *manners*, as they are denominated, rapidly, because they have a genius for the study.'

It was of course social, cultural, as well as linguistic pressures, rather than this laudatory 'genius', which in reality combined to reinforce these patterns of social sensibility towards language which are so often singled out as characteristic of women in such accounts. Language attitudes, as we have seen, can indeed be effective in influencing patterns of behaviour, as well as of belief, in terms of these notions of 'proper' language, often encouraging convergence in the more formal registers of the language when people (both men and women) are concentrating particularly on what they are saying. Nineteenth-century texts, however, often stress the superior responsiveness of women in these ways and, more empirically, the same patterns are again brought out in twentieth-century data on linguistic behaviour, so that the researches of Peter Trudgill, William Labov, and Suzanne Romaine, for example, have all recorded greater levels of receptivity for women (of all social groups) to the variants recognized as most statusful within the wider speech community.[123] These patterns moreover seem to emerge both in evidence of language attitudes by means of subjective reaction tests, and in the more statistical surveys carried out on individual variables so that, for example, women regularly utilize higher frequencies of [h] or [ŋ] (and lower proportions of [Ø] and [n] in relevant words) than might perhaps otherwise be expected.

Certainly, in the nineteenth century, those widely attested patterns of proscription which, as we have seen, habitually rely on the censure of 'vulgar' enunciations against those presented as infinitely more 'polite' and 'characteristic of the best speakers', were especially prominent in contemporary attitudes to 'proper' female behaviour, as well as being embedded in much contemporary writing, including that of an overtly non-prescriptive nature

---

[122] *The Manners of the Aristocracy. By One of Themselves* (London, 1881), 2–3.
[123] See e.g. Labov, *Sociolinguistic Patterns*; Trudgill, *The Social Stratification of English in Norwich*; and S. Romaine, 'Postvocalic /r/ in Scottish English: Sound Change in Progress?', in P. Trudgill (ed.), *Sociolinguistic Patterns in British English* (London, 1978), 144–57.

(such as fiction). It would therefore not be entirely unexpected that value-judgements of this kind might indeed exert some corresponding pressure on the actual linguistic behaviour of women long conditioned by prevailing feminine ideologies to be alert to the finest shades of delicacy and refinement, especially in their more formal speech. Comments made by a number of observers who are more reputable in terms of phonetics and the emergent descriptive tradition seem to bear this out. With reference to enunciations of [h], for example, Henry Sweet himself observed that the socially orientated prescription which articulations of this sound commonly attracted seemed to be far more effective for women than men: 'The Cockney dialect seems very ugly to an educated Englishman or woman' because, as he stressed, 'he— and still more she—lives in a perpetual terror of being taken for a Cockney, and a perpetual struggle to preserve that *h* which has now been lost in most of the local dialects of England, both North and South.'[124] Since contemporary constructions of ideal femininity exhorted avoidance of 'vulgarity', 'provinciality', or other linguistic infelicities wherever possible, such a heightened awareness of the shibboleths of [h]-usage would, of course, be fairly likely, not least since, as we have seen, [h] in itself had commonly assumed a role as a marker not only of the educated, but also of the truly 'ladylike'.

In terms of actual sounds, however, the use of /h/ was naturally not the sole phonemic nicety by which command of this necessarily 'ladylike' language could be revealed, and a number of other realizations came to share in these propagated notions of gender and propriety, and hence also in statements about the increased responsiveness of women to prevailing language attitudes (and contemporary stigmatization) in these contexts. Equally prominent in discussions about the 'proper' use of language, as well as its associated conventions of feminine propriety, are, for example, corresponding deliberations over the 'correct' sound to be accorded to the use of *a* in words such as *fast, bath*. Pronounced in the middle of the seventeenth century with a short *a* [æ] (similar to that employed in modern realizations of *mat, match*, for instance), the transition to that lengthened [ɑ:] which has now become a characteristic marker of RP was, as we have seen, not accomplished

---

[124] Sweet, *A Primer of Spoken English* (London, 1890), pp. vi–vii.

without a certain amount of controversy.[125] It was some considerable time before the use of [ɑ:] securely assumed those social values with which it is now imbued.

The actual situation was of course, as already indicated, somewhat more complex than prescriptive accounts suggest, and it seems clear that [æ] and [ɑ:] coexisted to an extent among both 'polite' and 'vulgar'. Even Benjamin Smart, in spite of his favoured binary absolutes, admitted in 1812 that use of the lengthened variant is in reality 'adhered to by some speakers above the vulgar',[126] conceding likewise that the realization [æ] which he himself advocates is, by some, considered 'affected', a position which is supported by a number of other writers. Such descriptive impulses do clarify in some respects the nuances of linguistic reality (and its attendant variations), but nevertheless they do not impede the barrage of comment, liberally endowed with social, cultural, and aesthetic specifications, which continued to surround this sound change in progress. Moreover, given the fact that both of these variants were imbued with connotations capable of negative interpretation, the one of 'vulgarity' and 'cockneyism', the other of 'affectation' and the 'mincing', it is not perhaps entirely unexpected that fashionable prescription should seize on another, intermediate sound as the one which was to be adopted by those desirous of true elegance. It is, in turn, this which becomes so associated with notions of femininity and the accents of the Proper Lady during the nineteenth and early twentieth centuries.

Realized neither in the 'broad' [u.] nor in the 'mincing' [æ], notions of a 'middle sound' located somewhere between the two can in fact be traced back to the early evidence of Cooper in 1687, whose descriptions suggest something like [æ:] in relevant words. The difference in the nineteenth century, however, lies in the new connotations which such a sound acquired in the joint realms of linguistic etiquette and prescriptive theory. Smart in 1836, for example, maintains a system of values slightly different to those he had set forth in 1812, and, countering the 'vulgarity' of [ɑ:] with the 'affectation' of [æ], he now concludes that 'a medium between the two extremes is the practice of the best speakers'.[127] 'Avoid a too broad or too slender pronunciation of the vowel *a*, as in . . .

---

[125] See pp. 90–7.
[126] Smart, *Grammar of English Sounds*, p. xxv.   [127] Ibid., §17.

glass, pass', likewise cautions Smith in 1858, recommending instead
the avoidance of 'the extremes of affectation and vulgarity' by the
more 'elegant' selection of a middle sound.[128] Alger in 1832, Longmuir in 1864, and, most importantly perhaps, Ellis in 1869 all
unite in commenting on the marked affiliations of this compromise
'middle sound' with accents of intentionally greater delicacy, status,
and correctness.[129]

Alexander Ellis is, of course, a linguistic observer characterized
both by his intended objectivity and his attempted empiricism,
features which he deliberately sets against the bias and preconception which had so often pervaded the comments of his predeces-
sors (and which were, in fact, also to infiltrate the work of not a
few of his successors). Though not exempt from failings of his
own in the notions of a 'standard' he deployed,[130] Ellis's evidence
is yet presented with a clarity of understanding which is often
absent from other writers on the language. Aware of the factors
outside language which may operate to influence its use, he stresses,
for example, like modern sociolinguists, the importance of variables
which are dependent on speaker and style, such as age, status,
formality, and, in addition, gender, in all considerations of language
use. As he points out, 'the sounds of language are very fleeting.
Each element occupies only a very minute part of a second.' In
discussions of pronunciation, it is therefore necessary to take into
account the fact that such 'elements' do not exist in a vacuum,
either in terms of sound, or indeed of society: 'many', he states,
'are much hurried over, and all are altered by combination, expression, pitch, intonation, emotion, age, sex'.[131] This position is
amplified in further comments, the role of gender as a significant
speaker variable again making its appearance: 'Every speaker has
individualities, and it is only by an intimate acquaintance with the
habits of *many* speakers that we can discover what were individualities in our first instructor. Not only have age and sex much
influence, but the very feeling of the moment sways the speaker.'[132]

This recognition of the import of gender in considerations of
speech and its analysis is not merely restricted to general principles,

---

[128] C. W. Smith, *Hints on Elocution and Public Speaking* (London, 1858), 34.
[129] See p. 93.
[130] See L. C. Mugglestone, 'A. J. Ellis, "Standard English" and the Prescriptive
Tradition', *Review of English Studies*, NS 39 (1988), 87–92.
[131] Ellis, *Early English Pronunciation*, iv. 1088.   [132] Ibid.

but it appears equally in Ellis's discussion of individual sounds and sound changes. 'We merely wish to know what *are* the sounds which educated English men and women really use when they speak their native language', he declares in setting forth his aims.[133] 'Educated English women' appear most often, however, in Ellis's comments on the realization of *a* in lengthening position, and particularly in his accounts of a female preference for the use of [æ], and, more especially, for the use of a 'middle sound' in what seems to be [æ:]. A range of currently acceptable realizations for *a* in these positions is, as we would expect, described by Ellis, entirely in keeping with his avowed intention to describe 'what *is*, rather than decide what *should* be' in language.[134] It is nevertheless evident that, as today, the tendency to favour [ɑ:] as the dominant prestige marker was well established and that it was indeed becoming more so. In spite of this, it is also apparent that, for those sensitive to the shades of prescriptive symbolism, the old stereotypes of 'vulgarity' and 'cockneyism' surrounding this [ɑ:] had by no means fallen entirely into disuse. The intentionally 'educated' and 'refined', as we have already seen, instead favoured other, more 'aesthetic' realizations. Ladies, urged to make manifest their superior delicacies and sensibility by the all-encompassing canons of feminine conduct, likewise seem to have been influenced by such perceptions.

Ellis notes, for example, that 'ladies in the South and many educated gentlemen' tend to adopt those elegant 'middle sounds' earlier praised by Smart.[135] Similarly, 'those who do not like broad sounds' (such as [ɑ:]) prefer instead [æ:]; this select company comprises, as Ellis adds, 'especially ladies'.[136] Such stated female preferences for the use of more 'delicate' middle sounds are alluded to on a number of other occasions. On page 593 Ellis again observes that [æ:] 'is sometimes heard in 19. [nineteenth century], especially from ladies, as a thinner utterance of (aa) than (aah) would be', and he verifies this apparent gender-preferential variation with reference to his own transcriptions from a performance of *King John*: 'In a performance of *King John*, I heard Mrs Charles Kean speak of "(kææf) skin", with great emphasis, and Mr Alfred Wigan immediately repeated it as "(kaaf) skin", with equal distinctness.'[137]

[133] Ibid. iv. 1089–90.   [134] Ibid. iv. 1204.
[135] Ibid. ii. 597.   [136] Ibid. iv. 1148.
[137] Ibid. The (aa) in Ellis's notation can be taken as signifying [ɑ:].

Notions of social value, and attendant value-judgements, of the use of these sounds had long been made explicit in writings of the prescriptive tradition, and these are given some prominence in Ellis's explanations of this pattern. Placing the social clichés of prescription in inverted commas, Ellis records that it is the 'delicate' and 'refined' who avoid the use of [ɑ:] which they consider 'too broad'. More than that, however, he links such avoidance to conceptions of propriety firmly vested in the visual authority of the written language: 'this dread arises from the fear that if they said (aask, laaf), they would be accused of the vulgarity of inserting an *r*, and when *arsk*, *larf*, are written, they "look so very vulgar".'[138] Of course <r> had commonly been used as a diacritic of length since the loss of rhoticity in final and post-vocalic positions in the eighteenth century (though, as already discussed, prescriptive fictions had resolutely endeavoured to suggest that only amongst 'illiterate speakers' was such 'deviation' common).[139] Notions of 'illiteracy' and associated 'incorrectness' clearly again come into play here and, as Ellis infers, it is the perceived 'repulsion of such sounds which drives the educated, and especially ladies, into the thinness of (ah, æ)'.[140]

Such aesthetic sensibilities towards the use of language and pronunciation had indeed formed a constituent part of feminine ideology, many writers, as we have seen, deliberately emphasizing the detrimental effect of perceived 'inelegance' and 'vulgarity' in conceptions of ladylike identity. The Reverend D. Williams, for example, stressing in general the incontrovertible credentials of breeding and refinement presented within nuances of voice, gives heightened emphasis to their importance as social signifiers in the feminine ideal: 'the most beautiful young female, who silently forms a kind of divinity, is', he opines, 'reduced at once to common earth, when we hear a few inelegant words from her lips.'[141] Domestic angels were to require equally angelic voices, and manifestations of superior linguistic delicacy and refinement were prized. As Ellis surmises, such commonly expressed attitudes could well

---

[138] Ibid. This attitude is of course precisely that exploited by many novelists in the nineteenth century who, wishing to indicate 'vulgarity' of speech, transform *laugh* into *larf*, or *fast* into *farst*, relying on this graphemic deviation to supply the intended connotations. See also pp. 231–2.

[139] See pp. 99–102.   [140] Ellis, *Early English Pronunciation*, iv. 1152.

[141] Williams, *Composition*, 5.

have influenced to some extent the patterns of variation he describes, the connotative values of 'middle sounds' in turn ensuring their adoption as an external signal of that delicacy revered as a marker of the appropriately 'ladylike' and 'refined'.

Ellis is not alone in his observations on this matter, and the phonetician Walter Ripman in the early years of the twentieth century likewise attests similar feminine preferences for realizations other than [ɑː]. In *The Sounds of Spoken English* (1906), he thus records that '[a] and [æ] occur, particularly in the speech of ladies', and he comments further on the value-judgements, and associated evaluative paradigms, which he assumes lie behind these patterns of variation: 'It is sometimes found that precise speakers, through an excessive desire to avoid any suspicion of cockney leanings in their speech, substitute [a] for [ɑː] . . . ; it is particularly ladies of real or would-be gentility who commit this mistake.'[142] The fact that this is specified as a 'mistake' underlines, however, a shift in attendant social sensibilities. From remarks Ripman makes elsewhere, it becomes clear that pronunciations with [ɑː], as in present-day English, were assuming the dominant role as prestige marker in relevant words, ousting even perceptions of that long-attested and ladylike 'delicacy' with which 'middle sounds' had traditionally been imbued. In the second edition of *The Sounds of Spoken English*, published in 1914, these references do not appear.

Both Ripman and Ellis (as well as Sweet) are, of course, phoneticians, ostensibly aiming therefore to give objective rather than subjective accounts of language use. Certainly the details they provide on these particular facets of language offer something potentially more than the mass of general prescription about those superior delicacies in speech which, ideally, the lady is to make manifest. All three certainly make marked attempts to move from language attitudes to something of the linguistic realities of usage as they perceived it. In some ways therefore, their evidence could also be seen as paralleling the insights into language and gender available from modern sociolinguistics; just as Sweet records this greater female preference for the use of the 'proper' [h] in realizations of relevant words, so do Trudgill's (rather more statistical investigations) in twentieth-century Norwich record the same thing, albeit in far more detail. As he reveals, women in all social groups

---

[142] Ripman, *Sounds of Spoken English*, 55.

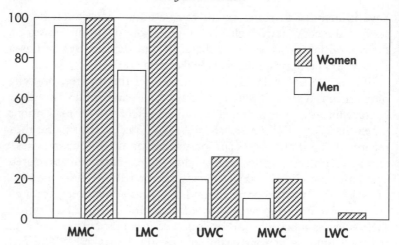

FIG. 4.1. Histogram for (ŋ), showing differences based on class and
sex

tend to adopt higher frequencies of [h] in contradistinction to
[Ø], or [ɪŋ] in contradistinction to [ɪn] than do men of the same
age and social ranking, as is shown in the histogram (from Coates,
1986) in Figure 4.1.[143]

Such findings form a staple of the quantitative research carried
out by Labov in New York, Trudgill in Norwich, Newbrook in
Wirral, or Romaine in Edinburgh. Irrespective of location, all
these studies reveal the significant operation of gender as a speaker
variable, marked for women in the systematic tendency, in the
patterns of variation which emerge, to use a smaller percentage of
the variants stigmatized within prevailing language attitudes as less
'correct', and especially in their more formal speech. As in that
(admittedly far less empirical) evidence cited by Ellis or Ripman,
the social values with which variants are imbued do indeed seem
to lead to patterns of preferential variation which are aligned quite
clearly with notions of gender.

The similar use in modern sociolinguistics of self-evaluation tests,
in which the facts of observed usage are compared with what
speakers *think* they say, also bears out patterns of distinctive gender
identities which are constructed through, and within language.

[143] J. Coates, *Women, Men and Language* (London, 1986), 64.

Female informants regularly (though not, of course, invariably) attest that they use a greater proportion of the statusful forms associated with usage of the standard variety than they do, in fact, actually employ, a fact which likewise bears out the import of language attitudes in this context. Such patterns of female 'over-reporting' are, however, to be placed alongside corresponding patterns of 'under-reporting' in evidence obtained from men questioned in the same studies. Signally unlike women, male speakers seem instead to assume that they use less rather than more prestigious variants of language than actually appear in their speech, a distribution which perhaps indicates the existence of differing notions of status and different norms of 'appropriate' language.

The explanations presented for these disparities within modern linguistic evidence have, predictably, been many and various, ranging from notions of the greater 'politeness' of women (in keeping with their status as a subordinate group), through interpretations based on a greater female sensitivity to notions of status *per se*, and including the frequent discussion of assumptions in which, in the absence of ways in which to mark other aspects of status by means of property or occupation, women have instead traditionally prioritized the social significance of language. In terms of the nineteenth century, such explanations can appear attractive. Certainly female identity tended to be defined (outside of language) in particularly male terms of reference; as Mrs Gaskell noted in *Cranford*, 'a married woman takes her husband's rank by the strict laws of precedence' while an unmarried women simply 'retains the station her father occupied'.[144] Legal statements enshrined the same processes of assimilation, and Sir William Blackstone's *Commentaries on the Laws of England* set forth the fundamental status divides which allowed incorporation of female identity within male, but not male within female. As Joan Perkin comments on this phenomenon, 'In Orwellian language', the woman after marriage 'became an "unperson".'[145]

The recognition of such patterns did indeed seem to inspire a marked female attention to other aspects of social identity. Davidoff notes, for example, of the social meanings subsumed within the nuances of dress, that 'every cap, bow, streamer, ruffle, fringe,

[144] Mrs Gaskell, *Cranford* (London, 1853), ed. E. P. Watson (Oxford, 1972), 143.
[145] J. Perkin, *Women and Marriage in Nineteenth-Century England* (London, 1990), 2.

bustle, glove and other elaboration symbolised some status category for the female wearer'.[146] Appearance is, as we have seen, indeed often foregrounded in contemporary conceptions of the 'lady' and her associated markers, and language too is regularly included in such frameworks; Ellis himself, in his accounts of ladylike preferences for the use of 'elegant' middle sounds, stresses the notion of appearance in partial explanation for this propensity, as does Sweet. Writers such as David Williams in the middle of the century were still more explicit on the adverse affects of 'inelegant' language upon female identity and appearance; using language without the requisite connotations of refinement can, he asserts, destroy entirely the angelic image which women otherwise might, and moreover, should create.[147] The education of girls was also to place regular emphasis on the significance of how they looked, behaved, and spoke as elements within the appearance they were to cultivate. Within prevailing social, cultural, and language attitudes, such features were presented as integral to their attractiveness, and their future success in life. As the promoter (and critic) of women's education Maria Grey attests of the young girl in nineteenth-century society, 'appearance [is] the one object for which she is taught to strive'.[148] Or as Hannah More had earlier noted at the end of the eighteenth century, it was behaviour and appearance of this order, rather than knowledge *per se* which in itself constituted the best proof of female education: '[it] is not often like the learning of men, to be reproduced in some literary composition, nor ever in any learned profession; but it is to come out in conduct.'[149]

Language, widely proclaimed by prevailing tenets of 'proper' behaviour as an undoubted marker of 'refinement', could thus logically be expected to take on heightened importance within the feminine context. Just as Trudgill in the twentieth century raises the greater significance of appearance for women in their construction of gender and identity as a potential explanation of the greater incidence of prestige forms habitually found in the speech of women, so too in the nineteenth century would similar patterns, from this point of view, tend to agree with this hypothesis.

---

[146] Davidoff, *The Best Circles*, 93.   [147] See p. 198.
[148] M. Grey and E. Shirreff, *Thoughts on Self-Culture. Addressed to Women* (London, 1854), 135.
[149] More, *Strictures on the Modern System of Female Education*, ii. 1.

Isolating another cultural stereotype endowed with continued validity, Trudgill hence draws attention to the fact that women and men have traditionally been evaluated differently by the outside world, men particularly by what they do (though other factors can also be important), but women especially by how they look, and by the external markers which go to make up appearance as a whole. He suggests therefore that pronunciation too may be subsumed for women within this notion of 'appearance', a notion which thus might usefully serve in the interpretation of this often greater use of 'proper' variants by women, outside that often-propagated belief in a greater female sensitivity to notions of status in its own right.

This hypothesis, though not developed further by Trudgill, is, as we have seen, one given potential support in a number of nineteenth-century writings on language and on gender. There are, however, other ways of looking at this problem. Self-evaluation tests, as already indicated, seem to confirm marked differences in the identities (and preferred identities) which men and women own by means of language. Though no parallels to suggest diachronic patterns of male under-reporting can be obtained from the nineteenth century, the affinities between gender and language thereby revealed nevertheless remain of interest, again in terms of the explanations which may be offered. Modern conceptions of overt, and conversely, of covert prestige are, for example, often introduced in attempted explanation of the resulting patterns of gender and variation, being used to confirm similarly contrastive applications of status which can themselves be influenced by behavioural norms and expectations dependent on gender. Masculine values, as a number of writers have asserted, are often perceived as residing in greater measure in the forms of the vernacular in contradistinction to those of the 'standard'. Associated with the connotative values of 'toughness' or 'macho' strength and behaviour, such vernacular variants, as well as preferences for their use, can, from such a psycho-symbolic position, be used to reveal the existence of a form of 'covert prestige'. This, it is stated, can in turn materially influence self-reporting of speech by male informants. The forms of the 'standard' are, as we might expect, conversely endowed with 'overt prestige', and with associations of the 'polite' and 'proper' in which cultural constructions of the feminine excel. Cultural prescription, and its attendant linguistic stereotypes, would as a result still seem to correlate 'feminine' with notions of superior linguistic propriety, allying both with the 'overt prestige' of the standard variety. As Vandenhoff had stressed in 1862, for the woman, 'the speaking of her native language with purity and elegance of pronunciation . . . and an easy, fluent utterance . . . carry with them the *prestige* of refinement and high breeding'.[150] Notions of linguistic acceptability are thus, as both nineteenth- and twentieth-century accounts of language reveal, likely to be strongly conditioned by corresponding norms of gender, as indeed are their explanations. In turn, such pervasive ideas are, importantly, more than capable of conditioning actual language behaviour, as well as attitudes to language use. Norms rarely exist in a vacuum, a fact which should perhaps be kept in mind when considering the implications of that wealth of prescriptive information on 'ladylike' language and accent from centuries before our own.

As Lesley Milroy has asserted: 'although phonology is not directly linked with meaning, vernacular phonological norms typically have a social *significance* (not meaning) of maleness, youth, working class identity or whatever.'[151] In her subsequent discussion, she thus usefully moves away from the purely class-based models of behaviour which are so often adopted in these contexts, looking instead at the value of underlying stereotypes of 'masculine' and 'feminine' behaviour—such indeed as are widespread in language attitudes and which are not necessarily correlated with these (potentially problematic) notions of prestige. As we have seen throughout this book, such stereotypes can indeed be of marked value, not only in terms of language attitudes (and associated beliefs) but also in influencing actual behaviour. Evident in the avoidance of the elisions and assimilations of ordinary speech by speakers of adoptive RP (in all its heightened 'correctness'),[152] such notions of 'proper' language can also be illuminating in this context too, especially in terms of the superior proprieties of language so often stressed in prevalent cultural constructions of the feminine. As in the nineteenth century, modern twentieth-century evidence can offer compelling proof of the operation and effects

---

[150] Vandenhoff, *The Lady's Reader*, 1.

[151] L. Milroy, 'New Perspectives in the Analysis of Sex Differentiation in Language', in Bolton and Kwok (eds), *Sociolinguistics Today*, 175.

[152] See pp. 158-9.

of a ubiquitous 'double standard' with reference to gender (and gender stereotypes) in both language and society. A study by John Edwards, carried out in 1979, provides, for example, particularly striking confirmation of this fact, as well as of the pervasiveness (and influence) of these behavioural norms and expectations for women as for men.[153]

An exercise in perception, Edwards's study merely required a set of adults to note down the sex of children from tape-recordings of forty children's voices. The children were of an age before the onset of distinctive pitch differences (i.e. before the voices of the boys had broken), but nevertheless the voices of girls, as well as those of boys, were, on the whole, identified without apparent difficulty. It was, however, in the systematic patterns of mis-identification which occurred that the major interest of this study was found to lie. The children were differentiated not only by sex, but also by social level; of forty voices, twenty were from the working class, twenty from the middle, and in the mistakes made by the listeners, significant patterns of error in this context came to light. Exposing notions of behavioural norms which are clearly dependent on gender (a cultural construct), rather than on sex (a biological one), in each case of 'mistaken identity' working-class girls were misidentified as boys, while middle-class boys were perceived as girls. Girls, in other words, are expected to sound 'middle-class', while these allocations of male identity confirmed the masculine associations of working-class language as already revealed in the data of self-evaluation tests. As Edwards's data therefore suggest, these orientations are dependent not on notions of 'covert'/ 'overt' prestige, but instead on the workings of social psychology, and the social, cultural, and linguistic stereotypes which are pre-valent within it. The perceptions of a second set of adult listeners within the same study further corroborated the existence of such cultural norms. Asked to specify the values generated by the differ-ences in accent, working-class voices were rated as rougher, lower, and more masculine. Middle-class voices instead took on evalu-ations of smoothness and femininity. The existence of another stereotype in modern British society in which higher-status male

---

[153] J. R. Edwards, 'Social Class Differences and the Identification of Sex in Children's Speech', *Journal of Child Language*, 6 (1979), 121–7.

voices are regularly deemed effeminate likewise bears out these findings.[154]

Such accounts provide empirical evidence of the way in which gender is firmly embedded, in the twentieth century as in the nineteenth, in the attitudes and expectations which surround language use. Stereotypes of gender, identity, or language are, it seems, not discarded easily and their effects can still be perceptible in language behaviour (and language attitudes) in line, in many ways, with those prescriptions set out with such explicitness in the nineteenth century. In these terms, just as the cultural stereotypes of the twentieth century exert their own influences upon actual language behaviour in the context of gender, so in the nineteenth century can corresponding processes be assumed to have taken place, as women modified their actual linguistic behaviour, as Ellis and Ripman indicate, in line with that abundant proscription and prescription supplied under this head. Correlations between perceived femininity and those 'proper' accents deemed appropriate as its markers were, as we have seen, prescribed with little reserve in the nineteenth century, and their legacies are, in a number of ways, thus still made manifest in the quantitative findings of the twentieth, exemplifying those more subtle ways in which such stereotypes of 'talking like a lady' (or indeed like a 'proper man') can be encoded in language attitudes, expectations, and subsequently even in language use itself. Other comments from the nineteenth century confirm the presence of equally heightened female sensitivities to the use of other widely stigmatized forms, or to their 'proper' variants; the 'best' articulation of *ing*, the use of [hw] rather than [w] in words such as *which*, the use of the 'delicate' palatal glide in enunciations of words such as *kind* /kjaɪnd/[155] all regularly appear in the context of discussions of the greater proprieties (and greater femininity) which the Proper Lady manifested in her speech. Such stereotypical perceptions can indeed also still be manifested in modern attitudes to RP, as Elyan *et al.* have demonstrated; 'RP women', as they note, are consistently 'rated higher on the femininity trait than Northern accented females'.[156] Stereotypes can and do 'contain

---

[154] See L. Milroy, 'New Perspectives', 177.   [155] See pp. 233–4.

[156] O. Elyan, P. Smith, H. Giles, and R. Bourhis, 'RP-accented Female Speech: The Voice of Perceived Androgyny', in P. Trudgill (ed.), *Sociolinguistic Patterns*, 129.

a measure of truth', contends Deborah Cameron,[157] and it is indeed undeniable that cultural norms of appropriate language can still differ for men and women, and not only in traditional areas of linguistic taboo and the differential acceptabilities of swearing.

[157] Cameron, *The Feminist Critique of Language*, 23.

5

Literature and the Literate Speaker

THE ideal of the 'literate speaker', defined in terms of social and cultural, as well as linguistic values, was, as we have seen, adopted as an important tenet of phonemic propriety within many works on language published during the late eighteenth and nineteenth centuries.[1] It was a precept encapsulated perhaps most effectively in Dr Johnson's dictum on the nature of elegant speech ('For pronunciation the best general rule is, to consider those as the most elegant speakers who deviate least from the written words')[2] as well as in the frequent iterations this received in later years. Resulting notions of 'literacy' were applied to spoken as well as written forms, regularly influencing popular notions of correctness. As Thomas Sheridan in 1762 had, for example, adjured, 'good' speech was to be dependent upon 'giving every letter in a syllable, its due proportion of sound, according to the most approved custom of pronouncing it'.[3]

In spite of the manifest incompatibility of grapheme and phoneme in English,[4] the focus on literate speech which emerges is marked in language attitudes of the late eighteenth and nineteenth centuries. Smetham in 1774, for instance, illustrates a prevalent cultural equation in his evident belief that it was only provincial accents which deviated from the non-localized (and invariant) norms established in the written forms of words:

It may not be amiss here to mention some practices which ought always to be discouraged; namely, the pronouncing words totally different from what they are spelled, according to the dialect which prevails in the particular county where the speaker was born, or perhaps brought up; a provincial dialect should always receive a check.[5]

Glossed as 'rude' and 'unpolished' by Johnson, 'provincial' is readily incorporated into prevalent paradigms of 'knowledge' versus

---

[1] See pp. 97–9.   [2] Johnson, *Dictionary*, a2ᵛ i.
[3] Sheridan, *Course of Lectures*, 35.   [4] See p. 135.
[5] T. Smetham, *Practical Grammar*, 36.

'ignorance' in speech, drawing on associated prescriptive fictions by which such variations were necessarily flawed.[6] In these particular manifestations of the standard ideology, literate speakers (in contradistinction to the 'provincial') were to make manifest superiorities of status, education, and breeding by the assumed correlations they evinced between spelling and the spoken word. Illiterate speakers, 'those who cannot read', are conversely seen to 'catch sounds imperfectly and utter them negligently', as Johnson also averred.[7]

Such convictions arose, as Sheridan made plain, as a result of the 'habitual association of ideas' which existed between written and spoken languages. 'These two kinds of languages are so early in life associated, that it is difficult ever after to separate them; or not to suppose that there is some kind of natural connection between them', he stressed on the opening page of his *Course of Lectures in Elocution*. Dichotomies between the awareness of such principles, and their subsequent application, are, however, easily discovered in Sheridan's own work. Sound and alphabetic symbol should, for true propriety, be aligned as 'body and shadow', he declares on page 243 of the *Course*. His normative rulings on the pronunciation of unaccented syllables further exemplify susceptibilities in this respect: since the final syllables of words such as *actor, baker,* or *altar* are, in spite of their graphemic disparities, all commonly pronounced alike (in /ə/), speakers are urged to conquer such habitual 'negligence', and to articulate the sounds clearly in accordance with the letters on the page, rather than in line with the requirements of internal word-stress. Walker shared this vacillation. Likewise aware of the weaknesses in any unquestioned correlation of grapheme and phoneme, he too was nevertheless to appeal time and time again to visual authority as a guide to oral norms. On the pronunciation of the word *boatswain*, for example, he notes that though 'this word is universally pronounced in common conversation' as]bŏ'sn[, in reading aloud 'it would savour somewhat of vulgarity to contract it to a sound so very unlike the orthography'. As he adds, 'it would be advisable, therefore, in those who are not of the naval profession, to pronounce the word when they read it, distinctly as it is written'. His comments on the words *quoit, clef* and *fault* exemplify similar assumptions about the role of graphemic norms in appraisals of phonemic correctness. In

---

[6] See p. 15.   [7] Johnson, *Dictionary*, A2^r.

such ways, spelling was often to be adopted as a guide for 'correct' speech, influencing not least the rise of /h/ as social symbol (and its introduction in words such as *humble*, *herb*, and *hospital* where it had previously been absent)[8] as well the pronunciation of scores of individual words from *chap* to *forehead*, *waistcoat*, *fault*, *falcon* and *clef*.[9]

Given the prevalence of these assumptions, in prescriptive tenets as well as in popular attitudes to the language, it is perhaps hardly surprising that representations of speech in literature should trade on many of the same ideas. Authors are, in this as in other ways, a product of the age in which they live; that consciousness of the spoken word and its needful proprieties operates upon them just as on other members of the population. Sensitization to the social import of accent, prescriptive sensibilities about correctness (and its converse), perceived correlations between accent and mind, intelligence, character, status, and gender, were, as we have seen, widely discussed and disseminated as issues over the late eighteenth and nineteenth centuries. In turn, poets, authors, and dramatists rarely proved unwilling to exploit the potential thus offered to them for the depiction of the nuances of direct speech, readily manipulating the resonances of the standard ideology in line with common socio-cultural attitudes towards speech. The cultural ideal of the 'literate speaker' was in consequence frequently incorporated in literary texts, as 'gentlemen' and 'ladies' (in accordance with the stereotypes already discussed), members of the upper and middle classes and, of course, heroes and heroines were regularly given speech which reproduced the orthographical patterns of the standard language without deviation. Servants, members of the lower ranks, Cockneys and rustics were instead habitually made to deploy patterns of speech in which the absence

---

[8] See pp. 117–18.

[9] *Chap*, for example, defined by Walker as 'to divide the skin of the face or hands by excessive cold', is also given by him in 1791 (and in succeeding editions of the *Critical Pronouncing Dictionary*) as one of 'those incorrigible words, the pronunciation and orthography of which must ever be at variance'. Attested as having a pronunciation identical to that of *chop* for much of the 19th c., such 'incorrigibility' was eventually to be defeated by the pressures of graphemic authority. *Waistcoat*, *forehead*, and *fault* shared similar patterns of restitution, from forms in the late 18th c. in /wɛskət/, /fɒrɪd/ and /fɔːt/ to their modern forms in which greater attention is given in pronunciation to distinctions manifest in writing. *Clef*, now /klɛf/, was commonly pronounced /kliːf/ in the late eighteenth century, as Walker records in his dictionary.

of expected graphemes, and the presence of others equally unexpected, was marked.

This affiliation of sociolect and spelling traded on the implicit
assumption that the non-localized norms of the written language
were, in themselves, to be understood as representative of that
non-localized accent, the possession of which had, throughout the
late eighteenth century and onwards, increasingly been presented
as the hallmark of the 'best' speakers. As Sheridan had asserted,
to use an accent which conformed to the norms of polite London
speech, irrespective of one's geographical origins, served as 'a
proof that one has kept good company'. It is this belief which, in
literary terms, is hence made to inform the differences within the
discourse of, for example, David and Barkis in *David Copperfield*.
' "If you was writin' to her, p'raps you'd recollect to say that
Barkis was willin" ', says Barkis. ' "That Barkis is willing" ' repeats
David in the next line: ' "Is that all the message?".'[10]

In spite of the compromises which such equations of spelling,
sound, and social status involved, it was nevertheless this which,
in terms of literature, was often to embody the set of equalities
and inequalities which differences of accent had come to suggest.
Divergent patterns of language in, for example, Dickens's *Martin
Chuzzlewit*, as in this exchange between Mrs Gamp and John
Westlock, can hence provide innumerable illustrations of the ways
in which the differentiated deployment of standard and non-
standard spellings can be used to form a highly effective, and
contrastive, social discourse:

'Don't I know as that dear woman is expectin of me at this minnit . . .
with little Tommy Harris in her arms, as calls me his own Gammy . . . his
own I have been, ever since I found him, Mr. Westlock, with his small
red worsted shoe a gurglin in his throat, where he had put it in his play,
a chick, wile they was leavin of him on the floor a lookin for it through
the ouse and him a chokin sweetly in the parlour. Oh, Betsey Prig, wot
wickedness you've showed this night, but never shall you darken Sairey's
doors agen, you twinin serpiant!'
'You were always so kind to her, too!' said John, consolingly.[11]

Literary fictions of speech such as this bear clear witness to
corresponding fictions of that social divide, and its manifestations

[10] *David Copperfield*, 56.
[11] C. Dickens, *The Life and Adventures of Martin Chuzzlewit* (London, 1844), ed.
M. Cardwell (Oxford, 1982), 755.

in the terms of 'literate' speech, which were regularly deployed within prescriptive ideology. As Fulton and Knight had stressed in 1833: 'Nothing gives us a greater impression of ignorance and vulgarity, than bad spelling, and awkward or provincial pronunciation.'[12] Conventions of direct speech in nineteenth-century literature, however, were to draw on both these social shibboleths simultaneously, choosing to depict 'ignorance' and 'vulgarity', and their respective social correlates, by the use of 'bad spelling' as a device which, in itself, would be able to signify the requisite awkwardnesses and provincialities of pronunciation. Mrs Gamp is therefore made to drop letters with ease. Forms such as *gurglin*, *chokin*, *ouse* demonstrate those stereotyped social associations already discussed in Chapter 3, while constructions such as *wot*, *agen*, or *wile* suggest other notions of 'illiteracy' as social marker which will receive further discussion later. John Westlock, of course, has by contrast direct speech which is composed entirely of unmarked forms, serving to allocate him (in this particular implementation of language attitudes) with 'polite' rather than 'vulgar', and with 'knowledgeable' instead of 'ignorant'. The perfect graphemic propriety of his discourse functions, by means of that 'habitual association of ideas' discussed by Sheridan, to suggest a parallel propriety of enunciation. No letters, whether visual or oral, are dropped.

The substance of literary discourse can, in such ways, be materially affected not only by *what* is said, but also by *how* it is depicted as being said, precisely in line with the rulings of a number of writers on both language and society. Mrs Gamp's use of pseudophonetic forms such as *minnit*, or elsewhere, the allocation of parallel forms such as *spazzums* to Mrs Crupp, David Copperfield's landlady in London ('Mrs Crupp was a martyr to a curious disorder called "the spazzums", which was generally accompanied with inflammation of the nose, and required her to be constantly treated with peppermint')[13] serve moreover to reveal other aspects of the 'illiterate speaker' in literary terms. The visual disharmonies of such spellings acting as unambiguous markers of intended deviation, they are, in the representation of direct speech, thus overtly made to suggest corresponding failings in utterance; their connotative

---

[12] G. Fulton and G. Knight, *A Dictionary of the English Language Greatly Improved* (Edinburgh, 1833), Advertisement.
[13] *David Copperfield*, 330.

values establish a highly effective sub-text, marking out the fictional divisions in social space. In *David Copperfield*, Peggotty uses *pritty*, David himself, *pretty*. In Gissing's *The Town Traveller*, the contrastive use of 'hyjene' rather than 'hygiene' aligns sociolects and speakers with ease: 'They had a decent little house in Kennington, managed—rather better than such homes usually are—by Mrs Parish the younger, who was childless, and thus able to devote herself to what she called "hyjene".'[14] In Meredith's *The Ordeal of Richard Feverel*, *leftenant*, *fashen*, and *joolry* again demarcate 'vulgar' and 'polite' in the characters we meet. Notions that what looks 'right' must also sound 'right' (and vice versa) dominate in an era preoccupied with linguistic mastery as an art of profound social significance, even when, as in all these instances, the fictions of 'inferior' speech are patently transparent for those who care to attend with ear rather than eye. Both *pritty* and *pretty*, irrespective of the difference of <i, e> grapheme, can only signify /prɪtɪ/ in speech, *fashen* and *fashion* receive an identical realization /fæʃn/ in the spoken language. *Hygiene* and *hyjene* can only be realized as /haɪdʒiːn/.

Prescriptive ideologies of the literate speaker are, in ways such as these, themselves made entirely literal within the realms of literature. *Minnit, leftenant, joolry, spazzums*, and the rest, though manifesting prevalent notions of 'illiteracy', equally act as accurate transcriptions of enunciations which would not, in real terms, be out of place in the most polite discourse. It is, however, the assumed authority of graphemic propriety, and the dominance of connotative over denotative values, which serve to reveal the 'best' speech in these particular contexts. Employing *du* rather than *do* (a favourite device of Thackeray), or *collidges* rather than *colleges* signifies, at least intentionally, the 'illiterate' speaker, whose pronunciation is, in consequence, assumed to be profoundly 'negligent'.

The relevant paradigm is that set out by Graham in 1869: 'whatever may be the recognised standard of pronunciation, there will always be a refined and a vulgar mode of speech', he stated, 'one adopted by the cultivated and well-informed, and the other used by the rude and illiterate.'[15] Just as Walker had commented on the words *business*, *busy*, and *bury* that 'we ought rather to blush

---

[14] G. Gissing, *The Town Traveller* (London, 1898), 139.
[15] Graham, *A Book About Words*, 159.

for departing so wantonly from the general rule as to pronounce them *bizzy*, *bizness*, and *berry*',[16] so too did authors regularly extend such conceptions, endorsing the implicit censure of 'custom' in these respects by allocating parallel, and seemingly 'illiterate' transcriptions only to those outside the 'polite'. 'Rude', as Walker confirmed, was to be 'coarse of manners' as well as 'inelegant'; later, in 1870 Ogilvie provides the synonym 'illiterate' too. In these terms, Mrs Gamp's occupations include an interest in *berryin* rather than *burying*, and *bizness* instead of *business* occupies a diverse range of characters such as Mark Tapley in *Martin Chuzzlewit*, Samuel Weller in *The Pickwick Papers*, and the coachman in Cuthbert Bede's highly popular *The Adventures of Mr Verdant Green*. ' "I knows my biz'ness . . . and I'd never go for to give up the ribbins to any party but wot had showed hisself fitted to 'andle 'em" ', says the latter, his speech leaving little ambiguity as to its intended social markings,[17] in spite of the fact that again, *business* and *biz'ness* represent identical sound patterns ([bɪznəs]) in the realities of direct speech.

Realism is clearly not the aim. Nevertheless, the set of conventions which evolve around the detailed representation of speech in literature do, in a number of ways, deserve further consideration, as indeed do the patterns of distribution assigned to these conventions. Literature, as Roger Fowler reminds us, is a social discourse; in turn the fictions of speech deployed within it readily draw on corresponding fictions, and fallacies, of speech which influence that wider world outside its own particular confines. Similarly, as Brook notes in his own work on the language of Dickens, 'the use which any author makes of language' must be seen as 'part of the history of that language'.[18] Readings of texts which incorporate such diachronic knowledge can therefore, in a number of ways, offer certain advantages, especially if awareness of language history is taken to include knowledge not only of the language in isolation, but also of prevailing attitudes to its use, and of those value-judgements (both social and linguistic) which may encompass its patterns of variation. The heightened prominence of accent as social symbol, common reactions to certain sound changes in progress, or prescriptive resistance to phonemic

---

[16] Walker, *Critical Pronouncing Dictionary*, 1st edn. (1791), §178.
[17] C. Bede, *The Adventures of Mr. Verdant Green, An Oxford Freshman*, 3rd edn. (London, 1853), 22.
[18] G. L. Brook, *The Language of Dickens* (London, 1970), 13.

mergers seen as characteristic only of 'unskilful' speakers, are all foregrounded with no little detail in the literature of the nineteenth century.

But the effectiveness of such notions of deviation does not depend solely upon that shift in prescriptive sensibilities towards the role of accent as social symbol, nor indeed, at least in isolation, upon these paradigms of accuracy and error which so often came to be imposed upon details of enunciation. Literary representations of 'standard' and 'non-standard' in pronunciation by means of the graphemic patterns employed must, for example, depend equally upon the clear, and widespread, recognition of a written norm. In pragmatic terms, it is therefore the near-standardization of spelling during the eighteenth century, coupled with the rise of the dictionary as popular reference book (especially after Dr Johnson's own endeavours in this respect), and the gradual extension of public norms of spelling into private use, which all contributed to facilitate increased detail in this respect, especially since such developments were also combined with a general increase in levels of literacy, of education, and of exposure to the written word. Whereas some variation did continue, <dote>, for example, often appearing as <doat> in nineteenth-century texts, <frowzy> as <frouzy>, <diplomat> as <diplomate> or <develop> as <develope>, the growing sense of a written standard did nevertheless render it increasingly easy for writers (and readers) to discriminate between the use of significant, and non-significant variation. Mrs Gamp's selection of *piller* for *pillow*, *wotever* for *whatever*, or *pizon* for *poison* was seen as being of a completely different order from the use of <controul>, or <boddice> in the same text (forms used moreover outside the confines of direct speech). The artistic intent apparent in the former group functions of course as an important aspect of Mrs Gamp's characterization, employed alongside her idiophonic fondness for /dʒ/ ('this indi-widgle roof', 'a surprige in-deed').

Deliberate principles of deviation in terms of the spoken language and its representation had of course appeared in literature long before this date. Chaucer in the *Reeve's Tale* made early use of Northern forms of speech, allocated to the two Cambridge University men Aleyn and John within the London dialect which Chaucer himself employed. The absence of a non-localized written language in the fourteenth century, however, could and did present problems on occasion; the scribe of the Paris manuscript of the

Canterbury Tales, for example, effectively 'translates' the whole text into Northern dialect, thus eliminating the intentionally contrastive modes of speech (*fares* instead of *fareth*, *sal* instead of *shall*) which had been inserted by Chaucer as an integral aspect of his tale. Even with the subsequent rise of a written, and above all, a printed mode of English used on national rather than merely localized levels, it must nevertheless be remembered that printers, as well as private individuals, have by no means always adhered to a single spelling for each word. Extra graphemes were, for instance, commonly inserted by earlier printers in order to justify the lines, so that a word such as *freedom* could appear as *fredom*, *fredome*, *freedome*, or indeed as its preferred modern version, *freedom*. In such circumstances, the finer nuances of orthographical deviation such as those later deployed by Dickens, Eliot, or Gaskell would certainly have been reduced in effectiveness. Though writers generally maintained control of the substantives of their texts, its accidentals, the spelling and punctuation, were, as this indicates, largely dictated by the printers themselves.

Where deliberate orthographical variation was used, writers instead tended to rely on broader schema of deviation which were less liable to potential misinterpretation, and distortion—as in Vanbrugh's marked use of <a> for <o> to depict the affected modes of speech adopted by Lord Foppington in *The Relapse* ('Now it is nat possible far me to penetrate what species of fally it is thau art driving at', 'That, I must confess, I am nat altogether so fand of ').[19] Many writers indeed chose to depict deviation (and its social correlations) not in terms of these attempted graphophonemic correspondences, but rather in terms of lexis or grammar, levels of linguistic organization in which consciousness of non-localized norms, and sensitization to requisite proprieties, was in any case more advanced. This is the method preferred, for example, by Wycherley in *The Country Wife*, in which paradigms of knowledge versus ignorance are worked out in terms of fashionable slang and familiarity (or otherwise) with metropolitan modes of language; these do not, at least explicitly, include the phonemic.[20]

[19] J. Vanbrugh, *The Relapse; or, Virtue in Danger* (London, 1697), V. v. 174–5 and II. i. 203.

[20] See e.g. II. i. 33–4, in which Mr Pinchwife is greeted by his new spouse: 'Oh my dear, dear Bud, welcome home; why dost thou look so fropish, who has nanger'd thee?', *The Country Wife* (London, 1675), in *The Plays of William Wycherley*, ed. A. Friedman (Oxford, 1979), 226.

Though these methods were used to an extent in Restoration drama, it was the novel which was to provide the most effective vehicle for increased linguistic nuance in the modes of speech adopted by various characters. Smollett and Fielding, as we have seen, provide early examples of those 'illiterate speakers' who were later to populate the nineteenth-century novel in such numbers.[21] Later authors were to extend immeasurably the patterns of linguistic deviation and attendant social meanings depicted in such works, uniting a complex of grammatical, syntactic, and intentionally 'phonetic' markers to portray alignments within the social hierarchy. Clearer conceptions of 'standard' norms in pronunciation, and the details of enunciation by which their use was to be recognized, thus in turn provide a far greater awareness of the non-standard, and indeed sub-standard, in literature as in life. Austen's characters, as has often been remarked, are distinguished by shades of usage in grammar and lexis which betray close correlations with precepts enforced in prescriptive writings on the language. Other writers were instead to foreground that consciousness of accent as prime social signifier which had been inculcated at such length by Sheridan and others. Austen is, in *Emma*, content merely to remark on Mr Martin's perceived 'want of gentility' in this respect: 'I am sure you must have been struck by his awkward look and abrupt manner—and the uncouthness of a voice, which I heard to be wholly unmodulated as I stood here', as Emma tells Harriet, betraying her own misjudgements of manner and matter, external and inner worth.[22] Later authors such as Dickens, Meredith, Reade, Gaskell, Eliot, and, perhaps most notably, Gissing would, however, scarcely have been satisfied with anything less than a full representation of such 'uncouthness', using all the conventions at their disposal.

Such patterns of representation were indeed envisaged as a potentially important aspect of the writer's role. Since 'of accent, as well as of spelling, syntax, and idiom, there is a standard in every polite nation', as Beattie set forth as early as 1788,[23] authorial manifestations of these 'standards' were deemed not only significant but also of possible exemplary value. 'In all these particulars',

---

[21] See pp. 138–41.
[22] J. Austen, *Emma* (London, 1816), ed. R. W. Chapman, 3rd edn. (Oxford, 1933), 33.
[23] Beattie, *Theory of Language*, 92.

Beattie continued, 'the example of approved authors, and the practice of those, who, by their rank, education, and way of life, have had the best opportunities to know men and manners, and domestick and foreign literature, ought undoubtedly to give the law.' Literary methods of indicating accent in 'narrow' rather than 'broad' formats in fact evolved with some rapidity, and if not actually establishing 'laws' of linguistic usage, they certainly traded on the social resonances of contemporary shibboleths and stigma in terms of accent to no little effect. Missing <h>s and missing <g>s, as we have seen, performed roles in literature precisely in line with that more general shift in attitudes towards the needful proprieties of speech,[24] and even the pronunciation of individual words, and their representation in literature, encoded the new social sensibilities (and ideological implications) which had come to surround contemporary attitudes to correctness.

Oblige, for example, was pronounced with propriety as /əbliːdʒ/ in the eighteenth century. Pope rhymed *obliged* with *besieged*, as well as *oblige ye* with *besiege ye*. The social meanings of such enunciations were, however, gradually to shift: allied with the 'affected' and 'vulgar' by Chesterfield, by the mid-nineteenth century /əbliːdʒ/ had almost without exception been affiliated to the latter, as the modern pronunciation /əblaɪdʒ/ came to dominate in questions of acceptability. John Kemble, the actor, is even reputed to have corrected the monarch on a phonemic *faux pas* in this context, as Graham records in 1869: 'When George III. said to him: "Mr Kemble, will you 'obleedge' me with a pinch of your snuff?" [Kemble] replied: "With pleasure, your Majesty; but it would become your royal lips much better to say 'oblige' ".'[25] Literary texts regularly assimilated these changed social values, the contrastive use of *obleedge/oblige* being deployed as an unambiguous marker of differentiated status, complete with appropriate graphological deviation. Habitual enunciations by Silas Wegg in *Our Mutual Friend*, or Mr Peggotty in *David Copperfield* adopt the former: ' "I'm much obleeged to her, I'm sure" ',[26] ' "I'm obleeged to you, sir, for your welcoming manner of me" ',[27] and the speech of Mrs Tester, the bedmaker in Cuthbert Bede's comic *The Adventures of Mr. Verdant Green* is likewise distinguished by the

---

[24] See Ch. 3.   [25] Graham, *A Book About Words*, 158.
[26] *David Copperfield*, 27.   [27] Ibid. 90.

emphasis assigned to this form: ' "So long as I can obleege the gentleman" ', ' "it's obleeged I feel in my art" '.[28] Kate Nickleby instead employs *obliged* (' "I'm very much obliged to you, uncle" '), a usage dependent upon her hereditary and social status as gentleman's daughter, rather than her socio-economic class as a milliner earning seven shillings a week.[29]

The use of enunciations of *cucumber* as *cowcumber* is similarly made to pertain to prevalent social and linguistic stereotypes. Though Walker in 1791 had lamented that it 'seemed too firmly fixed in its sound of *Cowcumber* to be altered', giving reluctant sanction to the acceptability of this pronunciation, later observers, and indeed later editors of his own dictionary, stressed instead that ' "best usage" had ceased to pronounce the first syllable like *cow*'. 'When people of fashion relinquish an absurdity, men of letters should be deeply grateful', as the lexicographer Townsend Young added in approbation,[30] celebrating this triumph of graphemic propriety. Iterations of *cowcumber* and *cucumber* again combined to form a binary pair of marked social value for nineteenth-century writers, and it is in this deeply unfashionable mode of speech in which Mrs Gamp, for example, is made to request a cucumber to give that extra piquancy to her meal: ' "In case there should be sech a thing as a cowcumber in the ouse, will you be so kind as to bring it, for I'm rather partial to 'em, and they does a world of good in a sick room".'[31] Dickens's selection of the form with ~~cow~~ hence signifies the outmoded and deliberately *déclassé* use of [aʊ] ([kaʊkʌmbə]), an articulation opposed to those more 'correct' enunciations in [u:] ([kju:kʌmbə]) which were suggested, and reinforced, by the spelling. As Levante was later to declare of this word in 1869, 'None but the most illiterate now pronounce it other than it is written',[32] and it is of course in such paradigms of 'illiterate' versus 'literate' speech that Mrs Gamp's usage is to be placed. Alternations of *sparrowgrass/asparagus, faut/fault* or *sodger/ soldier* all serve similar functions, their newer spelling-pronunciations encoding the proprieties of literate speech, whereas their traditional

[28] *The Adventures of Mr. Verdant Green*, 92.
[29] C. Dickens, *The Life and Adventures of Nicholas Nickleby* (London, 1839), 92.
[30] T. Young (ed.), *A Critical Pronouncing Dictionary of the English Language* (London, 1857), note under the word *cucumber*.
[31] *Martin Chuzzlewit*, 411.
[32] Revd E. R. de Levante, *Orthoepy and Orthography of the English Language* (London, 1869), 148.

enunciations are habitually used in literature to signify the massed ranks of artisans, rustics, Cockneys, and other members of the lower classes, as well, in fact, as the 'hypercorrect' forms of the aspiring parvenu. Such details encoded the social divide in literary and linguistic terms with a marked sense of contemporaneity for the nineteenth-century reader. Graphological deviation, often regarded, as by Leech and Short, as 'a relatively minor and superficial part of style' is,[33] as a result, made fundamental to the perception, and presentation, of the social meanings stressed as omnipresent in pronunciation. When Meredith, for example, introduces Farmer Blaize in *The Ordeal of Richard Feverel* (1859), it is graphology, and its assumed relationship with an underlying phonetic reality, which proclaims his status as merely yeoman rather than gentleman farmer (and which by contrast establishes Richard in the superior position—in spite of the latter's transgressions in poaching, as well as in setting fire to the aptly-named Blaize's haystack):

'Now', said he, leaning forward, and fixing his elbows on his knees, while he counted the case at his fingers' ends, 'ascuse the liberty, but wishin' to know where this 'ere money's to come from, I sh'd like jest t'ask if so be Sir Aust'n know o' this?'
'My father knows nothing of it', replied Richard.[34]

Forms such as *'ere* for *here*, *wishin'* for *wishing*, or *o'* for *of* become meaningful in the social world created within the novel, trading as they do on common assumptions about language, status, and identity which were widely prevalent outside such fictional confines. Deliberate modifications of orthography function as important aspects of foregrounding, qualitative deviation from established or expected norms hence assuming markedly expressive roles. Italicization, capitalization, the use of diacritics, patterns of hyphenation and punctuation, and especially the respelling of words to suggest correspondences between visual and vocal disharmony can all share in this aspect of stylistic technique. Diacritics mark perceived deviance in Dickens's representation of American speech in *Martin Chuzzlewit*: ' "In my country", said the gentleman, "we know the cost of our own prŏ-dūce" ', ' "we will not pursue the

---

[33] G. N. Leech and M. H. Short, *Style in Fiction: A Linguistic Introduction to English Fictional Prose* (London, 1981), 131.
[34] G. Meredith, *The Ordeal of Richard Feverel* (London, 1859), i. 172.

subject, lest it should awaken your prějudīce" '.[35] Capitalization, as we have already seen, serves to mark the heavily emphatic discourse of Mr Podsnap in explaining the social meanings of /h/ in *Our Mutual Friend*.[36] It is, however, the combined resources of spelling and punctuation which prove of greatest value in literary delineations of accent.

In this, authors commonly purposed, as did Hardy, to convey the 'spirit' of the spoken word,[37] and methods, as a result, are more often impressionistic than entirely systematic. ' "Accordin' as the world went round, which round it did rewolve undoubtedly, even the best of gentlemen must take his turn of standing with his ed upside down and all his air a flying the wrong way" ', philosophizes Mr Plornish in *Little Dorrit*,[38] betraying principles of variation (*accordin'*, *flying*, *standing*, or *his*, *ed*, *air*) which owe more to literary selection than sociolinguistic insight. It is enough if the illusion of speech is given, and indeed providing more than this risked certain dangers. Gaskell's more conscientious attempts to depict the nuances of Yorkshire speech in *Sylvia's Lovers* met, for example, a number of reactions which were less than favourable: 'the continual use of the common dialect of the north-eastern shores of England is both useless and fatiguing' declared an unsigned review in the *Observer* in 1863. Using 'the broad vernacular Yorkshire dialect' although giving 'local colour', is 'a drawback to the comfort of the reader, and fatiguing to the eye' confirmed Geraldine Jewsbury in the *Athenaeum*. The *Daily News* was still less responsive: 'it is trying the patience of readers too far to compel them to wade through three volumes of unpronounceable *patois* and miserable incidents'.[39] Such constraints alone served to inhibit absolute accuracy, as well as extensive representation, of speech within the novel.

Patterns of deviation moreover often tend to imply a certain distance, both from authorial viewpoint, and in addition from that of the implied reader—that hypothetical entity who, as Leech

---

[35] *Martin Chuzzlewit*, 344, 367.   [36] See p. 116.
[37] T. Hardy, 'Dialect in Novels', *Athenaeum*, 30 Nov. 1878, 688.
[38] *Little Dorrit*, 712.
[39] Unsigned review of *Sylvia's Lovers*, the *Observer*, 1 Mar. 1863, 7; Geraldine Jewsbury, unsigned review of *Sylvia's Lovers*, the *Athenaeum*, 28 Feb. 1863, 291; and unsigned review of *Sylvia's Lovers* in the *Daily News*, 3 Apr. 1863, 2. cited in A. Easson (ed.), *Elizabeth Gaskell: The Critical Heritage* (London, 1991), 440, 432, and 445-6.

and Short point out, is assumed to share with the author not just background knowledge, but equally 'a set of presuppositions, sympathies, and standards of what is pleasant and unpleasant, good and bad, right and wrong'.[40] It is this distancing which often tends to endow with comic resonance those characters whose language differs from that standard variety in which the narrative is primarily constructed, and which, in addition, tends to exempt heroes and heroines from the demands which might otherwise be imposed by verisimilitude in these respects. Little Dorrit hence employs not the language of the debtors' prison, as one might expect, but instead is endowed by Dickens with a perfect propriety of grammar and grapheme (and presumably therefore of phoneme as well). Oliver Twist's ignorance of the linguistic foibles of the lower classes is similarly remarkable, given a social environment formed of workhouse and thieves' den. Even Gissing, heavily censorious of Dickens's practice in these terms ('Granted that Oliver was of gentle blood, heredity does not go as far as this'[41]), is forced to comply with conventional fictional expectations in his own work, so that in *Demos*, although we are told of Richard Mutimer's 'struggles with the h fiend', they are never shown, lest their use invite a ridicule incompatible with heroic status, and with those wider issues Gissing was endeavouring to explore through Mutimer's rise and fall.

Though absolute realism was therefore neither intended nor attempted in this context, it is the presence of what we have already described as 'linguistic contemporaneity' which on many occasions renders a close examination of literary conventions of speech in the nineteenth century rewarding. Commonly drawing on prevailing attitudes to 'right' and 'wrong', 'statusful' and 'statusless' in speech, of which the implied reader of the nineteenth century would likewise have been aware, fictional delineations of accent often embody with striking precision and clarity the normative framework (and accompanying ideologies) in which language use was placed. 'Ideology tells people how to act in prescribed, socially acceptable ways', writes Blake of conceptions of literature as a social process,[42] and the same is true of the

---

[40] Leech and Short, *Style in Fiction*, 259.
[41] G. Gissing, *Charles Dickens. A Critical Study* (London, 1898), 206–7.
[42] A. Blake, 'The Place of Fiction in Victorian Literary Culture', *Literature and History*, 11 (1985), 204.

linguistic processes and assumptions which it too can enact. Binary divisions of 'well-bred' and 'vulgar', which, as we have seen, form a regular feature of the prescriptive tradition, are, for example, transferred into the fictional dimension with ease. Prescriptive fictions that only the more 'careless' speaker would employ colloquial forms of speech in which elision of syllables takes place similarly provide a regular source of socially contrastive language use within the domains of nineteenth-century literature. *P'raps* and *perhaps*, *s'pose* and *suppose*, *guv'nor* and *governor* are as a result used in structured ways in many novels, mapping out preconceptions about literate speech and social status, entirely irrespective of linguistic reality, and the varying demands of situation, register, or stress. ' "I don't know which is the freshest, the freshman or his guv'nor" ', says the Oxford shopkeeper in Bede's *The Adventures of Mr. Verdant Green*; ' "I heard from my governor that you were coming up" ' says an undergraduate, ' "I suppose the old bird was your governor".'[43] Forms such as *int'rest* and *corp'ral*, with elision of medial unstressed syllables, likewise assume marked social correlates in Bulwer Lytton's *Eugene Aram*, the intended sense of deviation being heightened further by the presence of other accompanying infelicities: 'that's the reason they all takes so much int'rest in their profession', 'when he comes for to get as high as a corp'ral or a sargent'.[44] Again, [ɪntˈrɛst] and [kɔːprəl] would form the habitual enunciations of the majority of speakers, in upper as in underclass, in the 'real' speech of the nineteenth century.

Just as Dr Johnson had equated the 'colloquial' with the 'licentious', and Smart had excluded 'familiar and consequently negligent discourse' as having no place in the linguistic descriptions of a dictionary, so too did nineteenth-century writers respond to such prevalent language attitudes and ideals, presenting the elisions and contractions of informal speech in contexts which implicitly shared prescriptive antipathies on this point. Weakly stressed (and perfectly normal) forms such as *an'* for *and* or *ev* for *have*, are in turn made to fulfil similar functions by their differential allocations: ' "I've been a mother to her, an' a good mother" ', says Mrs Peckover in Gissing's *The Nether World*, 'only wait till I've ad my tea', says her daughter earlier in the same novel,[45] the expressive

[43] *The Adventures of Mr. Verdant Green*, 39, 47.
[44] E. Bulwer Lytton, *Eugene Aram* (London, 1832), ii. 42.
[45] G. Gissing, *The Nether World* (London, 1889), i. 106, 110.

powers of the rewritten word being employed to suggest deviation even though such patterns are both long established and entirely characteristic of normal connected speech, even in RP.[46] Variant forms such as *an'* (for *and*) or *'ad* (for *had*) which naturally occur in all connected speech in response to patterns of rhythms and stress are thus regularly ascribed only to the lower classes, and assimilated into the fictional non-standard which results. Mrs Lucas in Mrs Humphry Ward's *Marcella* is given utterances such as 'I've talked to 'er', whereas Marcella's own speech (much as in the 'corrected' forms of modern adoptive RP)[47] maintains intact the unelided forms of the written language: ' "How long has she been like this?" ',[48] in spite of the fact that an accurate transcription of the latter, even in 'good' speech, would have to acknowledge identical [h]-loss in unstressed grammatical words such as *had* and *her*: /haʊ lɒŋ əz ʃɪ bɪn laɪk ðɪs/.[49] Such circumstances present us with a paradox which is frequent in literary depictions of the spoken word, evident here in the fact that whereas authorial observations of the stress patterns of speech may indeed at times give highly accurate indications of the rhythms of English speech, chosen distributions of these patterns within the fictional world can instead erroneously tend to suggest their role as a differentiating feature of marked social import. Literary fictions that the 'polite' pronounce all words and syllables as if under equal stress can, in consequence, be foregrounded out of all relationship to reality.

Similar paradigms are mapped on to the elision of /l/. ' "It's almost time you went" ', says John Rokesmith in *Our Mutual Friend*, ' "I a'most believed as you'd giv' me the slip" ', says Rogue Riderhood in the same novel, further encoding popular assumptions that while heroes, heroines, and members of the upper classes articulate with proper graphemic propriety, only those in the lower ranks display the simplifications of speech which, at least to a phonetician, are characteristic of all informal spoken English. Authors as well as writers on the language, however, aligned accent barriers and social barriers with some rigidity in the ways in which they chose to represent these nuances of speech. Elision was construed as 'negligence', and dichotomies of *a'most/almost*, or *a'ready/already* appeal unashamedly to the social prejudices which result.

---

[46] See e.g. Ch. 3 n. 2.   [47] See p. 158.
[48] Mrs Humphry Ward, *Marcella* (London, 1894), iii. 54.   [49] See p. 107.

Liberally assigned to servants and subordinates (' "A'most all the red washed out of it" ', says Molly the servant in Mrs Henry Wood's *Johnny Ludlow*, ' "Back a'ready?" ' asks Rogue Riderhood), an unnatural exemption from such features is regularly granted to those characters located in the middle and upper sections of society. As such features indicate, common language attitudes in terms of 'good' and 'bad' usage could achieve a notable currency in their working out within these fictional spheres.

Notions of the realization of /hw/, as in *which* and *what*, provide a further case in point, concisely revealing the ways in which fiction made use of contemporary images (and associated evaluations) of speakers and of speech to marked effect. Words such as *which* had, of course, traditionally been distinguished from potential homophones such as *witch* by the quality of the initial consonant. In phonetic terms, whereas *witch* uses an initial labio-velar semivowel /w/, *which* opened with /hw/, a glide cluster which can, in relevant words, be traced back to Old English: *whale* derives from *hwael*, *while* from *hwil*. Though confusion between the two is evident even in early Middle English in occasional spellings, this long-established pattern of differentiation began to fade rapidly even before the late eighteenth century, /hw/ and /w/ merging in pronunciation in /w/, as yet another example of '[h]-dropping' was apparently made manifest. Prescriptive reaction to this development was predictable, and negative. Traditionally excluded from 'educated' speech, Thomas Batchelor (1809) specifies that its use is a clear indication of 'depraved provincial pronunciation', and John Walker conversely proscribes it as a Cockney fault of the natives of the metropolis which tends to 'weaken and empoverish the pronunciation': 'The aspirate *h* is often sunk, particularly in the capital, where we do not find the least distinction of sound between *while* and *wile*, *whet* and *wet*.' As remedy, offenders are recommended to 'collect all the words of this description from a dictionary, and write them down', afterwards forcibly enunciating them with an initial aspirate until perfection is attained. The well-attested reliance on visual authority as the rightful guide to 'good' pronunciation is made abundantly clear by the terms of this proffered counsel, and similar comments appear throughout the nineteenth century as variation between [hw] and [w] in relevant words is, at least in theory, imbued with marked social correlations, demarcating 'well-bred' and 'vulgar', 'educated' and 'ignorant' with seeming precision. Its loss, by many writers, is affiliated solely to the 'negligent' and 'careless', and to the sheer social unacceptability of those who dare, in any circumstance, to drop an [h].

Authors too were readily to embrace the use of /hw/ and /w/, <wh> and <w>, as another useful symbol of the linguistic polarities of status. Mrs Gamp is made to select *wile* and not *while*, *wen* and not *when*. In *Nicholas Nickleby*, it is this which (among other things) serves to distinguish the direct speech of the repossessing bailiffs from that of the dispossessed owner Mr Mantalini: ' "*What's* the demd total ?" ' demands the latter. ' "A good half of *wot's* here isn't paid for I des-say, and *wot* a consolation oughtn't that to be" ', announces Mr Scaley, one of the bailiffs, as he assumes control of the property.[50] Magwitch in *Great Expectations*, Benjamin, the 'young retainer' at Mrs Todger's London boarding-house in *Martin Chuzzlewit*, the vast armies of the London poor in Gissing's œuvre, and the clerkly Mr Polly of H. G. Wells, are all intentionally united in their inferior social status by their disregard for the graphemic, and assumed phonemic, properties of the <h> in this respect. In the sporting world of Surtees, it is this which is foregrounded to great effect in the horse dealers and grooms we encounter. ' "If a man gets spilt it don't argufy much wether its done from play or from wice" ', asseverates Benjamin Buckram, combining his infelicities of <w>/<wh> with alternations of <v> and <w>, the intended social resonances of which are too familiar to need discussion. Mr Sponge's horse-groom is accorded the same complex of features: ' "one of them tight-laced candlestick priests wot abhors all sorts of wice and immorality" '.[51] To use *wether* for *whether*, *wich* for *which*, or *wot* for *what* is thus, in both fictional and prescriptive sensibilities, to contravene the assumed proprieties of 'elegant speech' and thus to be consigned, almost automatically, to the lower reaches of society.

Such demarcations of norm and deviation, falling so neatly alongside demarcations of status, form the stuff of fiction in more ways than one. In actual fact, as even a careful reading of Walker's comments in 1791 on this head reveal, the loss of distinctions between [hw] and [w] was prevalent far outside his specified confines of the 'vulgar'; as Eric Dobson later points out, even in

---

[50] *Nicholas Nickleby*, 196, emphasis added.
[51] R. S. Surtees, *Mr Sponge's Sporting Tour* (London, 1853), 13, 31.

'educated' speech this had been common by the end of the eighteenth century. Smith in 1866 makes the compromises being made with reality on this score particularly clear. In accordance with prescriptive sensibilities, the 'omission of *h* after *w*' is duly given as 'a fault highly detrimental to correct pronunciation'. It is, however, also specified immediately afterwards as one which 'is committed by the majority of educated people'.[52] Alexander Ellis three years later patiently stressed that 'in London and in the South of England (wh) is seldom pronounced', pointing out furthermore the weaknesses in the assumption that 'to write *wot* for *what* is thought to indicate a bad vulgar pronunciation'.[53] As such comments indicate, fictions of speech in this context were evidently widespread far outside the discourse of Mrs Gamp, Magwitch, and Pip, as notions of correctness continued to advise the 'correct' use of /hw/ long after its loss for the mass of the population. Henry Sweet, by the end of the nineteenth century, is scathing about speakers who retain this use of /hw/ in accordance with elocutionary tenets and artificial notions of correctness, rather than with the realities of the language:

If we look at the tendencies of natural speech, we must confess that it is nearly extinct, although it cannot be denied that many born Southerners pronounce it in ordinary speech. The question is, do any of them do so naturally, apart from the influence of elocutionary habits, or Scotch or Irish parentage? This question I am inclined to answer doubtfully with no: we must, I think, admit that though (wh) is a Standard English sound, it is not a *natural* Standard English sound.[54]

As Sweet's comments serve to indicate, however, language attitudes in this context again contribute to the 'unnatural' retention of /hw/ in real terms too—especially, we may imagine, in the more formal registers of speech when speakers are most often concerned to retain (and reproduce) the accepted proprieties of the 'best' language.

In both prescriptive and literary works, it was the connotative rather than the denotative which was to be privileged in appropriate readings in this context; ' "You've told me *what* you think will happen" ', says Dr Seward in Bram Stoker's *Dracula*, ' "The

[52] Smith, *Mind Your H's and Take Care of Your R's*, 4.
[53] Ellis, *Early English Pronunciation*, i. 188.
[54] H. Sweet, *The Elementary Sounds of English* (London, 1881), 7.

gard'ner *wot* didn't remember" ', says Mr Bilder, the keeper of the zoological gardens to whom he is talking.[55] The implied social values of *what* and *wot* are again profoundly dissimilar even though, in actual fact, respective pronunciations of both would usually have been identical. This use of *wot* rather than *what*, was, in particular, to rise into a pervasive marker of 'illiterate speech' throughout nineteenth- (and twentieth-) century literature. Trading on the system of social resonances, and accompanying social stereotypes, which ensued from prevailing assumptions about the correctness of continuing to differentiate *which* and *witch*, *what* and *watt*, writers came to use graphemically divergent forms such as *wot* as a habitual leitmotif of the lower classes: ' "Wot job?" ', asks the long-legged young man who runs off with David's box in *David Copperfield*, ' "I know wot it is to be loud, and I know wot it is to be soft" ', says Rogue Riderhood in *Our Mutual Friend*. The relevant (though erroneous) equation is again that what looks 'wrong' must also sound 'wrong', and the aesthetic disharmonies of *wot*, indeed 'illiterate' though perfectly accurate in terms of sound, have in fact proved remarkably enduring in these socio-symbolic associations. Though modern phoneticians reject the proprieties of /hw/ in English[56] with little dissimulation ('those who use it almost always do so as the result of a conscious decision: persuaded that /hw-/ is a desirable pronunciation, they modify their native accent in this direction. Thus /hw/ is nowadays in England found principally among the speech-conscious and in adoptive RP'),[57] language attitudes still retain marked continuities with the past in terms of what is regarded as 'better' enunciation; as in the nineteenth-century, the actualities of linguistic usage are regularly disregarded. In literature likewise, the old stereotypes can still survive, the use of *wot* continuing to generate these well-established, and entirely connotative values of ignorance and of lower social station too, in spite of the evident incompatibilities which occur

---

[55] B. Stoker, *Dracula* (London, 1897), 142, emphasis added.

[56] The use of [hw], or perhaps more precisely, that of the voiceless labio-velar fricative, is retained in Scots, as well as in some rural areas in the far north of the country.

[57] J. C. Wells, *Accents of English*, ii. 228–9. As he also comments: 'Present-day RP usage could be described as schizophrenic. For most RP speakers /hw/ is not a 'natural' possibility. The usual RP form of *whine* is /waɪn/; similarly *what* /wɒt/ ... Other RP speakers use /hw/, and say /hwaɪn, hwɒt/ ... , and this usage is widely considered correct, careful, and beautiful.'

between subjective fiction and objective fact for the majority of
English speakers in this respect.

Similarly exact correlations between prescriptive fictions of
speech, and appropriate delineations of speech in fiction, are well
attested on a number of occasions. Phonemic mergers, for example, regularly formed a target for proscriptive censure as writers
on the language endeavoured to constrain a force of change which
manifestly reduced distinctions in the spoken language, while
differentiations in the written language remained intact. Attitudes
to the vocalisation of /r/, as well as to the import of intrusive
/r/, have already illustrated this particular set of preconceptions.[58]
The continued graphemic distinctions between the <er>, <ir>
and <ur> in words such as *fern, fir*, and *fur*, in spite of a phonemic
identity traceable to the seventeenth century (and certainly well
established by the end of the eighteenth)[59] were, in parallel ways,
to lead to considerable resistance being maintained among writers
within the prescriptive tradition.[60] Walker, amongst many others,
decisively promotes the loss of such 'correct' distinctions as an
unmistakable symbol of a social identity outside the polite and he
excludes it from the 'standard' he intends to document; it has,
he asserts, 'a grossness in it approaching to vulgarity'.[61] Such
enunciations standing as evidence of 'a coarse vulgar pronunciation',[62] he stresses therefore that the 'delicate difference' of the
'true sound' should be maintained for all those who wish to align
themselves with 'good' speech.

Prescriptive lexis again enforces subjective connotations (and
subjective inequalities), as the 'true' and 'delicate' is opposed to the
'coarse', 'vulgar', and 'gross'. Both the 'true' and the 'delicate' are,
however, also entirely fictive at this date, as a careful reading of
Walker's text reveals: the 'true' position is in fact that in which a
merged sound in /ɜ:/ was, as now, used by 'polite', as well as 'vulgar'
for all relevant words in that emergent standard he describes.
Though prescriptive ideology and phonemic reality again diverge,
the legacy of the former in this particular context nevertheless

[58] See pp. 99–103 and pp. 156–9.
[59] This merger has not occurred in most Scottish accents.
[60] See L. C. Mugglestone, 'Prescription, Pronunciation, and Issues of Class in
the Late Eighteenth and Nineteenth Centuries', in D. M. Reeks (ed.), *Sentences
for Alan Ward* (London, 1988), 175–82.
[61] Walker, *Critical Pronouncing Dictionary*, 1st edn. (1791), §110.
[62] Ibid., note under the word *earth*.

again tends to linger on throughout the nineteenth century in literature as well as works on language. Batchelor, Smart, and Vandenhoff (among many others) all attempted, with much inconsistency and self-contradiction, to sustain these prestigious patterns of the past. Likewise, authors too came to share, and even to collude, in this pattern of cultural stereotyping, willingly drawing on conceptions of the 'vulgarity' of pronouncing <er>, <ir> and <ur> as a single phoneme by incorporating significant patterns of respelling within the paradigms of ostensibly 'illiterate' speech they adopt. Smollett's characterization of Win Jenkins as an 'illiterate' speaker (and writer) early made good use of this feature, giving such forms as *shurt* for *shirt*, *murcy* for *mercy*, *burth* for *birth*. Firmly embedded in the standard ideology (and its socio-cultural correlates) Gissing too was willingly to utilize conceptions of articulations of this kind as stigmas of vulgarity, especially Cockney vulgarity; iterations of *girl* and *gurl* mark out intended contrasts in acceptability, in spite of objectively identical realizations in /gɜːl/. Similarly, in *Oliver Twist*, the social degradation of Oliver's birth is further compounded by its location in the *wurkus*, the suggested enunciation of the initial syllable by the nurse who brings him into the world effectively being made to convey the realms of the ignorant and uneducated, regardless of the fact that the pronunciation thereby suggested was again not incompatible with the speech of those in the highest ranks: ' "Lor bless her dear heart, when she has lived as long as I have, sir, and had thirteen children of her own, and all of 'em dead except two, and them in the wurkus (/wɜːk/-) with me, she'll know better than to take on in that way, bless her dear heart." '[63] The grammar and idioms used nevertheless do offer unambiguous confirmation of these intended affiliations of <wurk>.

Allocating pronunciations of this order to underclass alone in the fictional world of the novel serves, however, to confirm both prevalent prejudices about pronunciation, as well as to endorse the relevant criteria of acceptability, both social and linguistic, which were seemingly to be imposed upon variation and its attendant developments. Revealing parallel illustrations of ideological bias to those already discussed in the context of [h]-dropping or

---

[63] C. Dickens, *The Adventures of Oliver Twist* (London, 1846), ed. K. Tillotson (Oxford, 1966), 2.

the use of /r/, literature, as John Lucas reminds us, does not tend to be 'a straightforward representation', either of language or society. As he adds, 'it rather suppresses, congeals and refracts . . . revealing itself in its internal contradictions and omissions as not external to, but as part of, a total social process.'[64] Language attitudes to the perceived 'vulgarity' of using the lengthened *a* and *o* (/ɑ:/ and /ɔ:/) before voiceless fricatives, as in words such as *last*, *bath*, or *off* are, for example, frequently refracted in literature in parallel ways. Though iterations of *orf* ([ɔ:f]) now suggest old-fashioned RP (or the Royal Family),[65] while enunciations such as [klɑ:s] are regarded as a common marker of the non-localized norms of 'good' speech, in the eighteenth and nineteenth centuries, as we have seen, such forms were conversely depicted in much prescriptive writing as emblematic of sociolects outside the socially acceptable,[66] and as redolent in particular of the negative linguistic prestige of the Cockney. They therefore often appear in the literature of the period in functions which tend further to amplify these perceived social values, trading on the negative implications (and social stereotypes) thereby implied.

Gissing's first novel, *Workers in the Dawn*, for example, makes use of relatively dense notations of lower-class London speech to this end, 'deviant' enunciations of relevant words figuring highly alongside other diacritics of the non- and sub-standard. ' "I'll learn yer . . . I'll say the words first, an' then you say 'em arfter" ', dictates Mrs Blatherwick, a slatternly London landlady, to the young Arthur Golding. ' "Now, if I'll pay for the lad . . . will you tackle Hannah Clinkscoles, and make her let him horff his work two or three nights a week for an hour or so?" ', says Ned Quirk, baked-potato seller, in the same novel.[67] Forms such as *arfter* and *horff*, just like the use of *horsespitle* (for *hospital*) by Jo, the Cockney crossing-sweeper in *Bleak House*, or *parsties* by Barkis in *David Copperfield*, signify by their inorganic <r> conventions of 'illiteracy' which were apparently to predispose so many speakers against using these lengthened sounds. As Ellis records in attempted explanation, it was in part the aesthetic demerits of such forms

[64] J. Lucas, 'Editorial Preface', *Literature and History*, 1 (1975), 2.
[65] See 'Human After All', *Sunday Times*, 1 Mar. 1987, magazine section, 61, where Princess Anne is recorded as using *orf*.
[66] See pp. 90–2, and 194–5.
[67] G. Gissing, *Workers in the Dawn* (London, 1880), i. 97–8, 146.

which seemed to contribute to that sense of disfavour which could surround their use: 'this dread arises from the fear that if [speakers] said (aask, laaf), they would be accused of the vulgarity of inserting an *r*, and when *arsk*, *larf*, are written, they "look so very vulgar".'[68] Certainly the repeated use of *orf* and *arsk* in the discourse of, for example, the zoo-keeper in Bram Stoker's *Dracula*, given the cumulative effect of other usages which are likewise intentionally excluded from standard forms of speech (*'owling* for *howling*, *makin'* for *making*, as well plentiful elisions) would contribute to such an impression, standing as they do as intentionally unambiguous diacritics of lower social status.

It was precisely these socio-cultural overtones on which contemporary novelists drew. Though the <r> was inserted merely as a diacritic of length, writers were of course by no means unconscious of the symbolic potential of 'vulgarity' embedded within the resulting visual deviations. The large group of words in which <er> had traditionally been pronounced with /ar/, such as *serve*, *service*, *certain* or *verdict*, provides ample illustration of this same principle, as attitudes to the language increasingly shifted tenor on this feature too, encoding its use as unfashionable, uneducated, and therefore untenable.[69] Walker, for example, notes under the word *merchant* in his dictionary that though enunciations as *marchant* had been entirely acceptable thirty years earlier, and had even been sanctioned by Sheridan, they were now 'gross and vulgar, . . . only to be heard among the lower orders of the people'.[70] Sensitization to this new unacceptability, inspired as it was by the patterns of the written language, is marked in literary texts: ' "he makes hisself a sort o' sarvent to her" ', says Mr Peggotty of Ham in *David Copperfield*, ' "he sarves my turn" ', says Benjamin Buckram, the horse-dealer in *Mr Sponge's Sporting Tour*. ' "A pleasure you *may* call it, sir, with parfect truth" ', says the coachman in Cuthbert Bede's *Adventures of Mr. Verdant Green*. ' "My servant will show you the way" ', says the Master of Brazenface College in the same novel, in a contrast (*parfect/ser-vant*) which is well established in the prevailing social and linguistic structures, and their relevant shifts in extra-linguistic value.

---

[68] Ellis, *Early English Pronunciation*, iv. 1148.

[69] In early modern English, *e* before *r* often became *a*: *carve*, for example, derives from OE *ceorfan*, *war* from OE *werre*. Spellings with <e> were, however, often retained, as in *clerk*, *Derbyshire*.

[70] *Merchant* derives from OFr *marchant*.

Literature and the Literate Speaker   233

An awareness of such synchronic and diachronic contexts in
language and social meaning can in fact often usefully illuminate
the less obvious details of enunciation which are, on occasion,
employed. One habit of pronunciation regularly assigned by
Dickens to Mr Peggotty in *David Copperfield* provides a case in
point: ' "Mas'r Davy, . . . You han't no call to be afeerd of me:
but I'm kiender muddled" '; ' "When she did, she kneeled down
at my feet, and kiender said to me, as if it were her prayers, how
it all came to be" '; ' "My niece was kiender daughter-like to
me." '[71] Additional examples are sprinkled elsewhere throughout
the text. Confined exclusively to the speech of Mr Peggotty, this
restricted distribution perhaps renders it tempting to assume that
these repeated forms represent an idiophonic pattern along the
lines of that fondness for /dʒ/ in the speech of Mrs Gamp. This
is not, however, the case. On the contrary, utterances of *kind* as
kyind, or *garden* as *gyarden* are well attested in writings on the
language as they rise in and fall from favour over the late eighteenth and nineteenth centuries, Dickens's acuity in terms of
language merely leading him to explore their use as an additional
means of encoding the social divide within his novels.[72] *Kiender*,
with its <ie> digraph, is thus selected as the means by which
Dickens may effectively denote the presence of a palatal glide
/j/, a frequent and once highly fashionable phenomenon occurring
after the consonants /k/ and /g/ in words such as *kind* and *garden*,
but one which was clearly, by the mid-nineteenth century, sliding
considerably down the social scale. Walker, for example, at the end
of the eighteenth century is still stressing the use of this feature as
a fundamental marker of refinement in speech: enunciations such
as 'ke-ard', 'ke-art', 'ghe-ard' or 're-ghe-ard' (for *card*, *cart*, *guard*,
and *regard*) are specified as characteristic of 'polite pronunciation'
and his comments in his *Rhetorical Grammar* are still more emphatic
of the social values which such realizations comport. The glide
/j/ is described as a 'smooth and elegant sound' in forms such as
ke-ind, *ke-ard* or *re-geard*, its presence indeed 'sufficient to mark
the speaker as either coarse or elegant, as he adopts and neglects
it'.

[71] *David Copperfield*, 390, 619, 584.
[72] Early evidence of the use of similar forms with a palatal glide /j/ after /k, g/
can be traced in, for example, John Wallis's *Grammatica Linguae Anglicanae* (Oxford,
1653), in which clearly equivalent enunciations in *gyet* and *begyin* are given for the
words *get*, *begin*.

Such distinguishing marks of elegant speech were, however, to suffer a rapid decline, and by 1825 Oliver deploys an identical binary divide to demarcate not the 'coarse' and 'elegant', but instead the 'affected' and ordinary, the palatal glide standing as a signifier of 'affected speakers wherever they be among us'.[73] Ellis, in *Early English Pronunciation*, confirms the reversal in its pattern of social allegiances: 'old-fashioned', 'antiquated', and 'rapidly dying out', it is liable to be the hallmark of the socially inferior rather than of the truly refined.[74] It is of course in such values that its utility was recognized by contemporary authors. Realizations such as 'gjurl' or 'gjell' for *girl* thus come to stand as additional markers of phonetic impropriety, used alongside [h]-dropping and double negation in the novels of Gissing, for example, as in this speech by Mrs Cheeseman in *The Town Traveller*: ' "Now, see 'ere, Polly. You're a young gyell, my dear, and a 'andsome gyell, as we all know, and you've only one fault, which there ain't no need to mention it." '[75] The use of the palatal glide in such ways becomes part of that armoury of features by which social, cultural, and linguistic values may be conveyed to the discerning reader, the graphemic distortion which its use involved presenting yet another aspect of 'illiterate' speech over the course of the century.

Such patterns, whether of *wos* or *wot*, or *gjell*, *sarvice*, or *'ill* all serve to emphasize the social landscape in many novels of the nineteenth century, the graphemic irregularities which are depicted trading on attitudes and assumptions about pronunciation which were commonplace in much popular comment on language. Authors were, of course, on the whole writing from the point of view of the standard and the standard ideology, which in itself, as we have seen, readily applied labels of non- and sub-standard to features of pronunciation which were either new, or which indeed merely differed from those more ideal states of the language which many writers would have liked to see in existence. As many of these examples illustrate, common nineteenth-century reactions to sound changes in progress were also to provide a useful source of such intentionally contrastive markings. Given a London-based literary culture, as Norman Page has noted, 'provinciality' in all

---

[73] Oliver, *General Critical Grammar of the Inglish Language*, 284 n.
[74] Ellis, *Early English Pronunciation*, iv. 1115, i. 206.
[75] *The Town Traveller*, 68.

its senses tends all too readily to be equated with inferiority;[76] this was of course the appropriate paradigm in which attitudes to accent, and representations of its use, are (regardless) worked out in literature and works on language alike. As such, literary works filled a potentially important role in the ways in which they too were able to contribute to, and even disseminate, the prevalent notions of 'right' and 'wrong' in speech. Blending entertainment with implicit instruction in the stereotypes of 'polite speech', as well as in those social alliances which such embedded value-systems suggested, the novels, poetry, and drama of the age were able, in a number of ways, to reinforce 'that habitual association of ideas' between the proprieties of grapheme and phoneme discussed by Thomas Sheridan in his own intention to disseminate awareness of a national standard of speech. Literature, like works on language themselves, can hence partake in that process by which that 'consciousness' in Sheridan's terms may be 'awaken'd'—not least in the ways in which such preconceptions about pronunciation were regularly presented in terms of a dominantly social discourse in which comedy may attend error, and respect will almost inevitably accompany its absence.

As we have, for example, already seen, from all accounts Dickens's influence in this respect was potentially great, and a number of observers note that Uriah Heep's iterations of *umble* seemed to have predisposed most speakers decisively in favour of enunciations with [h] in this traditionally [h]-less word.[77] It must nevertheless be remembered that most novels (and poetry) reached a relatively narrow audience, even given the much greater levels of literacy attested in the nineteenth century than in earlier centuries. Their price alone proved a barrier to widespread circulation, rendering them commodities of luxury rather than necessity; a copy of Scott's *Ivanhoe* would, for example, have cost 30s. in 1820 in spite of its well-attested popularity. In 1810, his *Lady of the Lake* was priced still higher at 42s. Though the cost was gradually to decrease,[78] the average price of a book by the mid-nineteenth century was

---

[76] N. Page, *Speech in the English Novel* 2nd edn. (London, 1988), 58.

[77] See pp. 144–9.

[78] This is particularly evident in the second half of the 19th c., when, as a result of the introduction of steam power for printing in the 1840s and the use of machine-made, rather than hand-made, paper, printing costs began to decrease.

still between 8*s*. and 9*s*., a relatively substantial amount given that a shipwright in the late eighteenth century might be earning a total of 32*s*. a week, or, by the 1830s, a skilled London worker would be earning only 30*s*. to 33*s*. a week.[79] To spend a third or even a half of one's weekly wages on the purchase of a single book required a commitment to literature beyond the range of most people in the middle and lower ranks of society. Even use of the circulating libraries was beyond the means of many: Charles Mudie, for example, charged one guinea for a year's subscription in 1842, and this was half as much as many of his rivals.

In a number of ways therefore, though literature did endorse popular fictions of correctness and incorrectness in the contrastive modes of speech it deployed, its influence was on the whole more limited than might perhaps initially be assumed. Dickens's decision to publish his novels in parts (like a number of other novelists such as Thackeray, Trollope, Ainsworth, and Lever) is, however, potentially of more interest in this context, securing, as it did, a far wider readership than would otherwise have been possible. Costing 3*d*. a week or 1*s*. a month, and thereby spreading the total cost of the novel over a considerable period of time, such a format, as Richard Altick notes, 'appealed to the great body of middle-class readers who could afford to spend a shilling every month but not to lay out a cool guinea or a guinea and a half at a time'.[80] Even in the long term, it proved a more economical way to purchase books, for, as Altick points out, if *Pickwick* had in the first instance appeared in book form, the price would have been around 31*s*. 6*d*.; as it was, even after buying all the parts separately, the total cost was only 20*s*., and only one further shilling was necessary to have the whole volume bound into book form.

The popularity of this method of publication was well attested. Chapman and Hall, for example, printed some 400 copies of the first part of the *Pickwick Papers*; by the end, they were instead producing over 40,000 copies of each monthly part. Around 50,000 copies of each number of *Nicholas Nickleby* were sold during its publication in 1838–9, Part I of *Our Mutual Friend* sold 30,000 copies in the first three days alone, and, as Altick notes, the 'penny edition' of *Oliver Twist* sold 150,000 copies in three weeks in 1871.[81]

---

[79] See Altick, *English Common Reader*, 58, 276.
[80] Ibid. 279.   [81] Ibid. 384.

Mowbray Morris in the *Fortnightly Review* claimed in 1882 that, in the twelve years since Dickens's death, the sale of Dickens's works in England totalled 4,239,000 volumes.[82] Given such figures, it is hardly surprising that Dickens's work and characters were to secure such a hold upon the national, and public, imagination, especially since each copy was presumably being read by more than one individual, not least given that emphasis placed on reading aloud within common Victorian eulogies on the pleasures of the home.[83] Few, however, would have reached as large an audience as that described in the (possibly apocryphal) tale of the Liverpool locksmith encountered by Lord Denham and Sir Benjamin Brodie. Having hired his monthly part of *Pickwick* from a circulating library for 2*d.*, he was described as reading it aloud to an audience of more than twenty men, women, and children. Few people, moreover, could read or still further listen to a Dickens novel without being aware of the important role which language, and significant variations within it, played in creating the overall texture of his work.

Dickens's own sensitivity to voice is well known; his early training in shorthand, his interest in the stage, and in the dramatic potential of the spoken word, as well as his own public readings of his work, all attest to a marked responsiveness to the nuances of speech. His imagination worked, as his daughter Mamie records, in profoundly aural as well as visual ways; she recalls him performing a 'facial pantomime . . . talking rapidly in a low voice . . . peopling his study with other men, women, and children, hearing other voices' in the process of composition.[84] His delineations of direct speech form, as a result, a salient facet of characterization within his novels, voices often being sharply individualized by means of his strategic manipulation of written and spoken interfaces. Though Walker appears explicitly by name only as one of Miss Blimber's preferred authorities in *Dombey and Son* (' "If my recollection serves me", said Miss Blimber, breaking off, "the word analysis, as opposed to synthesis, is thus defined by Walker . . . Now you know what analysis is, Dombey" '[85]), Dickens betrays a similar responsiveness to the fictions of prescriptive ideology and accompanying language attitudes in his depictions of speech. Early

---

[82] Cited ibid. 384.   [83] See pp. 175–7.
[84] P. Ackroyd, *Dickens* (London, 1990), 561.   [85] *Dombey and Son*, 184.

recognized as being fundamentally a '*class* writer',[86] he makes liberal use of perceived, and propagated, correlations between language and social status, encoding in abundance received stereotypes about the cultural and social, as well as linguistic values present within the structured variations of speech.

A plethora of marked and unmarked forms locate Dickens's characters in social space, the stratified distribution of orthographical improprieties corresponding clearly to the notional norms and deviations of nineteenth-century speech. Socially sensitive variables, such as the variation between [hw] and [w] or *obleege* and *oblige* are deployed, as we have already seen, in ways which reinforce established views on the properties and possession of literate speech. Hyperlects as well as basilects attract modifications of spelling designed to suggest divergence from a norm: ' "Have I brought ruin upon the best and purest creature that ever blessed a demnition vagabond! Demmit, let me go" ', exclaims Mr Mantalini in *Nicholas Nickleby*; ' "Then my ears did not deceive me, and it's not wa-a-x work" ', says Lord Frederick Verisopht in the same novel, his vocalic attenuations effectively conveying the affected drawl deemed typical of the aristocracy.[87] Orthographical variations, just like that more explicit comment on language within the prescriptive tradition, are often employed in distinctly evaluative ways. Magwitch's first utterances in *Great Expectations* reveal him as an outcast from polite society, while his status as convict is as yet unknown; Jo's use of language in *Bleak House* concisely establishes patterns of social equality and inequality by linguistic means: ' "They're wots left . . . out of a sov'ring as wos give me by a lady in a wale as sed she wos a servant, and as come to my crossin one night and asked to be shown this 'ere oust and the oust wot him as you giv the writin to died at, and the berrin ground wot he's berrid in." '[88]

The combination of such forms with malapropisms such as *malefactors* for *manufacturers* by Mr Plornish in *Little Dorrit*, or *consequential* for *consecrated* by Jo himself only serve to enhance a sub-text often founded on the appreciation of linguistic 'ignorance', placed against the conventional proprieties of the 'educated', reinforcing preconceptions, in terms of accent, of a literate norm

---

[86] *Blackwood's Magazine*; cited in Ackroyd, *Dickens*, 719.
[87] *Nicholas Nickleby*, 197, 176.   [88] *Bleak House*, 283.

located primarily in the middle and upper classes. For those middle-class readers who were indeed felt to be Dickens's true audience (as one reviewer in *Blackwood's Magazine* commented, 'it is the air and breath of middle-class respectability which fills the books of Mr. Dickens'[89]), the complex of marked forms which distinguish the speech of those lower down the social scale merely reinforced awareness of the normative patterns of linguistic and social behaviour to which stated conformity was important. As Dickens was well aware, his selections from among the range of possible options for the representation of speech were by no means value-free. Aligned within prevailing linguistic ideologies, and firmly embedded in the wider social and cultural environments of his readership, it is, as Carter and Nash affirm, precisely this 'intermeshing of language and style in the *context* of social systems and institutions' which serves to convey, at least in part, those more ideological dimensions of literature.[90] 'Particular linguistic or stylistic choices', they stress, 'are not innocent value-free selections from a system.' Instead such choices 'conceal or reveal certain realities rather than others, establishing or reinforcing ideologies in the process',[91] a precept which is equally important in terms of the standard ideology and the profound status-consciousness with which its manifestations, especially in terms of accent, were endowed.

The evaluative bias present within those fictions of speech used by Dickens (and other writers) is of course inescapable, the oppositions of 'literate' and 'illiterate' speech serving, as already illustrated, to encode prevalent stereotypes about the nature of 'class' and its linguistic correspondences, often largely irrespective of the facts of linguistic reality (though displaying marked conformity with the expressed tenets of language attitudes). The fact that lexical, syntactic, and grammatical choices can also intervene in this paradigm only serves to enhance its effectiveness. Dickens can, however, be much more subtle than such schematic patterns suggest, and it is often in his ability to confront directly such sociolinguistic stereotypes, and the fallacies behind them, that he is in fact most successful.

Manners, and their role in setting forth 'a culture's hum and

[89] Cited in Ackroyd, *Dickens*, 719.
[90] R. Carter and W. Nash, *Seeing Through Language: A Guide to Styles of English Writing* (Oxford, 1990), 21.
[91] Ibid. 24.

buzz of implication',[92] form of course a salient territory of the
novel, a fact equally significant in considering their specifically
linguistic aspects. When, in *David Copperfield*, Dickens presents
us with the graphemic propriety of David himself, of Betsey
Trotwood, and of Steerforth, and develops the contrast between
this and the heavy use of marked forms which characterizes the
speech of Mr Peggotty, we are tempted to assume, with Trilling,
that it is 'inescapably true that in the novel manners make man'.[93]
Demarcating the divide between 'polite' and 'vulgar', the distribution of marked and unmarked forms corresponds closely to the
evaluative norms of 'correctness', and 'incorrectness', 'literate' and
'illiterate', 'cultured' and 'provincial', or 'superior' and 'inferior'
which are deployed with such regularity in contemporary writings
on the language. Language, and especially accent, was seen as
denoting 'breeding', and 'moral' as well as 'intellectual' culture,
as *Talking and Debating* stressed in 1856.[94] Or as Williams expounded six years earlier, 'language, both oral and written, is the
exponent of the condition of the mind; when mean and inappropriate, it infers that the habits of life and the condition of the
mind are equally mean and uncultivated'.[95]

Certainly, it is this (amongst other things) which underpins
Steerforth's negative perceptions of Mr Peggotty and his family as
being merely 'that sort of people'.[96] The patterns of qualitative
foregrounding employed in the novel to represent speech effectively
serve to map out the relevant stereotypes of social and linguistic
inequality: ' "I'll pound it, it's wot you do yourself, sir" ', says Mr
Peggotty, addressing Steerforth, ' "and wot you do well—right
well!" '[97] Common cultural equations of accent and identity, of
external as a signifier of internal, and moreover of 'provincial' as
synonymous with 'inferior', are all involved in Steerforth's subsequent estimation of the nature of social distance, difference, and
deviation in this context.

'Why, there's a pretty wide separation between them and us', said
Steerforth, with indifference. 'They are not to be expected to be as sensitive
as we are. Their delicacy is not to be shocked, or hurt very easily. They
are wonderfully virtuous, I dare say—some people contend for that, at

---

[92] L. Trilling, 'Manners, Morals, and the Novel', in id., *The Liberal Imagination:
Essays on Literature and Society* (London, 1955), 206.
[93] Ibid. 216.   [94] *Talking and Debating*, 3; see also p. 129.
[95] Williams, *Composition*, 5.   [96] *David Copperfield*, 251.   [97] Ibid. 90.

least; and I am sure I don't want to contradict them—but they have not very fine natures, and they may be thankful that, like their coarse rough skins, they are not easily wounded.'[98]

David assumes that Steerforth is merely jesting in his iteration of common assumptions about the nature of the lower orders. Nevertheless, as subsequent events reveal, he was indeed in earnest.

Language informs the reader's perceptions of that 'separation' which is recognized by Steerforth, and while Steerforth himself is characterized by his 'nice voice', and the graphemic and grammatical proprieties which inevitably accompany his speech, Mr Peggotty is distinguished by the contrary. The value-laden forms of accent tempt common value-judgements in response. Dickens, however, in a highly successful form of linguistic didacticism, uses fiction to expose common fallacies about these prevailing sociolinguistic stereotypes, making it entirely clear that judgements made on such grounds may all too often be instead misjudgements, with all the inadequacies which such errors imply. 'Handsome is as handsome does' is of course the rightful adage to be applied, and it is deeds not words (and their pronunciation) which prove the gentleman. As Blake has noted in his own work on the use, and associations, of the non-standard in literature: 'An accent is no guide to a man's character, though people may make assumptions on that basis',[99] and it is precisely this process of mistaken assumption which takes place in *David Copperfield* (or, for that matter, in David Lodge's *Nice Work*).[100] Dickens, deliberately heightening the use of 'illiterate speech' by Mr Peggotty as we move towards realization of Steerforth's duplicity, exposes rather than endorses

---

[98] Ibid. 251.

[99] N. F. Blake, *Non-standard Language in English Literature* (London, 1981), 14.

[100] The same pattern of equation, and mis-equation, is, for example, deployed by Lodge in the introduction of Basil's girlfriend Debbie, whose speech is markedly Cockney and colloquial: ' "Held in a sorter castle. Just like a horror film, wonnit? . . . suits of armour and stuffed animals heads and everyfink." ' As Lodge comments on Robyn's reactions to such linguistic markers of 'identity': 'at first Robyn thought that Debbie's Cockney accent was some sort of joke, but soon realised it was authentic. In spite of her Sloaney clothes and hair-do, Debbie was decidedly lower-class. When Basil mentioned that she worked in the same bank as himself, Robyn assumed that she was a secretary or typist, but was quickly corrected by her brother when he followed her out into the kitchen when she was making tea.' Belying such initial categorizations by her ready recognition of Lapsang Souchong (' "Love it", said Debbie. She really was a very difficult girl to get right.'), Debbie is of course ultimately revealed as a foreign exchange dealer, with a salary far in excess of Robyn's own. *Nice Work* (London, 1988), 124.

the processes of value-judgement commonly invited by the stig-
matizing effects of graphemic deviation. Steerforth, endowed with
the delusive proprieties of 'gentlemanly' speech which to many in
the nineteenth century had come to signify associations of inner
worth too,[101] is instead decisively revealed as villain:

> 'Why, this here candle, now!', said Mr. Peggotty, gleefully holding out
> his hand towards it, '*I* know wery well that arter she's married and gone,
> I shall put that candle theer, just that same as now. I know wery well that
> when I'm here o' nights (and where else should *I* live, bless your arts,
> whatever fortun I come into!) and she ain't here, or I ain't theer, I shall
> put the candle in the winder, and sit afore the fire, pretending I'm ex-
> pecting of her, like I'm a doin' now. *There's* a babby for you', said Mr
> Peggotty, with another roar, 'in the form of a Sea Porkypine! Why, at the
> present minute, when I see the candle sparkle up, I says to myself, "She's
> a looking at it! Em'ly's a coming!" *There's* a babby for you, in the form
> of a Sea Porkypine! Right for all that', said Mr Peggotty, stopping in his
> roar, and smiting his hands together; 'fur here she is!'
> It was only Ham.[102]

Though forms such as *heer*, *art* (rather than *heart*), and *fur* (rather
than unstressed *for*) are liberally used within this (and later)
sections, the distancing effects of deviation are largely broken down,
displaced not only by the pathos of such sustained devotion but
also, and more significantly, by respect.

The construct presented within the contrasted schema of language in *David Copperfield* is again essentially that of subjective
inequality, the structured patterns of norm and deviation being
used to aid mistaken assessments about the nature of superiority,
inferiority, and the 'gentleman'.[103] Similar processes still take place
of course, as the data of subjective reaction tests reveal; by means
of accent speakers are judged 'friendly' or 'polite', 'intelligent' or
'well educated' and their arguments too, as Wells confirms, may
be found more or less persuasive 'depending on the qualities which
we implicitly attribute to them on the basis of their accent'.[104] In
the context of literature, as Leech and Short point out, the very
use of non-standard language similarly tends to suggest 'remoteness
from the author's own language, and hence from the central
standards of judgement in a novel'.[105] It is this habitual association

---

[101] See e.g. p. 61.　　　　[102] *David Copperfield*, 384.
[103] See pp. 58–9.　　　[104] Wells, *Accents of English*, i. 30. See also pp. 58–9.
[105] Leech and Short, *Style in Fiction*, 172.

of ideas which Dickens exploits so well in *David Copperfield*. He offers, for example, a similar pattern of assessment, and reassessment, in *Great Expectations*, as Pip's education into a 'gentleman', in at least its dominantly social senses, leads him into disregarding those truer gentlemanly virtues which, throughout the novel, form the hallmark of Joe's character. As we have already seen, the linguistic differentials of status are closely associated with the sense of social shame which surrounds Pip's associations with the forge once his acquaintance with Miss Havisham has begun.[106] They are perhaps brought out most clearly in the evident failure of discourse in Joe's meeting with the latter:

'Well!' said Miss Havisham. 'And you have reared the boy, with the intention of taking him for your apprentice; is that so, Mr Gargery?'
'You know, Pip', replied Joe, 'as you and me were ever friends, and it were look'd for'ard to betwixt us, as being calc'lated to lead to larks. Not but what, Pip, if you had ever made objections to the business—such as its being open to black and sut, or such-like—not but what they would have been attended to, don't you see?'[107]

As in *David Copperfield*, the widespread belief that it is external manners which alone make man, as well as which determine relevant estimations of social worth, is again brought to the fore. Pip, aspiring to the role of 'gentleman', and given an all-too-effective education in social and linguistic consciousness by Estella, is similarly made all too aware of Joe's seeming inadequacies in this respect. ' "You will not omit any opportunity of helping Joe on, a little" ', he urges Biddy before his departure, ' "Joe is a dear good fellow—in fact, I think he is the dearest fellow that ever lived —but he is rather backward in some things. For instance, Biddy, in his learning and his manners." '[108]

Pip, influenced by Estella's teaching, equates the provincial with commonness and 'disgrace', the non-localized with superiority. Joe has a surer perspective from the beginning: ' "Manners is manners, but still your elth's your elth." '[109] No 'improvement' of Joe is necessary, as later events reveal; one of 'Nature's gentlemen', though he may drop his [h]s, employ *wot* rather than *what*, and discuss *coddleshells* rather than *codicils*, it is, as Pip comes to realize, 'the wealth of his great nature' which is most important, and not

---

[106] See pp. 142–4.   [107] *Great Expectations*, i. 212.
[108] Ibid. i. 318.   [109] Ibid. i. 20.

those manners, linguistic or social, which Pip would first have remedied. As he acknowledges early in the novel: 'I wanted to make Joe less ignorant and common, that he might be worthier of my society and less open to Estella's reproach.'[110] By its end, such perceptions have been reversed, and it is his own unworthiness, in the face of Joe's unwavering fidelity, which he wishes to amend. The linguistic divide is rendered unimportant in the face of this greater truth, a corrective which many writers on the language (and on manners too) would have done well to observe in the pressures which they often attempted to exert upon their readers.

The connotative values of speech, their assumed social meanings, and the misconceptions to which they may lead, are, in such ways, made into an important element of Dickens's art. His treatment of the manners and mannerisms of speakers, on a number of occasions, functions not just as a diacritic of status (though this aspect is not neglected), but also as a means by which larger themes and issues may be explored. Almost simultaneously therefore, Dickens endorses prevailing images of speech and speakers, allocating graphemic deviations in abundance to those located below the middle classes, and further encoding popular images of literate and illiterate speech and their assumed social correlations, yet he also offers within his work a timely reminder that such superficialities of speech may disguise a deeper reality which should not be ignored. Polished speech may conceal more serious errors; the accents and grammatical errors of the provincial or the lower class, in spite of their well-attested stigmatization in nineteenth-century attitudes to the language, will in no way serve as images of inferiority in all respects. As Trilling wrote of the treatment of manners in the novel, 'in this part of culture assumption rules, which is often so much stronger than reason'.[111] Dickens, in his treatment of Steerforth, Mr Peggotty, Pip, and Joe (among many others) offers clear illustration of the dangers and misconceptions which such unquestioned assumptions may lead to in the context of linguistic manners, and the phonemic and grammatical sensitivities of the age.

Dickens was thus both able to encode, and also to decode, the repercussions of prescriptive ideology upon language use and language attitudes in the nineteenth century. George Gissing is,

---

[110] Ibid. i. 232.   [111] Trilling, *The Liberal Imagination*, 207.

however, the novelist who perhaps demonstrates in fullest measure
the ways in which the evaluative paradigms within which accent
variations were so often placed could infuse literary depictions of
the social world. His novels, almost without exception, betray an
acute sensitivity to the nuances of speech, not only in the context
of its relatively detailed representation, but also within the range
of explicit comments on accent and its social overtones which
regularly appear throughout his work. Conceptions of the extra-
linguistic values which accent could convey can rarely have been
expressed with such clarity within the domains of literature. Sharing
a lexis which has marked affinities with that employed by Walker
in his moments of greater prescriptive excess, accents which deviate from the increasingly non-localized norms of the standard
are described as 'gross', 'hateful', or 'vilely grotesque'. Voice is
developed into a signifier of more than merely social resonance,
so that the presence of perceived 'refinement' in its tones is regularly
used to suggest corresponding interior qualities. Descriptions of
its nuances accompany the introduction of new characters, as in
the description of Stephen Lord in *In the Year of Jubilee*: 'His pronunciation fell short of refinement, but was not vulgar. Something
of country accent could still be detected in it. He talked like a
man who could strike a softer note if he cared to, but despised the
effort.'[112]

Hugh Carnaby in *The Whirlpool*, 'the well-bred, well-fed Englishman' is likewise distinguished by 'his tongue' which 'told of age-
old domination', and Alma's reactions to him are expressed in
precisely the same terms: 'She was impressed by a quality in the
voice, a refinement of utterance, which at once distinguished it from
that of the men with whom she had been talking. It belonged to
a higher social grade, if it did not express a superiority of nature.'[113]
'There was no flagrant offence in the man. He spoke with passable
accent', Gissing notes of Mr Cusse in *Born in Exile*.[114] In *The
Emancipated*, the acquisition of non-localized nuances of speech is
presented as a marker of evident achievement in our first encounter
with Cecily Doran: 'Her enunciation had the peculiar finish which
is acquired in intercourse with the best cosmopolitan society, the
best in a worthy sense. Four years ago, when she left Lancashire,

---

[112] G. Gissing, *In the Year of Jubilee* (London, 1894), i. 46.
[113] Id., *The Whirlpool* (London, 1897), 9, 181.   [114] *Born in Exile*, i. 101.

she had a touch of provincial accent . . . but now it was impossible to discover by listening to her from what part of England she came.'[115]

Such distinctions, of language and of class, are, for Gissing, often fundamental to his perceptions of the struggles of his characters. Assimilation to the norms of refined London speech, and the corresponding suppression of the provincial, mark the experiences of Richard Mutimer in *Demos* or Godwin Peak in *Born in Exile*. Exile from the cultured classes is often specifically seen in linguistic as well as social terms, and to the still-exiled, and socially aspiring, their language is to be emulated, if not to be revered. Gissing's *Born in Exile*, for example, details an alienation which manifests itself in barriers of accent as well as wealth, the sociolinguistic stigmas of low birth forming a recurrent topic in the novel. Born himself into the lower reaches of the middle class ('a social sphere in which he must ever be an alien'),[116] Godwin Peak, the central character, is yet endowed with an exquisite sense of social and linguistic nuance which is continually disturbed by the language, and especially the accents, of the 'vulgar' who surround him. With 'an ear constantly tormented by the London vernacular', his reactions to those who do not share his aural sympathies are extreme:

I hate low, uneducated people! I hate them worse than the filthiest vermin! . . . they ought to be swept off the face of the earth! . . . All the grown-up creatures, who can't speak proper English and don't know how to behave themselves, I'd transport them to the Falkland Islands.[117]

Peak himself thus becomes a casualty of that prevalent impulse towards social, cultural, and linguistic cohesion, as the evaluative paradigms imposed on accent, together with their cultural correlates, constantly pervade his thoughts, his reactions to others, and above all perhaps, his reactions to himself:

No less introspective than in the old days . . . Peak, after each of his short remarks, made comparison of his tone and phraseology with those of the other speakers. Had he still any marks of the ignoble world from which he sprang? Any defect of pronunciation, any native awkwardness of utterance? Impossible to judge himself infallibly, but he was conscious of no vulgar mannerism. Though it was so long since he left Whitelaw, the

---

[115] G. Gissing, *The Emancipated* (London, 1890), i. 40.
[116] *Born in Exile*, i. 84; see also p. 249.   [117] Ibid. i. 63.

accent of certain of the Professors still remained with him as an example;
when endeavouring to be graceful, he was wont to hear the voice of Dr
Nares, or of Professor Barber who lectured on English literature. More
recently he had been observant of Christian Moxey's speech, which had
a languid elegance worth imitating in certain particulars. Buckland
Warricombe was rather a careless talker, but it was the carelessness of a
man who had never needed to reflect on such a matter, the refinement
of whose enunciation was assured to him from the nursery. That now
was a thing to be aimed at.[118]

Emulation, imitation, the problems of signifying a status he does
not possess in an accent which he has assumed, impinge without
respite upon Peak's consciousness. Continually monitoring his
speech for the inflections which might betray his lowly origins, his
obsession with speech is precisely aligned within recommendations familiar from the social and linguistic dicta of books like
How Should I Pronounce?, *How to Shine in Society*, and *Vulgarities
of Speech Corrected*. Peak has learnt his prescriptive lessons well,
perhaps too well.

Those correlations of accent and identity, readily encompassing
cultural and intellectual, as well as social values within much contemporary writing on the language, are, as this indicates, woven deep
into the texture of Gissing's work. Notions of literate speech, and
its associated polarities of 'education' and 'ignorance', are in turn
reinforced with little compromise: 'Another word of which Mr
Cullen is fond is "strattum",—usually spelt and pronounced with
but one *t* midway', Gissing notes in *Demos*.[119] Few other authors
can rival Gissing's perspicacity in the sphere of the connotative
values which accent, by the late nineteenth century, had inextricably
come to impart. In him language attitudes received their best
exponent, though the limited circulation of his work clearly meant
that no great conversions were (perhaps fortunately given his characteristic vehemence) likely to have been achieved by such means.
Readily engaging with prevalent fictions of speech, and encoding
dominant stereotypes of speaker and speech with ease, Gissing
has nevertheless an unerring eye for the detail which will convey
residual vulgarity, or the fact of low origins still not entirely transcended. Hence of Richard Mutimer, working-class socialist whose
transformation into wealthy capitalist occupies much of *Demos*,

---

[118] Ibid. i. 248.   [119] *Demos*, i. 118.

we are told: 'It was unfortunate that Richard did not pronounce the name of his bride elect quite as it sounds on cultured lips. This may have been partly the result of diffidence; but there was a slurring of the second syllable disagreeably suggestive of vulgarity.'[120] In spite of his almost achieved ambition to marry a 'lady', the stigma of his social origins, embodied in his speech, still hampers Richard's progress towards acceptability. As Gissing adds in a typical aphorism: 'The vulgarity of a man who tries hard not to be vulgar is always particularly distressing.'[121]

It is this emphasis on accent as an unmistakable signifier of vulgarity or, conversely, of refinement which works so strongly in Gissing's novels to reinforce the system of value-judgements with which variations of speech were popularly imbued. The due proprieties of female speech were also to receive corresponding attention, his aesthetic sensibilities in this respect revealing precise alignments with that gendered bias which is, as we have seen, so perceptible in many accounts of language as it should be used. Ideologies of the feminine voice, and corresponding notions of 'talking like a lady' form, in fact, recurrent motifs in his characterization of women. As George Vandenhoff had proclaimed, delicate enunciation ensures both status and attractiveness for the lady,[122] and female readers of Gissing's work would certainly have found no lack of confirmation of such views. The attraction Lilian holds for Denzil in *Denzil Quarrier* is thus initially phrased in terms of voice ('I managed to get a word or two with her, and I liked her way of speaking'),[123] and Will's proposal to Bertha Cross in *Will Warburton* refers to the linguistic as much as love in his account of the beginnings of his admiration: 'As you talked to me that morning, I knew what I know better still, that there was no girl that I *liked* as I liked you, no girl whose face had so much meaning for me, whose voice and way of speaking so satisfied me.'[124] Whereas defeminized speech mars the 'new woman',[125] it is the external refinements of voice which reveal the true 'lady', her linguistic perfections designed to please the fastidious (and predominantly male) ear, whilst her vocalic purity is often made to take on those more widely emblematic properties often expounded

[120] Ibid. ii. 33.   [121] Ibid. ii. 35.
[122] See p. 167.   [123] *Denzil Quarrier*, 103.
[124] G. Gissing, *Will Warburton. A Romance of Real Life* (London, 1905), 322.
[125] See p. 191.

in nineteenth-century texts on the Proper Lady.[126] The possession
of such linguistic virtues indeed provides one of the most significant
revelations for Godwin Peak in *Born in Exile*, the voices of the two
girls he overhears at the Whitelaw prize day serving to bring home
a further facet of his social exile to him, here presented explicitly
in terms of gender and of voice:

He had not imagined that girls could display such intelligence, and the
sweet clearness of their intonation, the purity of their accent, the grace
of their habitual phrases, were things altogether beyond his experience.
This was not the English he had been wont to hear on female lips. His
mother and his aunt spoke with propriety; their associates were soft-
tongued; but here was something quite different from inoffensiveness of
tone and diction. Godwin appreciated the differentiating cause. These
young ladies behind him had been trained from the cradle to speak for
the delight of fastidious ears; that they should be grammatical was not
enough—they must excel in the art of conversational music. Of course
there existed a world where only such speech was interchanged, and how
inestimably happy those men to whom the sphere was native![127]

Voice, as we have seen, provides a joint symbol of exclusivity, and
of exclusion throughout *Born in Exile*, and this is perhaps one of
its most telling expositions, as Peak listens attentively to the superior, and truly feminine, diction of these young ladies, yet is unable
to enter into converse with them.

The voice that is soft, gentle, sweet, and low, often presented
in popular ideologies of the feminine as one of the most essential
properties within contemporary stereotypes of the 'lady',[128] thus
finds one of its best advocates in Gissing. In *Will Warburton*, for
example, the 'soft and musical' voice of Will's mother is given
prominence in her introduction in the novel, while that of
Rosamund is 'always subdued', with 'a range of melodious expression which caressed the ear, no matter how trifling the words she
uttered'.[129] Evelyn Cloud in the short story 'Our Learned Fellow-
Townsman' is likewise depicted in terms of her 'soft, kindly accents'
and her 'intonation of peculiar gentleness'.[130] These and other
nineteenth-century Cordelias populate Gissing's novels, their articulatory 'gentleness' often inextricably linked with notions of status,

---

[126] See Ch. 4.   [127] *Born in Exile*, i. 82–3.
[128] See pp. 173–5.   [129] *Will Warburton*, 53, 225.
[130] G. Gissing, 'Our Learned Fellow-Townsman', in id., *A Victim of Circumstances* (London, 1927), 278–9.

just as the shrieking tones of other women are made to signify their own vulgarity, and corresponding alienation from the refined and 'literate' spheres of ladies and gentlemen.[131]

Other authors, however, were to explore this particular aspect of the prevalent fictions of speech and their specifically feminine proprieties with perhaps more caution, able to encode, but also to expose undue emphasis on these stereotypes of 'ladylike' speech. George Eliot, a novelist whose command of language in assigning nuances of identity has often been praised, deploys an awareness of prevailing language attitudes in this context with some skill. Heightened feminine sensibilities towards 'proper' linguistic behaviour in fact come to form a recurrent aspect of her novels: the Miss Gunns in *Silas Marner*, Esther Lyon in *Felix Holt*, and Rosamond Vincy in *Middlemarch* are all linked by their concern for conformity with the avowedly 'ladylike' ideal, and by their corresponding preoccupation with its linguistic manifestations. Daughters of a wealthy wine-merchant from Lytherley, the Miss Gunns, for instance, readily condemn Nancy Lammeter for linguistic infelicities they regard as incompatible with their own assumptions of status and ladylike identity:

The Miss Gunns smiled stiffly, and thought what a pity it was that these rich country people, who could afford to buy such good clothes . . . should be brought up in utter ignorance and vulgarity. [Nancy] actually said 'mate' for 'meat', ''appen' for 'perhaps', and ''oss' for 'horse', which, to young ladies living in good Lytherley society, who habitually said 'orse, even in domestic privacy and only said 'appen on the right occasions, was necessarily shocking.[132]

In George Eliot's work, such perceptions, and the value-judgements on which they are based, tend, however, to be assimilated into a wider moral framework, as, like Dickens, she willingly confronts the fallacies which can rest behind the common fictions of speech. As David Daiches stressed in 1963, for example, Eliot's novels regularly reveal the presence of an 'acute ear for differences in conversational idiom', which is employed as 'a means of

---

[131] See e.g. the short story 'One Way of Happiness' in the collection *A Victim of Circumstances*, and the descriptions of voice accorded to Mrs Budge and Mrs Rippingdale, Cockney housewives, and profoundly negative exemplars of the feminine ideal: 'They talked in a high key, laughed in a scream', we are told on p. 39, and their 'screeching' tones and 'high-pitched remarks' are described with disfavour two pages later.

[132] G. Eliot, *Silas Marner: The Weaver of Raveloe* (London, 1861), 184–5.

emphasizing human variety and at the same time of linking that variety with a central moral pattern'.[133] In representations of notions of the ladylike in speech, and the superior sensibilities which ladies, and most notably, would-be 'ladies', are supposed to affect in this context, a similar pattern is apparent. While the Miss Gunns react with disfavour to forms they see as 'vulgar' in Nancy's speech, their own 'vulgarity', that of 'exclusiveness', is simultaneously revealed. The paradigm is that set forth by Eliot in 'The Natural History of German Life' in her precept that 'More is done towards linking the higher classes with the lower [by] obliterating the vulgarity of exclusiveness, than by hundreds of sermons and philosophic dissertations.'[134] Language in her novels, and attitudes to it, prove to be particularly useful ways of expounding this belief, as the notions of linguistic exclusion and linguistic exclusivity so readily endorsed within contemporary language attitudes are instead transposed into vehicles of moral as well as social meaning.

Morals and manners are, as in Dickens, set into opposition, and characters such as Esther Lyon and Rosamond Vincy provide striking examples of women who, in their initial adherence to ideologies of the feminine and ladylike as adequate emblems of identity, are unable to transcend the dissimulations of language (and of status) to penetrate to the underlying and moral realities. Social status provides, for example, a major preoccupation for Esther Lyon in *Felix Holt*. Though her father's role is that of independent preacher, her own ideals rest in 'refined society', and the identity of a 'lady'. Appropriately refined and ladylike airs are cultivated with some assiduity, the bust of George Whitfield in her father's study being covered up because of its squint, and her olfactory sensibilities requiring the purchase of wax rather than tallow candles. Her sensitivities to accent are similarly precise. Her father abides by his own moral code: 'I abstain from judging by the outward appearance only',[135] but Esther instead adheres to the converse; the only point in Felix's favour is that 'he speaks better English than most of our visitors'[136] and she registers a similar approval of Harold Transome, in spite of his moral nullity. As Eliot points out:

[133] D. Daiches, *Middlemarch* (London, 1963), 67.
[134] G. Eliot, 'The Natural History of German Life', *Westminster Review*, NS 10 (July 1856), 51.
[135] G. Eliot, *Felix Holt, the Radical* (London, 1866), ii. 108.   [136] Ibid. i. 133.

[Esther] was alive to the finest shades of manner, to the nicest distinctions of tone and accent; she had a little code of her own about scents and colours, textures and behaviour, by which she secretly condemned or sanctioned all things and persons. And she was well satisfied with herself for her fastidious taste, never doubting that hers was the highest standard.[137]

Such 'fastidious taste' is itself satisfied once Esther is removed, Cinderella-like, to Transome Court. Accent is again used to form a prime index of acceptability: 'over and above her really generous feeling, she enjoyed Mrs Transome's accent, the high-bred quietness of her speech'.[138] The pleasure which attends listening to the latter's family stories is likewise enhanced, for this highly susceptible auditor, by 'that refined high-bred tone and accent which [Mrs Transome] possessed in perfection'.[139] This mastery of the symbols of social exclusivity is, however, also accompanied, as Esther gradually comes to realize, by a corresponding command of social exclusion, as had indeed already been apparent in Mrs Transome's first meeting with Rufus Lyon:

Mrs Transome hardly noticed Mr Lyon, not from studied haughtiness, but from sheer mental inability to consider him—as a person ignorant of natural history is unable to consider a fresh-water polype [*sic*] otherwise than as a sort of animated weed, certainly not fit for table.[140]

As Eliot stated in *Theophrastus Such*, 'a chief misfortune of high birth is that it usually shuts a man out from the large sympathetic knowledge of human experience which comes from contact with various classes on their own level'.[141] It is this which Esther comes to understand, in her dawning sense that moral sympathy can be fatally incapacitated by both egoism and an undue concentration on a superiority defined solely in terms of external markers rather than internal virtue. Esther's moral growth in the novel is presented in these terms, her own shifting attitudes to accent being made to mirror the growing realization that the possession of material fortune, and even the markers of both social and linguistic superiority, will rarely be adequate to grant exemption from a more serious, and moral, disaster.

Esther's earlier and spurious value-judgements being abandoned,

---

[137] Ibid. i. 139.   [138] Ibid. ii. 78.   [139] Ibid. ii. 100.   [140] Ibid. ii. 72.
[141] G. Eliot, 'Looking Backward', in id., *Impressions of Theophrastus Such* (London, 1869), 36.

her habitual symbols of superiority thus gradually lose the inviolable meanings with which they had previously been invested. While the love of Harold Transome is seen to give 'an air of moral mediocrity to all her prospects', and life at Transome Court proves '*not* the life of her day-dreams',[142] other events, such as the visit of the old Rector, Jack Lingon, reveal the way in which attitudes to accent are again made to fuse with the widening sympathies, and diminishing egoism, of the heroine:

> Esther was always glad when the old Rector came. With an odd contrariety to her former niceties she liked his rough attire and careless frank speech; they were something not point device that seemed to connect the life of Transome Court with that rougher, commoner world where her home had been.[143]

Snapping the 'silken bondage' of Transome Court, Esther returns to the world she had once inhabited, now equipped, however, with a truer index of superiority which is independent of the surface markings of social status.

Recurrent references to language, and the values with which it may be invested, can hence operate as significant indices of moral growth and standing in Eliot's work, a schema employed here in *Felix Holt*, but given its clearest exposition in *Middlemarch* in the character of Rosamond Vincy. A product of Mrs Lemon's school for ladies in which propriety of discourse forms part of the curriculum (as do proper modes of ascending into, and descending from a carriage) Rosamond displays a sensitivity to the social symbolism of accent which in fact surpasses much of that advice proffered to the aspiring 'lady' (and discussed in Chapter 4). Language, in exact accordance with contemporary dictates on the social values of speech, is presented as a prime means of asserting her own social identity, and assessing that of others.

Her preoccupation with such signifiers is described on a number of occasions in the novel: ' "It always makes a difference, though, to be of good family", said Rosamond, with a tone of decision which showed that she had thought on this subject.'[144] Sure of the fact that ' "you would never hear me speak in an unladylike way" ',[145] she readily corrects perceived vulgarities in her mother's

---

[142] *Felix Holt*, ii. 149.   [143] Ibid. ii. 152.
[144] G. Eliot, *Middlemarch, A Study of Provincial Life* (London, 1871), i. 175.
[145] Ibid. i. 170.

speech, and deems the young men of Middlemarch unfit as potential suitors on similar grounds: 'They were Middlemarch gentry,
. . . embarrassed in their manners, and timidly jocose: even Fred was
above them, having at least the accent and manner of a university
man.'[146] Accent determines acceptability, and Rosamond's misplaced sensibilities in this respect are perhaps most evident in her
reactions to the visit of Lydgate's cousin, Captain Lydgate. Her
judgement clouded by social status, his conversation charms her
'fine ear', not indeed by virtue of what he says, but rather by how
he says it:

> to most mortals there is a stupidity which is unendurable and a stupidity
> which is altogether acceptable—else, indeed, what would become of social
> bonds? Captain Lydgate's stupidity was delicately scented, carried itself
> with 'style', talked with a good accent, and was closely related to Sir
> Godwin. Rosamond found it quite agreeable and caught many of its
> phrases.[147]

The linguistic trappings of social identity are thus made to act as
one of the ways in which Rosamond's relationships are determined; swayed only by an attention to the superficial, language
is given exaggerated value as a standard by which she evaluates
others. Status triumphs over substance, and Rosamond, unlike
Esther, remains rooted in her egoism, continuing to place her
trust in such delusive symbols of 'superiority'.

Of course, using 'correct English' is not in itself an immediate
correlate of either snobbery or egoism. Dorothea Brooke, for example, uses English with perfect and unstudied propriety, so much
so that to Rosamond she forms 'one of those county divinities . . . ,
whose slightest marks of manner or appearance were worthy of
her study'.[148] Dorothea herself, infused by moral and not social
ardour, grants little significance to such details; her dress is plain,
her hair unadorned and simply coiled behind. Snobbery, of language, manner, or dress, is alien to her character. Attitudes to the
Garth family who, as Daiches has noted, 'provide an important
moral centre in the novel',[149] further amplify these antitheses between Dorothea and Rosamond. The Vincys, with the exception
of Fred, largely disdain to acknowledge the socially inferior Garths.
Dorothea instead refutes such snobbery, and in spite of a social

---

[146] Ibid. ii. 77.   [147] Ibid. iii. 283.
[148] Ibid. iii. 5–6.   [149] Daiches, *Middlemarch*, 47.

position far above that of the Vincys themselves, accords Caleb
Garth and his family both respect and admiration.
The Garths, however, equally form a linguistic as well as moral
centre of judgement in the novel. Mrs Garth's use of English is,
for example, characterized by its propriety; she is, for her husband, 'a treasury of correct language', and as Eliot elsewhere notes,
'in a general wreck of society [she] would have tried to hold her
"Lindley Murray" above the waves'.[150] As the image of Murray's
Grammar surviving the deluge aptly indicates, Mrs Garth endows
good usage with no little value, though the nature of this value
differs significantly from that with which it is invested by Rosamond. Linguistic propriety is important, as the former makes clear
in teaching her children, but for the purposes of communicating
one's ideas rather than signifying one's social position. Without
grammar, as she instructs her son, ' "You would use wrong words,
and put words in the wrong places, and instead of making people
understand you, they would turn away from you as a tiresome
person. What would you do then?" '[151] Whereas for Rosamond
notions of correctness had been the basis on which she decided
whether to turn away or not, in Mrs Garth's moral (and linguistic)
scheme, it is to be prized precisely because it may prevent this,
and so may facilitate rather than impede a truer communication
between individuals irrespective of their class. Accent is also included within this reorientation of priorities. ' "These things belong
only to pronunciation, which is the least part of grammar" ', stresses
Mrs Garth to her children,[152] negating those heightened sensibilities
which tended, in contemporary culture and social thinking, to
foreground its nuances as a prime determiner of social, cultural,
and even intellectual acceptability. Though using an accent which
would not affront even Rosamond's standards of speech, Mrs
Garth attaches little importance to this fact: 'she rarely forgot that
while her grammar and accent were above the town standard,
she wore a plain cap, cooked the family dinner, and darned all
the stockings'.[153]
Largely in contrast to Gissing therefore, Eliot informs her
treatment of attitudes to accent, its ladylike proprieties, and the
social values with which it was so often imbued, with a vision

---

[150] *Middlemarch*, ii. 33.   [151] Ibid. ii. 34.
[152] Ibid. ii. 33.   [153] Ibid. ii. 30.

which aligns it within the complex of moral symbolism she employs. Assigning exaggerated importance to notions of linguistic correctness becomes in Eliot's novels a way by which misplaced values, and misjudgements of external and internal worth are to be revealed. Patterns of exclusion and exclusiveness, fostered in linguistic terms by the value-laden descriptions of norm and deviation which littered popular and prescriptive comment on language, are rendered insignificant in the broader, and rightful, vision of characters such as Dorothea, or Mrs Garth.

Literary depiction of the prevalent fictions surrounding speech, its associated values, and value-judgements, is thus in many ways closely informed, as we would expect, by the tenor of the individual author's writing. Whether made into a vehicle for moral exploration in Eliot, or made to signify the social exile and the barriers of class in Gissing, its nuances are nevertheless emphasized in the literature of the nineteenth century with a detail which offers close parallels with much contemporary, and non-literary, writing on language and its socio-symbolic dimensions. Just as writers such as Sheridan, Walker, or Smart stressed the social values of literate speech, and the social unacceptability of its converse, so too did authors such as Dickens, Meredith, or Gissing extend such equations into their own delineations of the spoken word, drawing on conceptions of 'good' and 'bad' in usage which were commonplace within that prescriptive legacy which had proved so pervasive in attitudes towards language, correctness, propriety, and status. Using spelling and significant variations within it to convey the nuances of sociolect and social acceptability, such writers further encoded the prevalent stereotypes of speech and speaker, disseminating preconceptions about, for example, the differentiation of *what* and *wot*, or *girl* and *gurl*, in line with widely recognized, normative, and essentially non-localized ideals of language.

More influential perhaps in the context of disseminating these ideals were, of course, journals such as the *Family Herald* or the *London Journal*, the stories of which, as well as the letters page, often displayed a concern with the due propriety of grapheme and phoneme, and their associated and extra-linguistic values, for audiences which comprised 300,000 readers by 1855. Children's literature too ensured early exposure to notions of norm and deviation, and the appropriate criteria of acceptability to be applied, as indeed did the educational precepts of many schools, as we shall see in the following chapter. Fictional discourse, whether in journal, novel, poetry, or moral tales for children, was, in such ways, frequently rendered similar by its shared modes of depicting accent, and its shared attitudes to the social and regional distinctions of speech. Implicitly, and often explicitly, notions of a non-localized standard accent were promoted as emblematic of social and cultural superiority, and though Dickens and Eliot might attempt to redress the simplistic nature of many of those value-judgements which hinged on such perceptions by their own forms of linguistic didacticism, the common stereotypes of speech and speaker were not dispelled. 'Commonness' stands as the correlate of the 'broad Brummagen accent' used by Mrs Rymer in Mrs Henry Wood's *Johnny Ludlow* and the stigma of the 'provincial' is worked out primarily in terms of status and of speech. Correlations of accent, status, and identity, a frequent topos in writings on the language throughout the nineteenth century, infused the representation of fictional discourse, its depiction transmuted not by only by notions of 'literate speech' but also by the inescapable connotations of 'refinement' and 'vulgarity', 'educated' and 'ignorant' with which accent, in its role as a dominant social construct of the age, was imbued.

6

Educating Accents

B y the end of the nineteenth century, popular notions of 'educatedness' were, as we have seen, strongly associated with the possession of a set of standard pronunciation features, which were regularly taken to comprise the presence of [h] where deemed proper, the use of [ɪŋ] rather than [ɪn] in words such as *walking*, articulating words such as *servant* as [sɜːrvənt] and not [sɑːvənt], and, amongst other things, the avoidance of intrusive /r/. Such stated affiliations of accent and education, in line with those paradigms of 'knowledge' and 'ignorance' already discussed, were, in fact, commonplace in attitudes towards the language; 'the tone of the voice indicates character; the mode of speaking shows training and education', as Nichols proclaimed in 1874.[1] 'The true standard of pronunciation in any country is that which prevails among the best educated of its inhabitants', *How to Speak or Write English with Perspicacity and Fluency* averred two years later.[2] Within a few years of the Education Act of 1870, which promised elementary education for all, it is clear, as Nichols contends, that optimism surrounds expected standards of learning and of speech; 'compulsory education' will, he states, end not only illiteracy but will also eradicate the 'evil habit' and 'absurd and perverse fashion' of [h]-dropping.[3] These attitudes did not, of course, arise merely with this new legislation in the sphere of education. Even earlier, for example, in a lecture 'On the Art of Delivery and the Influence of School Discipline', Alexander Bell had in 1855 expressly urged the fact of educational responsibility in matters of phonemic propriety as in reading. Accent, he stressed, is a marker not only of status but of education in itself, and its nuances provide 'distinctive marks,—which, if they do not always tell the place of birth, do, in a manner liable to little mistake, proclaim where and how

---

[1] Nichols, *Behaviour*, 59.
[2] *How to Speak or Write English with Perspicacity and Fluency* (London, 1876), 20.
[3] Nichols, *Behaviour*, 63.

each individual has been educated'.[4] As well as securing facility in the three Rs, the role of education was, in such formulations, envisaged as able to equip the child with proficiency in the non-localized norms of 'proper' speech. All other accents were to be discouraged: 'The formation of such habits should be counteracted from the first, and in every stage of education, IN THE SCHOOL, where that pure and classical parlance should prevail, which indicates, not a province, but the legion of good society.'[5]

Such conceptions of education as an institution which, in the ideal world, should aid and inculcate the transmission of the 'right' accent alongside the 'right' ways of spelling, addition, or subtraction, are by no means rare. Not only manuals of manners, or works on pronunciation, but directives on education by the state, reports by Her Majesty's Inspectors on educational standards and achievements, or assessments of the suitability of educators for their appointed tasks all habitually refer to the perceived significance of accent and its alignment with the 'proper' and 'educated' norms of speech. Notions of a 'standard' in speech were, both overtly and covertly, to be implemented in educational ideology, as the cultural and social hegemony of 'talking proper' came to constitute a recurrent topos in estimations of education and its benefits. Language attitudes moreover tend to be no respecters of denominational differences within the type of school, nor even of levels of wealth and the great divides between state and more élite forms of instruction; elementary schools, 'public' schools, schools for Quakers, new schools in the traditions of the grammar schools of ancient foundation, and even Sunday schools all witnessed (and endorsed) in various ways the diffusion of these ideas.

Language attitudes thus here too have their repercussions; pronunciation, in the eyes of many, was in itself to form an index of achievement within as well as outside the school, with praise or blame being allotted accordingly. 'Attempts are made, with considerable success, to combat the peculiarities of the Lancashire pronunciation', observed T. M. W. Marshall, one of Her Majesty's Inspectors of Schools, while assessing a school in St Albans in 1849. 'I was struck with the absence of provincial accent, particularly in

---

[4] A. M. Bell, *A Lecture on the Art of Delivery and the Influence of School Discipline on Public Oratory*, delivered to the Edinburgh Local Association of the Educational Institute of Scotland, 21 Oct. 1854 (Edinburgh, 1855), 8.
[5] Ibid.

the monitors', he comments, visiting a school in Preston. 'There is a remarkable absence of provincial accent in the elder girls', he similarly commends St Mary's in Nottingham.[6] As such remarks suggest, paradigms of norm and deviation, and of 'provincial' versus 'standard', were in a number of ways to have a bearing on issues of 'proper' education as indeed upon the 'proper' language which it should purvey. Their consequences in such educational contexts were, however, perhaps to be even more far-reaching, not least given those equations of accent and intelligence which were widespread in contemporary attitudes to linguistic nicety.[7]

There is of course an indissoluble link between education and the 'standard', rather than non-standard, varieties of a language. 'Standard English is the dialect of education', as Trudgill affirmed in 1983; 'it is spoken by most teachers; it is the dialect normally employed in writing; and it is rewarded in examinations.'[8] Grammatical features common in many spoken dialects but proscribed in the standard variety itself (such as multiple negation, or the use of double comparatives) are therefore equally proscribed in educational precepts, being corrected as inappropriate and 'wrong' in the written discourse of children. Education can thus foster the same images of unidimensionality in language as are common in the prescriptive tradition, likewise advocating the monolithic above the heterogeneities of actual usage. Precisely the same processes operated in the nineteenth century, though they did so with perhaps even greater rigour given attitudes to a 'standard' which explicitly embraced hypotheses of inherent value rather than imposed norm.[9] Education, both officially and unofficially, was seen as an important part of the standardization process, involved in the conscious maintenance of standard norms, and, more importantly, in their dissemination. As this moreover indicates, it was also to be profoundly linked with associated ideologies of a standard, and the set of beliefs which came to surround conceptions of its 'proper' use, in

---

[6] General Report on Roman Catholic Schools for the Year 1849 By Her Majesty's Inspector of Schools T. M. W. Marshall, Committee of Council on Education: Reports on Elementary Schools, *Parliamentary Papers*, xliv (1850), 523, 527, 533.

[7] See pp. 62–3.

[8] P. Trudgill, 'Standard and Non-Standard Dialects of English in the UK: Problems and Policies', in M. Stubbs and H. Hillier (eds.), *Readings on Language, Schools and Classrooms* (London, 1983), 57.

[9] See e.g. p. 12.

spoken and in written forms. As attention shifted to pronunciation
and its needful proprieties, this too was often included within the
same paradigm, intentionally forming part of that 'taught' language
which was to distinguish 'educated' from 'uneducated', or the 'literate' from their converse. As James Buchanan, schoolteacher and
linguist in the eighteenth century, had early noted of this conjunction: 'he truly has attained the ends of education, who can speak
and write his own language fluently and correctly.'[10]

Buchanan's own *Plan of an English Grammar School Education*
was written in 1770, and, in keeping with these stated ideals, it
includes both instruction in the nuances of 'good' pronunciation,
and implicitly, an education in their social values too. Addressing
his text to 'the serious consideration of every sensible Parent and
Teacher in Great Britain', he makes it clear that since the speech
of the 'polite and learned' in the metropolis is the 'standard',
those who wish their learning to be taken seriously must also
assimilate their speech to these patterns: 'how unbecoming are
discordant and jarring sounds in the mouth of an otherwise polite
gentleman or lady, or in that of a man of learning.'[11] As part of
this conception, localized forms of speech are to be seen as fundamentally alien to the educational regime: 'it ought to be indisputably the care of every teacher of English, not to suffer children
to pronounce according to the dialect of that place or country
where they were born or reside, if it happens to be vicious.'[12] As
Buchanan adds in further warning: 'if they be suffered to proceed
in, and be habituated to an uncouth pronunciation in their youth,
it will most likely remain with them all their days.'[13] Advertisements
for his own school reveal the practice of these remedial principles;
'Youth are taught to read English by the Powers of the Sounds',
a procedure designed to inculcate 'standard' speech and eliminate
the 'uncouth' by rigorous training in articulation and its range of
'proper' phonemes in English. Children are moreover urged to come
into residence at the age of 4 in order to prevent, one assumes,
'contagion' from such essentially disadvantageous local habits of
speech.

A number of writers on the language apart from Buchanan
naturally endorsed, and endeavoured to implement, similar tenets

---

[10] J. Buchanan, *A Plan of an English Grammar School Education* (London, 1770),
title-page.
[11] Ibid. 45.   [12] Buchanan, *Linguae Britannicae*, p. xii n.   [13] Ibid.

in the late eighteenth century, as the new 'consciousness' of accent seemingly evolved alongside a parallel consciousness of the role which education too might play in these respects. Sheridan, for example, was to place particular emphasis on the agency which education could offer for the transmission of the non-localized accent he regarded as essential. His *British Education* was, in fact, published long before the later works on elocution for which he is now primarily remembered, already stressing in 1756 the need to incorporate English, and especially spoken English, within the schema of instruction offered to the 'gentleman'.[14] The arts of speech being made compulsory in his ideal syllabus, Sheridan is clear on the impetus which might thereby be given to the 'educated' accent and its standardization, providing 'rules' (as for grammar) from which the 'best' language might be learnt throughout the country, and moreover might be 'ascertained', or (as in the gloss provided in his dictionary) 'made certain, fixed, established'. Sheridan's rousing cry for increased sensibility towards pronunciation is, in such ways, framed by explicit references to the need for educational provision in this context too. 'Spoken language is not regularly taught', he asserts, and the consequences are all too clear; it is instead 'left to chance, imitation, and early habit; and therefore like all other things left to chance, or unsettled principles, is liable to innumerable irregularities and defects'.[15] Even members of the established élite could emerge from school with accents which, unlike those of the 'best speakers' of the metropolis, did not serve as the requisite 'proof that one has kept good company'. In the prescriptive terms adopted, their accents could therefore be 'uneducated' for, as Sheridan affirms in 1762, 'there are few gentlemen of England who have received their education at country schools, that are not infected with a false pronunciation of certain words, peculiar to each county'.[16] Recommending a new educational vigilance, he argues that the mission of education should therefore be integrated with the spread of the 'best speech' of London. His pronouncing dictionary of 1780 is in turn depicted as an important tool in the conformity which must result. The pronunciation of each word being presented as 'a certainty by fixed and visible marks', the dictionary offers potential for a new

---

[14] T. Sheridan, *British Education: Or, The Source of the Disorders of Great Britain* (London, 1756).
[15] Sheridan, *Course of Lectures*, 21.   [16] Ibid. 31.

era in education, whereby 'a similar uniformity of pronunciation . . .
may be spread through all parts of the globe, wherever English
shall be taught by its aid'.[17] The stereotype of the 'educated accent'
is, by its means, to be open to all.

Walker too endorsed the importance of these ideas. 'A clear
and distinct utterance' should unquestionably form a composite
part of education, he stressed in 1785,[18] and his own precepts on
this head were, for instance, implemented in the Reverend Dr
Thomson's School in Kensington (as well as presumably in the
school which he himself had run).[19] As Walker makes clear in the
dedication to his 'Academic Speaker', this academic balance was
apparently effective, Dr Thomson receiving commensurate praise:
'congratulating you on the successful experiment you have made
of uniting the most extensive study of Greek and Latin with a
regular course of reading and speaking English.'[20] A number of
other schools, as we shall see, were likewise to recognize the utility
of Walker's work in this respect, as indeed were inspectors of
education themselves.

In the late eighteenth century, however, perceptions of this
order were not limited simply to the authors of pronouncing dictionaries. The religious and educational writer David Williams,
for example, reflected a more general interest in these issues of
'good' speech (and their educational relevance) in his *Treatise on
Education* (1774). The 'objects of education' should, he declares,
comprise 'a distinct articulation' and 'an authorized and elegant
pronunciation'[21] and he duly sets up plans of education in which
English as a subject receives due attention. Williams, like Sheridan,
clearly envisages the school as a means by which the 'correct'
language sanctioned by the prescriptive tradition could be given a
scope hitherto unprecedented in its dissemination. Education and
standardization again fuse for, as he maintains, the explicit teaching

[17] Sheridan, *Rhetorical Grammar*, p. xviii.
[18] J. Walker, *A Rhetorical Grammar of the English Language*, 1st edn. (London, 1785), 1.
[19] As *DNB* notes, Walker, together with James Usher, had established a school in Kensington in 1769, though Walker's active involvement lasted only until 1771 when he began to devote more time professionally to his interests in elocution, beginning at that date to deliver his lectures on that subject which, as *DNB* adds, was 'henceforth to be his principal employment'.
[20] J. Walker, *The Academic Speaker* (Dublin, 1789), dedication.
[21] D. Williams, *A Treatise on Education* (London, 1774), 157.

of speech along these lines would necessarily give rise throughout the country to 'a proper and elegant pronunciation' which would 'take the place of provincial vulgarism, or fashionable affectation'.[22]

Views such as these, of course, tend to form the theory, and the ideal. Reality was usually somewhat different, as Williams was also to acknowledge, making plain the paradoxes inherent in an education system which, almost without exception in the grammar schools, had in fact traditionally chosen to teach Latin and Greek at the expense of English altogether:[23]

The language which a man is to speak and write in . . . ought certainly to be the principal object of his study, and not suffered, in our common school phrase, '*to come of course*'; nevertheless, it is the 'dead and useless languages' which are to be studied, and it is the 'living, useful, improveable one' which is '*to come of course*'.[24]

This concentration on the classical languages at the expense of English in the grammar and public schools (likewise lamented by Sheridan) will be discussed in more detail later in the chapter; what is important at this stage is the emphasis being placed by a number of writers and educationalists in the late eighteenth century on the perceived need not only to teach English as a formal subject in its own right, but also to teach it in spoken as well as written forms. It was a subject to which Locke too, in his own critique of educational methods as they existed in England, had drawn attention. 'To write and speak correctly gives a Grace, and gains a favourable attention to what one has to say', he stated, already in 1693 revealing the foundation of some of those patterns of subjective inequality later to be so prominent: 'since, 'tis *English* that an *English* gentleman will have constant use of, that is the Language

---

[22] Ibid. 162.

[23] There are exceptions to this pattern, as R. Wilson confirms in 'The Archbishop Herring Visitation Returns, 1743: A Vignette of Yorkshire Education', in J. E. Stephens (ed.), *Aspects of Education 1600–1750* (Hull, 1984) 92–130. A questionnaire sent out to the incumbent of each parish in the diocese of York following the election of Thomas Herring to the archbishopric devoted its third question to the topic of educational provision and elicited a 93.9% response. The data provided clearly reveal that a number of grammar schools in the area had added instruction in English to the classical syllabus. Schools at Worsborough and Tadcaster in the West Riding, for example, although specifically 'grammar only' according to the terms of their foundation, also taught reading, writing, and mathematics.

[24] Williams, *Treatise on Education*, 136.

he should chiefly cultivate, and wherein most Care should be taken to polish and perfect his Style.' Given the cultural climate which came into existence within the next hundred years, not least in terms of those codificatory ideologies of a standard (and their socio-cultural affiliations) which were so regularly propounded in contemporary attitudes to both language and 'correctness', it is perhaps not surprising that conceptions of this kind were, in consequence, likewise to impinge upon notions of 'good' education in a number of ways. As in Sheridan's own beliefs in prescriptivism as a mode of achieving a national accent for all,[25] language, education, and nationalism were frequently to fuse. Similarly, the stated correlations between education and accent were to consolidate still more closely in associated stereotypes of 'educated' and 'standard' speech. Such shifts in attitudes to linguistic propriety were moreover often mirrored in educational precepts, and educational practice too, especially as the nineteenth century advanced.

That this should be so is not entirely unexpected. Education does not take place in a vacuum, but is, as Irene Fox confirms, 'located within social space—[in] a society which has a history, structures, institutions, people, classes, and values'.[26] The role of the school as social institution, and of education as an important aspect of socialization thus in themselves tend to ensure a failure of immunity from prevailing behavioural norms and expectations. That this failure extends to language too, whether in terms of attitudes or usage, is equally clear. As Wolfram and Fasold indicate with reference to modern educational policy and practice, 'public education in our society serves the function of inculcating in children the values that are shared by the society in which they will be participating members'. They moreover make plain the fact that 'included in these values are attitudes and beliefs about language and language attitudes'.[27]

The same premises hold true in the late eighteenth and nineteenth centuries, before as well as after that increasing state involvement in educational issues which was to be a prominent feature of the age. The educational 'system' in the late decades of the eighteenth century, and the opening ones of the nineteenth is, of course, almost a misnomer. No 'system' as such existed, but

[25] See p. 29.   [26] I. Fox, *Public Schools and Public Issues* (London, 1985), 1.
[27] W. Wolfram and R. Fasold, 'Social Dialects and Education', in J. B. Pride (ed.), *Sociolinguistic Aspects of Language Learning and Teaching* (Oxford, 1979), 185.

instead a random collection of dame schools, ragged schools, charity schools, private schools (such as those established by Buchanan or Walker), grammar schools of old or more recent foundation, Sunday schools,[28] monitorial schools (after 1801),[29] Nonconformist academies, as well as private tutors, all existed in uneven distribution, and uneven quality, over the country. The first state provision for education, of £20,000, was not made until 1830, the first training colleges for teachers were not established until the 1840s. Moreover, access to education, and its varied manifestations, was determined primarily by class, a pattern which was in some ways to become increasingly apparent as the years went on, as many grammar and public schools engaged in ever more stringent policies of social exclusivity to the disadvantage of the local and impecunious scholars for whom such schools had, at least originally, been designed. Education was riven on all levels by the sense of a social divide; 'grade in the social system', as Thomas Wyse stated in 1836,[30] was the main influence on educational provision, whether the classical syllabus followed by the 'gentleman' (born or aspiring) which might last until the age of 18 or 19, or the four hours a day of the most elementary schooling granted to pauper children by the Poor Law Reform Act of 1839.

Wyse advocates a number of reforms in this context: 'There is a certain degree of developement and instruction, which ought to be common to the members of every civilised community, but beyond which it may not be for the interests of certain classes, or the community at large, to proceed.'[31] Although his latter clause suggests affinities with the position adopted by Mr Dombey on the subject of equal education for all (' "I am far from being friendly", pursued Mr Dombey, "to what is called by persons of levelling

---

[28] Robert Raikes of Gloucester is traditionally assumed to have pioneered the Sunday School in the 1780s. The system expanded rapidly: by 1833 1,550,000 pupils were in regular attendance, and by 1851, 2,400,000 children were on the registers of Sunday schools up and down the country.

[29] The monitorial system was based on the principle of using older children to teach the younger children within a school. Established in 1801 by Joseph Lancaster and Andrew Bell, it could lead to a school having up to 1,000 pupils but employing only one teacher, as in Lancaster's original school in the Borough Road, London, where 1,000 children were taught by 67 monitors and one teacher—Lancaster himself.

[30] T. Wyse, Education Reform; Or, The Necessity of a National System of Education (London, 1836), 49.

[31] Ibid.

sentiments, general education. But it is necessary that the inferior classes should continue to be taught to know their position, and to conduct themselves properly. So far I approve of schools." [32]), by the end of the century state involvement was in fact such as to bring about more or less the situation which Wyse had proposed. Compulsory elementary education for all was endorsed by Forster's Education Act of 1870, but a number of inequities in access to education still remained. Its provision by that date was, however, indisputably more systematic, more organized, and more controlled in the standards which were aimed at and which were, in turn, achieved.

Given this complexity, an examination of the ways in which attitudes to accent in the wider linguistic climate were also to influence education is by no means easy. This chapter will therefore consider first, the 'public' school system and its extension, not least in socio-symbolic terms, over the eighteenth and nineteenth centuries, then discuss the state system, its various ramifications, and its attempted implementation of the prescriptive canon of correctness as part of the 'elementary' training given to the children under its care. Stereotypes of 'talking proper' are, of course, most readily attached to the former rather than the latter, notably in the collocations of the 'public-school accent' and 'public-school English' which still remain in the late twentieth century; 'Public School Pronunciation' was, for example, the label selected by Daniel Jones to cover the type of speech he described in his 1917 *Pronunciation of English* (and which was replaced by 'Received Pronunciation' itself in the edition of 1926).

As *Good Society*, with its subheading '*A Complete Manual of Manners*', indicates, this was a socio-linguistic stereotype already apparent in 1869: 'The best accent is that taught at Eton and Oxford', it affirms. [33] Still earlier instances of this equation can also be traced. Murdoch, for example, in the stereotype edition of Walker's dictionary published in 1809, likewise expresses the perception that 'a polite pronunciation is an essential part of a genteel and liberal education', a fact given as 'incontestable'. [34] A 'liberal' education moreover, as Walker's dictionary itself explains, was that which 'becomes a gentleman'; 'genteel' has the corresponding gloss

---

[32] *Dombey and Son*, 62.   [33] *Good Society*, 91.
[34] Walker, *Critical Pronouncing Dictionary*, ed. J. Murdoch (1809), p. ii.

'polite, elegant in behaviour'. As with the disjunctions between ideology and process in terms of standardization,[35] there can, however, be a similar disjunction in these terms too. Murdoch's comment, for example, reveals the clear alliance of notions of the 'best' accent with corresponding notions of the 'best' education in ways which are entirely in keeping with the evaluative processes common within the prescriptive tradition. *Good Society* later reveals the continuity, as well as the further consolidation, of this idea, with its commendations of the accents which Eton, for example, was assumed to confer. It is nevertheless important to recognize that, in reality, English did not form a composite part of instruction in these institutions at all. As Dr Johnson had phrased it in his dictionary, a 'grammar-school' (as such schools were commonly referred to) was 'a school in which the learned languages are grammatically taught'—a definition later deemed of such authority that it was used in attempts to combat the extension of the syllabus in such schools into the more modern realms of science, or indeed into the non-learned languages (such as English). In addition, the very identity of these institutions as 'public schools' was another development which only emerged over the course of the nineteenth century, a fact which renders notions of their correlations with accent and the 'best speech' somewhat more complex than might initially be assumed. As *OED* confirms, the first official use of this mode of reference was in the 1861 appointment of the Royal Commission which was to investigate the schools recognized in this way; these in turn were formulated in the 'Act for the better Government and extension of Certain Public Schools' of 1867 as Eton, Westminster, Winchester, Harrow, Rugby, Charterhouse, and Shrewsbury.

'Unofficial' notions of the 'public school' were, however, current long before this date. 'By a public school, we mean an endowed place of education of old standing, to which the sons of gentlemen resort in considerable numbers', Sydney Smith (canon of St Paul's and founder of the *Edinburgh Review*) explained in the *Edinburgh Review* in 1810, and as the nineteenth century advanced, these conceptions were to become still clearer, as well as coming to include a number of other schools of 'newer' foundation too. Not only did modes of reference change during the late eighteenth and nineteenth centuries, but a number of the salient characteristics of

[35] See e.g. p. 55.

the public school tradition, important in a variety of ways in explanations of the 'public-school accent' too, also come to have their existence over this time. A swift survey of the history of these foundations makes this situation and the nature of its developments in the late eighteenth and nineteenth century somewhat clearer. A large number (though by no means all) of the grammar schools which are, for instance, now recognized as 'public schools' were founded a considerable time ago, Winchester in 1382, Eton in 1440, Westminster and Shrewsbury in 1560. The terms of their original foundation, as well as specifying an education in the classical languages, also specified that such education was, on the whole, to be received by the 'poor and needy' (*pauperes et indigentes*) of the local area, a formulation which offers no little contrast with their later social composition. Winchester as a result was initially able to take around seventy 'poor and needy' scholars, though the terms of the foundation also allowed ten noblemen's sons to be fee-paying members of the college, while the masters were, in addition, allowed to have private (fee-paying) pupils boarding outside the college. Eton presented more or less the same picture, with an original intake of seventy 'poor and needy', augmented by twenty sons of noblemen as fee-paying students. Harrow, founded in 1571 by John Lyon, was explicitly designated 'for the perpetual education, teaching, and instruction of children and youth of the same parish'. What is clear from this outline is that schools later seen as emblematic of an élite, and its attendant social values, were in their original conception almost entirely the converse, dominated by the financially less able and local, above the wealthy and non-localized. Other schools maintained similar patterns of intake. Westminster, for example, records the sons of an earl, a bishop, a Procurator of the Arches, a London vicar, a steward of Lord Zouch's estates in Northamptonshire, and of 'a keeper of the Orchard at Whitehall' among its members in the early seventeenth century. Merchant Taylors' School, founded in 1561, evinces an even wider social mix, with the sons of a barber–surgeon, a blacksmith, a bricklayer, a cook, and a poulterer mingling with the sons of a knight, a Fellow of Winchester College, the Secretary of the East India Company, and nineteen sons of gentlemen in 1645–6.[36]

[36] See *The Public Schools and the General Educational System: Report of the Committee on Public Schools appointed by the President of the Board of Education, July 1942* (London, 1944), 11 n. 18.

Though these patterns of social diversity were long the norm rather than the exception, a gradual change did take place as the rich and affluent came, in a number of schools, to displace the 'poor and needy'. The period 1660–1780, as Lawson and Silver note, saw in particular an increasing sense of hierarchy among the older grammar schools. It was, for example, during this period that 'a few . . . began to be patronized by wealthy and aristocratic families and so gradually to stand apart from the rest', though, as they add, 'there was as yet no attempt as in the more class-conscious nineteenth century to exclude boys because of their comparatively plebeian origins'.[37] The tendency for pupils from geographically distant (and disparate) places to form a large proportion of the intake also becomes perceptible at this time; of the students at Rugby at the end of the seventeenth century, around 80 per cent were not local boys. Though the direction of change is always towards the situation familiar today, the decisive patterns do not become entirely apparent until the end of the eighteenth century and the century which followed. These two elements, the rise of a non-localized intake and the more or less simultaneous consolidation of a sense of social exclusivity, already beginning to be apparent at this date, were to become even further established as the years advanced.

The eighteenth and nineteenth centuries were, as we have seen, witness to a set of momentous changes in the fabric and organization of society; industrialization, urbanization, the rise of 'class' as social construct, and of new notions of status, together with a new rich (and a new poor) are all perceptible as developments over its span. Education is equally embedded in this pattern of change, and the new mobility facilitated by the increased ease of communications, especially following the advent of the railway, aided the growth of boarding (and hence a non-localized intake) as particularly salient aspects of the public school system. Similarly, that growing awareness of the social values of education in the classical mould at schools such as Harrow, Shrewsbury, Westminster, or Eton is plain in the patterns of social homogeneity which gradually displace the heterogeneities of the past. As Gathorne-Hardy has noted, out of the 3,000 pupils who entered Eton between 1755

---

[37] J. Lawson and H. Silver, *A Social History of English Education* (London, 1973), 198.

and 1790, only thirty-eight were the sons of tradesmen.[38] Between 1821 and 1830, two pupils alone represent the lower classes; in the following decade this has dropped to zero, while entrance from among the sons of gentry reveals a more than corresponding increase, from 305 in the period 1801–10, to 430 by 1850. A similar pattern is evident in pupils from the titled sections of society, rising from 226 to 330 over the same period. As a result, though in previous decades it had been acceptable and even advisable for a gentleman to be educated at home—as Locke had asserted, 'how anyone being put into a herd of unruly boys . . . fits him for civil conversation or business, I cannot see'—by the end of the nineteenth century, the dominance of the public school tradition was such that this was the archetypical education for a gentleman, or for those who wished to be numbered amongst such. By implication therefore, this was at the same time no longer the typical education for the sons of ploughmen and clerks. Even where the social origins of boys in the same school did remain mixed, there likewise emerges a large body of evidence showing considerable differences in their treatment, the increasing sense of a social divide occasionally being made literal as well as metaphorical within the social world of the school. As the Report of the Schools Inquiry Commission of 1868 recorded on a number of occasions, patterns of overt segregation often separated foundationers from the fee-paying scholars:

At several schools the free scholars were made to sit in a different part of the room; at another the two sets of boys were separated by 'a partition breast high.' The use of the playground was a continual problem. In one it was divided 'by an imaginary line between the boarders and free boys and a penalty imposed on transgressors'.[39]

Nor was it necessarily the policy of the school which imposed this consciousness of exclusion, and exclusivity, upon its pupils. As the Schools Inquiry Commission observed of Repton School, the headmaster himself 'had clearly made a sincere attempt to break down the barriers between the local boys and the boarders'. He had, the report continued, met with 'little success':

[38] J. Gathorne-Hardy, *The Public School Phenomenon* (London, 1977), 49.
[39] Report of the Schools Inquiry Commission (1868); cited in *The Public Schools and the General Educational System*, 23.

He stated that he had had very numerous applications from 'persons of good standing in the world and good fortune', and that he had invariably been asked, 'What is the character, station and position of the home boarders?' When he had answered that they were 'of all classes down to the sons of blacksmiths and washerwomen', the application had immediately been withdrawn. Of these 'home boarders' he stated that he had 'succeeded in gaining them perfect fair play in school', but that he had had to separate them out of school and that 'mainly for the sake of the village boys'. He felt that if he allowed them to associate, 'he should have a constant fear of their being ill-treated'.[40]

As the headmaster pointed out: ' "It is not the fault of the boys, it is the fault of society, . . . I never yet saw a man who would send his boy to a school in order to associate with those lower than himself." '

Such perceptions make plain the foundation of the social stereotype of the public school boy in the eighteenth and nineteenth centuries. Social homogeneity, in these select applications of it, comes moreover to enforce a due sense of the social benefits which might thereby be derived from attendance at these schools. 'Social elegance' and 'refinement' were prime among the virtues of Eton, as the author of *The Eton System of Education Vindicated* states in 1834,[41] extolling recognition of this ideal. The shifting sense of identity of the public school itself thus in these terms gives rise to a particular sense of identity for the public school boy too, as well as for his associated cultural (and linguistic) stereotypes. Certainly it was in terms of such social characteristics that public schools, especially after Thomas Arnold's time as headmaster of Rugby, were frequently praised. As Sir Stafford Northcote stressed in 1864: 'These public schools were national institutions, and had an important bearing on the formation of the national character.'[42] The public school boy, in the popular images deployed over the nineteenth century, hence tends to become an amalgam of social elegance, refinement, wealth, good manners, and perfect gentlemanly conduct.

Manners were, for example, prioritized by Arnold himself above

---

[40] Cited in *The Public Schools and the General Educational System*, 23

[41] *The Eton System of Education Vindicated* (London, 1834), 30, 69.

[42] *Hansard*, clxxv. 139–40, 6 May 1864; cited in C. Shrosbree, *Public Schools and Private Education: The Clarendon Commission 1861 64 and the Public Schools Acts* (Manchester, 1988), 116.

academic potential in his pupils; as he directed his praeposters at Rugby: 'What we must look for . . . is, 1st, religion and moral principles, 2ndly, gentlemanly conduct; 3rdly intellectual ability.'[43] Though Lord Chesterfield had cautioned his own son (in the less exclusive days of the early eighteenth century) against the contagion of *bad* manners at Eton,[44] later commentators were to praise instead the contrary, portraying the acquisition of the right manner as an undeniable benefit of public school education. 'The general manners, from rudeness and vulgarity, have been rendered easy, courteous, and polite' as Carlisle, citing Erasmus, expounded in this context.[45] As this suggests, such schools were often thought to provide a social as well as a classical education, an attitude similarly reflected in real terms in the experiences of many of those who attended educational establishments of this kind at that time. Charles Merivale, historian and Dean of Ely, offers, for example, ready affirmation of the cultural hegemonies which could be enacted, recollecting the 'sense of social inferiority' which had been 'impressed' upon him at Harrow as well as his 'acute consciousness of rustic or homely manners and of means and domestic circumstances much below par at a first-class aristocratic school'.[46] Though he, and his brother, survived by dint of academic ability (such that they were able 'to command the respect of a set who would have been otherwise very prompt to despise and browbeat us'), the pressures exerted by the social homogenization of such schools were clear. For assimilation and acceptability within the social world of the superior school, conformity to those manners which makyth not only man, but also the 'gentilman' was apparently of importance.

Other first-hand accounts affirm the role of these specifically social sensibilities within the school, the reminiscences of John Mitchinson (1823–1918) recording the practical consequences of

---

[43] Cited in W. J. Reader, *Life in Victorian England* (New York, 1964), 20.

[44] Lord Chesterfield's admonitions in this context include the advice that his son, upon entering Westminster, must be 'sufficiently upon [his] guard . . . against awkward attitudes . . . and disgusting habits; . . . such as putting your fingers in your mouth, nose, and ears'. Cited in J. Cannon, *Aristocratic Century: The Peerage of Eighteenth-Century England* (Cambridge, 1984), 38.

[45] N. Carlisle, *A Concise Description of the Endowed Grammar Schools of England and Wales* (London, 1818), p. xxxvii.

[46] J. A. Merivale (ed.), *Autobiography and Letters of Charles Merivale, Dean of Ely* (Oxford, 1898), 43.

this emphasis in some detail. Mitchinson was, in fact, involved in education for much of his life; educated at Durham Grammar School (and Pembroke College, Oxford), he subsequently taught at Merchant Taylors' School and later became headmaster of the King's School, Canterbury. He is therefore, in a variety of ways, particularly well placed to comment on this aspect of the public school stereotype, being subject to its dictates as a pupil and, as we shall see, choosing to reinforce it in specifically linguistic ways as headmaster. The acquisition of the 'polish' which education should provide is, for instance, stressed as an undeniable marker of its success and its efficacy; Mitchinson notes, for instance, of George Hayton, a pupil at Durham Grammar School in the 1840s: 'he was the son of a Cumberland Estatesman, i.e. yeoman, or small freeholder . . . He came to us a ruddy, round faced, flaxen haired lad, but developed into a fine manly character, and took polish well.'[47] He 'took polish splendidly' is likewise recorded of Field, a pupil of similarly humble social origins at the King's School, Canterbury.[48] 'Social considerations . . . bulk large with boys', is the moral Mitchinson draws in explanation of this convergence.[49]

Social considerations were, however, to affect parents too, and the widespread belief in the public school as a social as well as educational process led in a number of ways to a demand satisfied only by large numbers of new schools being created along roughly similar lines to those already in existence. Marlborough was founded in 1843, Radley in 1847, St Nicholas's, Lancing in 1848 (aimed at the sons of gentry and the upper middle class), Wellington in 1852,[50] St John's, Hurstpierpoint, in 1853 (aimed at the sons of the well-to-do tradesmen), Haileybury in 1862. Education as both social process and social symbol was assimilated into strategies of cultural cohesion. As Bamford affirms, though 'the really important boys were at Eton and Harrow', as he adds, 'it

[47] Unpublished memoirs, from the Mitchinson Archive, Pembroke College, Oxford, ii: 'School Reminiscences', fos. 16–17.
[48] 'Canterbury: The King's School. Appendix: My Boys', Mitchinson Archive, vii, fo. 5.
[49] Ibid. ii, fo. 17.
[50] Those listed here merely constitute a representative sample of the new educational foundations of the 19th c. It should be noted that many of them preserved similar policies of social exclusivity to those increasingly practised by older schools. The first prospectus of Cheltenham College states, e.g.: 'No person shall be considered eligible who shall not be moving in the circle of Gentleman, no retail trader being allowed in any circumstances to be so considered.'

was the public school image as a type that was important, for similar schools produced similar products that spoke the same language'.[51] It was to this belief that notions of a corresponding linguistic stereotype were gradually added, ultimately providing one of the most enduring images of 'talking proper' that England has known.

The linguistic hegemonies which the public school might impose on pupils of rather disparate social origins from those most prominent in its composition are, for example, early made plain in *Practical Education*, a two-volume work written by Maria Edgeworth and her father, the author Richard Lovell Edgeworth. In it they offer a clear and unambiguous account of the paradigms of language, education, and advantage which were to surround the public schools, setting forth both their statusful associations and remedial values in terms which effortlessly assimilate contemporary emphases on imitative cohesion, and the accompanying stereotypes of the parvenu:

Persons of narrow fortune, or persons who have acquired wealth in business, are often desirous of breeding up their sons to the liberal professions; and they are conscious that the company, the language, and the style of life, which their children would be accustomed to at home, are beneath what would be suited to their future professions. Public schools efface this rusticity, and correct the faults of provincial dialect: in this point of view they are highly advantageous.[52]

Education of this order becomes a means by which the signifiers of the 'well-bred', amongst which language is specifically included, may be acquired. 'Rusticity', suggesting not rural charm but 'rudeness' ('coarseness of manners' as Walker explains), will by such means be remedied, and provincialites of dialect (a 'sign of disgrace' as Sheridan had averred) will be similarly displaced. As *Practical Education* reveals, education at this type of school was to be a means of integration into the linguistic as well as the social proprieties of those who might henceforth occupy positions within the 'liberal professions', and another way in which the hegemonies of the standard variety might be spread. Obviating the 'provincial' was, as this moreover reveals, seen in the distinctly normative

[51] T. W. Bamford, *Rise of the Public Schools* (London, 1967), 20.
[52] M. Edgeworth and R. L. Edgeworth, *Practical Education* (London, 1798), ii. 502.

terms of 'proper' language from which variations were to be viewed as 'faults'; ideologies of a standard are all too perceptible in the 'advantages' which, as the Edgeworths imply, will surely follow. Not all public schools are, however, to be regarded as equally efficacious in this process. Though it is given as a general principle that removal from the provincial and localized, together with subsequent immersion in a superior social environment, will do much to mitigate 'the faults of provincial dialect', it is also made plain that for a perfect command of 'talking proper', only a major public school will do:

We strongly recommend it to such parents to send their children to large public schools, to Rugby, Eton, or Westminster; not to any small school: much less to one in their own neighbourhood. Small schools are apt to be filled with persons of nearly the same station, and out of the same neighbourhood: from this circumstance they contribute to perpetuate uncouth antiquated idioms, and many of those obscure prejudices which cloud the intellect in the future business of life.[53]

Principles of linguistic and social purism again operate in tandem, the refined atmosphere of a select public school presented as being in itself some guarantee for the acquisition of a parallel refinement in language, one devoid of those localized forms which, as the nineteenth century advanced, increasingly consolidated their own role in the public mind as a prime marker of lower social standing. As William Enfield had early indicated, it was the absence of features such as these which was in particular to be regarded as a defining hallmark of the 'gentleman', and hence also for those who wished to be adopt this social label for themselves: 'These faults, and all others of the same nature, must be corrected in the pronunciation of a gentleman, who is supposed to have seen too much of the world, to retain the peculiarities of the district in which he was born.'[54] The non-localized education which public schools could provide was hence to be regarded as particularly important, securing a process of linguistic as well as social segregation, and purging speech of the regional forms which, as a variety of writers indicate, were thought to be inherently 'statusless'. Thomas Arnold himself offered similar confirmation of these ideas. As he remarked, separation from the social environment in the locality of the child's home often constituted a prime parental

<hr>

[53] Ibid.   [54] Enfield, *The Speaker*, p. xiv.

motive in sending a boy to public school: 'It is the object of the father, as a rule, to withdraw his son from local associations, and to take him as far as possible from the sons of his neighbours and dependants.'[55] That these 'local associations' included the local accent too is also clear, indicated not only in the educational theories which the Edgeworths expound, but manifest in a number of other comments on the virtues and value of this type of education throughout the century.

Especially commended in their remedial effects for the offspring of those 'persons who have acquired wealth in business', public schools of this order were for, instance, often to be included within the strategic patterns of assimilation which were adopted not just by the stereotypes of the 'new rich'. Real entrepreneurs too participated in this pattern: Wedgwood sent his sons to Rugby, while Arkwright's grandsons went to Eton and Harrow. Similarly John Gladstone, the Liverpool merchant, sent his sons to Eton, as did Matthew Boulton his grandson. 'What a good classical education did was confer or confirm the status of a man as an English gentleman', as Colin Shrosbree notes.[56] It was a process recorded in fictional form in Disraeli's *Coningsby* (1844) as the son of the manufacturer Millbank is sent to Eton, but it was far from being the stuff of fiction alone. As Shrosbree records, it was commonplace for the sons, and perhaps especially the grandsons of these new men of wealth to receive an education in this mode, consolidating advances in status and the social markers that accompany them. 'Men dress their children's minds as they dress their bodies, in the prevailing fashion', Herbert Spencer wrote in this context in 1861: 'a boy's drilling in Latin and Greek is insisted on, not because of their intrinsic value, but that he may not be disgraced by being found ignorant of them—that he may have "the education of a gentleman"—the badge marking a certain social position and bringing a consequent respect.'[57] Language too was naturally to be included in these paradigms.

Matthew Boulton, for example, the partner of James Watt, directed that his grandson should be sent to Eton, not in order to cement the familial ascendance in the social hierarchy (though

[55] Cited in J. Honey, *Does Accent Matter? The Pygmalion Factor* (London, 1989), 25.
[56] Shrosbree, *Public Schools and Private Education*, 89.
[57] H. Spencer, *Education: Intellectual, Moral and Physical* (London, 1861), 42.

that was presumably not unimportant), but also in order to obviate the dangers of acquiring 'a vicious pronunciation and a vulgar dialect', a contamination which would surely result if he remained in his native Birmingham.[58] Revealing a marked awareness of prevailing language attitudes, as well as the role which education too was assuming within associated ideologies of a standard (and its transmission), Boulton affirms the perceived values of the non-localized, in terms which comprise both school and accent. Markers of 'local' identity are not only unfitting for the 'gentleman' (as Enfield had already made plain) but they are in addition 'vicious': 'corrupt, having ill qualities', and connotative of 'vulgar' rather than élite. It is in such terms that Boulton responds to the cultural hegemonies so often asserted in prevailing language attitudes towards 'talking proper' and its 'educated' associations.

As the Edgeworths had early indicated, it was the fact of boarding (and in the right school) which was recognized as being of particular significance. 'Boys that are brought up at home and attend a Day School for instruction have seldom the tone . . . of those that are educated at a Boarding School', the Reverend G. Bartle later asserted in *A Few Words to Parents and Guardians on the Education of Youth*.[59] 'Tone', as many writers on the language (and its social values) had stressed, has of course its linguistic side too. As the anonymous author of *A Very Short Letter from One Old Westminster to Another* of 1829 asserts, it was part of the role of the public school to protect its pupils against 'those habits of faulty pronunciation, against those vulgar and offensive tones in reading and speaking which it is afterwards so contemptible to retain and so difficult to correct'. Boarding-school, in these conceptions, was to be seen as a sphere largely insulated from corrupting influences of this kind, an abode of 'proper' language where the pressures for convergence were enhanced by the increasing patterns of social exclusivity adopted. Evidently seen as a merit by Boulton, the principles of linguistic purism so clearly advocated are moreover used to support corresponding principles of social purism, informing this 'old Westminster's' account of the exclusion of a 'pot-boy' whose social (and linguistic) marking was such that the necessary conformity could not be conferred:

---

[58] Cited in Coleman, 'Gentlemen and Players', 105.
[59] Revd G. Bartle, *A Few Words To Parents and Guardians on the Education of Youth* (London, 1875), 21.

You cannot but remember the sturdy, flaxen-haired pot-boy, whom an ambitious and aspiring publican sent to Westminster in our times, as a qualification, doubtless, for the *bar*. He was neither bullied nor beaten. But he was taught, by unequivocal lessons from those he wished to make his playmates, that he had been *missorted*, and the blunder was rectified in little more than three months after its commission.[60]

'And so should it be with all such as intrusively flock' into such spheres, the author adds. Given such attitudes, it is hardly surprising either that the 'pot-boy' left, or that others rapidly chose to conform to those standards, of language as of behaviour, which were presented for their emulation. As Thackeray noted, boys in the public school tended to form ideal agencies for the manipulation of social shame: 'If your father is a grocer, you have been beaten for his sake, and have learned to be ashamed of him.'[61] Their sensibilities in terms of language were evidently no less acute.

Education, in whatever school, is of course much more than instruction in the academic subjects on the syllabus. As Durkheim noted, for example, it rather constitutes 'the methodical socialization of the young generation',[62] acting as a fundamental aspect in the creation and maintenance of notions of group identity. It is this emphasis which the Edgeworths endorse in their account of the other advances which a child might make by dint of such instruction. Involved in the transmission of cultural and social values (and value-judgements), education is, as they recognize, important in the ways in which it establishes, implicitly and explicitly, a set of attitudes, expectations, and behavioural norms which inform patterns of collective identity and peer-group pressure. Such notions were familiar in the late eighteenth century as well as afterwards; the child's 'sentiments; his conscience; his mind, must be regulated by the laws of this institution' as Williams wrote in his own *Treatise on Education* in 1774, long before the advent of educational

---

[60] *A Very Short Letter from One Old Westminster to Another, Touching Some Matters connected with Their School* (London, 1829), 9–10.

[61] W. M. Thackeray, *A Shabby-Genteel Story* (London, 1887), 12. Mitchinson's memoirs of his days at Durham Grammar School similarly recall that the influence of those 'social considerations which bulk large with boys' had, in effect, 'severed' some of the boys from the others. He notes of one Forster, for example, that 'he was the son of a small innkeeper, and from his tavern sign was known as Black Horse Forster' (Mitchinson Archive, ii, fo. 17).

[62] E. Durkheim, *Education and Sociology*, trans. S. D. Fox (Glencoe, Ill., 1956), 71.

sociology. The end result, as he added, should be that 'his soul will be moulded to the times, and he will come into the world perfectly fitted for it'.[63]

In terms of language the same implications again hold true, and 'moulding' (especially in view of the prescriptive tenor of the age) was in turn regularly to be recognized as important, and not least in the pressures for conformity exerted within the rarefied world of the school. Given the fact that few schools of this type engaged in explicit teaching of the norms of speech (though this will be discussed below), it is, however, the levels of what may be seen as implicit instruction which assume prime importance in the creation of these nineteenth- (and twentieth-) century stereotypes of the public school boy and his 'proper' speech. As Jonathan Gathorne-Hardy confirms, 'boarding communities where every one is in full view of everyone else are particularly conducive to codifying, elaborating, intensifying, and enforcing . . . aspects of behaviour';[64] in these terms, they are also particularly conducive to linguistic convergence, especially given that non-localized bias already discussed.

As the lesson of the 'pot-boy' in Westminster undoubtedly reveals, assimilation could be essential for acceptability. 'Protective imitation' is vital in the world of the school, Bertrand Russell observed, and certainly Anthony Trollope's failure to conform to the social norms of Winchester and Harrow (as a result of his father's poverty) left him ostracized and alienated. 'I became a Pariah', he noted of his experiences at the former, and he fared no better at the latter when he was sent there at the age of 15: 'an age when I could appreciate at its full the misery of expulsion from all social intercourse' as he recorded in his *Autobiography* (1883).[65] Such notions of exclusion, and exclusivity, meant that a marked sensitization to the issues of conformity could exist within the school, a pattern of behaviour also evident in the elaborate rules and social codes which many schools independently adopted. 'At no place or time of life are people so much the slaves of custom as boys at school', stressed Thomas Arnold in 1850[66] in

---

[63] Williams, *Treatise on Education*, 13.
[64] Gathorne-Hardy, *The Public School Phenomenon*, 51.
[65] A. Trollope, *An Autobiography*, ed. M. Sadleir and F. Page (Oxford, 1980), 9.
[66] T. W. Bamford (ed.), *Thomas Arnold on Education* (Cambridge, 1970), 50.

a statement endorsed time and time again by contemporary comment. 'Your weighty words they neglect, but they dare not set themselves against the sneers of their companions', wrote Hope, for example, in 1869 after years of association with boys in the public school: 'They are slaves to Mrs Grundy, bound with a heavier chain than even diligent votaries of the handbook of etiquette.'[67] Their slavery, as this indicates, was to 'propriety' (for which 'Mrs Grundy' stood as a dominant social icon in the nineteenth century) and the 'sneers' of companions were, in these terms, to exact due obeisance, revealing an awareness of shibboleths within the closed world of the school which clearly parallels that in existence outside its confines. It is this mode of 'informal' education which Kington-Oliphant commends, not least for its efficacy in ensuring the articulation of /h/ where deemed correct: 'Our public schools are often railed against as teaching but little; still it is something that they enforce the right use of *h* upon any lad who has a mind to lead a quiet life among his mates', he points out in approbation.[68] As the sub-text here suggests, it is the pupils, not the teacher, who enforce this pattern, conformity being the key to 'a quiet life', or, as C. Jarman confirms of the same pressures in the twentieth century, to the attempt to be 'one of them' ('I spent my first term in a private hell of homesickness and fear that the boys would find out that I was not "one of them" . . . I quickly acquired the right slang, and my parents were delighted with my new accent').[69] These sociolinguistic processes too seem to have endured as a similar aspect of the public school stereotype; Judith Okeley describes the role of accent as 'a sign and a weapon' in her own days at boarding school in the 1950s (and the strategic mimicry and ridicule applied to those, usually scholarship girls, whose accents deviated from the forms deemed 'proper'),[70] and so too, in boys' boarding-schools of the nineteenth century, did sensitization to accent often seem to ensure corresponding patterns of ostracism or acceptability. Conformity in these respects provided the means of camouflage for those, like Merivale,

[67] A. Hope, *A Book About Dominies. Being the Reflections and Recollections of a Member of the Profession* (London, 1869), 49.
[68] Kington-Oliphant, *Sources of Standard English*, i. 333.
[69] Cited in J. Wakeford, *The Cloistered Élite* (London, 1969), 48.
[70] J. Okeley, 'Privileged, Schooled and Finished: Boarding Education for Girls', in S. Ardener (ed.), *Defining Females* (London, 1978), 115.

made all too conscious of a social origin below that of the dominant peer group and its markers of identity.

It was, as Hales pointed out in 1867, the homogenization of social environment amongst the pupils at such schools which in itself prepared the ground for the homogenization of accent later associated with them. They reinforced notions of 'proper' English through a sense of collective identity in which this too operated as a sign of membership and integration. As Hales therefore commented, describing the typical public school boy of the 1860s: 'He can speak [English], because he has heard it spoken around him from his earliest years. If he has been born and bred in what I call well-educated society, he speaks it "with propriety". He shudders duly when he hears it spoken with impropriety.'[71] Conceptions such as these tended to function as a self-perpetuating paradigm, confirming the associations of the 'best' accent and the 'best' education in schools of this order by means of the emphasis given to the social composition (and social sensibilities) of their intake. School, as Hales too recognizes, provides an ideal environment for reinforcing the sense of a norm, here explicitly presented in terms of 'propriety' and 'impropriety' in the spoken word; the 'shudders' of the 'proper' schoolboy would undoubtedly have been equally efficacious at imposing this same awareness in those who had not 'been born and bred . . . in well-educated society,' likewise encouraging that convergence of which Arnold, Hope, and Kington-Oliphant all, in various ways, discourse. 'Education has often been perceived as the *central* pillar in group identity maintenance', Edwards notes in his own work on *Language, Society and Identity*.[72] Lord Houghton provides still earlier evidence of such perceptions in an essay expressly devoted to the 'social results' of this type of education; it was, as he adds, the social dominance of one set of society above others in schools of this order which guaranteed the use, and dissemination, of 'the tone of feeling and habits of demeanour that prevail in our best British homes'.[73]

Certainly education in the classical mould at these schools was regularly depicted as effective in the transmission of the hegemonies

---

[71] J. W. Hales, 'The Teaching of English', in F. W. Farrar (ed.), *Essays on a Liberal Education* (London, 1867), 293–4.

[72] J. Edwards, *Language, Society and Identity* (Oxford, 1985), 118.

[73] Lord Houghton, 'On the Present Social Results of Classical Education', in Farrar, *Essays*, 377.

of the 'best British homes' to those boys who were perhaps without the social markers of such advantages. Stereotypes of élite education, as the Edgeworths early reveal, were naturally to involve the associated standards of the 'best' speech as part of their conception; these ideas merely consolidate over the course of the century, though perhaps being best expounded in the series of essays and lectures assembled by William M'Combie in his book *On Education in Its Constituents, Objects, and Issues* (1857). This in fact provides one of the most telling expositions of the linguistic benefits which were often assumed to be intrinsic in these types of education.

In it M'Combie narrates the tale of his own encounter with a man who was returning from leaving his elder son at boarding-school. He gives a full account of the motives proffered by the father in (somewhat jubilant) justification of his decision to send his child so far away from the influences of his home:

> With that self-complacency which men are very apt to feel when conscious of having successfully completed a piece of work of special merit and difficulty, our companion dilated on the importance of education in order to success in life [*sic*], clenching his argument and concentrating the expression of his ideal of the matter in the exclamation—'Give them a good pronunciation, and there is no fear but that they will get on in the world.'[74]

Pronunciation is highlighted as the major benefit to be derived from the boarding-school; this 'clenches his argument' and is the focus of his ideal. It is a supposition which, as M'Combie is forced to acknowledge (in spite of his own conviction that it is 'absurd'), stands as a 'typification of the notion of education current with the majority of respectable people in our time',[75] a statement which in itself conclusively affirms the pervasiveness of these stereotypes of language and education at this time. Ideologies of a 'standard' and the means by which it was to be achieved hence unite in the stress placed by contemporary comment on a non-localized education as a particularly good route to that non-localized accent which, as we have seen, was itself embedded in language attitudes (and their attendant socio-cultural constructs) as a marker

---

[74] W. M'Combie, *On Education in Its Constituents, Objects, and Issues* (Aberdeen, 1857), 198–9.
[75] Ibid. 199.

of success. 'The *social* education offered by our schools is of immense value', wrote Farrar, praising the cohesion thereby achieved in the future upper levels of society; 'the end product' at least in its more ideal manifestations was, as Stone and Stone affirm, 'to be an homogenized gentleman by education, whose background was not detectable in his accent, behaviour or culture'.[76] It is clearly this at which M'Combie's own acquaintance aims, and its legacy is still apparent in the attitudes to education surveyed by Fox in her own work in this context, as parents in the late twentieth century still likewise stress their preference for a school 'with a strong emphasis on correct manners and speech', or echo the advantages of linguistic segregation in comments such as 'the advantage of an independent education is to get him away from the local boys who speak badly'.[77]

The social environment of the school is, however, made up of far more than schoolboys. Teachers too can exert an influence, and indeed, as the modern truism has it, 'all teachers are teachers of English'. Tutors in the public school tradition, themselves largely scholars and gentlemen, were by such implicit lessons also to reinforce the sense of a norm in a number of ways. Certainly, their pupils could be sensitive to notions of deviation in this respect, apparently applying the same stringent social testing to masters as they did to their fellow pupils. Merivale's experiences at Harrow are mirrored, for example, in the comments which Mitchinson records of the mathematics teacher at Durham. From his own perspective as a pupil, Mitchinson reveals the social sensibilities (and their consequences) which could operate in this context, noting with some disfavour: 'he was not in Holy Orders nor an English Graduate . . . Nor was he socially regarded or treated as a gentleman.'[78] The majority of masters and headmasters were nevertheless products of the public school tradition in which they taught; a whole series of Arnold's pupils at Rugby, for instance, subsequently became headmasters of other schools, including Marlborough, Harrow, Lancing, Haileybury, Sherborne, Cheltenham, Felsted, and Bury St Edmunds, a process which, as the Clarendon Commissioners recognized, was in itself conducive to certain homogeneities of approach. It offered an element of

---

[76] Stone and Stone, *An Open Élite?*, 27.
[77] Fox, *Public Schools*, 157.   [78] Mitchinson Archive, ii. fo. 6

continuity important in the generation, and the maintenance of a public school stereotype, as well as in conceptions of its associated proprieties: 'The great schools . . . it must be observed, train for the most part the Masters who are placed at the head of the smaller schools, and thus exercise not only a direct but a wide indirect influence over education', as the Commissioners pointed out.[79] Certainly it can appear that the 'gentlemanly' qualifications conferred by such 'indirect' means were at times of more importance than academic excellence; Mitchinson, for instance, describes his appointment of Richard Goodall Gordon at Canterbury in the following terms: 'he was a Second Classman in Mods:, a third in Lit: Hum:. He was a fair scholar, and a fairly good master, but not more; but he was a gentleman to the backbone, and his influence in that direction was invaluable.'[80] In such conceptions, the import of the third in Lit. Hum. was clearly negligible.

As this suggests, those exemplary aspects of behaviour and demeanour which might thereby be presented to pupils could be regarded as particularly invaluable. Specific recommendations for the teacher in this respect are set out most clearly perhaps in the formal manuals of teaching written by John Gill and Robert Robinson, reprinted in their thousands to cater for that escalating demand for instruction as England slowly moved towards a national educational system. Such statements are, however, equally relevant in the context of the grammar school tradition too in the exposition which they offer of the properties required in the ideal teacher, and the indirect influences which he (*sic*) would thereby wield. As Gill stressed in 1870 in his *Introductory Text-Book to School Education, Method, and School Management*, education in these terms was a process which allowed of no remit:

> The teacher does exercise a powerful influence on the habits and character of his young charge . . . In a certain sense he is teaching always, and often when he least thinks of it. The lessons which he gives insensibly are perhaps the most availing of all . . . He is constantly imposing his own likeness.[81]

That this 'likeness' has its linguistic aspects too is given some prominence in Gill's subsequent argument: 'The words which drop

[79] G. M. Young and W. D. Handcock, *English Historical Documents 1833–1874* (London, 1956), xii. 903.
[80] Mitchinson Archive, vii, fo. 21.
[81] J. Gill, *Introductory Text-Book to School Education, Method, and School Management*, rev. [10th] edn. (1870), 7.

unobserved from his lips . . . his daily habits and deportment, have that effect, and may be made subservient to the highest ends.'[82] In other words, since the teacher must of necessity set the standard, potentially imprinting his own habits upon the pupils in his care, his accent too assumes considerable value, offering an additionally instructive model and 'standard' in this sense as well to his pupils. As Gill adds:

reading and speaking are much influenced by imitation, from the inherent tendency to imitate those with whom we associate. This fact shows the importance of the teacher's speech being pure, distinct, deliberate, and impressive . . . The teacher is unwise who neglects so powerful an instrument as this.[83]

Writers who directed their comments specifically to the public school tradition make the same point, likewise stressing notions of the role the teacher was assumed to play in conceptions of group identity and peer group pressure. The recommendation was clear that both masters and headmasters must, in the ideal world, have accents which conformed to the non-localized norms which mark the 'gentil' and 'educated' man. As *Thorough English* observes, directing its comments to 'every Public School, Grammar School, or institution on a large scale': 'The headmaster . . . should write and speak the best English . . . His accent ought to be simply that of a well-educated Englishman, without any trace of local intonation, London or provincial, Scotch or Irish.'[84] Issues of 'proper' language, however, could in addition be made the subject of formal instruction, as the directives issued in *The English Vocabulary*, a textbook 'compiled for the use of Ackworth School' in 1852 make plain. Founded by the Quakers, Ackworth aimed to provide education in the public school tradition for children whose parents were of moderate means. *The English Vocabulary* to be used within its confines in turn unambiguously endorses that contemporary emphasis on 'good' speech which, as we have seen, was often portrayed as a composite part of the benefits the good public school should convey. In keeping with such conceptions, the *Vocabulary* stresses, for example, that the 'teaching [of] a distinct pronunciation' ought to form a significant part of educational provision in

---

[82] Ibid., p. iv.   [83] Ibid., 9th edn. (1863), 153.
[84] *Thorough English* (London, 1867), 9.

the nineteenth-century public school;[85] the responsibility of teachers is not only to impart knowledge on more conventional paradigms, but is also 'to instil a proper pronunciation' in their pupils. This, the author adds, is a feature which can 'scarcely be acquired with accuracy, except *vivâ voce*'.[86] The avowed intention is therefore that of promoting the existence of a 'standard' and uniform pronunciation within the school; any localized markers prominent in the speech of children when first placed in their care are to be eradicated in line with this intent. As we are informed, the impetus for the book had in fact 'been suggested by the peculiar dialects of children brought to this school from various parts of the kingdom', a statement which clearly reveals the alignments of 'standard' rather than 'non-standard' forms of English with the educational regime; modes of language connotative of the 'provincial' rather than the 'proper' and indeed 'educated' are, in these terms, to be 'counteracted.'[87] That these notions of a standard extend to spoken as well as written forms is moreover made plain by subsequent comments. The use of /h/, perhaps predictably, is, for example, foremost amongst the linguistic 'peculiarities' proposed for remedy by such instruction:

In some counties there prevails an unaccountable habit of omitting to sound the letter H when it ought to be pronounced, and of sounding it, not only when the generality of speakers consider it silent, as in *h*eir, *h*erb, &c., but very often when it does not exist in the word . . . In order to correct these errors, a number of words of this kind are inserted for the purposes of exercising pupils in them, by which there is no doubt that the habit may be generally overcome, in all young persons at least.[88]

Whereas major public schools, as the Edgeworths suggested, were almost effortlessly able to endorse requisite proprieties of speech,[89] it was, on the whole, the smaller or newer public schools (such indeed as Ackworth) which tended to resort to these more explicit measures in their attempts to constrain the effect of localized accents in an era sensitized to their use.

[85] *The English Vocabulary. Compiled for the Use of Ackworth School* (London, 1852), p. viii.
[86] Ibid., p. v.   [87] Ibid., p. viii.   [88] Ibid., pp. vii–viii.
[89] Christopher Sykes of Sledmere, sensitive, like Matthew Boulton, to the potential stigma of a local accent for his offspring, specified its eradication before he sent his sons to school, rather than relying on the agency of the school itself to effect this transformation. See pp. 42–3.

St John's, Hurstpierpoint, a school founded in 1853 to cater for the sons of well-to-do tradesmen, exemplifies some of the same points in the *English Primer* written by the headmaster, Edward Lowe, in 1867. A textbook which was employed throughout the school, it too contained a number of extensive directions on the spoken, as well as the written use of the English language. Section IV of the primer is, for example, devoted to 'The Mother Tongue', and it sets out for the instruction of pupils a range of socially sensitive variables in pronunciation, making plain that it is to these that individual usage should conform. The use of [ɪn] (rather than [ɪŋ]) in words such as *walking* or *riding*, and the 'correct' rather than 'vulgar' use of /r/ are all itemized (among other 'errors') under the heading 'Cautions in Pronunciation'. Paradigms of norm and deviation are applied as rigorously as they are to notions of incorrect spelling and, as the advice given on the subject of 'the letter *h*' additionally affirms, the aim is to conform as far as possible to perceptions of 'educatedness' in terms of spoken as well as written words: 'Reverence the letter *h*. Though our forefathers seem to have been very careless about it, no educated ear can now tolerate the omission of this letter.'[90] 'Educated' norms of accent are again explicitly imparted to those being instructed, a point which was presumably of no little significance for the aspiring tradesmen who chose to send their sons to the school.

John Mitchinson's own role as headmaster of the King's School at Canterbury reveals similar preoccupations, notably in his appointment of the Reverend Alex J. D. D'Orsey as 'Lecturer in Elocution'. Readily subscribing to prevalent ideologies of 'proper' speech, he notes that the utterance of his pupils had long been a source of some concern to him: 'I had long chafed at the indistinct and unintelligent utterance of my boys, seniors quite as bad as juniors, and I recognised that my remonstrances and strictures had no effect in abating the nuisance.'[91] As a result, he read with some interest an Advertisement by the Reverend D'Orsey, who described himself as an 'instructor of Peers, M.P.s and Clergy' in the finer matters of enunciation: 'I resolved to try him, and write to enquire whether he, the instructor of Peers, M.P.s and clergy, . . . would stoop so low as to try and cure mumbling among

---

[90] E. C. Lowe, *An English Primer* (London, 1867), 176. A second edn. of this text was produced in 1868.
[91] Mitchinson Archive, vii, fo. 23.

my hobbledehoys; and preoccupy the little folks lips & tongues with articulate utterance.'[92] D'Orsey responded eagerly: 'He caught at my proposal; it was a long cherished scheme of his', and set to work to correct the speech of the boys at Canterbury with some diligence. Mitchinson offers a detailed account of the proceedings which followed, and it is perhaps worthwhile to cite this in full, revealing as it is on the ways in which prevailing ideologies of correctness in speech, as well as the contemporary fondness for recitation and elocution, could be assimilated within the traditions (and emerging stereotypes) of a grammar school of older foundation too:[93]

I constituted myself policeman and sat on vigilant guard all day, lest haply some bolder spirit should try to pull his leg. His method was excellent. He began by warning them that he was an excellent mimic, & meant to bring his gift to bear on them, & bound them by a tacit promise not to be offended if he took them off with their little faults of utterance exactly reproduced,—and then he set to work. Calling up his first 'subject' for dissection, & posting him conspicuously, he put a book in his hand & bade him read. The result may be imagined; dull, lifeless, indistinct, faint murmuring. 'Thank you' he said, and took the book, dismissing the reader to his place. 'Now (remember your promise), listen.' He reproduced him exactly down to every little detail to the joy and mirth of all his comrades, which he checked by a reminder that their turn to have the mirror held up to them was close at hand. Next he would get them to criticise each other, & indicate faults of diction, throwing in rules and reasons for them,—quite simple and obvious as he frequently reminded them; no mystery. I sat and listened and laid to heart all that I heard.[94]

As Mitchinson adds, though he himself was decisively in favour of this course of instruction, and the education in phonemic nicety and public modes of discourse which it provided, 'the unanimous verdict of the upper boys was that it was all "rot" '.[95] King's was, however, not the only school to try this venture in the explicit teaching of elocutionary precepts. 'Thring of Uppingham fell in after my experiment' as Mitchinson records,[96] establishing

---

[92] Ibid. vii, fos. 23–4.
[93] The King's School at Canterbury was originally founded in A.D. 600, and though a boarding element was established in the 19th c., Mitchinson records (Mitchinson Archive, vii, fo. 27) that in his time there it was 'virtually a day school'. Given the reservations expressed by the Edgeworths on this head, this may explain his eagerness to secure specific instruction in the proprieties of spoken English.
[94] Mitchinson Archive, vii, fo. 24.   [95] Ibid.   [96] Ibid.

a similar focus in the school later to become the centre of the first Headmasters' Conference in 1869. Thring was of course a strong advocate of the teaching of English within the public school tradition; as he informed the Schools Inquiry Commission in 1868, his opinion was indeed that 'much more English is required to be worked into the public schools'. 'I have found it so throughout', he added: 'We teach English throughout the school in various forms, and I hold that the very highest results have been attained in a great degree by it.'[97]

As this suggests, both consciously and unconsciously the normative values of 'good' spoken English were able to be implemented in a variety of ways in many of the major (and minor) public schools of the nineteenth century.[98] Masters and headmasters intentionally presented exemplary models of the 'gentleman' for whom 'talking proper' was judged a defining characteristic, while the boys themselves often endorsed paradigms of 'proper' English by the issues of exclusion and exclusivity manipulated in defining norms of group identity. In these terms, ridicule, social shame, the impulse to conform could all act as agents in reinforcing the sense of a 'standard', and while perfect uniformity was not, and indeed could not, be attained,[99] it is nevertheless clear that by the end of the century the public school boy was often seen in terms of that 'command of pure grammatical English' which, among other things, the Clarendon Commissioners of 1864 had deemed essential.[100] It was this which was gradually institutionalized as

[97] Report of the Schools Inquiry Commission, 1868, v. 103; cited in B. Hollingsworth, 'The Mother Tongue and the Public Schools', in A. K. Pugh, V. J. Lee, and J. Swann (eds.) *Language and Language Use* (London, 1980), 187.

[98] The devotion each year of a six-week period at Eastertime to the recitation and learning of sections from 'the chief English poets' at Winchester may be assumed to have contributed to the same sensibilities towards the 'proper' use of the English language. Report of Her Majesty's Commissioners, 1869, i. 144; cited in Hollingsworth 'The Mother Tongue and the Public Schools', 186.

[99] As John Honey notes, Sir Robert Walpole, though attending both Eton and Cambridge, 'all his life sounded like a Norfolk squire' (*Does Accent Matter?*, 24). Similarly, Gladstone, a product of Eton and Oxford, retained traces of his Liverpool origins in his speech.

[100] The Clarendon Commission was appointed in 1861 to inquire into the state of the education provided in the public schools of Winchester, Eton, Westminster, Charterhouse, Harrow, Rugby, Shrewsbury, St Paul's, and Merchant Taylors', and its report was made in 1864. Language, especially English language, occupied a considerable space in its recommendations, not least in terms of the proprieties of usage which ought to characterize the public school product. As John Honey points out, the resulting stereotype was associated most closely with the products

part of the public school ethos, embedded in popular images of the 'gentlemen' who attended such schools as well as undoubtedly being fostered by their escalating, and increasingly deliberate, social exclusivity. Schools within the emergent state system offer a slightly different picture. Diversified, as already indicated, by quality, size, aims, and intake over the entire country—as one inspector noted, 'there are few, if any, occupations regarded as incompatible with school-keeping . . . Domestic servants out of place, discharged barmaids, vendors of toys or lollipops . . . cripples almost bedridden' all formed some of those who had set up schools within London in 1861[101]—the resulting situation, especially before the Elementary Education Act of 1870, is one about which it is often impossible to draw general conclusions. Dame schools could provide what was, in effect, a basic childminding service, offering (like that attended by Pip in *Great Expectations*) only the most rudimentary forms of instruction. Private schools could provide commendable levels of instruction, or be run by out-and-out charlatans whose only qualification for establishing a school was monetary greed. Like Dotheboys Hall in *Nicholas Nickleby*, the educational rewards they offered could be minimal, or instead, like that attended by Dickens in his own childhood, they could be run by a highly competent clocution master.[102] Nevertheless, most schools, even if they aimed no higher, endeavoured to provide some acquaintance with the habits of reading, writing, and arithmetic, and it is here that, overall, a considerable amount of information on attitudes to education, to the spoken language, and to its necessary proprieties, can be traced.

As in the grammar and public schools already discussed, the repercussions of that set of beliefs surrounding notions of the 'best' English could, in many instances, be seen to influence materially

---

of these public schools, and in general with those in the south rather than those in the north ('it seems to have been more effective in Southern public Schools than in that minority of public schools which are in the north'). J. Honey, ' "Talking Proper": Schooling and the Establishment of English "Received Pronunciation" ', in G. Nixon and J. Honey *An Historic Tongue: Studies in English Linguistics in Memory of Barbara Strang* (London, 1988), 213–14.

[101] Report of Dr W. B. Hodgson, one of Her Majesty's Inspectors of Schools on the State of Education in the Metropolitan District, Report from the Commissioners on Popular Education, *Parliamentary Papers*, xxi: III (1861), 93.

[102] See Ackroyd, *Dickens*, 41.

corresponding notions of 'good' and 'bad' in education, an equation effortlessly extended to include pronunciation. 'To facilitate the improvement of the Pupil by the simplest and most easy methods, should be an object with all Tutors and authors of elementary works', as Coysh wrote in his own manual of education in 1837, addressing those involved in the practice of elementary education: 'a correct pronunciation is of paramount importance'.[103] For both teacher and pupil this was to form a pervasive theme within the provision of elementary education, endorsed by training colleges for teachers, by manuals of teaching addressing both theory and practice, and later, by inspectors' reports and the assessments they provided. Since the role of education was to teach the 'proper' forms of English, habits of enunciation in which [h] was habitually lost, or which included regional uses of [ɪn] rather than [ɪŋ] were, by extension, to be regarded in the same light as the double negative, or lack of concord in the sentence. They were 'mistakes' out of keeping with the aims of education, for, as *The Elementary Catechisms* of 1850 stressed, this was specifically to be in standard, rather than non-standard, forms of speech:

Q. Why is it, that if we can speak our own language, it is necessary to learn grammar?

A. From habit we often use many unsuitable words, and incorrect modes of speech; and as dialects differ from the standard in various parts of the country, it is therefore requisite to learn grammar.[104]

John Poole's *The Village School Improved* provides early illustration of the inspiration which prescriptive notions of correctness with reference to the spoken word could exert in such educational contexts. Published in 1813 with the explicit aim of facilitating 'in some degree the introduction of a new system of education into village schools',[105] the book stands as an account of the teaching of reading and pronunciation in Enmore School in Somerset over the previous five years. Employing the monitorial system developed by Bell and Lancaster, and with an intake composed of local village children, notions of the 'educated accent' and its seemingly

---

[103] G. Coysh, *The British Pronouncing and Self Instructing Spelling Book* (Topsham, 1837), p. iii.

[104] *The Elementary Catechisms* (London, 1850), 5.

[105] J. Poole, *The Village School Improved; Or, A New System of Education Practically Explained, and Adapted to the Case of Country Parishes*, 2nd edn. (Oxford, 1813), 1.

inherent proprieties are fervently embraced. Poole, the rector of Enmore, describes in some detail the methods by which 'correctness' in these spheres was to be obtained.

Vigilance on the teacher's part is, in particular, presented as vital, for each mistake in enunciation made by a pupil was to be immediately detected, and then corrected: 'Throughout the whole lesson the utmost attention and vigilance are requisite on the part of the teacher: it being a fundamental rule of the school that no error, however slight, shall be suffered to pass unnoticed, or uncorrected.'[106] The child's performance is hence constantly supervised in auditory terms, his or her ranking in the school being made dependent on respective levels of failure or success. Relevant paradigms of norm and deviation are rigorously implemented, and the progress of the reading lesson is, it seems, continually interrupted by the enforcement of these normative dictates:

If a child omits, or mistakes, a word, or even a letter, he is liable to degradation; as it is the duty of the teacher instantly to pass to the next child, and, if necessary, to all the children in succession; and on no account to rectify the mistake himself, until the whole class has been tried. Even a coarse or provincial way of pronouncing a word, though sanctioned by the general practice of the district, is immediately noticed by the teacher; and exposes the child, who uses it, as much to the correction of those below him, and consequently to the loss of his place, as any other impropriety in reading would do.[107]

This notion of 'linguistic exposure' as a direct consequence of using localized 'error' rather than the 'proper' and non-localized markers of standard speech is an important one, clearly relying on imprinting upon the child a sense of shame surrounding his habitual forms of speech. Forming a staple of prescriptive attitudes to language, it serves to provide an additional perspective on the ways in which, as Labov contends, language attitudes tend to be uniform throughout the linguistic community.[108] Regardless of actual patterns of usage, such statements deploy notions of collective linguistic identity which rely not on linguistic reality (the forms 'sanctioned by the general practice of the district' which are instead construed as 'coarse' and 'provincial') but instead on forms sanctioned by a broader (and far more unidimensional) view of 'proper' language. 'Flawed' pronunciation in these terms thus leads

---

[106] Ibid. 40.   [107] Ibid. 40–1.   [108] See p. 56.

to 'degradation', a word which in itself conveys not only 'demotion' ('to put one from his degree' as Walker's 1791 definition explains) but also 'devaluation' in a far wider sense: 'to lessen, diminish the value of', as Walker also notes.

Whereas the negative repercussions which such policies may have (not least in the sense of alienation, either from family and home, or indeed from the school itself) often leads to their categorical condemnation in modern work on language and educational psychology, nineteenth-century writers had little interest in such matters. 'It is difficult to belittle a speaker's language without belittling the speaker as well', states Trudgill, for example, in his own work in this field;[109] 'by rejecting a child's accent, or even some features of it, we run the risk of his feeling we are rejecting *him*';[110] Few scruples of this kind bothered Poole, or indeed many of the other writers and educationalists who followed him over the nineteenth century; these issues of rejection could, it was felt, merely enhance the convergence deemed both necessary and 'correct'. Though as Poole admits, 'it was easy to foresee, that the immediate effect of this strict attention to correctness and propriety, would be to embarrass the child', his priorities remain clear. 'This embarrassment is merely temporary' but 'permanent advantages . . . are sure to follow if the method be patiently persevered in'.[111]

Poole had learnt his own lessons well; just as Sheridan proclaimed that regional forms were emblematic of social disgrace, pleading for educators to take heed of the methods his work offered for the creation of national uniformity in speech, so too did Poole wholeheartedly embrace the hegemonic potential of notions of a 'standard' accent, endorsing prevalent attitudes towards 'talking proper' in the system of education he advocates for village schools all over the country. Displacing the 'negligence' of local accents with the 'propriety' of the chosen norm, this achievement, in spite of any initial difficulties the child may have, is presented as exemplary:

Experience has fully proved to us, that although at the commencement the progress of the learner is continually checked and interrupted, yet by degrees habits of accuracy and propriety are formed; which terminate at length in an intelligent, discriminating manner of reading, and a purity of pronunciation, which are seldom, if ever, attained under the old system.[112]

---

[109] P. Trudgill, *Accent, Dialect, and the School* (London, 1975), 67.
[110] Ibid. 58. [111] Poole, *The Village School Improved*, 41. [112] Ibid. 41–2.

Regional 'impropriety' is to be replaced by non-localized 'purity', and the modes of reading which result are furthermore 'intelligent', an adjective which likewise reveals the adherence to those models of accent and cognitive adequacy which in themselves tend to form a recurrent topos in language attitudes over this time. Since *The Village School Improved* went through three editions in a mere five years, it may moreover be assumed that other educators too recognized the stated validity of Poole's ideas.

Elementary education was, in fact, to become a sphere in which the common value-judgements about language, advantage, and disadvantage were to be encoded with remarkable frequency. Given then prevalent conceptions in which accent (as indeed in modern subjective reaction tests) could be taken as an unquestioned index of intelligence, and manner as a guide to matter, such policies were perhaps understandable. As Bainbrigge later emphasized in *Early Education* (1881), the import of *what* was said could be materially influenced by *how* it was said: 'Whatever powers of mind or extent of knowledge we possess, it is the voice which gives them utterance, and their influence in a large degree depends on skilful modulation; and without it, accuracy of thought, cogency of argument, and brilliancy of conception lose much of their force.'[113] Many writers concluded from such precepts that if children were to have systematic access to education, they must therefore also have equally systematic access to teaching in the spoken language: ' "Pronunciation" and accent cannot be taught too early, too assiduously, too perseveringly', as Wyse declared in his own earlier work on education reform, expressing an opinion that many were to share.[114]

The teaching of reading was, in particular, influenced in no small measure by the practical application of such maxims. Prominence was regularly given to its capacity for decoding to sound, especially to the 'correct' sound, as well as (and, occasionally, even at the expense of) its capacity for decoding to meaning. *Chambers's Educational Course: Simple Lessons in Reading*, a text written 'for use in schools and for private instruction', made this view of reading plain in 1841: 'it is necessary that the child should be taught to *read*— that is, to apprehend at a glance the appearance of the written

---

[113] W. H. Bainbrigge, *Early Education* (London, 1881), 124.
[114] Wyse, *Education Reform*, 100.

symbols of his native language, and to pronounce these symbols according to the most approved manner.'[115] Other definitions of reading tended to endorse these insights. Gill's textbook on school method and management, widely used in teacher training colleges, notes that 'correct reading also includes purity of pronunciation, which consists in giving each letter its right sound, and to each word its proper accent'.[116] Graham, author of *An Introduction to the Art of Reading* (1861), specifies that aptitude for reading requires 'a correct as opposed to a vulgar or provincial pronunciation'.[117] Notions of reading as an oral as well as a visual experience were thus closely aligned with prescriptive notions of correctness, as well as with the often-avowed ambition to standardize the spoken language. *Chambers's Educational Course*, stressing the advantages of disseminating accurate modes of articulation by means of this educational bias, hence offers a view of a future and perfect uniformity which will result from the implementation of such thinking in the school: 'by these means, vulgar and provincial dialects will be gradually extirpated, and purity of speech introduced.'[118] Such aims were by no means rare.

Reading, as the Reverend Fussell, one of Her Majesty's Inspectors of Schools, asserted in 1859, was indeed one of the most important subjects of instruction in elementary schools: 'no secular subject comprised in the time-table is of greater importance than *reading*',[119] and the methods by which it might best be taught received considerable attention. As in the public school, and as Poole (1813) has already indicated, the role and responsibilities of the teacher were perceived as salient. The central axiom was that set out, with appropriate rhetorical balance, by Livesey in 1881: 'If [the pupil] constantly hears good and correct speaking, he may learn to speak correctly and well.'[120] Other writers were more stringent, if less rhetorical, in the specification of the standards to be required in the 'good' teacher in this respect:

---

[115] W. Chambers and R. Chambers (eds.), *Chambers's Educational Course: Simple Lessons in Reading* (Edinburgh, 1841), 4.
[116] Gill, *Introductory Text-Book*, rev. [10th] edn. (1870), 149.
[117] J. G. Graham, *Introduction to the Art of Reading* (London, 1861), 3.
[118] Chambers and Chambers, *Chambers's Educational Course*, 7.
[119] Report of the Committee of Council on Education 1859–60; General Report for the Year 1859, by the Revd J. C. G. Fussell, *Parliamentary Papers*, liv. (1860), 20.
[120] T. J. Livesey, *How to Teach Grammar: Illustrated in a Series of Lessons* (London, 1881), 3.

Teaching to read requires that the teacher should often read for imitation by the learner. Here, as in other things, the example of the teacher is necessary to explain his precept. But more than this, reading and speech are much influenced by imitation, from the inherent tendency to imitate those with whom we associate. This fact shows the importance of the teacher's speech being pure, distinct, deliberate, and impressive; for the school will image forth these qualities if found in him, or will be deficient in them if he is so.[121]

Gill's notion that the accents of pupils would mirror their masters' speech (for good or ill) itself forms a notable and recurrent image in educational writings over the course of the nineteenth century. 'From not hearing good reading the children will never read well themselves' is given as undeniable in the General Report for the years 1848–9, by Her Majesty's Inspector of Schools, the Reverend H. W. Bellairs: 'a master should set a good copy to his children, should read frequently with them during a lesson, and take pains to correct their incorrect pronunciation, e.g. the prevalent provincialisms of the district.'[122] The ideal thus described reveals the ways in which ideologies of a standard, applied to spoken as well as to written discourse, were fully assimilated within notions of what 'good' elementary education could and should comprise. The teachers' own training exemplifies this bias even more, as accent is made into an aspect of their own assessment, as well as of that of the pupils they will teach. 'Intelligence, clear pronunciation, and good intonation are the main qualities we require to secure a high mark', the Reverend B. M. Corrie stated in his report on the Church of England Training Colleges for Schoolmasters in 1859.[123] Regional accents, connotative of 'ignorant' rather than 'educated', were indeed increasingly considered incompatible with the office of the schoolteacher: 'The intonation is good, and it is impossible to doubt that great pains have been consistently taken to correct any faults of pronunciation which students may previously have contracted', the Reverend F. C. Cook commented on the National Society's Training Institution at Whitelands,

---

[121] Gill, *Introductory Text-Book*, rev. [10th] edn. (1870), 152–3.
[122] General Report for the Year 1849, by Her Majesty's Inspector of Schools, the Revd H. W. Bellairs, Committee of Council on Education, *Parliamentary Papers*, xliii (1850), 119.
[123] Report of the Committee of Council on Education, *Parliamentary Papers*, liv (1860), 295.

Chelsea. 'This is a point of great importance for a teacher, and is no unfair test of mental cultivation and training.'[124] The teacher was thus to set the standard, not only in learning itself but also in the modes of language deemed emblematic of it. Recommendations of how the requisite modes of speech are to be acquired appear daunting in the extreme, as manuals of pronunciation, courses of elocution,[125] unremitting vigilance in terms of the teacher's own accent (as well as towards that of others), together with a full knowledge of articulation and phonetics, are all urged as essentials in the quest for that perfect propriety of enunciation which must distinguish the 'good' teacher. 'Provincialisms', suggestive, as Dr Johnson had declared, of the 'rude and uncultivated', did not befit those in charge of education; as *The Teacher's Manual of the Science and Art of Teaching* warned, the retention of such markers would be liable to establish erroneous models for the children in the school. The teacher is advised 'to guard himself' against their use, for 'if his intercourse with others accustom him to erroneous modes of pronunciation and speech, he will be in danger of setting these up as standards'.[126]

Such features, as already indicated, were similarly proscribed by inspectors of schools. D. A. Fearon, for example, gave their use or otherwise by the teacher as one of the salient points to be noticed during the assessment of the school: 'Does [the teacher] use provincialisms or avoid them, and check the use of them in the Scholars?'.[127] All provincial modes of speech were ideally to be eradicated in the teacher before any tuition in the school could begin. 'Help in curing provincialisms has been found in certain Training Colleges by the use of a little book called the 'Manual of English Pronunciation',[128] the *Science and Art of Teaching* helpfully advised. Gill too stressed the utility of this particular textbook, recommending in addition that both teacher and teaching assistants should transcribe into appropriate notation all lessons to

[124] Minutes of the Committee of Council on Education, *Parliamentary Papers*, xliii (1850), 24–5.
[125] Elocution as a study was commended for its evident utility in the training of teachers in the Training Institution of the British and Foreign School Society in the Borough Road, Southwark, by J. D. Morell, one of Her Majesty's Inspectors, Report of the Committee of Council on Education, *Parliamentary Papers*, liv (1860), 389.
[126] *The Teacher's Manual of the Science and Art of Teaching* (London, 1874), 225.
[127] D. A. Fearon, *School Inspection* (London, 1876), 33.
[128] *Teacher's Manual*, 225.

be given, hence further ensuring that 'correct' standards of speech would be maintained: 'An aid to this would be to mark the quantities and accents in the "Teacher's Lesson Book",—the doing so being a part of the preparation of the reading lesson required from his apprentices.'[129] In such ways, the training colleges established from the 1840s onwards were also to promote and endorse the normative standards of linguistic behaviour familiar from the prescriptive tradition and its associated ideals of standard speech. For teacher as for pupil, estimations of relative success could depend upon conformity in these respects. *Moffat's How to Teach Reading*, a popular text in educational training, makes this emphasis particularly clear, giving a full description of the levels of articulatory awareness which were required:

The teacher has to train the vocal organs to produce sounds distinctly and correctly. To do this, he will have to acquaint himself with the functions of the various organs concerned in the production of speech. He will have to be able to detect and correct bad habits and defects of utterance, and show the children how to use tongue, teeth, lips, and palate, in order to articulate distinctly.[130]

The teacher's education in 'proper pronunciation' was, however, to extend even beyond this formal instruction in phonetics and speech training provided by a number of the training colleges. On the subject of pronunciation, as Morrison's *Manual of School Management* advised, learning could never stop. A text frequently used in such institutions, being 'examined and gone into minutely' at, for example, the Free Church Training College at Glasgow,[131] its precepts encoded a process of continual monitoring (and intentional improvement) with regard to the accent of the teacher:

whenever the young teacher hears a good speaker pronounce a word differently from what he has been accustomed to, he ought to note it, and never rest satisfied until he has ascertained the correct pronunciation. He will be amazed at the benefit which such a course will confer, and, in a short time he will find himself master of the majority of words.[132]

---

[129] Gill, *Introductory Text-Book*, 9th edn. (1863), 156.
[130] T. J. Livesey, *Moffat's How to Teach Reading* (London, 1882), 2.
[131] Report on the Free Church Training College at Glasgow for the Year 1859, by Her Majesty's Inspector of Schools, C. E. Wilson Esq., Report of the Committee of Council on Education, *Parliamentary Papers*, liv (1860), 465.
[132] T. Morrison, *Manual of School Management* 3rd edn. (London, 1863), 126.

The teacher's stated role in disseminating as well as embodying
the norms of 'proper' speech tended to enhance still more that
importance placed upon linguistic mastery in these terms. Like
missionaries, teachers were often seen in terms of their abilities
in 'spreading the good word', appropriate criteria of 'good' and
'bad' of course again being dependent on relevant estimations
of 'standard' and its converse. It was an analogy made explicit
by Alexander Ellis: 'Education, which sends teachers as missionaries into remote districts to convey the required sounds more or
less correctly . . . does much to promote uniformity of speech'.[133]
Morrison's instructions on the duties of the teacher once he (or
she) is established in a position unhesitatingly reveal the wider
significance of these notions: 'We advise the teacher, whenever he
finds himself located in a particular parish, to observe carefully
the prevalent peculiarities; and, when he has done so, vigorously
to set himself to correct them among his pupils.'[134] Markers of
localized speech again being labelled as 'peculiarities', it should
perhaps be no surprise to find them being treated in a number of
textbooks on the art of teaching under the heading of 'Defective
Intelligence', for which, as Gill forcibly asserts, 'the cure is with the
teacher, who alone is to blame if there exists much incorrectness.'[135]

Gill's own section on 'Defective Intelligence' opens with the subject of pronunciation:

The most troublesome class of incorrect pronunciations are provincialisms, the substitution of one sound for another, as û for ŭ and *vice versa*;
the addition of sounds, as idea-r, and the omission of sounds, as of the
aspirate. These faults partake of a mechanical character, belonging to the
ear and habit, as much as to defective intelligence. The best mode of
dealing with them is to take up a systematic course of orthoepy.[136]

Stigmatized as a marker of 'ignorance' in more ways than one,
these assumed cognitive as well as elocutionary errors are, Gill
tells us, to be recognized by various habits of speech: enunciations
more typical of 'provincial' than 'metropolitan', the use of the [ʊ]
(as in *bull*) where one might expect the [ʌ] as in *cut* (and vice versa),
the use of intrusive /r/ and, of course, the loss of [h]. The last of
these regularly being interpreted as a signifier of lack of education

[133] Ellis, *Early English Pronunciation*, i 19.
[134] Morrison, *Manual of School Management*, 127.
[135] Gill, *Introductory Text-Book*, 9th edn. (1863), 156.   [136] Ibid. 155–6.

in itself, its use in accordance with accepted canons of correctness was deemed particularly important, often being depicted as enough to confound (or confirm) notions of 'educatedness' *per se*. As Wilkinson, for example, stressed in his lectures on education, its socio-symbolic value was such that merely by virtue of its presence 'it promotes refinement and assists in the cultivation of proprieties of manner'.[137] Other writers took a more practical approach to its inculcation, and assessments of teaching proficiency regularly refer to its use. *The Elementary School Manager* likewise specified in its directives for the monitoring of good teaching: 'In particular, are mistakes as to *emphasis, punctuation,* and *aspirates* noticed and corrected with even the youngest children? Is distinct and audible utterance enforced?'[138] School inspectors reinforced the same preoccupations, adjudging superiority or inferiority in the teacher on these grounds. As Mr Nevill Cream asserted in 1861, 'inferior teachers tell me it is useless to try and teach the children to [pronounce [h]]; that the parents at home unteach, by their conversation, whatever is taught at school; that it is provincial, and make a good many other excuses'.[139] Such excuses are evidently not to be accepted, nor are they proffered by that icon of the 'good' teacher: 'On the other hand, a good teacher says nothing, but sets to work; and the next year every child, from the oldest to the youngest, pronounces the *h* with correctness.'[140] The pressures exerted by such stereotypes were presumably not inconsiderable, not least since comments of this kind were regularly inserted in manuals of training for the hapless teacher.

'Every time a teacher corrects a pupil's spelling or a grammatical form, some process of standardization is taking place', Stubbs affirms in *Educational Linguistics*.[141] In the nineteenth century, this process was, in terms of educational theory, extended equally to the sounds of speech, encompassing not only the widely recognized shibboleth of /h/, but also a range of other (localized) markers stigmatized within the prescriptive tradition. Directives for the 'good' teacher hence frequently specify attention to their pupils' use of [ɪŋ] rather than [ɪn] in words such as *walking*, to the

[137] Revd W. F. Wilkinson, *Education, Elementary and Liberal: Three Lectures Delivered in the Hall of the Mechanics' Institute, Derby, Nov. 1861* (London, 1862), 56.
[138] Perceval Graves and Rice-Wiggin, *The Elementary School Manager*, 116.
[139] Cited in Robinson, *A Manual of Method and Organisation* 3 n.
[140] Ibid. 3.   [141] M. Stubbs, *Educational Linguistics* (Oxford, 1986), 84.

avoidance of the use of intrusive *r*, or to the 'proper' distribution of /ʊ/ and /ʌ/ as in *bull* and *cut*, as well as to the enunciation of a range of other sounds. As Gill counselled, 'when cases occur of indistinct pronunciation of particular sounds, as *s*, *r*, or *h*, it is desirable to give daily exercises thereon, directing the child's attention to yourself while uttering them'.[142] 'No faults should pass without correction', he adds. Graham's *Introduction to the Art of Reading* reflects the operation of similar principles; intrusive *r* is specified as a mark of 'vulgar pronunciation' and is therefore incompatible with the educational benefits being offered. Likewise of /h/ the author notes: 'there can scarcely be anything more disagreeable to a correct ear, than that of sinking the initial *h*, in words where it ought to be heard.'[143] Daily exercises to secure proficiency, in pupil and teacher alike, are again recommended as of prime utility.

The level of detail which children were at times apparently required to assimilate is striking. Even before the institution of the annual inspection and the demands it subsequently made in this area, individual schools frequently implemented prescriptive tenets with praiseworthy diligence, as the example of Poole in 1813 has shown. The 'seminary' run by the Misses Wilmshurst in Maldon provides a later and equally instructive example of the ways in which preoccupations with phonemic detail could exert considerable influence on methods of tuition.

The First Part of the Progressive Parsing Lessons was printed in 1833 'for the use of Miss Wilmshurst's Seminary', though its usefulness for other schools was, of course, not denied. It offers a comprehensive examination of the way in which reading is to be taught, asserting as a central principle that 'the importance of an early knowledge of every simple elementary sound in the English Language, is generally acknowledged'.[144] What is, in effect, a series of elementary lessons in phonetics follows, and though the details provided do at times verge on the incomprehensible, a thorough survey of pronunciation and its role in 'proper' reading is attempted: '*Ar* must be pronounced with the tip of the tongue pressed against the gums of the under teeth, to prevent the *r* having its rough or consonant sound', 'the close *o* is pronounced

---

[142] Gill, *Introductory Text-Book*, 9th edn. (1863), 155.
[143] Graham, *Introduction to the Art of Reading*, 30.
[144] *The First Part of the Progressive Parsing Lessons* (Maldon, 1833), p. iv.

with the lips drawn up as far as possible'.[145] Exercises on parsing
are, in addition, extended to phonemes as well as parts of speech,
and an illustrative section on how to apply this knowledge is presented in the typical 'question and answer' format of schoolbooks
of the day:

TEACHER. Tell me the vowel sounds in *barn yard*.
PUPIL. *Barn* middle *a*, *yard* middle *a*.
T. *Bee-hive*.—P. *Bee* long *e*, *hive* long *i*.
T. *Blue-bell*.—P. *Blue* long *u*, *bell* short *e*.[146]

Walker likewise appears as a prime educational authority, his
pronouncing dictionary presented as indispensable in teaching the
spoken language in ways which would have gratified Sheridan's
earlier ambitions in this respect: 'Mr Walker observes that when
the *o* ends a syllable immediately before or after the accent; as in
polite, impotent, &c, there is an elegance in giving it a sound nearly
as long as the long *o*', 'The *a* in the words *past, last, France*, . . . &c,
is sometimes prolonged in a sound between the short *a* and the
middle *a*.' 'Mr Walker does not approve of this sound', as they
add.[147]

It might, of course, be argued that concentration on the spoken
word to this level is a feature expected in a school professing to
teach 'young ladies'; as we have seen, elocution was depicted as
a necessary accomplishment within prevailing ideals of 'proper'
femininity for girl, wife, and mother.[148] However, it rapidly becomes clear that elementary education in general was often to display a similar focus, concentrating, for example, on teaching reading
by methods of phonic analysis which were designed to impart
'proper' rather than 'improper' ways of pronouncing sounds. As
Moffat's How to Teach Reading noted, 'phonic analysis' was to be
recommended for its thoroughness in this respect, guaranteeing
familiarity with the range of 'proper' sounds in English.[149] Detailed
descriptions of how to teach reading thus frequently present 'proper'
education in these terms too. 'Lessons must be given on each
sound of a vowel, the short ones before the long ones. Each
following lesson should also contain the sounds taught in preceding
lessons', instructed J. J. Prince in another central textbook on

---

[145] Ibid. 63–4.   [146] Ibid. 66.   [147] Ibid. 71–2.
[148] See pp. 175–7.   [149] Livesey, *Moffat's How to Teach Reading*, 10.

school organization and method.[150] Gill's account of the approved methods to be used in infant classes similarly emphasizes instruction in articulation as a necessary accompaniment to the art of reading: 'This method consists in slowly uttering a word, and drawing attention to the mouth while doing so, then the learner to utter the word, and this process to be continued until the child discerns how a particular sound is produced.'[151] Ideal lessons for the infant class specifically include 'orthoepy' as well as spelling, as definitions of reading as an oral activity are vigorously prioritized by this emphasis on articulatory prowess. Though the 'look and say' method of learning to read (in which 'children are taught to recognise and pronounce *whole words* at a single effort without stopping to spell them')[152] is acknowledged as achieving the quickest results, nevertheless, as Gill stresses, methods of teaching reading which incorporate these methods of 'phonic analysis' are to be preferred, primarily on the grounds that 'oral reading incorporates much more than recognition of the words': 'it includes, among other things, purity and distinctness of pronunciation. Hence it is desirable to have, current with the reading lesson, lessons on pronunciation and spelling, on the method of phonic analysis.'[153]

Though such methods were not without their critics, White in 1862 averring that they constituted 'too complicated a machine for teachers to handle, involving a process too difficult for children to encounter',[154] the focus on sound as well as spelling in the teaching of reading received, on the whole, a favourable response. As Prince noted in 1880, 'the pronunciation by this method will be much more accurate than any other',[155] an important achievement given that intermeshing of attitudes to a spoken standard within educational thinking of the time. Even the Report of the Privy Council Committee on Education in 1842 had seconded the values of Walker's pronouncing dictionary in the school: 'The master should have at hand also a good English Dictionary (Walker's may be purchased for 4s. 6d.), and not be afraid to

---

[150] J. J. Prince, *School Management and Method* (London, 1880), 225–6.
[151] Gill, *Introductory Text-Book*, 9th edn. (1863), 145.
[152] Livesey, *How to Teach Grammar*, 21.
[153] Gill, *Introductory Text-Book*, 9th edn. (1863), 163.
[154] G. White, *A Simultaneous Method of Teaching to Read Adapted to Primary Schools* (London, 1862), 25.
[155] Prince, *School Management*, 79.

make frequent use of it in the presence of his pupils.'[156] Grover's *New English Grammar for the Use of Junior Classes in Schools* attempted to make such necessary information about the sounds of English more palatable for young children by presenting it in rhyme: 'The *liquids* you may quickly tell, | They are but *four*—*m*, *n*, *r*, and *l*.| *Mutes* the rest are said to be, | Such are *b*, *d*, *c*, and *f* and *t*. . . .'[157]

Even outside the reading lesson, however, these pressures did not necessarily diminish for either teacher or child. While an unremitting vigilance towards matters of accent was, as we have seen, presented as integral to the teacher's role as linguistic standard, duties in this respect were also to extend to a form of constructive eavesdropping to be practised upon pupils wherever possible. Griffiths, for example, specifies that to confine dissemination of the desired norms of speech to the reading lesson alone is to limit vital opportunities for impressing these lessons upon children: 'The teacher should be scrupulously careful in exacting correct and distinct utterance in *all* school exercises, not merely in the formal reading lesson, but in all the intercourse of the children.'[158] Other manuals setting forth the theory and practice of teaching unreservedly endorse this view: '[the teacher] should carefully correct every mispronunciation made by the children, both in the reading lesson and out of it',[159] 'the gross errors in pronunciation which children acquire from the conversation of their contemporaries . . . can only be eradicated by correction at all times when they occur, either in the reading lesson, or in ordinary conversation'.[160] Robinson in fact specifies that it is in such informal circumstances that inculcation of the requisite norms of speech may be best achieved, and he advocates, wherever possible, the correction of 'local peculiarities . . . in that conversational intercourse that always exists between the teacher and children during school

[156] Cited in *Extracts from the Reports of Her Majesty's Inspectors of Schools* (1852), 192.

[157] A. Grover, *A New English Grammar for the Use of Junior Classes in Schools* (London, 1877), 11.

[158] R. J. Griffiths, *An Introduction to the Study of School Management* (London, 1872), 21.

[159] Livesey, *Moffat's How to Teach Reading*, 63.

[160] *Handbook on the Teaching and Management of Elementary Schools* (Manchester, 1872), 52.

hours'.[161] Any feelings of alienation, or indeed persecution, which might result from the full implementation of this process are not, of course, considered.

Robinson's emphasis on the need to teach pronunciation outside, rather than inside the reading lesson does, however, receive some justification from his account of the negative consequences which could, and did, attend that undue concentration on accent recommended in many manuals of teaching. As he stresses, prominence could be given to the correction of perceived 'errors' in enunciation far in excess of the attention paid, on occasion, to the acquisition of reading itself. '[Teachers] pass over the child's comprehension of the text, and the force and correctness with which he makes himself understood almost entirely, in their extreme desire to secure purity of utterance',[162] he points out with disapprobation. The reports of Her Majesty's Inspectors occasionally offer similar criticisms, revealing the ways in which an exaggerated emphasis on phonemic propriety could sometimes operate to the seeming exclusion of the true purposes of teaching reading. The Reverend Mr Grant in 1860 offers, for example, a graphic description of teachers 'lying in wait for provincialisms', and, as they occur, making constant interruptions in order to align 'faulty' utterance with the normative paradigms of 'proper' speech.[163] Robinson himself provides a similarly informative critique of contemporary practices in the teaching of reading, censuring the methods in which 'by their captious manner, and their constant fault-finding [teachers] worry and distract their children until they force them to commit, in their perplexity, errors of which they otherwise would have been quite innocent'.[164]

On the whole, this was unfortunately the position which seems most often to have been adopted, as school inspectors, themselves products of a cultural and linguistic climate in which notions of accent as social symbol had been assimilated into prescriptive and popular thought as never before, stressed the need to 'improve' English in ways which unambiguously proscribed localized accents as a marker of 'ignorance'. Inattention to the perceived oral proprieties is regarded with disfavour, attracting disapproving comments in the yearly reports: 'the reading lessons of the lower

---

[161] Robinson, *Manual of Method and Organisation*, 2–3.
[162] Ibid. 2.   [163] Cited ibid.   [164] Ibid.

classes are conducted with but slight regard to clearness of articulation or correctness of pronunciation', the Reverend Fussell
complained in 1859 of schools in Middlesex.[165] 'Reading is only
good in the best schools. The great fault in the lower classes is
want of real correctness, good articulation, and mastery of the
pronunciation', as the inspector for the schools of the West Central
division of England affirmed in 1887. 'Long-inherited peculiarities
of mode of speech and pronunciation' inhibit achievement in
Cumberland, Mr Parez reports in the same year, concluding: 'It
is not in Cumberland that for a generation or two good reading
will be found.'

Following the introduction of the Revised Code in 1862, and
the principle of 'payment by results',[166] one can imagine that such
comments would have exerted still more force on the normative
principles teachers were supposed to adopt, especially since the
modes of oral examination employed by inspectors would have
brought to the fore facility or otherwise in those modes of speaking
regularly presented as essential in principles of elementary education. As, in his role as inspector of schools, Matthew Arnold
himself was to comment on the elementary school and its assessment, 'how great a part [of the work] consists in the reading; and
what an advantage for making a favourable impression on a
spectator have those elementary schools in which the tone and
accent of the reading are agreeable'.[167] Notions of 'agreeableness',
and even of 'good' and 'bad' could, however, as Arnold realized,
depend all too often upon the evaluative assumptions, and accompanying notions of subjective inequality, which were commonly
enshrined in language attitudes.

That educational aims explicitly came to include the dissemination of a spoken standard on national rather than local scales is
therefore both openly acknowledged, and entirely in keeping with
the linguistic temper of the age. As *Chambers's Educational Course:
Simple Lessons in Reading* specified, the increasing use of modes of
oral instruction in the question and answer method, rather than

---

[165] *Parliamentary Papers*, liv (1860), 20.
[166] The terms of the Code made payment of the government grant for education
dependent on both the average attendance of pupils in the school, and on the level
of performance in the (often largely oral) examinations conducted by the inspectors
in their rounds.
[167] Matthew Arnold, *Reports on Elementary Schools 1852–1882*, ed. F. Sandford
(London, 1889), 42–3.

the learning by rote which had often dominated in the past, offered undeniable advantages for the child, not only in terms of the greater stimulation of the intellect, but also in the prominence thereby given to exemplary linguistic usage and its dissemination by means of the teacher:

> One very material advantage of this improved method of teaching is, the cultivation of the *art of speaking*. The master should speak in the best English, and take care that the answers are equally correct ... *Clearness of articulation* should be most carefully inculcated, as indistinctness acquired in childhood can hardly ever be removed. By these means, vulgar and provincial dialects will be gradually extirpated, and purity of speech introduced.[168]

Extirpation, defined by Johnson as 'the act of rooting out; eradicating; excision' and 'destruction', was to be applied as an important philosophy in educational terms with regard to the displacement of dialect and its associated markers of speech. Evoking the binary oppositions of 'pure' and 'impure', 'vulgar' and 'polite' common in much prescriptive writing, precepts such as these effectively embodied the ways in which the connotative and cultural values accorded to divergent linguistic varieties in the world outside the school were embedded within it too. Educational theory and inspectors' assessments, the training of teachers and expectations placed on pupils, all came to enforce ways of looking at language which prioritized the monolithic at the expense of the localized and variable. Only one form of language was, in theory, to be sanctioned as acceptable in the atmosphere of the ideal school.

Textbooks on recitation for the use of schools make this particularly plain. Commended by Arnold as 'the special subject which produces at present, so far as I can tell, most good',[169] recitation was popular in many schools, and works such as William Enfield's *The Speaker* went through many editions, its original ambition 'of assisting the students at Warrington in acquiring a just and graceful Elocution' being applied, in effect, on a national scale. 'Just' and 'graceful', as our analysis of Enfield's work has already revealed,[170] are readily chosen as epithets appropriate for the accent of the gentleman, that cultural and linguistic icon of the nineteenth century. That such conceptions popularly came to be seen as appropriate

---

[168] Chambers and Chambers, *Chambers's Educational Course*, 7.
[169] Arnold, *Reports on Elementary Schools*, 163.   [170] See p. 66.

for the 'educated' too, even those receiving instruction at the most elementary levels, is concisely revealed in a textbook from a century later: *Recitation. A Handbook for Teachers in Public Elementary School* by A. Burrell.

Published in 1891, Burrell's *Recitation* endorses those now familiar ideas by which 'distinct and correct pronunciation' was to form a part of the taught language from the first to the most senior class at school. Systematically analysing each sound and sound combination for the benefit of the pupil, the standardizing intent is clear; attention to such details provides the means by which provenance may be disguised, and assimilation to the non-localized as social norm achieved. On the realization of *a* in words such as *father* and *bath*, Burrell thus notes:

Remember, as I have said, that the person who pronounces the āh thinly (as ăh) *must* come from the northern part of England; but the person who pronounces the āh long and full *may* come from any part of England; and it is the business of educated people to speak so that no-one may be able to tell in what county their childhood was passed. Once more, I repeat this: the ăh is not wrong; *but it is provincial*.[171]

With a curious blend of description and prescription (refusing to specify the selection of [æ] in words such as *fast* as 'wrong', but nevertheless still condemning it effectively by attaching the label of 'provincial' to its use), Burrell stands in many ways as representative of the position adopted by the end of the nineteenth century in educational thinking on the 'standard language' in terms of accent. 'Good' accents being those unmarked by signifiers of the regional, these are the ones 'rightly' to be taught in schools; 'bad' accents are, conversely, to be made 'better' by educational processes which emphasized the spoken word in the teaching of reading, and regularly included recitation, with the right accent, as part of the syllabus. *Brandram's Speaker*, another text book of the same kind, adopting as central tenet on its titlepage Macbeth's line 'Stay, you imperfect speakers' (I. iii. 70), specifies still further that regional accents are compatible with the precepts of the taught language only when 'appropriately assumed with particular characters in dramatic recitation'. Otherwise, the message runs, they are to be 'conquered'.[172]

---

[171] A. Burrell, *Recitation. A Handbook for Teachers in Public Elementary School* (London, 1891), 24.
[172] S. Brandram, *Brandram's Speaker* (London, 1885), 15–16.

Even Sunday schools pursued the same principles and priorities, readily employing similar martial imagery in which victory attends those with command of the non-localized norms of speech, and defeat is the portion of those who fail in this respect. As *Groombridge's Annual Reader*, a manual of recitation 'for the use of schools' had stressed in 1867, 'Speech is a gift of God which accompanies reason', and 'the habit of speaking correct English . . . next to good morals, is one of the best things in this world'.[173] Such equations being set up between 'good' language and good behaviour, the extension of appropriate paradigms of norm and deviation with reference to accent in the Sunday school is perhaps a logical step. *The Sunday School Teacher's Manual*, published by the Sunday School Union, hence advises the teacher to give close attention to the language employed within the Sunday school, and to bear in mind his (or her) role as linguistic as well as Christian exemplar:

Next to sound Biblical information we would urge upon the teacher the cultivation of *correct English* . . . The Sunday School teacher is an *oral* instructor, not a wielder of the pen. He depends, instrumentally, on the power of the tongue; and therefore on the language which he employs— on what he says, and how he says it—his influence over his pupils must largely depend. Consequently, to be able to speak his own tongue with correctness, force, and facility is an acquisition to be sought after with all possible earnestness and perseverance.[174]

Knowledge of 'proper' English being second in this presentation only to 'godliness' and knowledge of the Bible, the instructor is urged to strive for an improvement appropriate to his role. After all, as the author pointed out, the voice is 'God-given', employed for reading out the book of books, for which speech which 'mangles the Queen's English' is sadly out of place: 'There is one powerful motive for the cultivation of correct tones and pronunciation, viz., the importance of being able to *read the Bible aloud* with accuracy, dignity, and force in the class, and to train the scholars to do the same.'[175] As in the elementary school, the avowed aim is that children, provided with such illustrative models for their imitation, will happily emulate linguistic as well as moral behaviour, leading naturally to a general improvement of 'tone' throughout the nation.

---

[173] M. A. Lower, *Groombridge's Annual Reader* (London, 1867), pp. iv, v.
[174] W. H. Groser, *The Sunday School Teacher's Manual; or, The Principles and Methods of Instruction as Applied to Sunday School Work* (London, 1877), 37–8.
[175] Ibid. 39.

Other books intended for the Sunday school foster similar precepts, though also encouraging on a number of occasions the use of explicit as well as implicit modes of teaching for the spoken word. The author of *The Sunday School Spelling Book* of 1823, dedicated 'To the Patrons and Teachers of Sunday Schools', focuses, for example, on the importance of the reading lesson for both teacher and pupil in the Sunday school, drawing attention, in particular, to those defects of pronunciation which can often mar instruction in this context. His own book is offered as a remedy for these problems:

It must have been observed by all . . . that children repeatedly read the same lesson without understanding or correctly pronouncing many of the important words. To obviate these evils, he has introduced . . . an Explanatory Dictionary . . . The Spelling Lessons have also been particularly attended to, and the natural and correct pronunciation of each word has been attempted to be conveyed to the mind of the pupil.[176]

Sunday schools, elementary schools, training academies for teachers, private schools such as that run by the Misses Wilmshurst in Maldon hence all embraced the theory that teaching the 'proper' accent was to form a vital part of educational provision, and that, by such means, regional modes of utterance, regularly construed in works on education as 'evils', 'vices', 'defects', 'faults', and 'peculiarities', were to be eliminated. Not only in England, but in Scotland, Wales, and Ireland were such principles openly adhered to. In the 1823 Statement by the Directors of the Edinburgh Academy, it is, for example, explicitly noted of the master of English that not only must he possess the highest qualifications in other respects, but also that he 'shall have a pure English accent'.[177] The School Board of Aberdeen likewise stressed that elocution, on specifically English models, was to form an integral part of the syllabus implemented in the region's schools; *Macleod's First Text-Book in Elocution*, developed in response to these requirements, went through three editions, and well over 6,000 copies, within the space of a few years.[178]

The theory by which these perceived standards were to be

---

[176] *The Sunday School Spelling Book* (London, 1823), 1.

[177] *Statement by the Directors of the Edinburgh Academy Explanatory of the Scheme of that Institution* (Edinburgh, 1824); cited in K. Robbins, *Nineteenth-Century Britain: England, Scotland, and Wales, The Making of a Nation* (Oxford, 1989), 133.

[178] A. Macleod, *Macleod's First Text-Book in Elocution With A Scheme for Acquiring Correct Pronunciation* 3rd edn. (Edinburgh, 1881).

fostered was therefore widely recognized. The practice, however, and that systematic training in non-localized norms which was so often recommended, may of course have differed. Ideologies of a standard and the associated processes of standardization naturally tend to maintain their disjunctions within as well as outside the school, and though many writers stressed the role of education as an agency of standardization, again this was to be revealed most clearly in the widespread diffusion of language attitudes (the 'errors' of dropping [h], the 'negligence' of intrusive [r]) rather than in any systematic linguistic conversions which the school, in reality, might achieve (especially in terms of the habitual patterns of speech which speakers use). As Robinson noted already in 1863, for example, though involved to some extent in perpetuating these requirements himself,[179] educational aims to standardize the accents of English in favour of a non-localized norm were in truth both unrealizable, and unrealistic:

If any teacher expects that he will ever be able to eradicate all traces of such errors, I am afraid that he will be sadly disappointed. The time will never come, most likely, when all the people of Great Britain and Ireland will speak exactly alike, and yet it is for this unattainable uniformity that men are struggling.[180]

Language attitudes and language use again diverge. That 'uniformity' espoused as ideal within the prescriptive tradition (and its educational manifestations too) is indeed 'unattainable' as Robinson rightly states. Though generations of writers on education had, for instance, stressed the utility of the teacher as model, notions of group identity and of peer groups too are, as already illustrated, far more complex that these simplistic equations suggest. Similarly, regardless of instruction in the patterns of 'proper' speech, children will tend to articulate identity in ways which, though perhaps conforming to more formal norms within the school, will outside it instead adhere to the usage of the speech community in which they have their being, and where 'talking proper' (as in Martha's Vineyard) may well be construed as 'talking posh' and a sign of not 'belonging'. Where educational precepts did perhaps achieve most success was, of course, in this dissemination of attitudes to language and in furthering awareness of those forms which

---

[179] See p. 306.   [180] Robinson, *Mannual of Method and Organisation*, 2.

constitute 'proper' as opposed to 'improper' English. The 'ridicule' recommended by school inspectors as remedial measures for the regional, and the deliberate manipulation of notions of shame so often implicit (or even explicit) within specifications of the nineteenth-century reading lesson did not exist in a vacuum. It was the stereotype of the 'educated' accent which was above all encoded by these means. Teaching, in other words, tended to reinforce the hegemony of the standard ideology and those forms of language associated with it, and though boarding schools, especially those in the south, went some way towards achieving a sense of the realities behind such ideals, they were aided in this by factors which it proved largely impossible for the elementary school to emulate. The emergent RP remained, in educational terms, largely the preserve of these rather more élite establishments, where the correlations of scholars and gentlemen, and the pressures of social (and linguistic) homogenization which did not end with the conclusion of the school day, were particularly in evidence. For the average child at elementary school, the impetus to conform in these respects was largely absent, for, as Morrison recognized, it would alienate him (or her) from local speech communities, from friends, family, and from the pressures of peer groups which urged conformity in other, far different, respects.[181] Reversing this pattern of emphasis, Morrison thus felt it necessary to warn the aspiring teacher that undue (or careless) censure in this context could in fact lead to his own alienation and estrangement from the surrounding community:

this, however, must be done with caution, and without any parade of ostentation; for, if the teacher, with the view of showing off his own acquirements, holds up to ridicule any local peculiarities, he will be sure to enlist the sympathies of the neighbours against himself, and will find his efforts at improvement thwarted at every step.[182]

Nevertheless, the ideal of education as a tool by which non-localized norms of speech were to be enforced over the nation remained an evocative one, endorsed in the twentieth century by still more writers on education and still other government officials. Though the endeavours of the nineteenth century had largely failed ([h]-dropping was still prevalent in those below the higher status groups, people based north of the Humber continued to use the

---

[181] Morrison, *Manual of School Management*, 127.   [182] Ibid.

'wrong sort of *u*' in words such as *cut*, or the 'wrong sort of *a*' in words such as *fast*), the Newbolt Report of 1921 (*The Teaching of English in England*) was to recommend still more strenuous efforts in this direction, the vigilance of past decades clearly having been inadequately implemented, and insufficiently thought out:

English, we are convinced, must form the essential basis of a liberal education for all English people, and in the earlier stages of education it should be the principal function of all schools of whatever type to form this basis.

Of this provision, the component parts will be, first, systematic training in the sounded speech of standard English, to secure correct pronunciation and clear articulation; second, systematic training in the use of standard English, to secure clearness and correctness both in oral expression and in writing; third, training in reading.[183]

Like Sheridan, the Newbolt Report prioritizes the teaching of the spoken language as an important desideratum in education. Like Sheridan too, it envisages this as a means of eradicating social distinctions in the nation.[184] Accent, laden with social values, and constituting a prime marker of social identity, is, as writers throughout the nineteenth century had stressed, divisive. Betraying the triumph of optimism over experience, the Newbolt Report thus notes:

We believe that such an education based upon the English language and literature would have important social, as well as personal, results; it would have a unifying tendency . . . If the teaching of the language were properly and universally provided for, the difference between educated and uneducated speech, which at present causes so much prejudice and difficulty of intercourse on both sides, would gradually disappear.[185]

'Prejudice' of a linguistic sort is, of course, pervasive in the report itself, as localized forms of language are stigmatized in moral terms, as well as being presented as virtual embodiments of evil: 'The great difficulty of teachers in Elementary Schools in many districts is that they have to fight against the powerful influence of evil habits of speech contracted in home and street. The teachers' struggle is thus not with ignorance but with a perverted power.'[186]

---

[183] *The Teaching of English in England* (1921). All citations from extract in T. Crowley (ed.), *Proper English? Readings in Language, History and Cultural Identity* (London, 1991), 196–206.
[184] See pp. 29–31.   [185] Newbolt Report, 200.   [186] Ibid. 202.

Dialect no longer being conceived of as disgrace, but instead as outright 'perversion', one cannot wonder at the emotive pleas the report contains, censuring teachers who 'make no serious effort to win' this moral crusade against defective language, and readily employing metaphors of 'fight', 'struggle', and 'race':

Teachers of infants sometimes complain that when the children come to school they can scarcely speak at all. They should regard this as rather an advantage. There is often a kind of race as to which should succeed in setting its stamp upon the children's speech, the influence of the teacher, or that of the street or home.[187]

The race is, of course, to confer the forms of standard speech, and is to be won by 'speech training' which is to be 'undertaken from the outset and . . . continued all through the period of schooling'.[188] The prize, for teacher, and for child, is 'the first and chief duty of the Elementary School'—'to give its pupils speech' and thus to 'make them articulate and civilized human beings'.[189] Articulacy is, however, determined only in the terms of the standard ideology, and the forms of speech with which it was associated. It is 'standard', and not 'dialect', which endows the child with 'civilization', and it is the 'right' of the child to receive this: 'the accomplishment of clear and correct speech is the one definite accomplishment which the child is entitled to demand from the Infant School.'[190] Though ostensibly dialect is not to be denigrated,[191] the sub-text is clear, as are affinities with earlier writers on education. As in Livesey's work on the teaching of reading in 1882, even if it should be true that 'the teacher can scarcely hope to eradicate completely the errors of a district', nevertheless the central maxim is that 'he need not let them, like seed heads, thrive and run to seed'.[192]

---

[187] Ibid. 203.   [188] Ibid.   [189] Ibid. 202.   [190] Ibid. 203.
[191] Ibid. 205: 'We do not advocate the teaching of standard English on any grounds of social 'superiority', but because it is manifestly desirable that all English people should be capable of speaking so as to be fully intelligible to one another.'
[192] Livesey, *Moffat's How to Teach Reading*, 65.

7

Conclusion

'I N the present day we may . . . recognise a received pronunciation all over the country, not widely differing in any particular locality, and admitting a certain degree of variety', wrote Alexander Ellis in 1869.[1] Documented extensively throughout the five volumes of *Early English Pronunciation*, it was this 'received pronunciation' (or RP) which in many ways came to constitute the legacy of that attention which had so prominently been paid to issues of accent and of status over the late eighteenth and nineteenth centuries. Non-localized, betraying little (if anything) of the speaker's place of birth, 'received pronunciation', and approximations to it, were to meet that desire for a geographically neutral accent which Sheridan and so many others had earlier proclaimed. As, in the late eighteenth century, Sheridan had noted of his ideal of a spoken standard, it should be such as would evince no 'disgrace of dialect' nor any of that 'rustic pronunciation' which at that date had still been able to mark gentry as well as commoner. A standard accent would instead be founded on the dissemination of metropolitan modes of speech to all, eradicating 'those odious distinctions between subjects of the same King, and members of the same community, which are chiefly kept alive by differences of pronunciation . . . for these in a manner proclaim the place of a man's birth, whenever he speaks, which otherwise could not be known by any other means in mixed societies.'[2] Grammars and dictionaries, informed by the prescriptive tradition, would impose norms of correctness and, just as double negation had come to be seen as unacceptable in terms of 'standard' grammar, so would the 'dropped letter' come to be seen in the same way as 'consciousness' in the context of pronunciation too was raised to new heights. Equality and harmony, as we have seen, overtly predominate in the visions which Sheridan (and others) have of the non-localized

---

[1] Ellis, *Early English Pronunciation*, i. 23.   [2] Sheridan, *Course of Lectures*, 206.

norms for all which must surely result. Education also would play its part. Sheridan's own optimism was marked:

Upon the whole, if such a Grammar and Dictionary were published, they must soon be adopted into use by all schools professing to teach English. The consequence of teaching children by one method, and one uniform system of rules, would be an uniformity of pronunciation in all so instructed. Thus might the rising generation, born and bred in different Countries and Counties, no longer have a variety of dialects, but as subjects of one King, have one common tongue. All natives of these realms, would be restored to their birthright in communage of language, which has been too long fenced in, and made the property of a few.[3]

The prescriptive persuasions of Sheridan's rhetoric do not, of course, entirely disguise the realities of language and its developments over the course of the late eighteenth and nineteenth centuries. Dictionaries and grammars were indeed, as he had hoped, assimilated into the educational endeavours of a variety of schools and their respective policies, Walker's own *Critical Pronouncing Dictionary*, as we have seen, frequently being recommended for the erudition of teacher and pupil alike. Even in the early decades of the twentieth century these ambitions, as the Newbolt Report suggests,[4] could continue largely intact and notions of the 'educated accent', at least in their common stereotypes, had undeniably come to fulfil the ambitions Sheridan had earlier expressed: ' "it is the business of educated people to speak so that no-one may be able to tell in what county their childhood was passed', as Burrell, for example, stressed in 1891.[5] 'Culture', 'refinement', status and superiority were, according to popular belief, all able to be conveyed within the accents one assumed. As Ellis affirmed of these attitudes to pronunciation which were, in so many ways, a hallmark of the nineteenth century: 'there . . . prevails a belief that it is possible to erect a standard of pronunciation which should be acknowledged and followed throughout all countries where English is spoken as a native tongue, and that in fact that standard already exists, and is the norm unconsciously followed by persons who, by rank or education, have most right to establish the custom of speech.'[6]

A closer examination of Ellis's words reveals, as we might expect, certain reservations about the spoken standard which others are

---

[3] Sheridan, *Dissertation*, 36.   [4] See pp. 314–15.
[5] Burrell, *Recitation*, 24.   [6] Ellis, *Early English Pronunciation*, ii. 264.

so willing to attest and to endorse; as he stresses, it was indeed 'belief' rather than behaviour which was the most significant and the most widespread in any 'standard' of pronunciation which had been achieved by this date. Ellis strove to clarify notions of an inviolable standard accent: 'A large number of words are pronounced with differences very perceptible to those who care to observe, even among educated London speakers'.[7] 'Men of undoubted education and intelligence differ in pronunciation from one another, from pronouncing dictionaries, and from my own habits, so the term "educated pronunciation" must be taken to have a very "broad" signification',[8] he likewise averred, seeking to introduce a due sense of linguistic reality into attitudes to language which, as we have seen, so often projected accent as a signifier of 'educatedness' or, in Phyfe's terms, 'mental standing' in itself. 'It is certain that nothing marks more quickly a person's mental and social status than his practice in this regard', as the latter, for example, stated in 1885.[9]

Ellis was of course right in the correctives he attempted to endorse. Language, then and now, is variable: 'nothing approaching to real uniformity prevails', Ellis set forth in the first volume of *Early English Pronunciation*, reiterating it at intervals thereafter. Accents exist on a continuum, influenced by variation in style and context, age and gender, as well as in regional location. Alongside those notions of a non-localized and 'best' 'standard' promoted with such determination in prescriptive texts, literary works, and manuals of etiquette and elocution alike, vernacular norms of speech continued to have their being, just indeed as multiple negation continued to be used in the spoken English of many dialects alongside that 'standard' norm of single negation which alone was reinforced in dicta on 'talking proper' and the proprieties of public, printed, or more formal discourse. Accent, as already indicated, works to locate the user in a multi-dimensional social space in which assimilation to the stated norms of the 'best' English is not always adequate. It is this which, fundamentally, lies at the heart of the nineteenth-century failure to impose those paradigms of 'one word: one pronunciation' on all speakers of English in the same way as each word had, for example, received a spelling from

---

[7] Ibid. ii. 629.   [8] Ibid. iv. 1208.
[9] Phyfe, *How Should I Pronounce?*, p. v.

which variation was roundly labelled error. Accent proved an image of identity which was far too complex for such simplistic operations to succeed.

Nevertheless, as Ellis also indicates, it was undeniable that notions of a non-localized 'received pronunciation' had, in some ways, come into being by the later nineteenth century and Henry Sweet provides similar corroboration of this fact. 'Standard English', as Sweet states with reference to pronunciation in *The Elementary Sounds of English* (1881), is both variable in its details, and non-localized in its essentials. 'Approximated to, all over Great Britain, by those who do not keep to their own local dialects', it is based 'on the educated speech of London and Southern England generally' and, as he adds, 'it need scarcely be said that this dialect is not absolutely uniform, but varies slightly from individual to individual, and more markedly from generation to generation.'[10] As modern sociolinguistics also stresses, it consisted of variations, of quantitative patterns of 'more or less' rather than of absolutes, and though ideas of unidimensionality (in both social and linguistic senses) had been adopted by writers within the prescriptive tradition as an essential part of their methodology, reality, as Sweet continued to emphasize, was, as always, somewhat different. As he notes of that ideal of the 'correct speaker' who, as we have seen, had so often been advanced in the attempt to proscribe certain realizations of sounds at the expense of others: 'I have for some years been in search of a "correct speaker". It is very like going after the great sea-serpent ... I am inclined to the conclusion that the animal known as a "correct speaker" is not only extraordinarily shy and difficult of capture, but that he may be put in the same category as the "rigid moralist" and "every schoolboy"—that he is an abstraction, a figment of the brain.'[11]

The 'correct speaker' in these terms was indeed myth rather than actuality, a product of the prescriptive imagination and its own images of wish-fulfilment, used to foster images of convergence towards (and proscribe deviation from) a rather idealized norm in which, for example, intrusive /r/ was never used, and nor /r/ in any circumstance 'dropped'. Sweet offers instead a vision of the future objectivity and empiricism which was henceforth to characterize descriptive rather than prescriptive approaches to

[10] Sweet, *Elementary Sounds*, 7.   [11] Ibid. 5–6.

language: 'it is absurd to set up a standard of how English people *ought* to speak, before we know how they actually *do* speak—a knowledge which is still in its infancy', he reminded readers of his *Primer of Phonetics*.[12] In this, like Ellis, Sweet too points the divide which could, and did, exist between the processes of standardization and associated ideologies ('belief' as Ellis terms it) of a 'standard'; the two are by no means the same, a fact which has of course been brought out on many occasions in this book. Only in its broader senses, Sweet affirms, could a 'standard' for the spoken language be said to exist, a framework which in no way served to parallel the standardization of the written language where both the processes of standardization, and that set of beliefs in 'correct' and 'incorrect', 'right' and 'wrong' did appear to engage in somewhat closer harmonies. 'Standard English is . . . unusual in that it is spoken with a large number of different accents', Peter Trudgill stresses in this context in the twentieth century, and the same was naturally true of the nineteenth century too where 'educated' speakers could avoid the grammatical solecisms of multiple negation or double comparatives in their use of 'standard' grammar, while simultaneously retaining features such as rhotic /r/ or monophthongal (rather than diphthongal) enunciations of words such as *boat, coat* (i.e. /boːt/ not /bout/). 'Most speakers of the (more or less regionless) standard English dialect, however, speak it with a (usually not too localized) regional accent', Trudgill continues, 'so that most educated people betray their geographical origins much more in their pronunciation than in their grammar or lexis.'[13] RP itself, in its 'purest' and most non-localized forms, is spoken only by 3–5 per cent of the population.

What the prescriptive tenor of the late eighteenth and nineteenth century served to do therefore was to put the emphasis firmly upon these non-localized forms of accent as the 'standard', manipulating language attitudes to good effect as it did so with the result that, as in those notions of collective 'right' and 'wrong' in the speech community which, as Labov has shown, are often at variance with the language habits actually evinced, speakers did indeed come to be highly responsive to this sense of a norm. As Sweet wrote to James Murray of the drive for information on matters of linguistic correctness in this context:

---

[12] Sweet, *Primer of Phonetics*, §8.
[13] Trudgill, 'Standard and Non-Standard Dialects', 51.

Twenty years ago people would not have gone to the dictionary for the *facts* of contemporary English pronunciation; on the contrary, they would have expected you to set up a *standard* by which they could 'correct' their own natural utterances, and the more artificial and unreal that standard, the more they would have been pleased.[14]

Certainly the prescriptive tradition of the late eighteenth and nineteenth centuries had catered for (and fostered) linguistic insecurity in a way impossible within a more scientifically valid and objective discipline, as Sweet indicates from his vantage-point firmly within the descriptivism of the late nineteenth century. Even he, however, was to be somewhat optimistic about the influences which this descriptive approach might wield: 'Now people are beginning to see that before setting up a standard, we must find out what the natural pronunciation is, how far it varies locally, chronologically, and according to rank, occupation etc.'[15] Though himself setting up principles which are, in a number of ways, significant in the methodology later applied to the study of linguistic variation, Sweet was, as subsequent events reveal, indeed naïve about the education in linguistic reality which ordinary speakers might receive from the operations of descriptivism. Belief in a 'standard' continued, and continues, to exist, regardless of the variations and complexities which, in reality, attend linguistic usage in the articulations of sounds.

In the nineteenth century, what did, however, also clearly exist, as Ellis confirms, was a set of regionally neutral 'standard pronunciation features', from the [h] which it would be 'social suicide' to omit in the wrong place, to the [ŋ] which 'polite speakers' all over the country required, from the diphthongal enunciations of the *a* in words such as *gate* and the *o* in *dote*, to the vocalization of *r* in words such as *bird*, and the use of /ʌ/ rather than /ʊ/ in words such as *cut*. It was the sum of features such as these (as well as the connotative values with which they were liberally endowed) which served to create perceptions of a 'standard', adhered to by those above the 'vulgar', or, as Ellis notes, by those who assumed, or attempted to assimilate 'the educated pronunciation of the metropolis, of the court, the pulpit and the bar'. These formed

---

[14] Letter written by H. Sweet to J. A. H. Murray, 22 Mar. 1882; cited in M. K. C. MacMahon, 'James Murray and the Phonetic Notation in the New English Dictionary', *Transactions of the Philological Society* (1985), 104 n. 25.
[15] Ibid.

the fundamental markers of 'received pronunciation', bound to no region in their use but instead establishing common signifiers of one type of speech all over the country. In other ways, however, as Sweet and Ellis combine to suggest, the 'standard' achieved was heterogeneous rather than monolithic, non-localized (as Sheridan had wished), but still open to slight differences in articulation which removed it in many ways from that more decisive standard so ably reached for most words in matters of orthography.

The rise of a spoken standard, albeit in these somewhat vaguer terms than had originally been hoped, was in addition by no means to achieve the eradication of those 'odious distinctions' within society as Sheridan (among others) had anticipated, but instead, as we have seen, it created new ones, erecting accent barriers which run along the fault lines of status and its attendant hierarchies. As in the late eighteenth century, the 'standard' remained the preserve of an élite, though an élite of which the composition had changed (and broadened) over the decades which had ensued. 'Received pronunciation', Ellis adds, for example, was spoken by the products of 'superior schools', and the phonetician Daniel Jones later confirms the correlations which had emerged in terms of the non-localized intakes of such schools, and the homogenization of accent which they were also assumed to enact. As he stated in his *English Pronouncing Dictionary* of 1917: 'the pronunciation used in this book is that most generally heard in the families of Southern English persons whose men-folk have been educated at the great public boarding-schools. This pronunciation is also used by a considerable proportion of those who do not come from the South of England but who have been educated at these schools.'[16]

In the early twentieth century, 'received pronunciation' was, in some ways, thus only to consolidate further its hold as a social symbol of peculiar dominance, its nuances transcribed in Jones's *English Pronouncing Dictionary* in ways which, in spite of his disclaimers ('Many suitable standards of English pronunciation might be suggested, e.g. educated Northern English, educated Southern English, the pronunciation used on the stage, etc.') again effortlessly reinforced perceptions that this was the 'right' way of speaking English. As Henry Wyld noted in 1934, similarly confirming the continued operations of the standard ideology in spite of his repute

---

[16] D. Jones, *An English Pronouncing Dictionary* (London, 1917), p. viii.

as a scholar of the English language, this was 'the best English': 'a type of English which is neither provincial nor vulgar, a type which most people would willingly speak if they could, and desire to speak if they do not',[17] superior in 'beauty and clarity' to all other forms of spoken English. 'It is not, however, easy to free oneself from the influence of pre-conceived notions', Edwin Guest had stressed in his own (remarkably accurate) account of pronunciation in the mid-nineteenth century,[18] and the truth of this is still self-evident. 'The 'best' speakers . . . have perfect confidence in themselves, in their speech, as in their manners', Wyld elaborates, illustrating the ways in which essentially subjective reactions to the forms of speech can influence perceptions which impinge far beyond the mere articulation of sounds: 'both bearing and utterance spring from a firm and gracious tradition. "Their fathers have told them"—that suffices. Nowhere does the best that is in English culture find a fairer expression than in Received Standard speech.'[19] Even now, as Tom McArthur notes, such perceptions can still exert 'a considerable gravitational pull throughout the UK, with the result that many middle- and lower middle-class people speak with accents more or less adapted towards it'.[20] In the nineteenth century, similar approximations would presumably have taken place, especially in terms of the most prominent markers (the presence of /h/, the use of /ŋ/, the vocalization of /r/ after vowels and in final position) of this mode of speech.

Its heyday, however, as McArthur confirms, coincided in many ways with that of the Empire, and, perhaps even more specifically, with the early days of the BBC, which, in the hands of John Reith, was also in a number of ways to embrace ideologies of a 'standard' with zeal. Just as Sheridan had seen the agency of the pronouncing dictionary as potentially significant in the spread of 'correct' standards of speech all over the nation, so too did Reith in the twentieth century (in spite of later assertions to the contrary) tend to see the role of the BBC. It was to function as educator as well as entertainer in matters of language as all else. 'One hears the

---

[17] H. C. Wyld, *The Best English: A Claim for the Superiority of Received Standard English*, S.P.E. Tract No. xxxix (Oxford, 1934), 605.
[18] Guest, *History of English Rhythms*, i. 303.
[19] Wyld, *The Best English*, 614.
[20] T. McArthur (ed.), *The Oxford Companion to the English Language* (Oxford, 1992), 851.

most appalling travesties of vowel pronunciation. This is a matter
on which broadcasting may be of immense assistance', Reith
stressed in his 1924 text of *Broadcast over Britain*,[21] endorsing the
exemplary roles which announcers were to assume: 'we have made
a special effort to secure in our stations men who, in the presentation of programme items, the reading of news bulletins and so
on, can be relied upon to employ the correct pronunciation of
the English tongue.'[22] These men were to form the foundation of
that other stereotype which accrued around definitions of 'talking
proper'—that of 'BBC English', a label initially current among
BBC staff, resentful, as McArthur adds, 'of the better prospects
of speakers with public-school accents', but one which was later
to assume general currency, designating, *OED* records, 'standard
English as maintained by BBC announcers'. Just as the announcers were instructed to wear dinner jackets for their evening broadcasts, so were their accents to be equally elevating, setting (at least
in theory) standards of decorum and tone throughout the nation.
Though instances of the Cockney or Yorkshire were, of course,
to be heard upon the airwaves, these were limited to the merely
comic, a distribution which likewise confirms those socio-cultural
stereotypes in terms of speech which persisted into the twentieth
century. Such accents were 'in general frowned upon by the young
BBC which prided itself on what it was doing to raise the standards
of speech',[23] as Asa Briggs affirms.

Even later attempts to reduce the hegemony of RP in more
serious genres of broadcasting were regularly to fail: Wilfred Pick-
les, employed to read the news during the Second World War on
the premiss that the Germans would find it impossible to imitate
his Halifax accent, encountered a number of complaints as listeners
criticized his voice. Without the accents of authority embedded in
contemporary attitudes to RP, listeners claimed that they could
not believe the news when conveyed in such Yorkshire tones, and
that its integrity was compromised by such deviation. As Reith
himself had earlier pointed out, being equally subject in this to the
cultural constructs of 'proper speech' and its attendant beliefs:
'No one would deny the great advantage of a standard pronunciation of the language, not only in theory but in practice. Our

---

[21] J. C. W. Reith, *Broadcast Over Britain* (London, 1924), 161.   [22] Ibid.
[23] A. Briggs, *The BBC: The First Fifty Years* (Oxford, 1985), 68.

responsibilities in this matter are obvious, since in talking to so vast a multitude, mistakes are likely to be promulgated to a much greater extent than before.'[24] Such beliefs tended in themselves to endorse the processes of sociolinguistic stereotyping which the early BBC evinced; as Marwick confirms in *Class: Image and Reality*, the consequences of this could be striking and, as well as suppressing working-class politics on occasion, television could also engineer decided status expectations in terms of voice. Marwick, for example, describes one of a series of talks on 'Modern Industry and National Character' in 1934 in which a car worker, William Ferrie, was to set forth his opinions about the 'British working man'. 'The unsophisticated technology of the thirties did not allow for the pre-recording of talks, which instead had to be very carefully edited and rehearsed, then read word-for-word from an approved script', Marwick notes; this 'editing' also extended to what could be said, so much so that when Ferrie did in fact reach the microphone he declaimed not his allowed speech (which he deemed 'a travesty of the British working class') but instead decried the 'censorship' of the BBC in its suppression of the real state of working-class politics in this context. Far more significant from our point of view is, however, the other accusation which Ferrie levelled at the broadcast: 'I also refused to drop my "aitches" and to speak as they imagined a worker does.'[25] These images persisted, as a listener in 1938 complained, again protesting at the reinforcements which the BBC offered for the prevalent evaluative paradigms of speaker and of speech: 'I certainly do feel that a limited income is all too frequently associated in broadcast talks with lack of intelligence and the omission of aspirates. Surely all clerks and similar persons earning around £4 a week do not necessarily possess these obvious indications of their inferiority?'[26]

That sense of 'responsibility' which Reith specified did, as these instances confirm, seem to guarantee no little subscription to standardizing ideals in terms of language and in ways such as these television was indeed to prove an additionally useful means of perpetuating the standard ideology in the public mind, further diffusing notions of the accents appropriate to various status groups and occupations. More than this, however, the BBC, and its own

---

[24] Reith, *Broadcast Over Britain*, 161.
[25] A. Marwick, *Class: Image and Reality* 2nd edn. (London, 1990), 154.
[26] Cited ibid. 156.

sensitization to notions of norm and deviation, became a means
by which the non-localized norms of speech adopted as 'correct'
by announcers and broadcasters could in themselves achieve a
non-localized and national exposure in ways which would have
delighted Sheridan. Within two years, the radio had secured an
audience which was estimated at around four million, a figure
arrived at merely from the licence subscriptions of 'legal' listeners;
as Reith adds, there was, in addition, 'definite evidence of a certain amount of evasion of the licence fee',[27] and of another set of
'illegal' listeners, equally gaining access to these exemplary tones
of British broadcasting.

Setting up the BBC Advisory Committee on Spoken English in
1926, broadcasting attempted to settle its own uncertainties on
the pronunciation of words, and though disclaiming the intent to
erect a uniform standard of speech ('There has been no attempt
to establish a uniform spoken language', as Reith averred in the
preface to Arthur Lloyd James's *Broadcast English*[28]), its concern
to establish certain parameters of 'right' and 'wrong' was nevertheless clear: 'The policy might be described as seeking a common denominator of educated speech.' It was this which constituted
the realities of that 'BBC English' which, both consciously and
unconsciously, was promoted through the agencies of the BBC.
As Reith stressed: 'There is now presented to any one who may
require it, an opportunity of learning by example.'[29]

Early evidence of the influence which the BBC might hold in
both the process and the ideology of standardization in terms of
speech was therefore regarded as important. Already in December
1922, *Popular Wireless* reported instances of the ways in which the
'perfect diction' of announcers 'had improved the accent and
pronunciation of large numbers of children'; this was, it is stated,
regarded as 'perhaps the most delicate compliment yet paid to
broadcasting'.[30] It was, in this sense, a compliment which was to
be frequently reiterated, as the educational potential of the BBC
apparently exerted pronounced appeal in terms of language itself
and the statusful variants it promoted. 'Children in particular
have acquired the habit of copying the announcer's articulation;
this has been observed by their teachers, and so long as the

---

[27] Reith, *Broadcast Over Britain*, 80.
[28] A. Lloyd James, *Broadcast English* (London, 1928), 5.
[29] Reith, *Broadcast Over Britain*, 161.   [30] Cited in Briggs, *The BBC*, 68.

announcer is talking good English, and without affectation, I find it much to be desired that the announcer should be copied', Reith confirmed in 1924.[31] In real terms, however, it was again that wider awareness of notions of 'talking proper' which was to be achieved with greatest success by the broadcasts of the BBC, rather than that convergent linguistic behaviour on a national scale which, at times, had indeed seemed to be envisaged. Like that escalating awareness of 'correctness' which Cockin documents as a consequence of the linguistic attentions of the late eighteenth century ('it appears therefore . . . that works of this nature may be at least as much service in teaching us to perceive as to execute'[32]), so too did the BBC aid in further increasing sensitization to issues of 'correct' English, this time, however, by means of the spoken word itself rather than by descriptions conveyed only in terms of the written text. In such ways, its illustrations of 'talking proper' gained an immediacy denied to the detailed descriptions, and socio-symbolic associations, documented by a Sheridan, or a Walker, or their many followers over the nineteenth century. As the phonetican Arthur Lloyd James (later given the official title of linguistic adviser to the BBC) noted in *Broadcast English* in 1928, commenting on the sensibilities inevitably aroused by the social meanings of speech:

it is nowadays considered essential that those who aspire to be regarded as cultured and educated should pay a due respect to the conventions that govern educated and cultivated speech. It would now appear that this interest in the niceties of our language is more alive than ever before, and it has been suggested that broadcasting is in some way responsible for this quickening.[33]

Lloyd James was presumably right, and in the early decades of the twentieth century the equation of 'talking proper' and 'received pronunciation' was propagated in ways which reinforced still further those shifts in thinking about accent which had been so perceptible over the course of eighteenth and nineteenth centuries. In his work on *The Pronunciation of English*, it was this, for example, which the phonetician Daniel Jones (himself a member of the BBC Advisory Committee on Spoken English) initially selected as the

[31] Reith, *Broadcast Over Britain*, 161.
[32] Cockin, *The Art of Delivering Written Language*, p. ix.
[33] Lloyd James, *Broadcast English*, 6.

form of speech to be described, and which he in turn endorsed as the norm for BBC announcers.[34] This formed the hallmark of those who, in the parlance of the day, were deemed to talk 'without an accent' at all, and it is, as already indicated, the non-localized features which this comports over which speakers of 'near-RP' and 'modified standard' attempt, on the whole, to have command, even though elsewhere in their accents they may retain traces of their regional origins. As these labels in themselves indicate, however, even RP itself cannot be given a categorical definition; it can be that spoken by the Royal Family with all its hyperlectal (or U-RP, upper-class RP) features; it can subsume that entity already discussed as 'adoptive RP' with its heightened responsiveness to the theoretical shibboleths of speech (such as intrusive /r/); it can, in 'near RP', assimilate closely (but not entirely) to the range of features generally deemed characteristic of this accent; it can be advanced, conservative, or merely of its time. Like any other accent, it is subject to variation and to change, and indeed to pressure from other accents. Even this therefore in no way constitutes that monolithic 'standard' which Sheridan had so hopefully advanced at the end of the eighteenth century, not least in the fact that attitudes to its use still imbue it with marked associations of privilege and prestige, the 'best' English of the 'best' speakers. It is presumably this fact, for example, which continues to validate its role as 'norm' for a great many people whose native cadences in no way resemble those they have come, in various ways, to adopt. As Susan Ramsaran further confirms, for example, of the convergences which can take place in this context: 'whatever the reasons, educated speakers of English do not speak with the broadest (or purest) forms of their local accents and the modifications are generally towards RP. So it can be argued that RP displays itself as a kind of standard, not necessarily deliberately imposed or

---

[34] Daniel Jones was, however, capable of giving more liberal interpretations of the status of a 'standard' in pronunciation, and his article 'On "Received Pronunciation"', *Le Maître phonétique*, supplement (Apr.–July 1937) stresses, for instance, that the attempt to impose RP on speakers of English via education should not be pursued: 'As far as English-speaking people themselves are concerned, I suggest that educational authorities should leave everyone to pronounce as he pleases, and that no attempt should be made to impose one particular form of speech upon anyone who prefers another form. Above all, it appears to me important that *no person should ever disparage the pronunciation of another*.' The latter ideal, as we have seen, was, however, already long past in the history of the language and language attitudes.

consciously adopted, . . . a standard in the sense that it is regionally neutral and does undoubtedly influence the modified accents of many British regions.'[35]

'Everyone in Britain has a mental image of RP, even though they may not refer to it by that name and even though the image may not be very accurate', wrote Wells in 1982. It is this 'image', as we have seen, which (with all its inaccuracies and assumptions of absolutes instead of variability) was, in various ways, created throughout the late eighteenth and nineteenth centuries, informing language attitudes and subjective reactions to speech in ways which have proved surprisingly enduring. 'Language provides the tickets of entry and exclusion in terms of simple conformity, and the consequences of missing aspirates can be a lot more damaging than a lordly witticism', the *Times Educational Supplement* declared in 1989 of the operations of these value-judgements and assumptions: 'The way people speak provides an instant signal as to whether they are one of us and, if not, what kind of outside or oddity they are.'[36] Likewise stereotypes of accent and intelligence still persist, in spite of the absence of any objective foundation for their correlation. The absence of accents approximating to RP can lead, as the empirical researches of Giles, Coupland, *et al.* affirm, to a certain 'intellectual downgrading' of speakers by their auditors; their studies of language attitudes and the social meanings of speech continue to attest the details of subjective inequality in ways which make plain the legacies of the eighteenth and nineteenth centuries in this context ('RP affords many social advantages for those who speak it in terms of competence, suitability for more prestigious jobs, and in eliciting co-operativeness from others. At the same time, social deficits accrue on dimensions of integrity, human warmth and caring').[37] Similarly, candidates scoring the highest grades in the GCSE English exams of 1993 could, for instance, still be accused of 'uneducatedness' if they dropped their [h]s, in ways which are precisely parallel to many of the attitudes

[35] S. Ramsaran, 'RP: Fact *and* Fiction', in id. (ed.), *Studies in the Pronunciation of English: A Commemorative Volume in Honour of A. C. Gimson* (London, 1990), 182–3.
[36] R. Barker, 'Cor Blimey, Belgravia and the Acute Loss of a Correct Accent', *Times Educational Supplement*, 25 Aug. 1989, 10.
[37] H. Giles, N. Coupland, K. Henwood, J. Harriman, J. Coupland, 'The Social Meaning of RP; an Intergenerational Perspective', in Ramsaran (ed.), *Studies in Pronunciation*, 209.

to accent expressed in the context of the nineteenth century. Objective and subjective reactions to language again diverge as, even in the late twentieth century, [h]-loss in these terms can suggest that academic achievement can be transcended by the subjective import of [h] with all the fallible value-judgements which its loss comports.[38] For all their fallacies, such attitudes can therefore prove remarkably pervasive as notions of 'standard' and 'non-standard', 'good' and 'bad' still continue to be fostered in the face of linguistic reality and linguistic change. Elision, /t, d/ deletion, the simplification of complex consonant clusters, all of which are long-established linguistic phenomena, all continue to attract censure and pleas for the salvation of the language: 'we're defiling our language for the sake of fashion . . . people deliberately drop their T's . . . join me in my campaign to get good English going again' as the subject of one recent interview declared,[39] in his asseverations against the stated 'slovenliness' of 'dropped letters' and the 'errors' of elision. Ideologies of a standard remain, as this suggests, in good health. The processes of standardization, on the other hand, can and will only reach completion in a dead language, where the inviolable norms so often asserted by the prescriptive tradition (and the absolutes of language attitudes) may indeed come into being—a fate, one assumes, which is not yet in store for English.

[38] Letter to the *Guardian*, 7 Sept. 1993.
[39] George Martin, *Sunday Express*, 21 Nov. 1993, magazine section, 62.

SELECT BIBLIOGRAPHY

Official Papers

General Report for the Year 1849, by Her Majesty's Inspector of Schools, the Revd H. W. Bellairs, Committee of Council on Education, *Parliamentary Papers*, xliii (1850).

Minutes of the Committee of Council on Education, *Parliamentary Papers*, xliii (1850).

General Report on Roman Catholic Schools for the Year 1849 by Her Majesty's Inspector of Schools T. M. W. Marshall, Committee of Council on Education: Reports on Elementary Schools, *Parliamentary Papers*, xliv (1850).

Privy Council Committee on Education, *Extracts from the Reports of Her Majesty's Inspectors of Schools* (London, 1852).

Report on the Free Church Training College at Glasgow for the Year 1859, by Her Majesty's Inspector of Schools, C. E. Wilson, Esq., Report of the Committee of Council on Education, *Parliamentary Papers*, liv (1860).

Report by J. D. Morell, one of Her Majesty's Inspectors, Report of the Committee of Council on Education, *Parliamentary Papers*, liv (1860).

Report of Dr Hodgson, one of Her Majesty's Inspectors of Schools on the State of Education in the Metropolitan District, Report from the Commissioners on Popular Education, *Parliamentary Papers*, xxi/III (1861).

General Report for the Year 1859 by the Revd J. C. G. Fussell, Report of the Committee of Council on Education 1859–60, *Parliamentary Papers*, liv (1860).

The Public Schools and the General Educational System: Report of the Committee on Public Schools appointed by the President of the Board of Education, July 1942 (London, 1944).

Anonymous Works

Advice to Governesses (London, 1827).
Advice to a Young Gentleman on Entering Society (London, 1839).
Boys and Their Ways. By One Who Knows Them (London, 1880).
Chambers's Encyclopaedia. A Dictionary of Useful Knowledge, 10 vols. (London, 1888–92).
Common Blunders in Speech and How to Avoid Them (London, 1884).

The Edinburgh Review. Containing an account of all the Books and Pamphlets Published in Scotland from June 1755 (to January 1756) (Edinburgh, 1755).

The Elementary Catechisms (London, 1850).

The English Vocabulary. Compiled for the Use of Ackworth School (London, 1852; rev. edn. 1854).

Errors of Pronunciation and Improper Expressions (London, 1817).

Etiquette for All (London, 1861).

Etiquette for the Ladies (London, 1837).

Etiquette for Ladies and Gentlemen (London, 1839).

Etiquette, Social Ethics and the Courtesies of Society (London, 1834).

The Eton System of Education Vindicated (London, 1834).

The First Part of the Progressive Parsing Lessons (Maldon, 1833).

Girls and Their Ways. By One Who Knows Them (London, 1881).

Good Society. A Complete Manual of Manners (London, 1869).

The Habits of Good Society. A Handbook of Etiquette for Ladies and Gentlemen (London, 1859).

Handbook on the Teaching and Management of Elementary Schools (Manchester, 1872).

Hard Words Made Easy (London, 1855).

Hints on Etiquette and the Usages of Society (London, 1836).

Hints to Governesses. By One of Themselves (London, 1856).

The History of Ackworth School (Ackworth, 1853).

How to Shine in Society (Glasgow, 1860).

How to Speak or Write English with Perspicacity and Fluency (London, 1876).

Live and Learn: A Guide for All who Wish to Speak and Write Correctly, 28th edn. (London, 1872).

The Manners of the Aristocracy. By One of Themselves (London, 1881).

The Manners and Tone of Good Society by a Member of the Aristocracy (London, 1879).

The Many Advantages of a Good Language to any Nation (London, 1724).

Mixing in Society. A Complete Manual of Manners (London, 1870).

Modern Etiquette in Public and Private (London, 1888).

The Mother's Home Book (London, 1879).

Observations Respectfully Addressed to the Nobility and Gentry on the Existing Importance of the Art and Study of Oratory (London, 1836).

The Popular Educator (London, 1864).

Private Education; Or a Practical Plan for the Studies of Young Ladies, 3rd edn. (London, 1816).

Society Small Talk. Or What to Say and When to Say It, 2nd edn. (London, 1880).

The Sunday School Spelling Book (London, 1823).

Take My Advice (London, 1872).

Talking and Debating (London, 1856).

The Teacher's Manual of the Science and Art of Teaching (London, 1874).

Thorough English (London, 1867).

A Very Short Letter from One Old Westminster to Another, Touching Some Matters connected with Their School (London, 1829).

Vulgarisms and Other Errors of Speech (London, 1868).

Vulgarities of Speech Corrected (London, 1826).

Woman: As She Is, And As She Should Be, 2 vols. (London, 1835).

Woman's Worth: Or Hints to Raise the Female Character, 2nd edn. (London, 1847).

The Young Housekeeper (London, 1869).

The Young Lady's Book. A Manual of Elegant Recreations, Exercises, and Pursuits (London, 1829).

The Young Mother (London, 1857).

Other Works

ABBOTT, C. C. (ed.), *The Correspondence of Gerard Manley Hopkins and Richard Watkins Dixon* (London, 1935).

ACKROYD, P., *Dickens* (London, 1990).

ALFORD, H., *A Plea for the Queen's English*, 2nd edn. (London, 1864).

ALTICK, R. D., *The English Common Reader: A Social History of the Mass Reading Public 1800–1900* (Chicago, Ill., 1957).

—— *Victorian People and Ideas* (London, 1974).

ARDENER, S. (ed.), *Defining Females* (London, 1978).

ARNOLD, M., *Reports on Elementary Schools 1852–1882*, ed. F. Sandford (London, 1889).

AUSTEN, J., *Emma* (London, 1816), ed. R. W. Chapman, 3rd edn (Oxford, 1933).

BAGEHOT, W., *The English Constitution* (London, 1867).

—— *Works*, ed. F. Morgan, 5 vols. (Hartford, 1891)

BAINBRIGGE, W. H., *Early Education* (London, 1881).

BAMFORD, T. W., 'Public Schools and Social Class, 1801–1850', *British Journal of Sociology*, 12 (1961), 224–35.

—— *Rise of the Public Schools* (London, 1967).

—— (ed.), *Thomas Arnold on Education* (Cambridge, 1970).

BANKS, O., *The Sociology of Education*, 2nd edn. (London, 1971).

BARKER, R., 'Cor Blimey, Belgravia and the Acute Loss of a Correct Accent', *Times Educational Supplement*, 25 Aug. 1989, 10.

BARRELL, J., *English Literature in History 1730–80: An Equal Wide Survey* (London, 1983).

BARTLE, REVD G., *A Few Words To Parents and Guardians on the Education of Youth* (London, 1875).

BATCHELOR, T., *An Orthoëpical Analysis of the English Language, including An Orthoëpical Analysis of the Dialect of Bedfordshire* (London, 1809), ed. A. Zettersten, Lund Studies in English, 45 (Lund, 1974).

BEATTIE, J., *The Theory of Language* (London, 1788).

BEDE, C., *The Adventures of Mr. Verdant Green, An Oxford Freshman*, 3rd edn. (London, 1853).

BEETON, I., *Beeton's Book of Household Management* (London, 1861).

BELL, A. M., *A Lecture on the Art of Delivery and the Influence of School Discipline on Public Oratory* (Edinburgh, 1855).

BELL, R. T., *Sociolinguistics: Goals, Approaches and Problems* (London, 1976).

BENZIE, W., *The Dublin Orator* (Leeds, 1972).

BICKNELL, A., *The Grammatical Wreath*, 2 vols. (London, 1796).

BLAKE, A., 'The Place of Fiction in Victorian Literary Culture', *Literature and History*, 11 (1985), 203–16.

BLAKE, N. F., *Non-standard Language in English Literature* (London, 1981).

BLOOMFIELD, L., 'Literate and Illiterate Speech', *American Speech*, 2 (1927), 432–9.

BOLTON, K., and KWOK, H. (eds.), *Sociolinguistics Today: International Perspectives* (London, 1992).

BOOTH, D., *The Principles of English Grammar* (London, 1837).

BOSWELL, J., *The Life of Samuel Johnson LL.D* (London, 1791), ed. L. F. Powell, 4 vols. (Oxford, 1934).

BRADLEY, I., *The English Middle Classes are Alive and Kicking* (London, 1982).

BRANDRAM, S., *Brandram's Speaker* (London, 1885).

BREWER, R., *What Shall We Do With Tom? Or, Hints to Parents and Others About School* (London, 1866).

BRIGGS, A., *The Age of Improvement* (London, 1960).

—— *The BBC: The First Fifty Years* (Oxford, 1985).

BRITTAIN, L., *Rudiments of English Grammar* (Louvain, 1788).

BRONTË, A., *Agnes Grey* (London, 1847), ed. H. Marsden and R. Inglesfield (Oxford, 1988).

BROOK, G. L., *The Language of Dickens* (London, 1970).

BROWNE, T., *The Union Dictionary* (London, 1806).

BUCHANAN, J., *Linguae Britannicae Vera Pronunciatio* (London, 1757).

—— *A New English Dictionary* (London, 1757).

—— *The British Grammar* (London, 1762).

—— *A Plan of an English Grammar School Education* (London, 1770).

BULLOKAR, WILLIAM, *Works*, ed. J. R. Turner, 3 vols. (Leeds, 1970).

BURNEY, F., *Evelina* (London, 1778), ed. E. A. Bloom (Oxford, 1968).

BURNLEY, J. D., 'Sources of Standardization in Later Middle English', in J. B. Trahern, Jr. (ed.), *Standardizing English: Essays in the History of Language Change in Honor of John Hurt Fisher* (Knoxville, Tenn., 1989), 23–41.

BURRELL, A., *Recitation. A Handbook for Teachers in Public Elementary School* (London, 1891).

BUTLER, J., *Memoir of John Grey of Dilston* (Edinburgh, 1894).

CAMERON, D. (ed.), *The Feminist Critique of Language: A Reader* (London, 1990).

CANNON, J., *Aristocratic Century: The Peerage of Eighteenth-Century England* (Cambridge, 1984).

CAREY, R. N., *Not Like Other Girls*, 3 vols. (London, 1884).

CARLISLE, N., *A Concise Description of the Endowed Grammar Schools of England and Wales* (London, 1818).

CARPENTER, J. E., *Handbook of Poetry* (London, 1868).

CARPENTER, T., *The School Speaker* (London, 1825).

CARTER, R., and NASH, W., *Seeing Through Language: A Guide to Styles of English Writing* (Oxford, 1990).

CHAMBERS, W., and CHAMBERS, R. (eds.), *Chambers's Educational Course: Simple Lessons in Reading* (Edinburgh, 1841).

CHANDOS, J., *Boys Together: English Public Schools 1800–1864* (London, 1984).

COATES, J., *Women, Men and Language* (London, 1986).

COBBETT, J., *A Grammar of the English Language in a Series of Letters. With an Additional Chapter on Pronunciation by James Paul Cobbett* (London, 1866).

COBBETT, W., *The Life and Adventures of Peter Porcupine* (Philadelphia, PA, 1797).

——*A Grammar of the English Language in a Series of Letters* (London, 1819).

COCKIN, W., *The Art of Delivering Written Language* (London, 1775).

COLEMAN, D. G., 'Gentlemen and Players', *Economic History Review*, 26 (1973), 92–116.

COLES, E., *The Compleat English Schoolmaster* (London, 1674).

COLLINS, W., *Basil* (London, 1852).

COOPER, C., *The English Teacher or the Discovery of the Art of Teaching and Learning the* English Tongue (London, 1687).

CORFIELD, P., 'Class by Name and Number in Eighteenth-Century Britain', *History*, 72 (1987), 39–61.

COUSTILLAS, P., *London and the Life of Literature in Late Victorian England: The Diary of George Gissing* (London, 1978).

COYSH, G., *The British Pronouncing and Self Instructing Spelling Book* (Topsham, 1837).

CRABBE, G., *The Complete Poetical Works*, ed. N. Dalrymple-Champneys and A. Pollard, 3 vols. (Oxford, 1988).

CRAIK, Mrs D. M., *Two Marriages* (London, 1881).

CRAMP, W., *The Philosophy of Language* (London, 1838).

CROWLEY, T. (ed.), *Proper English? Readings in Language, History and Cultural Identity* (London, 1991).

DAICHES, D., *Middlemarch* (London, 1963).

336 Bibliography

DAINES, S., *Orthoepia Anglicana* (London, 1640).
D'ARBLAY, MADAME, *Diary and Letters*, ed. C. Barrett, 4 vols. (London, 1876).
DAVIDOFF, L., *The Best Circles: Society Etiquette and the Season* (London, 1973).
DAVIS, M., *Everybody's Business* (London, 1865).
DICKENS, C., *The Life and Adventures of Nicholas Nickleby* (London, 1839).
—— *The Adventures of Oliver Twist* (London, 1846), ed. K. Tillotson (Oxford, 1966).
—— *Dombey and Son* (London, 1848), ed. A. Horsman (Oxford, 1974).
—— *David Copperfield* (London, 1850), ed. N. Burgis (Oxford, 1981).
—— *Bleak House*, 2 vols. (London, 1853).
—— *Little Dorrit* (London, 1857), ed. H. P. Sucksmith (Oxford, 1979).
—— *Great Expectations*, 3 vols. (London, 1861).
—— *Our Mutual Friend*, 2 vols. (London, 1865).
—— *The Life and Adventures of Martin Chuzzlewit* (London, 1844), ed. M. Cardwell (Oxford, 1982).
DISRAELI, B., *Coningsby; or the New Generation*, 3 vols. (London, 1844).
—— *Sybil; or, the Two Nations*, 3 vols. (London, 1845).
DOBSON, E. J., *English Pronunciation 1500–1700*, 2 vols., 2nd edn. (Oxford, 1968).
DORAN, J., *A Lady of the Last Century* (London, 1873).
DOUGLAS, S., *A Treatise on the Provincial Dialect of Scotland* (1779), ed. C. Jones (Edinburgh, 1991).
DOWNES, W., *Language in Society* (London, 1984).
DREW, E., *The Elocutionist Annual for 1889* (London, 1889).
DURKHEIM, E., *Education and Sociology*, trans. S. D. Fox (Glencoe, Ill. 1956).
EAGLESON, R. D., 'Sociolinguistic Reflections on Acceptability', in S. Greenbaum (ed.), *Acceptability in Language* (The Hague, 1977), 63–71.
EARLE, J., *The Philology of the English Tongue* (London, 1871).
EASSON, A. (ed.), *Elizabeth Gaskell: The Critical Heritage* (London, 1991).
ECCLES, E. A. S., *Harry Hawkins' H Book* (London, 1879).
EDGEWORTH, MARIA, *Letters from England, 1813–1844*, ed. C. Colvin (Oxford, 1971).
—— and EDGEWORTH, R. L., *Practical Education*, 2 vols. (London, 1798).
EDWARDS, J., *Language and Disadvantage* (London, 1979).
—— *Language, Society and Identity* (Oxford, 1985).
EDWARDS, J. R., 'Social Class Differences and the Identification of Sex in Children's Speech', *Journal of Child Language*, 6 (1979), 121–7.
ELIOT, G., 'The Natural History of German Life', *Westminster Review*, NS 10 (July 1856).
—— *Adam Bede*, 3 vols. (London, 1859).
—— *Silas Marner: The Weaver of Raveloe* (London, 1861).

—— *Felix Holt, the Radical,* 3 vols. (London, 1866).

—— *Impressions of Theophrastus Such* (London, 1869).

—— *Middlemarch, A Study of Provincial Life*; 4 vols. (London, 1871).

—— *Letters,* ed. G. S. Haight, 9 vols. (London, 1954–6).

—— *Essays,* ed. T. Pinney (London, 1963).

ELLIS, A. J., *On Early English Pronunciation,* 5 vols. (London, 1869–89).

—— 'Tenth Annual Address of the President to the Philological Society', *Transactions of the Philological Society* (1881), 317.

ELLIS, S. S., *The Women of England, Their Social Duties, and Domestic Habits,* 3rd edn. (London, 1839).

ELPHINSTON, J., *Propriety Ascertained in her Picture* (London, 1786).

ELYAN, O., SMITH, P., GILES, H., and BOURHIS, R., 'RP-Accented Female Speech: The Voice of Perceived Androgyny', in P. Trudgill (ed.), *Sociolinguistic Patterns in British English* (London, 1978), 122–31.

ENFIELD, W., *The Speaker: or, Miscellaneous Pieces, Selected from the best English Writers. To which is prefixed An Essay on elocution* (London, 1774).

—— *A Familiar Treatise on Rhetoric* (London, 1809).

ESCOTT, T. H. S., *England: Its People, Polity, and Pursuits,* 2 vols. (London, 1879).

FABER, R., *Proper Stations: Class in Victorian Fiction* (London, 1971).

FARQUHAR, B. A., *Female Education* (London, 1851).

FARRAR, F. W. (ed.), *Essays on a Liberal Education* (London, 1867).

FASOLD, R., *The Sociolinguistics of Society* (Oxford, 1984).

—— *The Sociolinguistics of Language* (Oxford, 1990).

FEARON, D. A., *School Inspection* (London, 1876).

FIELDING, H., *The Life of Mr Jonathan Wild* (London, 1743).

—— *The History of Tom Jones* (London, 1749), ed. F. Bowers (Oxford, 1974).

FOGG, P. WALKDEN, *Elementa Anglicana; or, the Principles of English Grammar,* 2 vols. (Stockport, 1796).

FOWLER, R., *The Languages of Literature* (London, 1971).

—— *Literature as Social Discourse* (London, 1981).

FOX, I., *Public Schools and Public Issues* (London, 1985).

FULTON, G., and KNIGHT, G., *A Dictionary of the English Language Greatly Improved* (Edinburgh, 1833).

FURBANK, P. N., *Unholy Pleasure: The Idea of Social Class* (Oxford, 1985).

GALSWORTHY, J., *The Island Pharisees* (London, 1904).

GASKELL, Mrs E., *Cranford* (London, 1853), ed. E. P. Watson (Oxford, 1972).

—— *North and South* (London, 1855), ed. A. Easson (Oxford, 1973).

GATHORNE-HARDY, J., *The Public School Phenomenon* (London, 1977).

GILES, H., COUPLAND, N., HENWOOD, K., HARRIMAN, J., and COUPLAND, J., 'The Social Meaning of RP: An Intergenerational Perspective', in S.

Ramsaran (ed.), *Studies in the Pronunciation of English: A Commemorative Volume in Honour of A.C. Gimson* (London, 1990), 191–211.

GILL, J., *Introductory Text-Book to School Education, Method and Management*, various edns. (London, 1857–82).

GIMSON, A. C., *An Introduction to the Pronunciation of English*, 4th edn., rev. S. Ramsaran (London, 1989).

GISSING, G., *Workers in the Dawn*, 3 vols. (London, 1880).

—— *Demos. A Story of English Socialism*, 3 vols. (London, 1886).

—— *The Nether World*, 3 vols. (London, 1889).

—— *The Emancipated*, 3 vols. (London, 1890).

—— *New Grub Street*, 3 vols. (London, 1891).

—— *Born in Exile*, 3 vols. (London, 1892).

—— *Denzil Quarrier* (London, 1892).

—— *The Odd Women* (London, 1893).

—— *In the Year of Jubilee*, 3 vols. (London, 1894).

—— *The Whirlpool* (London, 1897).

—— *Charles Dickens. A Critical Study* (London, 1898).

—— *Human Odds and Ends. Stories and Sketches* (London, 1898).

—— *The Town Traveller* (London, 1898).

—— *Will Warburton. A Romance of Real Life* (London, 1905).

—— *A Victim of Circumstances* (London, 1927).

—— *Collected Letters*, i: *1863–1880* ed. P. F. Mattheisen, A. C. Young, and P. Coustillas (Ohio, OH. 1990).

—— *Collected Letters*, ii: *1881–1885*, ed. P. F. Mattheisen, A. C. Young, and P. Coustillas (Ohio, OH. 1991).

GÖRLACH, M., *Studies in the History of the English Language* (Heidelberg, 1990).

—— *Introduction to Early Modern English* (Cambridge, 1991).

GRADDOL, D., and SWANN, J., *Gender Voices* (Oxford, 1989).

GRAHAM, J. G., *Introduction to the Art of Reading* (London, 1861).

GRAHAM, G. F., *A Book About Words* (London, 1869).

GRAHAM, J. C., *Principles of Elocution* (Edinburgh, 1837).

GRAVES, A. PERCEVAL, and RICE-WIGGIN, M., *The Elementary School Manager* (London, 1879).

GREENBAUM, S. (ed.), *Acceptability in Language* (The Hague, 1977).

—— *Good English and the Grammarian* (London, 1988).

GREENWOOD, J., *An Essay Towards an English Grammar* (London, 1711).

GREY, M., and SHIREFF, E., *Thoughts on Self-Culture. Addressed to Women* (London, 1854).

GRIFFITHS, R. J., *An Introduction to the Study of School Management* (London, 1872).

GROSER, W. H., *The Sunday School Teacher's Manual; or, The Principles and Methods of Instruction as Applied to Sunday School Work* (London, 1877).

GROVER, A., *A New English Grammar for the Use of Junior Classes in Schools* (London, 1877).

GUEST, E., *A History of English Rhythms*, 2 vols. (London, 1838).

GUMPERZ, J., *Language and Social Identity* (Cambridge, 1982).

GUTTSMAN, W. L. (ed.), *The English Ruling Class* (London, 1969).

GWYNNE, P., *A Word to the Wise*, 2nd edn. (London, 1879).

H., HON. HENRY, *Poor Letter H: Its Use and Abuse*, various edns. (London, 1854–66).

—— *P's and Q's: Grammatical Hints for the Million* (London, 1855).

H., H. W., *How to Choose a Wife* (London, 1854).

HALES, J. W., 'The Teaching of English', in F. W. Farrar (ed.), *Essays on a Liberal Education* (London, 1867), 293–312.

HALSEY, A. H., *Change in British Society* (Oxford, 1978).

HARDMAN, WILLIAM, *Papers*, ed. S. M. Ellis (London, 1925).

HARDY, T., 'Dialect in Novels', *Athenaeum* (30 Nov. 1878), 688.

—— *The Mayor of Casterbridge*, 2 vols. (London, 1886).

HARRISON, J. F. C., *Early Victorian Britain 1832–1851* (London, 1971).

—— *Late Victorian Britain 1875–1901* (London, 1990).

HART, J., *An Orthographie* (London, 1569).

HARTLEY, C., *Everyone's Handbook of Common Blunders in Speaking and Reading* (London, 1897).

HATFIELD, Miss, *Letters on the Importance of the Female Sex. With Observations on their Manners and Education* (London, 1803).

HILL, G., *The Aspirate* (London, 1902).

HILL, T. W., 'A Lecture on the Articulation of Speech. Delivered before the Birmingham Philosophical Society on January 29th 1821', in *Selections from the Works of the Late T. W. Hill* (London, 1860).

HOLLINGSWORTH, B., 'The Mother Tongue and the Public Schools', in A. K. Pugh, V. J. Lee and J. Swann (eds.) *Language and Language Use* (London, 1980), 185–97.

HOLMBERG, B., *On the Concept of Standard English and the History of Modern English Pronunciation* (Lund, 1964).

HONEY, J., ' "Talking Proper": Schooling and the Establishment of English "Received Pronunciation" ', in. G. Nixon and J. Honey (eds.) *An Historic Tongue: Studies in English Linguistics in Memory of Barbara Strang* (London, 1988), 209–27.

—— *Does Accent Matter? The Pygmalion Factor* (London, 1989).

HOOD, T., *The Wakefield Spelling Book* (London, 1868).

HOPE, A., *A Book About Dominies. Being the Reflections and Recollections of a Member of the Profession* (London, 1869).

HOUGHTON, LORD, 'On the Present Social Results of Classical Education', in F. W. Farrar (ed.), *Essays on a Liberal Education* (London, 1867), 365–84.

HOUGHTON, W., *The Victorian Frame of Mind 1830–1870* (Yale, 1957).

340   Bibliography

HOWATT, A., *A History of English Language Teaching* (Oxford, 1984).
HUDSON, R. A., *Sociolinguistics* (Cambridge, 1980).
HUGHES, G., *Words in Time: A Social History of the English Vocabulary* (Oxford, 1988).
HULLAH, J., *The Cultivation of the Speaking Voice* (Oxford, 1870).
JACK, F. B., *The Woman's Book* (London, 1911).
JAMES, A. LLOYD, *Broadcast English* (London, 1928).
JERNUDD, B. H., 'The Texture of Language Purism: an Introduction', in B. H. Jernudd and M. J. Shapiro (eds.), *The Politics of Language Purism* (Berlin, 1989), 1–20.
—— and SHAPIRO, M. J. (eds.), *The Politics of Language Purism* (Berlin, 1989).
JESPERSEN, O., *Modern English Grammar on Historical Principles*, 7 vols. (London, 1909).
JOHNSON, S., *The Plan of a Dictionary of the English Language* (London, 1747).
—— *A Dictionary of the English Language* (London, 1755).
JOHNSTON, W., *A Pronouncing and Spelling Dictionary of the English Language* (London, 1764).
JONES, D., *An English Pronouncing Dictionary* (London, 1917).
—— 'On "Received Pronunciation"', *Le Maître phonétique*, supp. issue (Apr.–July 1937).
JONES, S., *Sheridan Improved. A General Pronouncing and Explanatory Dictionary of the English Language*, 3rd edn. (London, 1798).
KENRICK, W., *A New English Dictionary* (London, 1773).
KENRICK, W., *A Rhetorical Grammar of the English Language* (London, 1784).
KINGTON-OLIPHANT, T., *The Sources of Standard English*, 2 vols. (London, 1873).
L., I. S., *Fashion in Language* (London, 1906).
LABOV, W., *The Social Stratification of English in New York City* (Washington, DC, 1966).
—— 'The Effect of Social Mobility on Speech Behaviour', *International Journal of American Linguistics*, 33 (1967), 58–75.
—— *Sociolinguistic Patterns* (Oxford, 1978).
LASS, R., *The Shape of English* (London, 1987).
LAUGHTON, W., *A Practical Grammar of the English Tongue* (London, 1739).
LAWRENCE, D. H., *Lady Chatterley's Lover* (Florence, 1928).
LAWSON, J., and SILVER, H., *A Social History of English Education* (London, 1973).
LEACH, A., *The Letter H. Past, Present, and Future* (London, 1881).
LEECH, G. N., and SHORT, M. H., *Style in Fiction: A Linguistic Introduction to English Fictional Prose* (London, 1981).

LEITH, D., *A Social History of English* (London, 1983).

LEPAGE, R., 'Projection, Focusing, Diffusion', *York Papers in Linguistics*, 9 (1980).

LEVANTE, REVD E. R. DE, *Orthoepy and Orthography of the English Language* (London, 1869).

LIVESEY, T. J., *How to Teach Grammar: Illustrated in a Series of Lessons* (London, 1881).

—— *Moffat's How to Teach Reading* (London, 1882).

LOCKHART, J. G., 'On the Cockney School of Poetry No. IV', *Blackwood's Edinburgh Magazine*, 3 (1818), 520–1.

LODGE, D., *Nice Work* (London, 1988).

LONGMUIR, J., *Walker and Webster Combined in a Dictionary of the English Language* (London, 1864).

LOWE, E. C., *An English Primer* (London, 1867).

LOWER, M. A., *Groombridge's Annual Reader* (London, 1867).

LOWTH, R., *A Short Introduction to English Grammar* (London, 1762).

LUCAS, J., 'Editorial Preface', *Literature and History*, 1 (1975), 1–2.

LYTTON, E. BULWER, *Eugene Aram*, 3 vols. (London, 1832).

—— *England and the English* (London, 1833), ed. S. Meacham (Chicago, 1970).

MCARTHUR, T. (ed.), *The Oxford Companion to the English Language* (Oxford, 1992).

MACAULAY, LORD, *Life and Letters*, ed. G. O. Trevelyan, 2 vols. (London, 1878).

M'COMBIE, W., *On Education in its Constituents, Objects, and Issues* (Aberdeen, 1857).

MACKARNESS, Mrs H., *The Young Lady's Book* (London, 1876).

MCKENDRICK, N., BREWER, J., and PLUMB, J., *The Birth of a Consumer Society: The Commercialization of Eighteenth-Century England* (London, 1982).

MACLEOD, A., *Macleod's First Text-Book in Elocution With a Scheme for Acquiring Correct Pronunciation*, 3rd edn. (Edinburgh, 1881).

MACMAHON, M. K. C., 'James Murray and the Phonetic Notation in the New English Dictionary', *Transactions of the Philological Society* (1985), 71–112.

MARSHALL, D., *Industrial England 1776–1851*, 2nd edn. (London, 1982).

MARTIN, B., *Institutions of Language* (London, 1748).

MARWICK, A., *Class: Image and Reality*, 2nd edn. (London, 1990).

MATTHEWS, W., *Cockney Past and Present: A Short History of the Dialect of London* (London, 1972).

MAY, T., *An Economic and Social History of Britain 1760–1970* (New York, 1987).

MAYNARD, J., *Matrimony: Or, What Married Life Is, and How to Make the Best of It*, 2nd edn. (London, 1866).

MEREDITH, G., *The Ordeal of Richard Feverel*, 3 vols. (London, 1859).

MERIVALE, J. A. (ed.), *Autobiography and Letters of Charles Merivale, Dean of Ely* (Oxford, 1898).

MILROY, J., *Linguistic Variation and Change: On the Historical Sociolinguistics of English* (Oxford, 1992).

—— 'Social Network and Prestige Arguments in Sociolinguistics', in K. Bolton and H. Kwok (eds.), *Sociolinguistics Today: International Perspectives* (London, 1992), 146–62.

—— and Milroy, L., *Authority in Language: Investigating Language Prescription and Standardization* (London, 1985).

MILROY, L., *Observing and Analysing Natural Language: A Critical Account of Sociolinguistic Method* (Oxford, 1987).

—— 'New Perspectives in the Analysis of Sex Differentiation in Language', in K. Bolton and H. Kwok (eds.), *Sociolinguistics Today: International Perspectives* (London, 1992), 163–79.

MITCHELL, S., 'The Forgotten Women of the Period: Penny Weekly Family Magazines of the 1840s and 1850s', in M. Vicinus (ed.), *A Widening Sphere: Changing Roles of Victorian Women* (Bloomington, Ind., 1977), 29–51.

MITCHINSON, J., unpublished memoirs of John Mitchinson, Pembroke College Archives (Oxford, 1823–1918).

MORE, H., *Thoughts on the Importance of the Manners of the Great to General Society* (London, 1788).

—— *Strictures on the Modern System of Female Education*, 2 vols. (London, 1799).

MORGAN, F. (ed.), *Works* (Hartford, 1891).

MORRISH, I., *The Sociology of Education*, 2nd edn. (London, 1978).

MORRISON, T., *Manual of School Management*, 3rd edn. (London, 1863).

MUGGLESTONE, L. C., 'A. J. Ellis, "Standard English" and the Prescriptive Tradition', *Review of English Studies*, NS 39 (1988), 87–92.

—— 'Prescription, Pronunciation, and Issues of Class in the Late Eighteenth and Nineteenth Centuries', in D. M. Reeks (ed.), *Sentences for Alan Ward* (London, 1988), 175–182.

—— 'Samuel Johnson and the Use of /h/', *Notes and Queries*, 243 (1989), 431–3.

—— 'The Fallacy of the Cockney Rhyme: from Keats and Earlier to Auden', *Review of English Studies*, NS 42 (1991), 57–66.

MURRAY, J. H., *Strong-Minded Women, and Other Lost Voices from Nineteenth-Century England* (London, 1982).

MURRAY, L., *English Grammar Adapted to the Different Classes of Learners*, 5th edn. (York, 1799).

NEALE, R. S., *History and Class: Essential Readings in Theory and Interpretation* (Oxford, 1983).

NEWMAN, F. W., *Orthoëpy: Or, a Simple Mode of Accenting English* (London, 1869).

—— 'The English Language as Spoken and Written', *Contemporary Review*, 31 (1878), 689–706.

NICHOLS, T. L., *Behaviour: a Manual of Manners and Morals* (London, 1874).

NIXON, G., and HONEY, J. (eds.), *An Historic Tongue: Studies in English Linguistics in Memory of Barbara Strang* (London, 1988).

NUTTALL, P. A. (ed.), *The Standard Pronouncing Dictionary of the English Language, Based on the Labours of Worcester, Richardson, Webster* (London, 1863).

—— *Walker's Pronouncing Dictionary of the English Language* (London, 1855, 1868, 1872, 1873).

OGILVIE, J., *The Comprehensive English Pronouncing Dictionary* (London, 1870).

OKELEY, J., 'Privileged, Schooled and Finished: Boarding Education for Girls', in S. ARDENER (ed.), *Defining Females* (London, 1978), 109–59.

OLIVER, S., *A General Critical Grammar of the Inglish Language on a System Novel and Extensive* (London, 1825).

OWEN, J., *The Youth's Instructor* (London, 1732).

PAGE, N., *Speech in the English Novel*, 2nd edn. (London, 1988).

PERKIN, H., *The Origins of Modern English Society 1780–1880* (London, 1969).

PERKIN, J., *Women and Marriage in Nineteenth-Century England* (London, 1990).

PHYFE, W., *How Should I Pronounce? Or the Art of Correct Pronunciation* (London, 1885).

POOLE, J., *The Village School Improved; Or, A New System of Education Practically Explained, and Adapted to the Case of Country Parishes*, 2nd edn. (Oxford, 1813).

POOVEY, M., *The Proper Lady and the Woman Writer: Ideology as Style in the Works of Mary Wollstonecraft, Mary Shelley, and Jane Austen* (Chicago, Ill. 1984).

PRICE, O., *The Vocal Organ* (Oxford, 1665).

PRIDE, J. B. (ed.), *Sociolinguistic Aspects of Language Learning and Teaching* (Oxford, 1979).

PRIESTLEY, J., *A Course of Lectures on the Theory of Language and Universal Grammar* (Warrington, 1762).

PRINCE, J. J., *School Management and Method* (London, 1880).

PUGH, A. K., LEE, V. J., and SWANN, J. (eds.), *Language and Language Use* (London, 1980).

PUTTENHAM, G., *The Arte of English Poesie* (London, 1589).

R., F. W., and X., LORD CHARLES, *The Laws and Bye-Laws of Good Society. A Code of Modern Etiquette* (London, 1867).

RAMSARAN, S. (ed.), *Studies in the Pronunciation of English: A Commemorative Volume in Honour of A. C. Gimson* (London, 1990).

READER, W. J., *Life in Victorian England* (New York, 1964).

REEKS, D. M. (ed.), *Sentences for Alan Ward* (London, 1988).

REITH, J. C. W., *Broadcast Over Britain* (London, 1924).

RICE, J., *An Introduction to the Art of Reading with Energy and Propriety* (London, 1765).

—— *Syllabus of a Course of Rhetorical Lectures in which the Art of Reading and Speaking the English Language with Elegance and Propriety will be Laid Down* (London, 1765).

RIPMAN, W., *The Sounds of Spoken English* (London, 1906).

—— *English Phonetics* (London, 1931).

ROBBINS, K., *Nineteenth-Century Britain: England, Scotland, and Wales, The Making of a Nation* (Oxford, 1989).

ROBINSON, R., *A Manual of Method and Organisation. Adapted to the Primary Schools of Great Britain, Ireland, and the Colonies* (London, 1863).

—— *Teacher's Manual of Method and Organization*, 2nd edn. (London, 1867).

ROBINSON, W. P., *Language and Social Behaviour* (London, 1972).

ROEBUCK, J., *The Making of Modern English Society from 1850* (London, 1973).

ROGERS, R. R., *Poor Letter R. Its Use and Abuse* (London, 1855).

ROSS, A. S. C., *How to Pronounce It* (London, 1970).

ROYLE, E., *Modern Britain: A Social History 1750–1985* (London, 1987).

RUBENSTEIN, W. D., 'New Men of Wealth and the Purchase of Land in Nineteenth-Century England', *Past and Present*, 92 (1981), 125–47.

RUSSEL, W. P., *Multum in Parvo* (London, 1801).

RUSSELL, B., *Education and the Social Order* (London, 1982).

SANGSTER, Mrs M., *Hours With Girls* (London, 1882).

SAVAGE, W. H., *The Vulgarisms and Improprieties of the English Language* (London, 1833).

SCOTT, J., *The Upper Classes: Prosperity and Privilege in Britain* (London, 1982).

SCRAGG, D., *A History of English Spelling* (London, 1974).

SHAPIRO, M., 'A Political Approach to Language Purism', in B. H. Jernudd and M. J. Shapiro (eds.), *The Politics of Language Purism* (Berlin, 1989), 21–30.

SHAW, G. B., *Androcles and the Lion, Pygmalion, Overruled* (London, 1916).

SHERIDAN, R. B., *Memoirs*, ed. J. Watkins (London, 1817).

SHERIDAN, T., *British Education: Or, The Source of the Disorders of Great Britain* (London, 1756).

—— *A Discourse Delivered in the Theatre in Oxford, in the Senate-House at Cambridge, and at Spring-Garden in London* (London, 1759).

—— *A Dissertation on the Causes of Difficulties, Which Occur, in Learning the English Tongue* (London, 1761).

—— *A Course of Lectures on Elocution* (London, 1762).

—— *A General Dictionary of the English Language* (London, 1780).

—— *A Rhetorical Grammar of the English Language* (Dublin, 1781).

—— *Elements of English* (London, 1786).

SHERMAN, L., *A Handbook of Pronunciation* (London, 1885).

SHROSBREE, C., *Public Schools and Private Education: The Clarendon Commission 1861–64 and the Public Schools Acts* (Manchester, 1988).

SIGSWORTH, E. M., *Black Dyke Mills* (Liverpool, 1958).

SMART, B. H., *A Practical Grammar of English Pronunciation* (London, 1810).

—— *A Grammar of English Sounds* (London, 1812).

—— *Walker Remodelled. A New Critical Pronouncing Dictionary* (London, 1836).

—— *Walker Remodelled* (London, 1846).

SMETHAM, T., *The Practical Grammar* (London, 1774).

SMILES, S., *Self-Help: With Illustrations of Conduct and Perseverance* (London, 1859), ed. A. Briggs (London, 1958).

SMITH, C. W., *Hints on Elocution and Public Speaking* (London, 1858).

—— *Mind Your H's and Take Care of Your R's* (London, 1866).

SMITH, D., *Conflict and Compromise. Class Formation in English Society 1830–1914* (London, 1982).

SMITH, W., *An Attempt to Render the Pronunciation of the English Language More Easy* (London, 1795).

SMOLLETT, T., *The Adventures of Peregrine Pickle*, 4 vols. (London, 1751).

—— *The Expedition of Humphry Clinker*, 3 vols. (London, 1771).

SPENCE, T., *The Grand Repository of the English Language* (Newcastle, 1775).

SPENCER, H., *Education: Intellectual, Moral and Physical* (London, 1861).

STEDMAN-JONES, G., *Outcast London* (Oxford, 1971).

STOKER, B., *Dracula* (London, 1897).

STONE, L. S., and STONE, J. C. F., *An Open Élite? England 1540–1800* (Oxford, 1984).

STUBBS, M., *Language and Literacy: The Sociolinguistics of Reading and Writing* (London, 1980).

—— *Educational Linguistics* (Oxford, 1986).

—— and HILLIER, H. (eds.), *Readings on Language, Schools and Classrooms* (London, 1983).

SURTEES, R. S., *Mr Sponge's Sporting Tour* (London, 1853).

SWEET, H., *Handbook of Phonetics* (Oxford, 1877).

—— *The Elementary Sounds of English* (London, 1881).

—— *A Primer of Phonetics* (London, 1890).

—— *A Primer of Spoken English* (Oxford, 1890).

—— *The Sounds of English* (Oxford, 1908).

TENNYSON, A., *Poems*, ed. C. Ricks (London, 1969).

THACKERAY, W. M., *Vanity Fair, A Novel Without a Hero* (London, 1848).

—— *A Shabby-Genteel Story* (London, 1887).

THOMAS, G., *Linguistic Purism* (London, 1991).

THOMPSON, F. M. L., *English Landed Society in the Nineteenth Century* (London, 1963).

TRAHERN, J. B. (ed.), *Standardizing English. Essays in the History of Language Change in Honor of John Hurt Fisher* (Knoxville, Tenn., 1989).

TRENCH, R. C., *English Past and Present* (London, 1855).

TRILLING, L., *The Liberal Imagination: Essays on Literature and Society* (London, 1955).

TROLLOPE, A., *An Autobiography*, ed. M. Sadleir and F. Page (Oxford, 1980).

TRUDGILL, P., *The Social Stratification of English in Norwich* (Cambridge, 1974).

—— *Accent, Dialect, and the School* (London, 1975).

—— (ed.), *Sociolinguistic Patterns in British English* (London, 1978).

—— 'Standard and Non-Standard Dialects of English in the UK: Problems and Policies', in M. Stubbs and H. Hillier (eds.), *Readings on Language, Schools and Classrooms* (London, 1983), 50–81.

VALENTINE, Mrs C., *The Young Woman's Book* (London, 1878).

VANBRUGH, J., *The Relapse; or, Virtue in Danger* (London, 1697).

VANDENHOFF, G., *The Art of Elocution* (London, 1855).

—— *The Lady's Reader* (London, 1862).

VICINUS, M. (ed.), *A Widening Sphere: Changing Roles of Victorian Women* (Bloomington, Ind., 1980).

WAKEFORD, J., *The Cloistered Élite* (London, 1969).

WALKER, J., *A General Idea of a Pronouncing Dictionary of the English Language on a Plan Entirely New* (London, 1774).

—— *Elements of Elocution* (London, 1781).

—— *A Rhetorical Grammar* (London, 1781).

—— *A Rhetorical Grammar of the English Language*, various edns. (London, 1785–1823).

—— *The Academic Speaker* (Dublin, 1789).

—— *A Critical Pronouncing Dictionary and Expositor of the English Language* (London, 1791, 1797, 1802, 1806, 1809); 1809 edn. ed. J. Murdoch.

—— *A Rhetorical Grammar of the English Language*, 27th edn. (London, 1823).

WALLER, P. J., 'Democracy and Dialect, Speech and Class', in P. J. Waller (ed.), *Politics and Social Change in Modern Britain: Essays Presented to A. F. Thompson* (Brighton, 1987), 1–28.

WALLIS, J., *Grammatica Linguae Anglicanae* (Oxford, 1653).

WARD, MRS HUMPHRY, *Marcella*, 3 vols. (London, 1894).

WARDAUGH, R., *An Introduction to Sociolinguistics* (Oxford, 1986).

WARDLE, D., *The Rise of the Schooled Society* (London, 1974).

WATTS, I., *The Art of Reading and Writing English* (London, 1721).

WEBSTER, N., *Dissertations on the English Language* (Boston, Mass., 1789).

WELLS, J. C., *Accents of English*, 3 vols. (Cambridge, 1982).

WHITE, G., *A Simultaneous Method of Teaching to Read Adapted to Primary Schools* (London, 1862).

WILKINSON, REVD W. F., *Education, Elementary and Liberal: Three Lectures Delivered in the Hall of the Mechanics' Institute, Derby, Nov. 1861* (London, 1862).

WILLIAMS, D., *A Treatise on Education* (London, 1774).

WILLIAMS, REVD D., *Composition, Literary and Rhetorical, Simplified* (London, 1850).

WILLIAMS, R., *Keywords: A Vocabulary of Culture and Society* (London, 1976).

—— *Writing in Society* (London, 1983).

WILSON, R., 'The Archbishop Herring Visitation Returns, 1743: A Vignette of Yorkshire Education', in J. E. Stephens (ed.), *Aspects of Education 1600–1750* (Hull, 1984), 92–130.

WOLFRAM, W., and FASOLD, R., 'Social Dialects and Education', in J. B. Pride (ed.), *Sociolinguistic Aspects of Language Learning and Teaching* (Oxford, 1979), 185–212.

WOLLSTONECRAFT, MARY, *Works*, ed. J. Todd and M. Butler, 7 vols. (London, 1989)

WORDSWORTH, WILLIAM, *Plays*, ed. A. Friedman (Oxford, 1979).

WYLD, H. C., *The Historical Study of the Mother Tongue* (London, 1906)

—— *Studies in English Rhymes from Surrey to Pope* (London, 1923).

—— *The Best English. A Claim for the Superiority of Received Standard English* (Oxford, 1934).

WYSE, T., *Education Reform; Or, The Necessity of a National System of Education* (London, 1836).

YONGE, C. M., *Womankind* (London, 1878).

YOUNG, G. M., and HANDCOCK, W. D., *English Historical Documents 1833– 1874*, xii/1 (London, 1956).

YOUNG, T. (ed.), *A Critical Pronouncing Dictionary of the English Language* (London, 1857).

INDEX